ENTRE ——————— NOUS

GRANT

*Between*

*the*

# ENTRE ——— NOUS

*World Cup*

*and Me*

FARRED

DUKE UNIVERSITY PRESS  *Durham and London*  2019

© 2019 Duke University Press
All rights reserved

Designed by Matthew Tauch
Typeset in Warnock Pro by Copperline Books

Library of Congress Cataloging-in-Publication Data
Names: Farred, Grant, author.
Title: Entre nous : between the World Cup and me / Grant Farred.
Description: Durham : Duke University Press, 2019. | Includes bibliographical references and index.
Identifiers: LCCN 2018044273 (print) |
LCCN 2018054839 (ebook)
ISBN 9781478005551 (ebook)
ISBN 9781478004097 (hardcover : alk. paper)
ISBN 9781478004707 (pbk. : alk. paper)
Subjects: LCSH: World Cup (Soccer) | Farred, Grant. | Messi, Lionel, 1987– | Suárez, Luis, 1987– | Tabárez, Oscar Washington, 1947—Influence. | Soccer players. | Sports—Philosophy. | Soccer—Social aspects. | Soccer coaches.
Classification: LCC GV943.49 (ebook) | LCC GV943.49 .F38 2019 (print) | DDC 796.3340922 [B] —dc23
LC record available at https://lccn.loc.gov/2018044273

Cover art: Soccer pitch with center circle. Photo by daitoZen/Getty.

POR JUANITA:
Gracias, mi amor

# CONTENTS

*Preface* ix

*Acknowledgments* xxv

**INTRODUCTION** 1

Entre-Nous: Between the World and Me

**CHAPTER ONE** 29

A Condemned Man: Between the Nation and the *Autonomista*

**INTERLUDE** 97

"Nog Lansur!"

**CHAPTER TWO** 163

The Shame of Loving the Condemned: The Philosophy of Óscar Washington Tabárez

**POSTSCRIPT** 219

*Notes* 225

*Bibliography* 251

*Index* 253

# PREFACE

> In all beginnings dwells a magic force
> —— HERMAN HESSE, "Stages"

Martin Heidegger knew nothing about *Mitsein*.
Martin Heidegger knew nothing about *Mitsein* because he never had the chance to see Lionel Messi, Football Club Barcelona's star player, "being-with" his fans after a miraculous, come-from-behind Champions League victory in 2017. Barça—as football fans the world over refer to the Barcelona team—had just emerged triumphant from its quarterfinal clash against Paris Saint-Germain (PSG) on Barça's home ground.

A philosopher, a double World Cup winner: a not-so motley cast of characters.

The Barça-PSG match will be dealt with at some length, shortly, but for now it is Martin Heidegger who demands our attention. After all, to claim that Heidegger knows nothing about *Mitsein* is little short of preposterous, a declaration that is philosophically unsustainable. No one, we can assert with absolute confidence, knows more about *Mitsein* than Heidegger.

But... let us tarry with the declaration a moment longer. Martin Heidegger, who in his boyhood days was a "useful left wing" in Meßkirch, his home town, and in his last years reportedly followed European football (*Fußball* to Heidegger) keenly, knew nothing about *Mitsein*. Heidegger knew nothing about *Mitsein* because, unfortunately for him, he died more than a decade before Leo Messi was even born.

In his final years Heidegger was (unsurprisingly, given his reputation for discipline) enamored of his countryman, the imperious Franz Beckenbauer. Nicknamed "Der Kaiser," Beckenbauer commanded respect from teammates, opponents and fans alike. In 1974 Beckenbauer captained the West German team to World Cup victory. On home soil, no less, with a 2–1 win over the Netherlands in West Berlin. In 1990, as manager of the last divided German team to play in a World Cup, Beckenbauer coached West Germany to victory.

On a train ride one day, Heidegger, who was "full of admiration for [Beckenbauer's] delicate ball control," according to his biographer, Rüdiger Safranski, "actually tried to demonstrate some of Beckenbauer's finesses to his astonished interlocutor," who happened to be the "director of the Freiburg theater."[1]

One can only imagine it. The now venerable philosopher, in his declining years, trying, as the keen Meßkirch amateur left-winger he'd once been, to make like Beckenbauer. On a moving train, showing no appetite for talk of the theater or literature, there, for all the world to see: Martin Heidegger, footballer. Martin Heidegger, trying to imitate Der Kaiser's football skills. The philosopher, an outdoors type (he liked to hike and he was no mean skier), exhibiting, in a moving train, his best football moves. The philosopher giving us a glimpse of what the philosopher as footballer looks like. The old philosopher retrieving, from gilded memory, the young footballer he once was. The old philosopher recovering, if only for a moment, the footballer in him. The footballer he imagined himself to have been. Albert Camus was a keen amateur goalkeeper. Jacques Derrida loved playing the game as a boy in El Biar, the Algiers neighborhood in which he grew up. And how could we forget Jean-Paul Sartre's insightful analysis of the game: "In football everything is complicated by the presence of the opposite team." What legendary coach has not arrived at exactly the same conclusion? Are all philosophers nothing but insufficiently talented footballers or underemployed color commentators?

*Zu sein wie.*

In the case of Heidegger's *Mitsein*, then, what we encounter is nothing other than the philosopher's (true; truest) desire: to be-with a great footballer. Heidegger could not know *Mitsein*, even with Beckenbauer, because he was (physically) too far removed from Der Kaiser. So he did the best could do: he tried to be-like: zu sein wie. To be-like Beckenbauer. Unlike Messi, at Camp Nou, Barça's stadium, where all the partisans were free to be-with their idol. As we will see shortly, Messi gave himself freely to them, and they, in their turn, gave themselves utterly to him. Heidegger did not give himself to Beckenbauer. Nor would Beckenbauer ever have imagined the possibility of *Mitsein* with Heidegger.

Still, Heidegger's is an admirable desire. Eschewing cultural expectation, Der Kaiser is subsumed into the athletic orbit—the aging body—of the "Maestro from Meßkirch." *Zu sein wie,* the meeting of the imperious Bavarian body (Beckenbauer) and the towering Baden-Württemberg mind (Heidegger). *Zu sein wie,* this is what it means to want to be-like the other. To be-like the other across (West) German generations, across vast discrepancies in athletic ability.

*Zu sein wie* is not *Mitsein* but it is what makes it possible for the amateur left-winger to give himself license, now nearing the end of his life, to believe that he is capable of reenacting the "delicate ball control" of a World Cup–winning captain and coach. In truth, zu sein wie, even more than *Mitsein,* may be the lifeblood of every amateur footballer, of every football fan: to imagine, for a moment, in a train carriage, on a dusty field, on a busy street, on a manicured training complex, no, to believe, with fervor and conviction, in the possibility of being-like your *Fußball,* football, *fútbol* heroes. To be-with is, for an instant, for a glorious instant, to be-like. As much as any amateur footballer, a community among whom I number, Martin Heidegger knew zu sein wie as such a dream, knew the dream of zu sein wie as momentary athletic transcendence, knew what it meant to dream of supping with the *Fußball* gods.

To correct the terms of this philosophical proposition, then, we can say that while Martin Heidegger knew "nothing" about *Mitsein,* he knew everything about zu sein wie. And, as such, all amateur and aspiring professional footballers are like, are with, Heidegger. *Mitsein.* In a footballing sense, as much as a philosophical one, there can be no doubt: Martin Heidegger is as much a master of *Mitsein* as he is of zu sein wie.

The left-wing philosopher.

The irony. Martin Heidegger, a philosopher infamous for his involvement—his May 1933 rectoral address ("Die Selbstbehauptung der deutschen Universität" [The Self-Assertion of the German University]) and so on—with the right wing of German politics, started out as a left-winger. Was Heidegger, like Leo Messi, left-footed? One wonders, was he left-footed but right-handed? As for the matter of "delicate ball control," football fans of a certain generation are more likely to associate this football skill with Messi rather than Beckenbauer. The always-imposing Der Kaiser was no slouch on the ball, and while he possessed impressive football technique, his was not on the order of Messi's. Football fans would be hard-pressed to name another footballer who has such immaculate technical skills, such an array of invention, and such a visionary range of passing skill.

But I digress, no doubt because I take too much pleasure at the prospect of an almost octogenarian Martin Heidegger reliving his ball-playing ambitions from his Meßkirch youth on a German train, ignoring the invitation to talk high culture. Who among us wouldn't pay good money to have been able to see that? Imagine what a historic spectacle all the passengers in that train carriage were witness to. They were with Heidegger zu sein wie Beckenbauer while Heidegger was being-with his younger, left-wing self. What a moment of triangulated (West) German zu sein wie und *Mitsein*. Heidegger, former member of Hitler's National Socialists (he and Carl Schmitt joined on the same day), enacting a being-like Beckenbauer, a footballer born in September 1945 in the ruins of postwar Munich, rising to lead both his country, West Germany, and his club, Bayern München, to footballing glory, a being-like that is, courtesy of Heidegger's athletic reenactment, extended to all (the passengers in the carriage) and sundry (metonymically, to all of Germany and the world beyond too).

*Mitsein* and zu sein wie, then, as that mode of being that forges a sustainable, perhaps unbreakable, connection between philosophy, replete with erudition and abstraction, and football, a sport that is so intensely about the body. Heidegger and Beckenbauer, arrived at through Messi, reminding us once that football is—at least—how the body thinks itself; football is how the body remembers its (younger, much younger,) self, is how the body, just for an instant, recovers its athleticism, skill, and, yes, its footballing dreams. Football, in Heidegger's case, is how the body accesses and archives (dare one say) a Meßkirchean paradise lost. This leads us to wonder as to when else (surely, there must have been other such reenactments) Heidegger was given to demonstrating his left-wing skills. Did they all, if there were others, every one of them revolve around Beckenbauer? Did he not want to make like the Brazilian Pelé? Or the English striker Bobby Charlton, naturally right-footed but almost as good with his left? Was Heidegger distraught after West Germany lost that epic 1966 World Cup final to England? That game where Geoff Hurst scored a hat trick (an event to which we will return in the "Interlude"), that game where a twenty-year-old then-central midfielder Beckenbauer was not yet quite so imperious, that Wembley final when he was not yet Der Kaiser, that final when he played in central midfield rather than central defense. In the history of football, of course, central defense is more readily identified as Beckenbauer's position. As it should properly be, because it was from his position as a commanding central defender that his greatest accomplishments were achieved.

"Stages," Herman Hesse's paean to the value of beginnings, achieves an ironic poetic resonance—a vivacity—in relation to Heidegger. "In all beginnings dwells a magic force / For guarding us and helping us to live." "To begin" marks an opening, it announces the onset of possibility. But "to live" again that which was, "to live" again in this spirit is to spontaneously experience the joy of living again, fully, that moment which was, just a minute ago, entirely lost to memory. What "helps us to live" is the joy of living again that which was once lived. There is an unadulterated pleasure to be found in beginnings, but in certain moments—or, perhaps, at a certain age—what gives true joy is the brief recapturing of a long-ago beginning. As such, we might say, to bring the argument full circle, the "magic" of the beginning is its ability—its "force"—to recast what was presumed to have ended as a "new" beginning. In this way, every beginning promises the prospect of retrieving that which was understood to have been lost.

Democracy, unbound.

Because of that Heideggerian moment in the train carriage, football as being-with and being-like achieves, paradoxically, subversively, mischievously, a kind of democratization. It is democratization of the sort that can only arise out of the philosopher's dream, Heidegger's desire to show off his (surely inconsiderable) skills. In football, it is the players' dreams that make all players equal, until that cruel moment that is athletic reckoning, when "delicate ball control" must actually be demonstrated rather than reenacted (when, as Sartre says, everything becomes complicated by the reality of the "opposite team"). On the football field, regardless of how big or small, fast or slow, tall or undersized, they are, regardless if they're (West) German or Argentine, all players are equal until they are not. That is, until they are distinguished according to their level of talent, when one player shows him- or herself to possess greater skill, to be able to execute delicate dribbles, to envision a pass that no one else could imagine. That is the moment of truth in football. To be equal on the football field, then, is always only a "technical" matter, because the means of judgment—skill, talent, discipline, stamina, the desire to win—is confounded by the individual body. By themselves, height, weight, muscle density, mean nothing—or very little. After all, in what other sport can a player standing five foot five, as Messi does, routinely and as a matter of course reign supreme over players who stand, as Beckenbauer does, around six feet? (Der Kaiser is half an inch short of six feet.)

Messi, for a second time of asking.

But, again, I digress. Again I am too much taken with that unknown left-winger, Martin Heidegger.

However, instead of lamenting my digression, I should perhaps be grateful for the lure that is *Mitsein*/zu sein wie, for the possibilities it opens up, for how it makes other thinkings—"beginnings"—of Leo Messi possible, of how the politics of sport, philosophy, and national expectation converge on the football pitch. (Beckenbauer, among that first generation of postwar Germans, understood—and accepted—the burden of national expectation more readily than most of his contemporaries.)

If Heidegger's affection for football is little known, reduced to a mere paragraph at the end of Safranski's biography of the philosopher, almost a footnote in work dedicated to a life of a thinker whose "passion was for questioning," then Messi stands in sharp contradistinction to his fellow left footer.[2]

In the contemporary game, Lionel Messi is a ubiquitous presence. In truth, however, it seems as if it has been that way since Messi first pulled on the *blaugrana* ("blue and red," or "maroon" rather than "red," if you insist) shirt of FC Barcelona on November 16, 2003. Football, *fútbol*, *Fußball*—in whatever language you choose, Lionel Messi is the game at its very best. With invention, grace, and sometimes nothing short of sublime beauty is how Messi plays the game. Millions around the world appreciate it. Many of those millions are not slow to show their appreciation for how Messi plays. I would venture that the older Heidegger would have been among those to sing Messi's praises.

Surely you've encountered Messi, whether you're a football fan or not. Look around as you stroll or hurry through the airport, kids and grownups alike sporting his number 10 FC Barcelona jersey; same thing when you're cruising your local mall, or when you drop your kid off at school. All this, of course, is to say nothing of the preponderance of Messi jerseys that can be spotted wherever pickup games are being played. Leo Messi strides across the planet, all five feet five inches of him, like a colossus, making more bank for Nike than any other athlete. (He is listed at five foot seven, but that's clearly a stretch, no pun intended.) Maybe Messi has made a football fan out of you. Maybe he has made an FC Barcelona fan out of your son or daughter.

Martin and Messi.

In one moment, in a single flash of insight (not quite a blinding flash, not quite an epiphany, but so close to both you'd hardly know the difference), Lionel Messi and Martin Heidegger came together. That is, in a single moment Heidegger's concept of *Mitsein* and not *zu sein wie*, I should be clear in all its philosophical complexity and density, was fully revealed. It was revealed through, or rather, in the person of Leo Messi. (That is, *Mitsein*, being-with, as the predominant concept but a positing of *Mitsein* in which the resonances, the desire to be-like, can be detected; sometimes those resonances are more, sometimes less, audible.) It is Messi who gave Heidegger's notion of "being-with" life in the most animated, the most politically entangled, and the most philosophically weighted way. Leo Messi made it possible to understand, in a single, wonderfully charged moment, *Mitsein*. In that moment, Messi might have been Heidegger's best friend in all the world (of football). Messi might have been, in that moment, the greatest advocate for what it means to "know" *Mitsein*. To know, for an instant, the signal difference between being-with and being-like.

But, in doing so, Messi might have, once more, raised the possibility that, in (footballing) truth, Heidegger never really knew *Mitsein*.

License, please: the match in which *Mitsein* came to life.

It is on account of this relation between the Argentine footballer and the German philosopher that philosophical license is asked for; a request that is, consciously, made in the name of hubris. Philosophical indulgence is asked for in the name of the game of football, for the game of football thought philosophically.

To begin with, an unsustainable negation, a claim that is, clearly, philosophically preposterous. No wonder, then, that license and a certain indulgence is requested. Martin Heidegger, philosopher of philosophers, philosopher for philosophers, knows nothing of *Mitsein*, one of his signature concepts. Heidegger could not have known what *Mitsein* truly was. Heidegger could not have known what *Mitsein* truly meant, although he spent his entire career thinking about it, because he had not met Lionel Messi.

What a great pity it is that Martin Heidegger, who died in 1976, did not live to see March 8, 2017. If he had, he would have seen *Mitsein* come fully to life. Come to life for the entire world to see what it truly means to be-with-the-other.

Let us recall this football match in which *Mitsein* made itself manifest in the world. It took place, as we know, on a Wednesday evening. On this early spring evening, *Mitsein* was "staged" at Camp Nou in the 2016–17 Champions League round of 16 clash between Messi's Barça and PSG.

The Champions League is Europe's top club footballing competition. It features the best teams from the continent—Liverpool (England), Barça, Real Madrid (Spain), Bayern München (Germany), and so on. It is divided into two stages. The first stage is known as the "group stages." In the first stage, four teams are drawn together in a group, and they play each other twice, on a home and away basis. The top two teams from every "group," labeled unimaginatively A, B, C, all the way to H, qualify for the "knockout stages." The second stage comprises eight matchups, in which the teams play each other, as in our case, Barcelona v. PSG; again, it's on a home and away basis. This time, however, the team that scores the most goals over the two "legs" goes through to the next stage. Following the round of 16 are the quarterfinals and the semifinals, culminating in the final, of course. In the "knockout stages" the rules are such—in order to encourage attacking play away from home—that in the event of the score being tied at the end of the second leg, it is not simply the team that scores the most goals but the team with the most away goals that is awarded the win. So, if the score is, as it might have been at Camp Nou in March 2017, say, 5–5, and PSG (as it did) boasts an away goal to its credit and Barça does not (again, this was the scenario for a minute or three), then PSG progresses to the quarterfinals.

In the first leg, PSG had run riot against a tepid Barça, winning comfortably 4–0 at their Parc de Princes stadium. This meant that in the return leg Barça would have to win 5–0 or by 5 clear goals in order to qualify for the quarterfinals. Messi's Barça started off well, going up 3–0 in the sixtieth minute and with half an hour to score two more. For a Barcelona team packed with offensive talent, this was not an insurmountable task.

The Uruguayan Luis Suárez, who is discussed in more detail later, scored a goal in only the third minute. A PSG "own goal" (the PSG left back, Layvin Kurzawa, deflected the ball into his own net) in the forty-first minute meant that Barça went into halftime up 2–0. In the fiftieth minute, Messi added an emphatic penalty for the third. 3–0.

Then disaster struck for Barça. Edinson Cavani scored that all-important away goal for PSG in the sixty-second minute. This meant that in the remaining time, some twenty-eight minutes plus whatever time the referee added on (five minutes, it turns out), Barça would have to score three goals without conceding another. A tall order, especially for a Barça team that seemed to have run out of steam and ingenuity after the Cavani goal. For the next twenty-six minutes Barça huffed and puffed, to no avail. Even when Barça's Brazilian striker, Neymar, struck an inch-perfect free kick in the eighty-eighth minute to make the score 4–1, Barça still needed two goals. It seemed to be over. Even when Barça was awarded a penalty in the ninety-first minute, which Neymar converted (5–1), there was still something of a mountain to climb. Maybe a hill, but the incline was sharp and time was running out. All PSG had to do was defend for the next four minutes.

It was so close that PSG could taste it.

So near, it turned out, and yet so far. So very far, so painfully far... It was all about to come crashing down.

In the ninety-fourth minute Messi took a free kick from the left side of the PSG defense. He curled it toward goal, but a Parisian defender met it with a stout header. The ball ricocheted to the middle of the park, about thirty meters from goal. There to meet it was Neymar, out of position, dead center. Neymar normally operates on the Barça left flank, but Messi took up that space with the free kick. From a Barça point of view, the ball dead center, so close to goal, was far from ideal.

But Neymar was equal to the task. He moved to his left, and with delicate precision chipped the ball, from some twenty-two or twenty-three meters out, toward the PSG goal. Sergi Roberto, native born-Catalan and without a goal in eighteen months, made a perfect diagonal run from the right flank. He stabbed his right foot at the ball, and in so doing redirected it past the hapless Kevin Trapp in the PSG goal. Pandemonium ensued. Gerard Piqué, Messi, and Neymar all rushed toward Roberto. The Barça fans went into a frenzied celebration. Camp Nou burst into uproar. Their heroes had just completed the greatest comeback in Champions League history.

The last minute of extra time was a mere formality. This Champions League tie had been dramatically settled.

A further irony.

In August 2016, for the princely sum of €222, Neymar signed for none other than PSG.

He was, he declared, 'following his heart."

The truth is less generous to Neymar.

As the new icon of Brazilian *futebol*, or, as his countrymen and -women say, joga bonito (the "beautiful game"), he could no longer tolerate life in Lionel Messi's shadow.

Such "being-with" had become intolerable.

In "being-with," the self at once, by turns, in the most contradictory of fashions, "gives up" (such is the logic and ethics of the team, sacrificing for the team is what is demanded, putting the self in the service of the larger—team, the collectivity of record—good) and "accrues" to itself. The self, the individual player, "gains" through the collective talent, skill, labor, and commitment of his or her teammates.

Playing with Neymar and Suárez was such a "gain" for Messi. And Messi clearly relished it. He plays unselfishly, providing goal-scoring opportunities for his fellow strikers, thriving on the ability to be able to lay the ball off to them. As such, Messi understands—embodies, once more—*Mitsein*. To be-with for him, playing alongside Suárez and Neymar, meant that he had more time, perhaps just a fraction of a second, but a fraction of a second is a lot of extra time on the ball for Messi; what is more, he used this fraction of more time to create for his teammates and to punish the opposition when they tried to defend the goal-hungry Uruguayan and the no-less-insatiable Brazilian. Messi, too, got his share of goals, but he seemed especially thrilled to be part of such a talented and deadly trio of marksmen.

Neymar, in hindsight, clearly did not.

So off to Paris he took himself.

Which leads one to at least two conclusions.

Firstly, if you can't play on a team with Leo Messi, you can't play on a team. At least not on a team where you (Neymar) are not the featured star. We could, in terms of the National Basketball Association, say the same thing about the Cleveland Cavaliers' LeBron James's former teammate, Kyrie Irving.[3] If you can't play with as unselfish a superstar as LeBron, ignominy should be your fate.

Secondly, Neymar, unlike Messi, as we're about to see, knows (as yet) nothing of *Mitsein*.

*Mitsein*.

When the final whistle blew, the Barça players offered heartfelt but perfunctory handshakes to the PSG players. And condolences. One imagines that was an act of mercy. Nobody in the visiting ranks wanted to linger on the Camp

Nou pitch any longer than they absolutely had to. The PSG players were shell-shocked and visibly distraught. Some were close to tears, Marquinhos foremost among them. It was a case of so near and yet so very, very far.

The TV cameras, however, were focused on the Barça players grouped in a delirious huddle, centered on Sergi Roberto, as unlikely a hero as one can imagine. And they caught the mournful glances of the PSG team, none so traumatized as the usually stoic Thiago Silva, who captains not only PSG but also Brazil. He had just been on the receiving end of his national teammate Neymar's magic. It must have felt strange to Silva to be a Neymar victim, after all those matches in which the boot had been on the other foot.

As Silva, Cavani, and the rest of the PSG team headed for their dressing rooms ("lockerroom"), the Barça players and coaching staff broke their huddle and jogged briskly out to their fans to share their joy (and disbelief, one imagines) at the incredible victory just achieved.

One of their number, however, had already disappeared into the crowd, held safely and lovingly in the arms of the Barça faithful. At the final whistle, Messi had virtually sprinted from his teammates, past the stricken PSG players, straight to the fans.

For a moment that seemed to last a lifetime he perched precariously on the advertising hoardings, his face aglow, the ecstasy of a historic win making his face almost beatific. He stood, his arms akimbo, welcoming all into the vast expanse of his embrace. And how they loved him. They surged toward him, the Barça partisans (historically known as the *cules*, the "half-asses"), their love mingled with excitement, their disbelief overwhelmed by the enormity of what they had just witnessed. They returned Messi's love for them.

And then he tumbled into the crowd and like a rock star surfed across the arms of his fans.

Leo Messi was a man who had finally, in that very moment of his leaping onto the hoardings, found himself, for the first time in his professional life, at home. This is what, in Heidegger's terms, it must feel like to know *Wohen* ("dwelling"): to know Being, to Be (fully) in Camp Nou, the professional dwelling you call home.[4]

This is what *Mitsein* looks like, this is what it feels like. Camp Nou, March 2017, is what it is like to witness *Mitsein* come to life before your very eyes. To be-with is to be enveloped by, is to give yourself into the arms of the other. Remind me again how it is that Heidegger understands *Mitsein*? Yes, that's it, "being-with-the-other." *Mitsein*, it is to feel safe enough to voluntarily cast yourself into the arms of the other; it is to trust yourself into the other's care. And the other's love. Yes, the other's love.

How I wish you could have seen it, Martin, how I wish you'd lived long enough to bear witness to the event of *Mitsein*. In the face of such an event, I doubt that a football fan and long-ago player such as you, you who loved the aesthetic and technical beauty of the game, would not have been moved. Ah, what moves you would have had for that theater director on a train ride should you have met on another occasion. Had you met in, say April 2017. How the other passengers would have marveled, in 2017 or 2018 or 2020, at your rendition of Messi at Camp Nou. After all, in Messi, because of Messi, the event of *Mitsein* that so preoccupied you was right there, right there to hand.

Might I render the event of *Mitsein* in the American vernacular, Martin? Might I suggest that until you have seen the event of *Mitsein* that is Leo Messi, well, Martin, "You ain't seen nothing yet"?

In the event of *Mitsein* that is Leo Messi there is nothing but the pureness of *Mitsein*: an event in which there is nothing between self and other. It is now possible to say we know what *Mitsein* looks like. It is a joyous thing. No, like grace is love beyond love, so *Mitsein* is joy beyond joy. Indeed, the truth of *Mitsein* might very well be that there is nothing other than love. The unfolding of love for all the (football) world to see. *Mitsein* is the event of love more true than love could ever have imagined itself to be.

For the most part, however, it is not love as such but Leo Messi and *Mitsein* that constitutes the governing problematic of the first chapter of this book. Messi being one with Catalunya is the condition of being that is thought in chapter 1. *Mitsein*, that is, and not love, as the epitome of being-with.

The "victims."

In the midst of all the joy, the tears, the palpable sense of the miraculous hanging over the stadium that is Camp Nou, the Catalan fans beside themselves, it was almost impossible not to feel sympathy for those two groups, one present as the historically unfortunate "opposite team," the PSG players, and others a continent removed, those who pledge their loyalty to Los Celestes, the Argentine national team.

Argentina is a nation with a proud, if tarnished, reputation in the world of football.

It was almost impossible not to "feel" ("to feel sorry") for the Argentines because they have never had the experience of *Mitsein* with Leo Messi, who captains their national team and is one of its three greatest players. In the Argentine pantheon, Messi is, in my judgment, sandwiched between the greatest of them all, the greatest footballer of all time, Alfredo Di Stéfano (the Buenos Aires–born striker who is most often remembered for his time with Real Madrid (1953–64), FC Barcelona's arch enemies), and the irascible but massively talented Diego Maradona.

Not for nothing is Leo Messi the central figure of *Entre-Nous*. It is through Lionel Messi that this book thinks that which is, in the spirit of Jean-Luc Nancy's work on Hegel, between-them-and-us; that which is, specifically, between Messi and the Argentine nation. It is a thinking that, in order to "get" what is at stake—a thinking that begins with the question of "essence," a thinking that cannot be disarticulated, in our supposedly postnational moment, as nothing other than the "essence" of the (Argentine) nation—in the ways that Messi gives life to Heidegger's *Mitsein*. Because of Messi, *Entre-Nous* wrestles with the philosophical and political difficulty that is *Mitsein* in two discursive modes. Predominantly, the first chapter offers a critique of the concept of entre-nous in a recognizably philosophico-political discourse, but it also interrupts this mode with a series of italicized reflections, reflections that provide an anthropological, shall we say, meditations on how Messi's relationship to Argentina registers in Buenos Aires at key moments in the qualifying campaign for the 2018 World Cup in Russia. The "anthropological" mode seeks to both explicate and animate what Messi means, how Messi is rendered, in the nation of his birth at a critical juncture in Argentina's footballing life. In short, how does *Mitsein* manifest itself when there is, a priori, overdetermined by history, no possibility of *Mitsein* culminating in love?

Crying for Argentina.

The event of *Mitsein* as such is, for Argentine fans, what they have been denied, what they have not experienced with Messi. For Los Celestes fans—and of this Argentines are sure beyond words—Barça is always Messi's preference. It is where, in Heidegger's terms, Messi is. It is where the truth—*die Wahrheit*—of Messi resides. It is where Messi's heart, his love, resides. Even if Argentines do not pronounce outright that they "know" that Messi's allegiance, his "first fidelity," if you will, is to Catalunya (and not Argentina, the country of his birth, that is, to "them," to their beloved Los Celestes), for them Catalunya, and Barça most especially, is what stands entre-nous, between him and them.

It is Messi's performances for Barça, especially in games such as the one against PSG, that confirms for the Argentines that Messi is decisively not theirs. He wears the Argentine colors and has pulled on the Los Celestes shirt more than 120 times to date (128 times, at the time of writing), most recently in his appearances for Argentina in the 2018 World Cup. (The last four appearances at the 2018 World Cup ended, as we know only too well, in painful defeat.) The captain's armband adorns his upper left arm, but his heart, Argentine national team fans suspect and quite often say (and loudly, too), is emblazoned with the yellow and red of the Senyera, the colors of the Catalan flag.

In the moment of the event that was *Mitsein*, I find it, for once, no matter the philosophical niceties of the argument that follows in these pages, hard to quarrel with Porteños, as the natives of Buenos Aires are called. I have a certain sympathy for them. For how they feel that they are outside of the possibility of the event of *Mitsein* (love) with Lionel Messi. His heart, as they say, belongs to the Catalans. How does one assuage such psychic hurt? How does one countenance such an abandonment of the nation? There is no case to be made against the South American nation in the face of the unarguable truth that was the PSG event. There is no gainsaying the force of *Mitsein*. Like love, *Mitsein* is a jealous mistress: there is only room for one.

The truth of the matter, then, is that while the governing rubric of *Entre-Nous* is the logic of that which is between-us, this argument is thrown into blessed relief by the event of *Mitsein*. This interplay between the titular concept, "entre-nous," and *Mitsein*, shapes each of the book's two chapters as well as the "Interlude." The dialectic that is "entre-nous" *Mitsein* grounds the Messi chapter as well as chapter two, which thinks the relationship between Luis Suárez and his national team coach, Óscar Washington Tabárez. Additionally, and much more so than in the Messi chapter, we find that because of what is entre-nous Suárez and Tabárez, love again demands to be thought.[5] This same dialectical logic permeates the "Interlude" where we encounter that what is between the author and himself is the incorrigibility of his place of origin. Once more we turn to love, this time a love that is complicated by, among other factors, time. In the "Interlude" the time of love is intensified by distance. However, for all that, love shows itself to be resilient, what is more, and a mode of sustaining the author, in the face of his uncertainty, in the diaspora.

For just one moment, one glorious, never-to-be-forgotten moment, the joy of being-with trumped everything. This is what Leo Messi gives us. This is his gift to us, his unique gesture, his almost indiscernible, gentle nod in the direction of Heidegger's (and Nancy's) philosophy.

The paradox, of course—and the power of the paradox must never be underestimated, as *Entre-Nous* makes clear—is that it would have been impossible to grasp the event of *Mitsein* without thinking (through) the concept that is entre-nous. And so, through the person of Messi, through Messi's "animation" of *Mitsein*, through the event of Messi bringing it to life, it becomes possible to understand how Messi's "being-with" Barça puts him in tension and often in outright conflict with his native Argentina. What is the nation-state to do when its most brilliant footballer shows such love, before the world, for the *autonomista* (the nominally, and not so nominally—as the independence stirrings in Catalunya attest—independent regions of Spain) among which he has lived since the age of thirteen? How can such a display of unadulterated love, passion, and commitment not be understood as an act of betrayal? How is Argentina not to feel as a lover spurned? Or, as Jean-Luc Nancy would have it in terms that are fundamental to the argument of this book, how is the demonstration of *Mitsein* (for/with the other) not to be experienced as (a) negation?

The path from Lionel Messi, as traced through *Entre-Nous*, is not so much one that leads from football to philosophy, or from philosophy to football. It is, rather, that this book proposes philosophy—as a mode of enjoying philosophy—as the only proper way to fully grasp, to comprehend with some authority, the actions of a Leo Messi. Leo Messi must be approached philosophically. To that end, *Entre-Nous* absorbs Martin Heidegger, Jean-Luc Nancy, Jacques Lacan, and others entirely into its thinking of Messi, Suárez, and Tabárez.

It is, then, not so much that Leo Messi made this all possible but rather that the invitation from philosophy to football, from football to philosophy, was already there. As such, *Entre-Nous* marks nothing more than the act of taking up a long-standing and, in truth, permanent invitation to think sport philosophically and to come to terms with philosophy through sport.

Still, there is something fortuitous about this "arranged" (or was it always preordained, preordained in that very moment that Heidegger sought to make like Beckenbauer?) engagement between Leo Messi and Martin Heidegger. Something on the order of a Hessian beginning: "So every virtue, so our grasp of truth, / Blooms in its day." "Our day," the day of the event of *Mitsein*, can be identified as March 8, 2017. That day allowed for a "blooming" of the question of *Mitsein*, which opened onto the possibility of "grasping" a Heideggerian "truth."

March 8, 2017, was an event. It was an event made, as Nancy would insist, in the "present." It was an event that brought to light, brought to life, the relation between football and philosophy. Or, following the "exchange" of terms between Heidegger and the German poet Paul Celan, it becomes possible to assert that *Entre-Nous* is the act of staking a claim to what Heidegger conceives of as the clearing (*Lichtung*); for his part, Celan takes the concept up as "*Lichtzwang*" (light compulsion)."[6] *Entre-Nous* is that creation made possible by thinking philosophy and football, by thinking football as a brief moment of an old left-winger's joy. And then, following that illumination of joy—the dream of making-like, zu sein wie—and the philosophical questions that emanate from it across the world of football, across the world because of football, *Fußball*, futbol, and, yes, even Neymar's world of *futebol*.

This can be done because Martin Heidegger cleared for us the way to think (and it must have been a slightly tentative if not creaky kind of making-like) what is entre-nous in/between Argentina and Barcelona; what is between the Uruguayan "Maestro" Tabárez and his star student Suárez, a star student who nonetheless tests his every limit as teacher; and what is between an amateur footballer from apartheid Cape Town and his teammates. (In truth, of course, the way was already "cleared"; such a thinking was permitted, from the very beginning. In fact, the beginning is that which, before all else, demands thinking. No matter, I take a certain pleasure in stamping *Entre-Nous* with Heidegger's seal of approval.) For thinking with joy, for demonstrating, as Heidegger did in that carriage on that now long-ago train ride, how it is to think the joy of football. The kind of joy, that is, that understands itself as free to take liberties with Heidegger; liberties that are, however, always taken affectionately.

Surely there can be no more pleasurable debt to Martin Heidegger than to acknowledge how *Mitsein* "compels" the joy of thinking football to "light." How brightly it sheds Celanian joy on that "light" that is our—my—love of football. And my love of Messi, Suárez, and Tabárez, and a now long defunct team named Lansur United Amateur Football Club that I loved playing on. A team from the working-class Cape Flats township of Hanover Park that was once a buffer against the stringencies of apartheid. Finally, *Entre-Nous* is a mark of how football does not so much resolve what is entre-nous as give the concept the opportunity to come fully to, to come fully into, the philosophical "light."

# ACKNOWLEDGMENTS

I had no intention, when I started writing *In Motion, At Rest: The Event of the Athletic Body* (published 2013), more than a decade ago, of producing three works on philosophy and sport. I had no idea that I would spend so much time, all of it enjoyably, thinking about the event in sport, the event and sport. And now that the time has come to acknowledge those people who helped in the process of writing *Entre-Nous: Between the World Cup and Me*, it seems abundantly clear that *Entre-Nous* is the final part of that project. In between, no pun intended, I published *The Burden of Over-representation: Race, Philosophy, Sport* (2018).

These three works do not so much echo each other as manifest a sustained (and sustaining) interest in sport and race, philosophy, and the event, and, perhaps most importantly, they articulate a commitment to producing a language for thinking sport that can bear the (philosophical, political) weight of thinking sport.

These acknowledgements, it is my hope, mark my final foray into this field. Time to call it a day. I've enjoyed the run, but there are other things I'd like to say. At least I'd like to try. Besides, three's a good number.

I've been fortunate, in this process, to have the benefit of truly incisive, sympathetic, and patient editors on all three projects.

*Entre-Nous* provided me with the opportunity to work with Courtney Berger. I've known Ms. Berger, mainly from a distance, for a while, going back to my time in Durham, where our paths crossed at Duke University Press and on the Duke campus. However, none of my previous interactions with her prepared me for Ms. Berger's response to the project when I first sent it to her. Her insight will remain with me. Verbatim: "I thought I would learn about sport through philosophy but instead I learned about philosophy through sport." Nothing could top that. In a single sentence, she grasped what I was trying to do. I am forever grateful for her confidence in the project, for the alacrity with which she responded. But, mostly, I will always be in her intellectual debt for that most incisive of remarks.

I first imagined *Entre-Nous* as a very different undertaking. For suggesting such a project to me, and talking me through (too) many, I am sure, of the initial drafts, I owe Aaron Jaffe a tremendous thank you. It was especially pleasurable to share the Heidegger-Messi moment with him. Without Aaron's prompting, I would not have written this book. My friends David Ellison and David Faflik were generous and patient with me. From Sydney and Brisbane, David Ellison pushed me to make the "Interlude" true to itself. David insisted that I dig deep, and then deeper still. He found, with unerring sharpness, those moments when my reticence won out. He would not permit it. Thanks for insisting. David Faflik made me see where the philosophical threads led, and he guided me along that path—I am sure he would name it "Hegel"—with a sure intellectual hand. Once more, Dr. Faflik, once more I have reason to be grateful to you. From Ljubljana, Jernej Habjan offered his usual insights, whip smart, and laced with a sense of humor sharp enough to make Dave Chapelle sit up and take notice. *Hvala.*

Jeff Nealon has been a consistent presence in all three projects. With each reading of my work, my regard for Jeff grows. With every critique he offers, I learn. Furthermore, I now find that when I am writing I try to imagine how Jeff might respond. It seems to me a good thing to be, in advance, haunted by Jeff Nealon.

Over the past eight years I have relied upon the administrative expertise, kindness, and friendship of Ms. Renee Milligan. Whatever thanks I offer her will be insufficient but, as things stand, it's the best I've got and so it will have to do. She, no doubt, will have something to say about my insufficiencies.

My research assistant, Dr. N. Bragg, was, as always, industrious and utterly reliable.

Ms. Sandra Korn, who assists Ms. Berger, is, above all, a sensitive partisan.

She does not take defeat lightly, a characteristic that has the fortunate effect of endearing her to other partisans. It is a pleasure to meet a fellow traveler.

To Sara "Mama" Leone: Billy Joel has something to answer for. Thank you for your excellent editorial labors.

Dirk Uffelmann provided invaluable assistance with my clumsy German translations. Followed by his ineluctably sardonic humor. *Danke.*

WM, as is his wont, provided access as it was needed and, again, without fail, offered "reassurance." "That's all you need." His words, and needed they were. Thanks.

Much of the rewriting, or perhaps the very first writing, of this book was undertaken in Minneapolis during the 2016 Christmas holidays. Steve, Mary, and ATrane were wonderful hosts to Nip, Jane, and me. Nip and his brothers, ATrane and Alex, had a great time hanging out, and Nip learned to cross the street all by himself. Mary served up a never-ending supply of good food, and Steve introduced me to a cool music store where I bought my first Lee Morgan LP.

I have long lived with that 1985 Lansur United team. Until our thirtieth reunion, I could not have imagined that I would one day be compelled to write about our experience. I am grateful to Shaheeda for organizing the reunion. To the eleven other guys on that team, and to four or five other guys who moved—either then or later—in its orbit, what I have tried to do here is honor our team. Now that Lansur United is gone, through *Entre-Nous* I have tried to remember. And it is my hope that I have paid homage to the lives we lived then.

If Alain Badiou, Gilles Deleuze, and Jacques Derrida are the figures who dominate *In Motion, At Rest*, and *The Burden of Over-representation* turns, decisively, on Derrida, then *Entre-Nous* owes almost everything to Jean-Luc Nancy. His work, *Hegel: The Restlessness of the Negative*, which I first pored over in Minneapolis and then in Ithaca, gave *Entre-Nous* its philosophical bearings.

Por Izzy, "Izz-Bizz," *mi guapa perra*.

For Nip, who regards Cape Town as at once a wonder and a mystery.

For Bug, who visited Baires with me and was decidedly underwhelmed.

Finally, por Juanita: *Gracias, mi amor*. I am sure that you will find it amusing to have a work that depends so extensively on abstraction dedicated to you. I'm afraid it's a burden you'll now have to bear. Thanks for putting up with it. I promise to try and do better next time, although I have no clue as what "better" will either look like or what it might yield.

# INTRODUCTION

Entre-Nous | *Between the World and Me*

> The instability and the fragility of an encounter, of a division, the unity of which cannot be arrested or pinned down.
> ——JEAN-LUC NANCY, "Sense"

> As soon as we encounter the other, as soon as we open our mouth or show our teeth, our economy fractures space (and) time, breaks away from the continuity of the Matrix thus always creating another reaction, another unexpected direction—another text, another violence—a move *of* and/or *in* the Matrix. ——JEAN-PAUL MARTINON, *After "Rwanda": In Search of a New Ethics*

RELATION THROUGH SEPARATION · It is impossible to think relation, Jean-Luc Nancy argues, without separation. Relation is what is established in relation to, in the aftermath of what is consonant with separation. (Something along the lines of what Nancy names "co-appearance," that which manifests itself in the moment of, as a consequence of the act of, separation. As such, relation must always be thought as grounded in, as a form of, negation. All relation, as thought here, is relation to negation. Relation is always a matter of the relation to negation; as such, negation is a concept that is critical for thinking, for the thinking of *Entre-Nous*.) So conceived, relation is constituted out of both what makes (that which makes up) separation and that which emerges out of that which divides; that which it divides, that which it divides into. That which, let us say, establishes difference from, puts "distance between," and, in so doing, forms the basis of the relation between what might be named A

FIGURE I.1  Lionel Messi celebrates Barcelona's 6–1 win over Paris Saint-Germain, March 8, 2017. Credit: Luis Gene/AFP/Getty Images.

and B. Rendered figuratively, in which the sign ↔ marks both, simultaneously, separation (divided from) and connection (related to), we can say that A ↔ B. A "and" B stand in relation: stand in a relation of conjuncture (joined to each other) that must be thought, in the same act, in the same moment, as simultaneously "bound" by separation as well being bound in/through negation.

We can count among the elements that constitute, make possible, that take as their goal, separation, an array of political forces and desires. All of these, without exception, are borne out of a commitment to one mode of being rather than another. These elements, in their individuality and their collectivity, demand a recognition of the plurality of histories that make up a singularity. If we follow the terms of Nancy's "being singular plural,"[1] we can say that these elements demand an accounting for the various "infrahuman" tensions that mark the life of every individual; those tensions that mark life itself, as such.

What exists in separation and, as such, as relation through/because of separation is something akin to the intricate way in which Nancy proposes, in his essay "Cosmos Baselius,"[2] that we understand the "unity of the world" as "not one" but, as it would follow, as a "multiplicity of worlds . . . within this world."[3] A "multiplicity of worlds" that composes a single world (a world of "exceptional singularity") denotes the presence of infinite tensions among the constituent elements; a "multiplicity of worlds" in which the "exceptional singularity" of a Messi finds himself located, whether he wants it or not, and sometimes in the same moment, sometimes by turn, sometimes in turn, in this "world" and that.[4] These elements, political forces, desires, articulations, commitments, and so on share the same time and space (Martinon's "space [and] time") and, as such, are always possessed of a certain combustibility. Out of the interplay between and among these elements there emerge, among other effects, the surging up of difference, conflict among the elements, jockeying for primacy or articulation; all these effects seem to be, in one way or another, the inevitable outcome of how these various elements respond to one another. Politically speaking, the effect of this interplay is that it renders individual subjects vulnerable to the force of judgment or, worse, indictment. We have already seen the latter effect play out, and we will see it again in greater detail shortly, with regard to Messi's relationship to Argentina. That is, Messi as "insufficiently" Argentine because of, in Goethe's terms, his "elective affinity" for FC Barcelona.[5]

That is not to say that *entre-nous* is an entirely "negative" political condition, because there is also another side to it. It is what one might describe as a conspiratorial mischievousness. *Entre-Nous*, as such, touches only very lightly on this effect, but the very concept of *entre-nous* turns on the notion of the (shared) secret. That is, following Jacques Derrida's work on the postcard, an understanding of the secret not as that (item of information, invariably highly politicized) which is largely unknown, but rather that which is publicly understood but, nevertheless, demands a conspiracy of "silence" for its functioning. That is, one whispers, with affection (or not), in jest (or not), about that person who is between us, that s/he is "really just out of it" or is silly to hold such-and-such an opinion. There is, needless to say, an extremely porous (and thin) line that divides conspiratorial mischievousness from outright judgment (that is, in its negative sense, as indictment or condemnation). Although it is, by and large, the negative aspects of what is *entre-nous* that engages this project, there are, nonetheless (especially in the "Interlude," that which, structurally, organizationally, typographically, literally stands between Messi and Luis Suárez) moments when the more playful possibilities of what is between manifest themselves, lending a certain levity—and, indeed, a kind of nostalgic, wistful pleasure—to *Entre-Nous*. As such, the possibilities that the conspiratorial and the mischievous (routine practices in daily life, after all) open should never be underestimated; and, because of this, should be enjoyed, politically and otherwise, all the more.

In this spirit, then, it would be wrong to name the primary deployment of *entre-nous* in *Entre-Nous* as purely "negative," as loss, absence, political deficiency. (All the while, of course, understanding how important "negation" as such is to the work of Jean-Luc Nancy, whose thinking is central to this project.) Rather, what is between is thought as an attempt to understand the effects of forces—and the forces themselves, of course—that obtain in and between and among what is the time and the space of *entre-nous*. The project, in short, is to think everything—or as much as possible—that constitutes (the) *entre-nous*, to think the forces of separation that make up, in their complementarity ("water and wine") and antagonism ("water and oil"), that which is *entre-nous* (Goethe, 52). It is to think what forces are present, how they are operative, what the nature of their work is, and—this is beyond question (difficult as they may be to "pin down")—to understand how they work incessantly, restlessly, toward and for separation. It is to recognize that there is no constitutive outside to relation. Everything is relation. However, this does not mean that "relation" as such operates in an overdetermined fashion. It must (still; that is, more than ever) be thought for, identified, explicated, struggled with and over. The precise nature of the relation must be specified under the condition of "no outside."

Let me cast the matter in the intensely racialized (the geopolitics of space) terms offered by Ta-Nehisi Coates in his work *Between the World and Me*, terms that figure prominently in *Entre-Nous* as a study of the politics and philosophy of relation. Describing the fatal sense of enclosure (incarceration, the overdetermined carcerality of urban black life, as it were) that he, his family, his friends, his neighbors, those other black kids he walked in mortal fear of, and the entire black community experienced as normative life in the West Baltimore of his youth, Coates offers a fatalistic declarative: "We could not get out."[6] We will return to the notion of the impossibility of escape as raised by Coates in the "Interlude," but suffice it to say for now that the irrepressibility of relation, the unrelenting demand to think relation, is precisely what stands, in *Entre-Nous*, as not only between the world and me but, indeed, *as* the world and me. The world as constituted out of nothing so much as the thinking of relation: the indefatigability of, shall we name it, the ubiquity, the constant need to negotiate the world as relation. In the terms that Goethe borrows from eighteenth-century chemistry and then renders as the discourse of thwarted love, "Just as each thing has an adherence to itself, so it must also have a relationship to other things" (Goethe, 52).

For Messi, as for Suárez, it is the political reality of the nation-state, a reality frequently experienced by Messi as oppressive; Suárez, for his part, encounters his native Uruguay as almost invariably demanding but also as supportive, as the source of solace that only the nation (or, perhaps only the nation that allows for the hegemony of a coach such as Tabárez), in its plenitude, can give. In the "Interlude," however, relation figures much more in Coates's (racialized and political) register. In the "Interlude," it is first the apartheid and then the (failures of the) postapartheid state, mediated as it is by a diasporic reality that complicates that already complex mode of being in relation to the world, that forms the political DNA of relation. The impossible struggle of "get out"; the struggle to remain in relation at all costs, to remain in relation from somewhere else (the diaspora); the unwinnable struggle to "get out," a psychopolitical inexorability (a battle against and with the self that is Sisyphean in cast) that is as much welcomed as it combatted as though it were a matter of life and death. Sometimes, it must be added, this battle is conducted more bitterly than others. Sometimes resignation wins the day.

Out of this tumultuous "unity" of (overdetermined political) fate and (the misguided belief in Nietzschean self-) will,[7] of opposition and complementarity, which we must pronounce as precarious and whose energy is almost impossible to "arrest," emerges, time and again, as something other than the forces of separation. What comes into being, what is released into life, what is made politically possible, just now and then, are those forces within separation that are themselves struggling to establish new modalities, new nodes, of relation. In relation, constitutively present, is separation; out of separation, relation; many of these relations we can, to some extent or other, anticipate; others are more likely to catch us entirely by surprise when they present themselves to us. And, if we are so fortunate, then, in Nietzsche's poetic terms, in that "autumnal hour of ripeness" we find ourselves as (Nietzsche's) beneficiaries: that moment when the relation of separation to relation reveals itself to us, "almost as a gift" (Nietzsche, 510).

Let us render this unruly, restless mode of philosophical production schematically, a representation that is important for understanding how relation works through separation in this project. That is, how the relation between relation and separation throws light on Leo Messi's relationship to the nation-state of his birth (Argentina; the nation he represents at the Copa Mundial) and the deep bond that marks his ties to Catalunya (where he plays his club football for FC Barcelona), and, of course, the amalgam of forces at work, active, politically intense, that constitute what is *entre-nous* Messi and Argentina/Catalunya; how that relation, and its numerous effects, cannot but be bound by and find themselves bound up within the logic of *entre-nous*.

Messi, of course, is recognized not only as the greatest player of his generation but ranks among the greatest of all time.[8] Born in Rosário, Argentina, in June 1987, Messi is the son of a factory manager (his father, Jorge Messi) and a magnet manufacturing workshop employee (his mother, Celia Cuccittini).[9] To watch Messi today is to be struck not only by his gifts as a footballer but to almost immediately recognize his "compromised" (it appears to us) physical stature. He plays as though he were bent over from the lower spine, so odd and arresting is his posture. His "compromised" body is the result of a childhood growth hormone deficiency, diagnosed when Messi was ten years old and playing as a junior for his hometown club, Newell's Old Boys. The treatment needed for Messi's condition was expensive, about $1,000 per month, and his father's health insurance covered it only for two years. Newell's had agreed to pay for treatment after his father's insurance ran out but reneged when the payment came due. The Buenos Aires–based River Plate,[10] one of Argentina's powerhouse clubs, was rumored to be willing to pick up the tab, but nothing came of it. (Historically, Argentine football has been dominated by the two dominant Buenos Aires clubs, River Plate and Boca Juniors.)

However, Jorge, who is partly Catalan, still had family there, and a trial was arranged for Lionel at Barça. (Messi's mother, as her name suggests, traces her origins to Italian immigrants.) Messi immediately impressed the FC Barcelona first team director, Charly Rexach, and, despite some hesitation on Rexach's part,[11] Messi was signed (on December 14, 2000). This contract was inked, so the story goes (it has reached apocryphal proportions by now), on a paper napkin, the only writing material that Rexach could find. The greatest player in the world, secured by a handy paper napkin—it makes for a good story. In February 2001, Messi and his family moved to Barcelona, and within a year young Lionel was installed at the La Masia de Can Planes (more commonly known by its Catalan name, "La Masia," or "The Farmhouse"),[12] Barça's famous youth training headquarters.[13] The generation of players whom Messi joined at La Masia was a distinctly very talented group, including the central defender

Gerard Piqué and the midfielders Cesc Fàbregas and Pedro;[14] not only were they talented—all of them would, for various lengths of time, eventually star for Barça—but they would constitute the core of the team for a considerable length of time, although by 2016 only Messi and Piqué remained. However, that generation that Messi encountered at the Barça youth headquarters, an old country house revamped to house some sixty members enrolled in the club's youth system, has become famous as the class of 1987—which designates, of course, the year in which all three were all born (Fàbregas in May; Piqué in February; and Pedro in July—Sergio Busquets, another of the stars, was born in July 1988).[15]

Messi's teammate at Barça, Luis Suárez, on whom the second chapter of *Entre-Nous* turns, was also born in 1987 (January 24, in Salto, Uruguay some 308 kilometers northwest of the capital Montevideo, and about 12 kilometers from the Argentine border town of Concordia). *Entre-Nous* is, quite unexpectedly then, also a book about a generation, a generation in football, a book about two of the best players of their generation. That Messi and Suárez were born exactly five months apart, to the day, separated by a single border and less than 200 miles (190 miles, to be exact, or 306 kilometers), adds its own relationality, a kind of national intimacy (the proximity of neighbors, with all the complication that such proximity entails, especially as it pertains to football in Latin America), if you will, to this project. These connections are, of course, intensified by the fact that (from 2014–) Messi and Suárez found themselves teammates on Barcelona.

After the central midfielder Sergio Busquets, Messi is thus the second-youngest of the 1987 quartet but, by some considerable measure, the standout performer. He is the key to Barça as a team, having won eight La Liga titles, four Champions League medals, and a host of individual awards, not least among them his five FIFA Ballons d'Or (the Ballon d'Or is FIFA's award for the best male player; it is voted on by international journalists, national team coaches, and captains). Messi is one of the only two players to have won this award five times (Ronaldo is the other)—four times consecutively, from 2009 to 2012.[16] Individually, the Ballons d'Or are a poor metonym for all the awards Messi has secured in his career, but they undoubtedly provide a handy place to begin the process of tabulating the many that have been afforded him. To count them all, an abacus or three would be advised. As such, what Messi has done is make of himself a truly defining figure in the history of football, a history that appears in need of revision every time Messi steps onto the football field, more often than not since the 2014–15 season in the company of Luis Suárez.

If *Entre-Nous* presents Messi as an intensely *"singular* plural" individual, his teammate Suárez is apprehended here in a much more interpersonal way. That is, Suárez is thought in relation to his Uruguayan national team coach, Óscar Washington Tabárez, so that we can say Suárez and Tabárez are always in a relation that is at once an intense(ly related), R, as befits a player-coach relationship, and separated, again, befitting because S marks the "spacing"—in terms of the hierarchy or chain of command that structures a football team, often more so when it comes to a national team setup, where the coach is presumed to shoulder most of the burden of responsibility for performance, for, that is, representing the nation. That is, the *entre-nous* that constitutes the R between self and other. Nevertheless, what is salient about the Suárez-Tabárez relationship are the affective and political forces that bind two individuals to each other, self-self, the intensity of "being-with-one-another," and the history and the political ideology that frame their relationship. There are forces operative here *entre-nous* Tabárez and his star striker Suárez that are equally, and simultaneously, it would seem, incendiary and affirming.

Suárez, who has scored more international goals than any other Uruguayan player (forty-nine goals in ninety-five appearances; a fantastic rate of more than a goal every two games), has worked his way up to the European elite after beginning his career with the Montevideo team Nacional, for whom he played only twenty-seven games (ten goals). Suárez moved to Montevideo from Salto at the age of seven, and his parents separated when he was nine. Growing up, Suárez worked as a street sweeper in Montevideo, and many speculate that his aggressive behavior on the pitch can be traced to his impoverished childhood. After Nacional he joined the modest Dutch team Groningen (twenty-nine games, ten goals), which led to a transfer to Ajax, historically the most successful club in the Netherlands (it was, as we know, also the great Dutch—and Barcelona player and manager—Johan Cruyff's first club). At Ajax Suárez became a star. In 110 games for Ajax, Suárez scored a phenomenal eighty-one goals, a strike rate that boggles the mind. In January 2011, he was transferred ("traded") to Liverpool, where he quickly established himself as one of the best players in Europe, with sixty-nine goals, in the much more competitive English Premier League, in the same number of games as he played for Ajax. After the 2014 Copa Mundial he left Liverpool for Barcelona.

Suárez is a player renowned as much for his prodigious and impish talent as for his ability to attract controversy. (He is something of, a concept I have deployed elsewhere,[17] an état *voyou*, a lovable, mischievous rogue with a commensurate capacity for getting into trouble. It is not only in the "Interlude" then, that mischievousness is manifest, but it is, both a priori and "post ipso facto," as it were, present with Suárez.) Playing in the quarter final of the 2010 World Cup in South Africa, Suárez deliberately handled the ball on the goal line. From the resulting penalty, the Ghanaian striker Asamoah Gyan hit the bar. Suárez, who was sent off for his offense, stopped before heading down the tunnel and cheered when Gyan missed. "I made the save of the tournament," an unrepentant Suárez declared as Uruguay triumphed 4–2 in the penalty shootout to advance to the semifinals against the Dutch. With the talismanic Suárez suspended, a game Uruguay lost 3–2 to the Netherlands. Suárez returned for the third-place game, which Uruguay also lost, 3–2 to Germany. Every time he touched the ball in that ceremonial game, the warm-up to the World Cup final between Spain and the Netherlands, Suárez was booed. A pyrrhic act of loud, *vuvuzela*-based solidarity between the South African crowd and their vanquished African neighbors to the northwest, one presumes.[18]

Suárez's other misdemeanors include diving (deliberately throwing himself to the ground in order to win a free kick; or, if the "offense" takes place in the opposition's penalty area, a spot kick). And he was involved in a nasty brouhaha about racism with an opponent, Patrice Evra, while playing for Liverpool, a charge that he has vehemently denied. However, what has won him the most notoriety is his propensity for biting an opponent, an offense for which he has been suspended thrice; first with Ajax and then with Liverpool.

However, it is the third biting incident, in the 2014 World game against Italy, that is determining for his relationship with Tabárez. It is also the biting incident that frames the chapter on him and Tabárez. In the seventy-ninth minute of a 2014 World Cup match that was scoreless, Suárez challenged for the ball in the Italian goal area and lunged into Giorgio Chiellini, the opposing defender, who clutched his shoulder. Suárez, in dramatic fashion, threw himself to the ground. Chiellini pointed to the bite marks on his shoulder, but the referee took no action. Uruguay scored from the resulting corner, the only goal in the game that knocked out Italy. However, after reviewing the incident, the FIFA disciplinary committee suspended Suárez for nine international games (the longest suspension in the history of the World Cup), ending his participation in the 2014 Copa Mundial and, effectively, with it Uruguay's chances of advancing.

Not only at home in Uruguay but also internationally Suárez's punishment was met with a significant show of support for the then-Liverpool striker. Even the victim of his aggression, Chiellini, pronounced the ban excessive. (Suárez apologized on Twitter, and Chiellini graciously accepted.) Among those who denounced the ban were Suárez's national team captain, Diego Lugano; the president of the Uruguayan Football Association (AUF), Wilmar Valdez; and Suárez's lawyer (who called it a "European-based campaign against Suárez"). (No matter, it seems, that the first two biting offenses were committed in Europe; in fact, it was Suárez's history of biting that lead to the severity of the ban—three bites and you're out, it would appear, at least from the Copa Mundial, if that's where the crucial third bite takes place.)[19] In general, the ban was received with scorn, skepticism, accusations of discrimination against a small Latin American country, and, quite remarkably, denunciation of FIFA by the Uruguayan president, José Mujica. The heavyset president, who has the avuncular appearance of an idiosyncratic relative (his coat doesn't quite fit and his sweatshirts are a little too roomy, all of which works to make his girth entirely comforting), pronounced the FIFA officials "una manga de viejos hijos de puta"—a bunch of old sons of bitches.[20] Such is the passion that Suárez inspired in his fellow Uruguayans, from the president's office on down.

However, *Entre-Nous* is specifically concerned with what emerges *entre-eux* Suárez and his national team coach, the highly esteemed "El Maestro" ("The Teacher," a position he did indeed once hold, as a primary [grade] school teacher), Óscar Washington Tabárez. A deep-thinking football man, Tabárez is an avid reader who regards the work of his fellow Uruguayan Eduardo Galeano highly. Tabárez is also a keen admirer of the Argentine-born revolutionary Ernesto "Che" Guevara (he named his daughter Tania after Che's last *compañera*), and perhaps the national coach best suited, in terms of political sensibility, to coaching República Oriental del Uruguay—the "Oriental Republic." Uruguay is known as the "Switzerland of Latin America," in part because it "boasts the highest levels of literacy in the continent and one of the lowest levels of corruption"; it is the second-smallest country in the Americas, and yet its tiny population, some three and a half million people, "enjoy the highest Index of Human Development, one of the most equitable distributions of income, and of the highest life-expectancy rates."[21] Tabárez and his native land were made for each other, in terms of how they understand being in the world and, of course, in football, where Tabárez's penchant for open, attacking football taps into the long tradition of playing *joga bonito* (the "beautiful game") beautifully. In the "Author's Confession," which opens *Football in Sun and Shadow*, Galeano gives voice to his love for beautiful football, a love that overwhelms any propensity for partisanship. "I've finally learned to accept myself for who I am," Galeano writes, "a beggar for good football. I go about the world, hand outstretched, and in the stadiums I plead: 'A pretty move, for the love of God.'"[22] A "beggar" impatient with partiality, and with decidedly aesthetic tastes, to boot, our Señor Galeano.

In Suárez, much like in former Uruguayan strikers such as Daniel "el castor" ("The Beaver") Fonseca and Diego Forlán, Tabárez appears to have found a man who most closely resembles him.[23] All three strikers share Tabárez's commitment to playing beautifully, to representing "Los Charrúas" with passion and joy. (Translating roughly as "The Plows," "Los Charrúas" stands more as an honorific dedicated to honoring the Amerindian population who lived in the area millennia ago. The indigenous Charrúa were driven south by the Guaraní thousands of years ago into regions that today incorporate parts of southern Brazil, Argentina, and Uruguay.) Suárez is, like the other ten most-capped Uruguayan players in the nation's history, the product of Proceso de Institucionalización de Selecciones y la Formación de sus Futbolistas—the careful organization of the Uruguayan national system, from the youth teams, under-13, and under-15 through to the senior side. Tabárez instituted "El Proceso" ("The Process") in 2006, when he began his second spell as national team coach. Through El Proceso, Tabárez has managed to provide the entire structure of Uruguayan football with an identifiable style of play.

It is the fact that Tabárez and Suárez seem to have so much in common that, as the second chapter of *Entre-Nous* argues, must have made it so difficult for Tabárez, a deeply ethical man (the *tecnico* who always wants to do right by his players and by history), to confront the event of Suárez's third biting offense. After all, Suárez's act effectively put paid to Uruguay's chances of advancing in the 2014 Copa Mundial, given that he was—and remains, for now—the national team's lynchpin. How Tabárez confronted the event of the Chiellini bite, how he addressed it, given what is *entre-eux*, between them, between Tabárez and Suárez, between *el tecnico* and his player, is what this chapter addresses. There is something about this relationship that makes one wonder if, as a former school master, Tabárez ever approaches Suárez as "the boy that no schoolmaster wanted,"[24] to use the language of George Augustus Moore, novelist and, with Lady Gregory and William Butler Yeats, the leader of the Irish Literary Revival. Suárez, the irascible, marvelously talented charge who cannot, ever, be brought fully to heel—and a good thing, too, Tabárez would say, one suspects, given the figures who dominate his political archive. It is worth remembering a famous sentence from Moore's autobiography, *Confessions of a Young Man*, that foreshadows Suárez's—or shares with Suárez—an inevitable doom. The fate that Moore suffered as a schoolboy, anticipates—somewhat uncannily—Suárez's footballing demise at the 2014 Copa Mundial: "I was a boy that no schoolmaster wants, and the natural end to so wayward a temperament as mine was expulsion."[25] The Catholic "schoolboy" from nineteenth-century County Mayo who claimed Sir Thomas More as an ancestor and the irascible street urchin from Montevideo both know the experience of "expulsion," albeit "expulsions" of a very different nature. Moore went on to read and write literature, and thereafter he helped found a nationalist movement; Suárez, in his turn, found himself "expelled" from one of the two greatest spectacles in modern sport (the other being the Summer Olympics), and in doing so he condemned his nation to more or less, in his absence, guaranteed defeat; and his "expulsion" presented his coach with an ethical and philosophical quandary to test the very fiber of Tabárez's political beliefs.

As such, what is *entre-eux* Tabárez and Suárez is, of necessity, at once evocative of and distinct from what is *entre-nous* Messi and the nation-state (Argentina) and the *autonomista* (Catalunya). *Entre-Nous* seeks to understand both what is shared among these figures from neighboring countries and how they each demand a distinct and complementary thinking (which requires an a priori openness to dialectical agonism) of what is *entre-eux*. That is, what is between Suárez and Messi, what is between Suárez-Tabárez and Messi, what is between Argentina and Uruguay, what is between an "elective affinity" to the *autonomista* and allegiance (*Wahlverstandtschaft* as both an "alchemical" and a chemical reaction, or, set of relations), however qualified, uncertain, or complicated, to the nation-state. The point, then, is not to "compare," an impossibility, in any case, Messi and Suárez/Tabárez but to think the ways in which they pose/propose different articulations of the concept *entre-nous*. A thinking, of course, that is brought into sharp and personal relief in the "Interlude," where what is *entre-nous* shows itself to be, in truth, not about football at all. In fact, we could say that in the "Interlude" football is only the pretext or the first provocation for writing—itself a loaded act—the (apartheid-inspired) politics of *entre-nous*.

Nonetheless, the two chapters stand as the architectural pillars of *Entre-Nous*, in no small measure because they inaugurate the difficulty of accounting for, simultaneously and by turns, how to think in a single gesture that is singular but never solitary or in isolation (from other such gestures), as regards the relation of *entre-nous* to *entre-eux*. How are they to be distinguished? Can the two terms, and the thinking of relation they impel, be kept separate, however momentarily? *Entre-Nous* approaches this conceptual conundrum by trying to establish, however provisionally and tentatively, what different kinds of tensions mark relation, as figured through Messi, and those that arise *entre-eux* Suárez and Tabárez. This line of inquiry leads to the question of what happens when the passage of relation runs through, that is, within, the nation-state rather than between nation-states, or their equivalencies. It also makes imperative an explication of what happens to the thinking of separation when it takes as its primary articulation that which is *entre-eux* rather than that which is—a question that the "Interlude" takes up, is compelled to take up (with existential consequences)—a line of inquiry that demands a neologism, in another language, a language truly "foreign" to a key political constituency in the "Interlude," *entre-moi-et-moi-même*. What is between me and myself? What language can bear that, surely among the most intimate of relations? What language must be, in two senses, *made* to bear that which is *entre-moi-et-moi-même*?

> *Signes et événements.* / Perhaps it is in the holes that movement takes place. —— GILLES DELEUZE, quoted in Michael Hardt, *Gilles Deleuze: An Apprenticeship in Philosophy*

Thinking what is *entre-moi-et-moi-même* is the source—the first thinking, the first articulation—of the "Interlude." It is about an amateur football team, Lansur United Amateur Football Club (AFC) and the ways in which the politics—the postulates, in and from which direction is thought emanating?—of what is *entre-nous* is explicated through a "singular plural" subject. Moreover, a "singular plural" subject emerging from out of the context of the history of apartheid and its effects on this football club from the coloured[26] ("mixed race") township of Hanover Park. Like many other coloured townships, Hanover Park was—and remains, to this day—home to a working-class community in a region of the Western Cape known as the Cape Flats. (The Cape Flats, often described as a windswept area with hardy, sparse vegetation, is located about sixteen kilometers (about ten miles) from downtown Cape Town. On a clear day, the splendor of Table Mountain in all its majesty is brilliantly visible, but the city and the wealthy, leafy, tree-lined suburbs that nestle on the slopes of the mountain are, in truth, a world away.) The "Interlude" uses *entre-nous* to think what it is exactly that marks, deforms, and persists in the relation through separation that is extant between the apartheid state and the individual who moves, relentlessly and restlessly, between the post-/apartheid state and the United States. (It is important to note that "restlessness" is a key term for Nancy in his thinking on Hegel,[27] as announced in the title of his book, *Hegel: The Restlessness of the Negative*; the term that is rendered here, in order to achieve the full Hegelian effect, as *Rastlosigkeit*—the most positive philosophical iteration of the term in German. *Rastlosigkeit* is, as such, distinguished from terms such as *Ruhelosigkeit*, which has a similar meaning but does not carry the same positive aspect, or *unruhig*, which would be the adjectival form.)

The "Interlude" is not quite of the diasporic order of Moore's notion that, as he puts it, "a man travels the world in search of what he needs and returns home to find it."[28] Nor is it as inexorable a rendering of the relation to nativity (the place of birth, its—perpetual, unbreakable—hold on the self), but there is nevertheless a certain Moore-like quality to the "Interlude." The "Interlude" is, as much as anything, an address to an amateur football club, a club now more than twenty years defunct, that provides not so much a passage to "connectivity," to invoke Nancy, but to weave the thread that is separation-intimacy, the intimacy of separation, and what it means to live (with the effects of) deracination, a thread and a threat that binds this book, no matter how fragile and speculative it might be, a threat/thread that runs through *Entre-Nous*. That thread that links, in ways both assertive and uncertain, the chapters on Messi and Suárez-Tabárez to the "Interlude," that thread which throws *entre-nous* into relief and animates the concept in entirely unexpected ways.

As such, the "Interlude" argues for *entre-moi-et-moi-même* as that mode of thinking relation that is, at once, derived from and more than simply the derivation of one concept from another. That is, *entre-moi-et-moi-même* as a less fully articulated concept but by no means a secondary one. What *entre-moi-et-moi-même* does is give voice to the thinking that first uttered—however haltingly, a voice eminently unsure of itself, a voice struggling to come into itself, to come into its own language—*entre-nous*, this project's organizing concept, as a philosophico-political difficulty. *Entre-moi-et-moi-même*, then, stands as the "first" address of (and to) Messi, Suárez, and Tabárez, from within the world that is between-us, the world that is between them and me. *Entre-Nous*, in this sense, is a project that begins in the middle. Not in medias res but a book that can be read from the middle. From the middle out. From the middle in either direction. *Entre-Nous* as a work whose "logic," if such a term might be permitted, "unfolds" either from the middle or chronologically. Or *Entre-Nous* as a book to be read toward the middle. *Entre-Nous* as a book that frees the reader to begin, in an absolute sense, anywhere, randomly. The "logic" of *Entre-Nous* can be constructed out of a multiplicity of arrangements. It is a book that invites its "logic" to be, again, *made*.

It is, in this regard, a project that affords a "spatial"—conceptual—latitude. Here Michael Hardt's sense of Deleuzean possibility, which invites us to do something with-in the "space" that Deleuze opens up, is apropos. Quoting his subject, Hardt says, "It is in the holes that the movement takes place." As such, the "Interlude" performs several philosophical functions at once. It serves to mark, anchor, and name the "hole," and one in particular, that one out of which the (Nancian/Deleuzian) "movement" obtained its (Nancian) "restlessness." Having identified the "hole" and recognized the possibilities for thinking that it engenders, it is also, then, to acknowledge that this "movement" toward Messi, Tabárez, and Suárez, to phrase the direction of thinking—the thinking of *Entre-Nous*—inelegantly, is the consequence of an a priori "upsurge." The "hole" as the space, and the time, of a fecund volatility; the "hole" as the domesticized space of restlessness, a restlessness that threatens to undo the very grounds of its domesticity; the "hole" as the time of struggle, of struggles, against apartheid, a struggle within the self, that has identifiable political names. Simultaneously, of course, the very attempt to impose a name finds itself confronted by that name's (innate) stubbornness: it is always on the verge of plotting an escape; or, it is always likely to refuse to submit to the force of nomenklatura.

The "movement in the hole," then, as the result of a straining against the (domestic) containment that was apartheid (and the inequities that have persisted into postapartheid South Africa), as much as it emerged out of a determined inclining in the direction of the world. As such, *Entre-Nous* "moves" in and through a variegation of worlds that cohere in the "singular plural" world that is football. *Entre-Nous* stipulates to a world at once (far, far) removed from the habitus of an amateur football club, a world that did not permit of any conceiving of a(n intimate) relation between-Messi-and-me, and the force with which that world (for which the name "apartheid" is nothing but a convenient shorthand) was—can be—drawn into that world where the likes of Messi, Suárez, and Tabárez manifest themselves and, yes, flourish. *Entre-Nous* thinks, exploits, we might even say, the philosophico-political possibilities that surge up out of that division, that fecundity that is (the) between-us. As such, *Entre-Nous* posits a world, worlds, that do not so much need to be "overcome" as inhabited, conceptually, imaginatively. Inhabited, yes, but never without, never before (again and again), making its way through the passage that is *entre-nous*. As much as anything, the "Interlude" speaks to the strength that is *entre-nous* and the intensity with which what is between-us is grappled with, struggled against, all the while lived-with, all the while, in its own way, and on its own terms, giving form and (footballing) content to that which is *entre-nous*. What is *entre-nous* is, then, never, as such, overcome, defeated, or even, much to the name's regret, refused. No, is it only ever, as such, endured ("lived-with"). Instead it provides that which is *entre-nous*, a "singular plural" mode of being self in its relation to the world—to the world of the football pitch, both the local apartheid one, and the one on which Messi and Suárez strut their stuff, that pitch, those training grounds, where Tabárez has and continues to put his stamp on the game.

However, one can begin to think the "Interlude" by acknowledging that between the greatest player of his generation, between the most prolific and successful Uruguayan striker of all time (and a player once beloved by the Liverpool partisans, myself included, on Lansur United AFC), between a coach much admired for developing El Proceso, there is, for the amateur footballer, a world. A world that cannot, as Nancy remarks (in a term full of poetic Nietzschean and Heideggerian allusions; allusions from which, as we shall see shortly, Nancy invokes as much he takes his distance from them), be "bridged." What is between is absolute, unbridgeable. That world where what is *entre-nous* is indeed, at least under the conditions of apartheid, apprehended as world that can never be accessed. And yet it out of this world, where the amateur coloured player under apartheid could only admire (and dream about, hopelessly), that world that the world knows as the Copa Mundial but never participates in, that *Entre-Nous* in all likelihood found its first, tentative articulation. What is between-us, between Messi, Suárez, Tabárez, and the constitutive "us" of Lansur United is not so disconnected as to be out of place, as to have no place, in *Entre-Nous*. Au contraire. It is for this reason that the "Interlude" must be understood as more than a break or a rupture, more than a moment for reflection, a moment of reflection on Hanover Park from some other place. *Entre-Nous* would try, in vain, to name who is, properly speaking, other, and so it cannot stand as of or apart from the enunciation of the other. The "Interlude," then, is located as it is in the very constitutive middle of this project because it is the philosophical heartbeat of *Entre-Nous*. What is *entre-eux*, as it were, makes possible a different, disruptive, or "rupturous" (the preferred neologism here) thinking of the difficulties, the philosophical prospects and promises, and the politics, in short, of that which constitutes the "world" of football. A thinking that may last only a moment, a moment possible only courtesy of a "singular plural" philosophical mode.

It is a world that encompasses, as *Entre-Nous* tries to faithfully do, the world that is the World Cup, the Copa Mundial, the Coup du monde, Weltmeisterschaft, the world of football in its entirety, as least as offered here, in order to apprehend the force of *entre-nous* at once from the very highest echelons of the game and from a level that is not only rudimentary but well outside the realm of conventional philosophical and cultural reflection. There may be, because of this rendering of the "Interlude," a more prosaic truth at work, a truth that should be but is not always easy to admit. In this regard, Elspeth Probyn's work on shame has something instructive, and not a little bracing (so effective is it in pulling the self up short), to say: "When you get very interested in something, it quickly seems that the whole world is revealed in its light. Falling in love is a good example."[29] *Entre-nous* is the act of interest, intense interest, in *entre-nous*. It should, of course, be—especially for someone who has written on sport before, and is likely (if putatively unwilling) to do so again in the future[30]—easier to acknowledge how much, to blend the unrelated terms of Probyn's argument, how "quickly" "interest" can spawn "love." But even this acknowledgement does not quite get to the heart of the matter. *Entre-Nous* is the effect of an "interest" that enabled the "revelation" in a host of disconnected, but persistently evocative, worlds; worlds that spoke to, and speak of, one another, in terms that are frequently dissonant (discordant, disrupting each other, erupting into each other) but also consonant (concordant, in harmony, "at home" with each other) in their ability to draw something out of each other. Each, in its turn, each, almost without fail, surprising in what it "reveals" about the other.

In this way, what *Entre-Nous* offers is not so much a "connectivity" but the recognition that the force of what is between-us, and between-them, operates, at least provisionally, unequally, that is to say, in different registers but sometimes in ways that are resonant, evocative, and, indeed, revealing, of similarities, echoes, hauntings, and, yes, love. That is, as much as it reiterates the difference of what is *entre-nous* in these different worlds. In thinking what is *entre-nous*, therefore, this project begins, began, who knows how long ago, from a subject (Lansur United, I, me) long since preoccupied with the force of *entre-nous*. A subject that "surges up" through the thinking, a subject constituted out of what is *entre-nous*. As such, *Entre-Nous* emerges out of the world that is, that was (apartheid, the amateur's lack of skill, if not ambition), between the World Cup and me, and the constitutive, metonymic, necessarily partial, Lansur United. And yet, it is out of precisely that between-us, because of that between-us, that makes it possible to address, to conceive of, *entre-nous* as an idea that is philosophico-political to its core. It is for this reason that the concept of *entre-nous* governs *Entre-Nous*.

*Entre-Nous* begins, then, with the constitutive insufficiency that is at the core of the "Interlude." It recognizes the tension, the appropriation at work, in recounting a moment in an institution that has disappeared from Hanover Park, beloved by all its members (at the very least, beloved by most of them), which makes of the "we," as Nancy says, a "'we' [that] is inevitably 'us all,' where no one of us can be 'all' and each one of us, in turn (where all our turns are simultaneous as well as successive, in every sense), the other origin of the same world."[31] There is thus in play, spoken or not, an entire series of "origins of the same world" so that *Entre-Nous* at once stakes its claim to the "origin" and understands that in speaking—on behalf of, as—the "all" of Lansur United, the account of the club is, in every act of speaking, in relation with the unspoken,[32] simultaneously and successively unarticulated "other origins." It may very well be that it is in this way, as the stirrings and hauntings of these "other origins," that the idiomatic Afrikaans, which occasionally punctuates the "Interlude," speaks most volubly. Township Afrikaans, a language inflected by race as much as by class and geopolitics, marks, as and in itself, more clearly than anything, the "other origins of the same world." As such, township Afrikaans is a discourse—a mode of being in the apartheid and postapartheid world—in which the traces of other languages, and here English is preeminent, are distinctly audible. (A sort of Spanglish of the Cape Flats, if you will, similarly spiced with a certain joie de vivre. In previous incarnations it was sometimes referred to as Kaaps, Afrikaans for, roughly translated, Cape, stamping the language with a geopolitical imprint in which, again, race and class figure prominently.[33]) It is, if such a description might be permitted, a decidedly "impure" discursive mode in which linguistic invention, borrowing and constant renovation, is the order of the day. The conceptual license taken with French (and German, too), then, can be said to be in the spirit of Cape Flats creativity.

THE OTHER SURGES UP · In those other names, in naming the other—in its abbreviation, in the prevalence of nicknames, names that speak affection and intimacy, yes, but also give voice to the unalterable, linguistically stubborn otherness of the other—as such the "other origin of the world" surges up into the world that is *Entre-Nous*. In the end, it is possible to say, to say rupturously, that what may emerge in both two chapters and the "Interlude" is at once a sense of pathos and the purest form of alienation, that which Nancy names the "bare exposition of singular origins."[34] The self, in being-with, stipulates to the immense difficulty involved in "achieving" being-with. Being-with is never, however it is desired, that which is always there for us to simply take, to take up, to "appropriate," to make our own, much as it presents itself to us, repeatedly, in one fashion, in one form or another. It is necessary to struggle to gain access to being-with. And, in significant ways, *Entre-Nous* grapples with the difficulty involved in achieving being-with as much as it tries to identify, without ever hoping to "overcome," that which stands in the way of its being-with.

For all that, this is a stubborn difficulty, as resistant to being named as it is averse to being "overcome." And we should not be surprised at the nature—and the philosophical persistence of the difficulty that being-with presents. After all, something of substance, politically, epiphenomenologically, is at stake. Nonetheless, being-with must be addressed because, as Nancy points out, the "themes of being-with and co-originarity need to be renewed and need to 'reinitialize' the existential analytic, exactly because these are meant to respond to the question of the meaning of Being, or to Being as meaning."[35] The "themes of being-with and co-originarity" constitute, as will be made clear especially in both chapters and in the "Interlude," each, in their own way, an argument for how to be in the world, and an address to the ways in which Being (*Sein*) pertains for each of the various protagonists. It is, in all likelihood, this struggle toward and for Being that animates *Entre-Nous* (the brief invocation of Nietzsche's will set us on our way toward the encounter with Being); more than even that, it may constitute its very core. Or it is this struggle that radiates out from the very core of *Entre-Nous*, consuming everything—every question, every line of thinking, every thought that is pursued, however successfully or not—with which it comes into contact.

To acknowledge Being as such, then, is to commit oneself to the act (thinking) as act (that is, to activate, to make something happen through philosophy; "thought is the penetration into the thing"), and to give the self over to the thing (thinking, the "object" being thought) itself.[36] It is Being as a "breaking or a sinking into the thing" that requires the paradoxical (and yet not) act of active "surrender": to do the work of "breaking into the thing" while also "submitting" to the "thing"—giving the self (over) to the force of Being (*Dasein*), to being one with Being (*Mitsein* of the highest order), no matter how difficult or impossible this desire might be.[37] In this way, the philosophical stakes that *Entre-Nous* raises has everything to do with football (the difficulty, shall we say, of Being, for Leo Messi is, as we will see, considerable, as it is for Luis Suárez), but the horizon of philosophical possibility also extends far beyond the purview of the field, certainly, and the game itself. In one articulation or another, it is the question of *Sein* that is the first and the last confrontation that *Entre-Nous* commits itself to. *Sein*, thought at once broadly and very narrowly, is what propels *Entre-Nous*. Or, in truth, it may be the confrontation, the question, that this book seeks most to address, no matter—or maybe because of—the impossible difficulty of thinking *Sein* as such, a difficulty of which Heidegger has long since made us aware.

THE SCHEMA · In each of the two chapters and the "Interlude," the logic of the schema, rendered as relation ↔ separation (R ↔ S) and separation ↔ relation (S ↔ R), operates on the following principle. Every instance of relation ↔ ("leads to," this is what the symbol designates) separation and every separation, in turn, without fail, leads to a new relation. That is to say, R ↔ S ≠ S ↔ R.

This means that, let us call it R1 (relation 1), the relation that produces the "first" separation might resemble the relation that emerges out of that separation, let us call it R2 (relation 2), but the two are in no way identical to each other. That is to say, every S (separation) produces an entirely new R (relation). Every separation produces a distinct R; and this means that every S must be understood as producing its own kind of rupture leading to a distinct R, every time. There might be similarity, but there can be no absolute replication of R.

THE EXISTING SINGULAR · This also entails that one not know exactly... what or who is an "existing singular," neither where it begins nor where it ends. ——JEAN-LUC NANCY, "Cosmos Baselius"

It is for this reason that every $R \leftrightarrow S \neq S \leftrightarrow R$ produces, to amend Nancy's terms, which has to do with the struggle for justice ("*au juste*") and spatiality (beginnings and endings), its own "existing singular."[38] What *Entre-Nous* is concerned with is less the specificity of spatiality or temporality (which we might name the "when" of), but the constituent elements—the constituting force—of the "existing singular" that makes up each R, that makes each R distinct from every other R because of the facticity of S. Every S produces its own individual R; or, as Nancy puts it, "What posits the distinct, and identifies it, is separation."[39] Positing every R in its particularity, in its separation (in what it is that makes it "distinct and identifies it"), however, "entails" a fair measure of constitutive uncertainty. That is because, even if we are rigorous in our fidelity to Nancy's notion of "separation," it remains difficult to know "exactly how" every "existing singular" R is distinct from every other one (At what point does it become "distinct?" At what point does it disarticulate itself from the R that precedes or succeeds it? How is the "distinction" marked?), especially the one that immediately precedes it, the one whose S out of which it has emerged, and upon which the distinction of R depends entirely. Nancy acknowledges this difficulty insofar as he recognizes that "every given unity" is composed of "something derived, deposited—a moment, unstable like every instant, in the movement that gives relation, in which relation gives itself."[40] It may be that the impossibility of relation "derives" from the very "movement" that makes relation possible. Without "movement," we can assume, relation itself cannot come into being; in other words, stasis, the lack of or refusal of movement will, sooner, rather than later, result in first the atrophying and then, inevitably, the death of R. It is, for precisely this reason, that what has been proffered here as the "indistinction," R that is always proximate to R through/despite the rupturous force of S, serves to explicate why it does not matter—or, at least, matters only very little—that one R be held utterly discrete from every other R, either the one that succeeds or precedes it. That $R_1$ is not $R_2$ matters, but it matters less than the ways in which $R_1$ and $R_2$ evoke each other. R is constituted out of itself; R is, when all is said and done, autogenerative of R.

Under these terms it becomes absolutely necessary, as an act of fidelity to the thinking of the schema, to recognize the importance of holding every R apart (as a part of other parts) and thinking it, to coin a Nancian phrase, as an "existing singular plural." That is, there are constituent elements that every R might share, and every S, too, for that matter; and these must be taken into account in thinking the distinctiveness of every R in relation to every other R. *Entre-Nous* is, then, engaged in the difficulty of thinking the "plurality" of the R while accounting, as rigorously and scrupulously as possible, for its resonant, constitutive, jealously enunciated "singularity." (Let us think it as an all-too provisional, contingent and transient sovereignty.) There is, for this reason, an ongoing struggle between the two signs. These two "logics," as it were, that designate inequivalence as much as equivocation, hesitation, uncertainty, a reluctance to pronounce too quickly, are locked in a productive tension; the one, let us say R, is not always in perfect relation to the other, but neither is it (ever) entirely without the propensity for relation (R) and separation (S). $R_1$ is never entirely discontinuous from $R_2$. It is for this reason that Nancy can confidently argue that "everything is at the same time separated in relation, everything is only separated and in relation."[41] It is because Nancy's writing on what is between, *entre-nous* (between-us; being-with-the-other),[42] *entre-eux* (between-them), and, not least, because his work on Hegel lends complexity and a restrained pathos to the concept of *entre-moi-et-moi-même* (between-myself-and-I, also rendered as "I-and-I"),[43] is so textured and attuned to the political in its many manifestations (desire, love, and caring not least among them, all of which figure prominently in this project) that his work is so central to *Entre-Nous*. (The pathos to which Nancy's work is attuned is especially resonant in chapter two, especially in light of Moore's trope of the "boy no schoolmaster wanted," except Tabárez, that is. A trope, of course, that is replete with Dickensian overtones as, before all else, the echoes of *Oliver Twist*'s

"Please, sir" ring in our ears.) These different modes of being (it would be very difficult to stipulate as to exactly how many, these different and distinct modes of what is *entre*) work to reinforce, complicate, and "fulfill" each other; or, to phrase it in a more rudimentary way, they "fill each other out." These various modes of being *entre* "complete" each other, insofar as "completion" is possible, enabling us to explicate "fully" each of the constituent elements, in both their singularity and their plurality, as well as, of course, their "singular plurality."

The term *entre-nous* is itself borrowed from Nancy in no small measure because his work recognizes the conceptual challenges that thinking what is between—between us, between myself and I, and so on—presents. In his long essay *Being Singular Plural*, Nancy offers a "definition" of the concept, one in which he insists upon (a characteristic with which we are already familiar) a "spatial" thinking of *entre-nous*. "This 'between,'" he says, "as its name implies, has neither a consistency nor continuity of its own. It does not lead from one to the other; it constitutes no connective tissue, no cement, no bridge.... it is that which is at the heart of a connection, the *inter*lacing [*l'entrecroisment*] of strands whose extremities remain separate even at the very center of the knot. The 'between' is a stretching out [*distention*] and distance opened up by the singular as such, as its spacing of meaning."[44] (Here Nancy refuses the "bridge" as a means of "relation"—a means of getting to the "other side." In *Was Heißt Denken?* and *Zarathustra* the "bridge" functions as the architecture of relation for Heidegger and Nietzsche respectively.) It is in just this "spacing of meaning" (which makes possible an extension—"distention"—into new meanings) that we encounter the various modes of what is *entre*. (So that, we might suggest, *Entre-Nous* stands as a series of "odes" to what is *entre*.) And it is in this "spacing of meaning" that the singular reveals its relation to the plural and, as such, makes it necessary to think the production of the singular under the condition of nonrelation, to name it poorly. As Nancy says, "One does not lead to the other," there is "no connective tissue, no cement, no bridge," so it becomes absolutely necessary to think separation (S) as constituting the core."[45] It is S that is at the "very center of the knot," and the "knots," in their turn, bring R into being.

As such, in thinking Messi, Tabárez, Suárez, and Lansur United as "knotted together" through the force of what is *entre*, in the several iterations that *Entre-Nous* raises, "knotted together" in such a way as to make its unknotting (if not its unraveling) an impossible undertaking, *Entre-Nous* begins with the difficulty of S. Or what it is that S makes possible in its relation to R. In Nancy's rendering, R is possible only through (that is to say, because of) S. Everything, then, turns on S. It is only through S that we understand how $R_1$ is related to $R_2$. In the absence of a "connective tissue," it is only through S that we can think the "extremities" in their relation to each other. In other words, *Entre-Nous* is that project that seeks to create a language—through its discursive exchange with Nancy as its central but by no means only mediating figure—for S: the language of separation, a language adequate to the politics of S.

*Entre-nous* is a language marked by the struggle to explicate relation through separation and, as such, to find in the concept of *entre-nous* a language that can bear the palimpsest nature of S. One articulation or uncovering of S, or revelation, of relation inexorably produces "another reaction," making possible "another unexpected direction," demanding yet another thinking of S and R. Every articulation of S and R is then, a priori, inadequate—it is never sufficient to the task of explicating relation—and generative—as Jean-Paul Martinon reminds us, it is the germ of "another text."

The "text" that follows "this" one (S or R) is also, however, the first word in the direction of a new "violence," the violence that may or may not explain the constitutive force of R or the rupturous (and equally, but distinct) force of S. S makes R, to present the schema another way.

However, it is important to recognize that the force of S, named "rupturous" here (as in, to rupture with—always potentially violent—intent), must be thought in relation to violence, both the violence that is present in the initial or "first" S, and the violence that is to come, *la violence à venir*, the violence that will inexorably emerge from the relation that R establishes. Needless to say, it is understood that such a violence is already present in every $R \leftrightarrow S$, has from the very first iteration of relation been present in that schema. Every thinking of relation constitutes, as it must, an act of violence *against* relation ($R \leftrightarrow S$) itself so that it is impossible to think R ($R \leftrightarrow S$) without doing violence to any thinking of relation or separation, R or S. And yet, without that "upsurge" of violence, to use one of Nancy's signature concepts (a forceful, surprisingly poetic noun), R itself, so foundational to *Entre-Nous*, will remain stubbornly unthought[46] (wherein resides the richness of the concept, of Nancy's thought), and, as such, possibly even unthinkable (which is precisely why it demands thinking). Such a prospect amounts to a philosophical intolerability because not thinking R in this way would constitute a violence, certainly a greater violence, to/against relation, and so, given what is at stake, relation must be engaged. Thinking R in the violence that is/of its unthought, is precisely what makes R that thought that must always be thought.

THE CONCEPTUAL LANGUAGE OF *ENTRE-NOUS* · In the three constituent essays, *Entre-Nous* sets itself in the direction of a language that might, if at all possible, bear the politics inscribed within R and S, and, of course, within its founding equation, R ↔ S.⁴⁷ Through these three essays on football, *Entre-Nous* locates the self in relation to the other; it delineates how the self stands in relation to itself; it stipulates what stands between, between-us, between-them, between-myself-and-I; it seeks to understand how R emerges out of S, emerges into its own singularity that is inextricable from (its constituent) plurality, and what it means for relations to endure and multiply in their singularity, what it means to write the R to the other, susceptible—constituted out of—as that R is to the inevitable force of rupture, S. In order to explicate the relation through separation, schematized as R →← S (the →← designates the "passage" of R through S; differently phrased, it is S that produces R so that R is the result of S and not the other way around), *Entre-Nous* attends to the inextricable bond that "connects"—with a precarious resilience, that "bridge" which is always under construction, which is always in danger of collapsing; but it is that "bridge" which can also make R possible—self to other. (A commitment, then, to thinking that inexplicability that so captivates Nancy.) This bond of being, of being unbearably vulnerable (to the other), is common to and constitutive of humanity and is, as such, unthinkable except in and through R →← S, the relation that is separation; or R = S, with all the complexity that constitutes what is between-them. Between self and other there is, as the "composition" (the politics) of what is, *entre-nous* insists, at once everything and nothing.

Between the world and I, the world-and-I, nothing: *il n'y a plus rien*, "there is nothing left," or so we are prone to thinking in moments. But there is only nothing because of what is and remains *entre-nous*, because of, as Nancy argues, the "negation" that demands a thinking of what was (constitutive of, what was once there). In thinking *il n'y a plus rien* it becomes possible to grasp what is between the world and I and, as such, to understand the world in its "unity," in the "mutual sharing and exposition of all its world." *Entre-Nous*, between the world and I, there is everything, a history, experience, experiences, shared: *nous avons un arrangement*, "there was an arrangement, an understanding," or so I thought. *Ce qui est maintenant entre nous?* Between the world and I: division and unity, diversity, plurality, singularity, all turned toward being (*Sein*); out of this emerges an encounter so singular as to be, at once, insignificant and eminently apprehendable (that which can, and must, be held in place, if only momentarily, in order to "fully" process what is at stake), and so momentous as to resist apprehension, in its very being, entirely.

This is an encounter marked by and in language and, to be precise, understanding that, as Nancy says, the "*speaker speaks for the world, which means the speaker speaks to it, on behalf of it, in order to make it a 'world.'*"[48] As such, this world, the one made in and through *Entre-Nous,* is a "world"—the world of football, internationally, in the cathedrals of the sport and locally, in relation to an amateur team that no longer exists but which still constitutes the "world of the speaker," the "world of the speaker" that has survived the death of the institution; the "world of the speaker" now endowing the institution which no longer is with an after-life; and, in some ways, writes its life for the first time—in which language assumes disproportionate importance.

This difficulty of language begins in the "Interlude," which is to say the difficulty of language was there from the beginning, in which the status, the "speaker speaking" English (the authorial "I") spoke English, in relation to football, with an intense awareness of the otherness of English in a football community where Afrikaans was the lingua franca (or, as has been pointed out, a working-class speaking of Afrikaans with a distinct regional inflection and politics). The difficulty of language, then, proceeds from English first and foremost, but the insistent turn to French (about which a word more, momentarily), the invocation of German, and the particular idiom of Afrikaans (of which, again, Kaaps—or Kaapse Vlakte, Cape Flats—is but a single designation of this mode of sociolinguistic engagement), one that, to be sure, one requires "translation," shall we say. It requires, at the very least, this idiom of Afrikaans, another rendering of names (nicknames, places, phrasings, and so on) in English, but most importantly what is acknowledged here is that all these languages combine to make the language of *entre-nous*, and, of course, of the "world" that *Entre-Nous* "speaks."

To sustain such a thinking of what is *entre-nous*, this project insists upon the language inherited as such, the acceptance of the gift made by Nancy in works such as *Hegel* and *Being Singular Plural*. That is the governing concept, *entre-nous*, as well as its constituent (and/or complementary) parts, *entre-eux* and *entre-moi-et-moi-même*, are all rendered in French so as to mark, beyond question, their "rupturous" quality. These terms, as Nancy might have it, are invoked to surge not only up and out of our thinking ("upsurge" is Nancy's preferred usage) but are used to retain their strangeness—that is, their unfamiliarity and, as such, their difficulty. In order to think what is between-us, *Entre-Nous* moves between and among discourses (philosophy, football history, politics, personal "reflection," and so on) and linguistic registers. Kaaps and French, to say nothing of switching of discursive codes (between say, Nancy's philosophy and Leo Messi's erudite left boot), are woven together—and only sometimes seamlessly—in order to "illuminate," to think, the philosophical concepts and political stakes that inhere in football.

*Entre-Nous* also, of course, moves between and among (formally speaking) languages, between, say, English and Kaaps, grounded as the project is philosophico-political concepts rendered in French. *Entre-Nous* crafts a language—a discursive apparatus—that can bear the weight of that which football, nominally and expansively conceived, reveals as *entre-nous*, as well as that which reveals what is *entre-nous* despite it being, initially, opaque to how it is football is thought. As such, *Entre-Nous* demands a dislocation, through language, a dislocation whose "passage" runs through a discursive, explicatory apparatus that requires that it, not so much first but simultaneously be approached—or, understood, translated, awkwardly, imperfectly, thinking in a language that belongs not to self or other but, inadequately, provocatively, rapturously, to both—and used as though it were itself, as Nancy might have, the "address."

The project of thinking *entre-nous* begins with *entre-nous* as the "first" address to be addressed. (It is an address to which we return, to which we turn, again and again, always as if it were entirely new to us, which, of course, it both is and is not; we know it, we know nothing of it.) That is, in every one of these constituent essays, each of these terms is tuned to its own "singular plural." Each of these constituent essays (to assign a generic term to the six "parts/pieces" that make up *Entre-Nous*) reinforces, challenges, and complicates the others, in order to produce not so much a "coherent" argument but an argument that can best give voice to the variegated issues and difficulties that emerge from thinking *entre-nous*. To this end, then, each essay is written in a "language" crafted specifically for its demands, crafted in that language that can best articulate the particular philosophico-political stakes it, by itself and in argument with the other essays, raises. Each essay, then, is at once discrete and complementary, distinct and a constituent part of the provisional whole that is *Entre-Nous*.

As such, the intention is not to produce that "bridge" or "connectivity" that Nancy warns us against, but to forge out of each essay, out of each (in their) together(ness), in each of their "being-with," a provisional "existing singular" that seeks not so much to identify where one ends and the other begins, or this one begins and that one ends, but to mark their disjuncture and their sharing. To mark, that is, those elements—of thinking, for thinking—that appear, in one articulation or another, incessantly, restlessly (*Rastlosigkeit*), again and again, never the same, as such, but always evocative of, always provoking a thinking of the other through the passage that is S →← R, that concept that runs, relentlessly, in a range of articulations, through *Entre-Nous*. S →← R is, in Hegel's terms, "*die Sache selbst* (the real issue)"[49] that preoccupies *Entre-Nous*. S →← R is the bond that, in all its knottiness and difficulty, in all its various philosophical shadings and political iterations, in the several discursive modes and linguistic registers, holds *Entre-Nous* together. Holds it together because it is what animates every essay, that is to say, every discrete and collective thinking, in *Entre-Nous*.

## CHAPTER ONE

## A Condemned Man | *Between the Nation and the* Autonomista

All this time the chestnuts and the jug went round and round; and by and by they had a song, about a lost child traveling in the snow, from Tiny Tim; who had a plaintive little voice, and sang it very well indeed. —— CHARLES DICKENS, *A Christmas Carol*

The *subject* is what it *does*, it is its act, and its doing is the experience of the consciousness of the negativity of substance, as the concrete experience and consciousness of the modern history of the world—that is, also, of the passage of the world through its negativity; the loss of references and of the ordering of a "world" in general (*cosmos*, *mundus*), but also, and thereby, its becoming-world in a new sense. It becomes immanent, and it becomes infinite. The world is only this world. —— JEAN-LUC NANCY, *Hegel: The Restlessness of the Negative*

TINY TIM: DICKENS AND HEGEL, HEGEL AND DICKENS · There is a distinctly Dickensian aspect to Lionel Messi's fate with Argentina's national team in the finals of international competitions such as the World Cup and Copa America. There is something Yeatsian about it too, but that will have to wait a moment.

This is not, of course, to suggest that Charles Dickens knew it all along. But it is to acknowledge a certain Dickensian prescience after Argentina's 2014 loss in the World Cup final, in extra time. In this regard, Dickens's gently ominous warning to Scrooge about his skinflint behavior around Christmas, "this Ghost's province was the Future,"[1] applies, regrettably, to the footballing fate that Messi has endured. Some would, and not without good reason, call that fate cruel. From 2014 to 2016, Leo Messi played in three finals, the World Cup (2014) and the Copa America competition (2015 and 2016), and he suffered defeats in all three finals. Hard not to argue about the cruelty of fate when a player some consider the greatest to have ever played the game loses finals, back-to-back-to-back.[2]

We can assert without fear of contradiction that as a footballer Messi, as Dickens phrases it, always "sings it very well indeed." His gift of "song," as it were, is especially evident when he wears the *blaugrana* (βław'ɣranə), the blue and deep red/maroon colors of his club, FC Barcelona, of Catalunya. The particularity of his gift, or the particular application of his gift, if you insist, brings us to the core difficulty of Messi's relationship with his native Argentina. This difficulty, which constitutes *die Sache selbst* ("the thing itself") of this chapter, can be summed up in the (*nacional*) designation Argentines apply to Leo Messi when he plays for the national team. They call him "El Catalán" ("The Catalan"), although it would probably be more appropriate to use "Catalano." Since the aspersion is so serious, the least that fans of the Argentine national team can do is get their terms of approbation right. They should hurl the linguistically accurate invective, "Leo Messi, *el Català*!" (the Catalan) at him. By naming him as they intend to, rather than as they do, Argentines would be acknowledging the history of Catalunya's long resistance to the hegemony of Castillia—that is, its desire for independence from "Spain" as we know it.

Messi, then, for all his gifts, and they are indeed many, and perhaps precisely because of these gifts, must be thought in excess of his talents. Messi must, as it were, be thought beyond his gifts, as that player in international football who, more than any other, demands that we, following Jean-Luc Nancy, "reorder" our understanding of the "'world' in general (*cosmos, mundus*)" in order to achieve a "new sense" of "becoming-world." In figuring Messi as deconstituted Argentine, the *cosmos* as such opens up to the prospect of "becoming-world," being in the world of international football, in a sense for which there has been, until Messi, no need. What is it that the "subject" Messi does that causes Argentines, and the world as such, to "lose its references?"

What is it about Messi in relation to Argentina (M →←→← A) that so unsettles Argentines? That causes them to "lose," if only for a moment, something more than their "references?" Causes them to lose something on the order of their minds?

*I was moved to ponder this on October 5, 2017, as I left a bar in the Recoleta district of Buenos Aires after watching Argentina draw ("tie") 0–0 with unfancied Peru in their World Cup qualifying game. The game had just been played at the nearby La Boca stadium, home to one of Buenos Aires' most storied teams, Boca Juniors. As the fans tumbled disconsolately out onto the street, I could not decide if a pall had just descended upon the city or if the utterly depressed fans cast that pall upon my beloved "Baires," my favorite city in the world. But I heard this, distinctly. Deadly afraid that this lackluster draw had sealed Argentina's fate, that because of this draw the team would not be going to the 2018 World Cup in Russia, the fans muttered darkly about how Messi couldn't fashion a goal for the national team whereas he always seemed to come through for Barça. In the Recoleta district, a fancy quarter with boutique hotels, designer stores, gourmet coffee and pastry shops, and, I am glad to say, old-fashioned bakeries, that quarter in "Barrio Norte" (the other two quarters that make it up are Retiro and Palermo) could not have been more somber. The Barrio Norte, where Jorge Luis Borges lived (on Quintana Avenue) and wrote, strolled and took his coffee, saw everyone hurry home with shoulders slumped. With only one match remaining in the qualifying round, and that against Ecuador, at altitude, in Quito, Argentina resigned itself to its fate. Gloomily.*

In the world that he is unmooring, Messi enables us to "experience the negativity of substance." That is, if we understand "negativity" as the first (Hegelian) principle. Freedom, being, and separation are all made possible by "negativity."

This means that, as Nancy argues, following his rendering of Hegel's famous phrase the "negation of the negation," that we are, firstly, released from the "position of the given" (the "fixity which holds back, freezes and annuls the movement of sense").[3] For Nancy there is no condition of being that can be presupposed, experienced as already determined or "given." Situating himself in a philosophical tradition that runs from Parmenides through Heidegger, Nancy argues that everything, every experience, must be subjected to the necessary force of thinking. Every "given" is, as such, nothing but the call to thought; every "given" demands thinking. If the "first negation is already freedom, but still only negatively experienced," then the project of "negativity" is fulfilled in the "second negation": the "negation of the negation" "denies that the first is valid on its own."⁴ As such, the "second negation" constitutes the "positive liberation of becoming, of manifestation, and of desire. It is therefore self-affirmation."⁵

As a "self-affirming negativity," as a "consciousness of negativity," to figure him in Nancy's terms, Messi's "acts" in relation to Argentina present a challenge to how we understand the singular footballer—unique, unreproducible, beyond the mimetic—in relation to the nation-state and in relation to the historic desire that the Copa Mundial evokes in Argentines. Messi's singularity is indeed singular: he is the greatest player in the world, by far the best player representing his country. Not for nothing, after all, is he the Argentine captain. He is absolutely necessary to his country and yet he instantiates the interplay, if that is the correct term and not just a seductive pun, between the "first" and the "second" "negations." (Into which must be introduced a contradiction: he is absolutely necessary to his country, but irreplaceable as he may be to Argentina's footballing fortunes, he is not understood as being *of* his country. That is to say, he is, at the level of "Argentineness"—"patriotism" is too ugly and ideologically oversaturated a term for our purposes here—presumed or condemned to be ontologically other; which is to say, he is affectively other; which is to say, "his heart is not in it"; his "heart," metaphorically understood, is not for Argentina. And even if his Argentine "heart" can be said to be in the "right place," a matter that is itself in grave doubt, his "soul," that is, who he is at his essence, is not. Following this logic, Messi is perceived to relate to the nation-state only at the level of representation, which is always secondary and as such never constitutive. As such, it is the test of ontology—the truth of his soul—that Messi fails.) Messi gives form to the "positive liberation of becoming" through his play (in it we recognize "freedom" and "self-affirmation" as we have rarely seen in football), and he is able to do so because his very "movement" is against the "fixity"—the stasis, the statist impositions of belonging, the state's appropriation of those born within its national borders—of the "givens."

In this way, every time that Messi touches the ball on a football field or on the practice ground, he is, inveterately, *entre-nous*: he is between the political force of birth (Argentina, national identity) and the political promise of life (the joy, as such, that is playing for Barça). But Messi's is not simply the experience of being *entre-nous*. He is not just "between," alluring as such a designation might be.

Messi's condition of being *entre-nous* is that of, in Nancy's sense, relentless movement, mimicking, as it were, his play on the field—where his style of play is about intelligent, seemingly unending motion. Leo Messi is, to invoke a phrase coined in relation to a different set of figures, the football "body in motion."[6] Messi's movement, as such, is fully Hegelian. It is movement in direction of becoming; it is, as Nancy phrases it, "infinite negativity in and as act."[7] That is, the "negativity" on the order of the "second negation," which works resolutely to, first, achieve "self-affirmation," and then, secondly, to transpose that "having-become" as the football body's motion, as the football body enacting itself as the thinking of the game, of movement itself as, above all, the effect of thinking: the body in motion as thinking.

The body in motion is the embodiment of the relentlessness of restless thought; restless thought knows no repose, as Nancy might phrase it. Like Messi, restless thought is always in search of producing a "new sense," a "new sense of the world," in football; and, possibly, through his *entre-nous* place in world football—the "world in general (*cosmos, mundus*)." For both those nation-states that aspire to participate in it (those for whom qualification is enough; for those who set the bar at the opportunity to just play in the Copa Mundial) and for those who set their sights higher (perennial challengers such as Brazil, Germany, Argentina, and Italy), Messi poses the difficulty of how to think the constituent self (the individual player) in relation to the nation.

In turn, in taking this turn, Messi himself is thrown into question. In *Being Singular Plural*, which begins as a critique of Heidegger's "one," Nancy argues that there is "no pure and simple 'one,' no 'one' in which 'properly existing' existence [*l'existant 'propement existant'*] is, from the start, purely and simply immersed."[8] "From the start," then, Messi is "immersed" not in the "one" but at once *entre la Catalogne et l'Argentine* (between-two, *entre-deux*) and *immergé dans deux* (immersed in two; national-/nation-state formations, that is). Messi is immersed in, made of, in unequal measure (it could not be otherwise because no equivalence is possible), both Argentina and Catalunya. *Entre-moi-et-moi*: between Messi and himself, because of Messi and himself, there can be no "one." Messi, the one that is not "one," can never be any such "one." "Messi" (birth/Argentina) is not so much the "negation" of "Messi" (life/Catalunya), as the condition of being *entre-moi-et-moi* (literally, "me and me," but invoked here to designate—what is—between the self and it-self), of "being between," renders Messi the "first negation" that makes imperative the "second negation." At the very least, Messi propels our thinking in such a direction so as to make possible the "positive liberation of becoming, of manifestation, and of desire." How can such a "desire" be spoken, how can it be achieved as a *"l'existant 'propement existant'"*—an existence "proper" to the desire out of which it arrives, from which it derives?

It is difficult, in our world, to account for the time and place of the "proper" place of origin, the origin of "desire." And yet, as Nancy argues through his evocative concept, the "singular plural," it is entirely possible that Messi presents us with precisely such an instance. It is not simply that Messi embodies the "singular plural" but that he embodies the "distance opened up by the singular as such, as its spacing of meaning."[9] Messi maps, in and because of his being, the distinct and "interlaced" "spaces of meaning": his birthplace, Rosário, the Argentine nation-state, Catalunya. In, and through, (the body of) his being *entre-nous*, Messi shows how these "strands of meaning" remain at once "separate" from and in "touch" with each other, discrete but invariably evocative of each other (how could they be otherwise?), inconsistently bonded, relentlessly disconnected, so that it becomes necessary to think the "space," the body (Messi's), the mode (football, on a global scale, as the imperious practice of international capital) from the "interlaced center of the knot" to its furthest reaches, there where various strands are most dispersed and "independent" (which is also to say "interdependent," within touching distance of each other) of each other; this is to say, in Nancy's terms, that the intensity and the degree of "immersion" of one space in the other, makes possible "penetration," that is, "negation" of the second order.

Such a thinking, the act of (making) meaning through spacing (απόσταση—apóstasi), or apprehending the meaning that emerges out of spacing, sets in motion nothing other, this movement from the "center" to the periphery, this movement back and forth, than a version of Nietzsche's "eternal return of the same." Repetition: to think again. To confront again that which already was. To know that just, but never exactly the same, such a confrontation will (always) be forthcoming. The same that "resembles" but does not, can never, must not be allowed to, emulate, itself. The ways, and the frequency with which, Messi moves between these "spaces of meaning," the ways in which he has long done so (since the age of thirteen, and well before, we can speculate, given his father's Catalan heritage), attests to the "originary plurality of origins and the creation of the world in each singularity, creation continued in the discontinuity of discrete occurrences," culminating in the "truth of this paradoxical 'first-person' plural."[10] Here one risks hyperbole (is there any other way to establish truth?), but the resonance is too insistent, too provocative, possibly even too unyielding in its hopefulness, to ignore. As such, the question presents itself: is it possible to discern, no to see, the "world" in the singular "singularity" that is Leo Messi? Is he not so much what stands between us, *entre-nous* but rather the "unique event whose uniqueness and unity consist in multiplicity?"[11]

Messi's is a "singularity" that makes imminent, and immanent, the "multiplicity" of origin and, as such, presents the possibility of a world that will not yield to anything other than the "creation of a world in each singularity." Messi is, as conceived on the philosophical terms that Messi instantiates (as explicated and made possible by Nancy), the event, the face, the *Sein*, of that world. Is that world also our world, the world we struggle toward? Is that world, a world that far exceeds that of the "world of football," already extant in Messi but one in which we, and possibly even him, are unable to be? We are called upon to answer: is Messi what, who, we want to-be, want to-be-with? Is Messi the absolute horizon of our *Mitsein*? Is he how we want to-be-with-the-other, as the infinite multiplicity of the "singular plural?" Is Messi what stands against the proclivity to return to, in the terms of Nietzsche's pejorative, those "humans" who are, as Zarathustra phrases it, "All-too-similar . . . to each other still?"[12] (Is Messi the "last man," the "bridge that passes over," and still we cannot recognize it? Recognize and account for it in him?) Those, we might say, who are entirely devoid of the capacity for the "singular plural"; or, worse, those for whom the "singular plural" is not at all visible, for whom it lies beyond the horizon of their thinking. The choice is stark: Messi, the "singular plural," or a (fatal?) return to the "all-too-similar?" Is Messi the enunciation in whom Nancy and Nietzsche converge?

**LEO MESSI IS NO GONZALO HIGUAÍN** · Gonzalo Higuaín was born in Brest, but no Argentinian fan would think to call him "The Frenchman," as they do with Messi when they provocatively call him "The Catalan." —— CLAUDIO MAURI, as quoted in the *Guardian*

The metric of *Mitsein* used by the "we," fans, players, all those footballing structures and nonfootballing forces that produces the nation itself, which constitutes the Argentine footballing community, is revealing. The litmus test turns out to be not place of birth (Rosário, Argentina, for Messi; as opposed to Brest, France, for the striker Higuaín), but the act of "giving" the self, in its "fixity," to the nation. Constructed as such, Messi does not measure up to Gonzalo Higuaín, the French-born Argentine international who has played for River Plate (Argentina), as well as Real Madrid (Spain), followed by his two stints in Italy, first with Napoli and now with Juventus (of Turin), where he currently stars. Higuaín was born in France because his father, Jorge, was then playing for Stade Brestois 29. Higuaín speaks no French but took advantage of the "accident" of his birth to secure French citizenship in 2007, making him a dual national.

Higuaín has proved himself a good footballer, at both international and club level, with 107 goals in 190 appearances for Real Madrid, and 37 in 61 for the Argentine national team. But, to state the obvious, Gonzalo Higuaín is no Lionel Messi (no one is, it goes without saying); such is the discrepancy in talent and accomplishment. Messi, as we know, has won the Ballon d'Or five times, and he has four Champions League medals to his credit. For Argentina, he has scored fifty-seven goals in 116 appearances to date.

The issue, as we well know, is not with Higuaín, and he is singled out here only because of his (French) place of birth. Other Argentine footballers who ply their trade in Europe, including Messi's former Barça teammate Javier Mascherano, are not condemned as traitors to the nation. (In January 2018, Mascherano moved to the Chinese side Hebei Fortune.) Mascherano is understood to be an Argentine professional who played in La Liga or who plays in China, but his national identification—his "fixity," as it were—is never in doubt. The same logic holds true for other European-based players in the 2014 World Cup squad, such as Ángel di María (Real Madrid, Paris Saint-Germain), Ezequiel Lavezzi (Napoli, Paris Saint-Germain, and now Hebei Fortune, with Mascherano), and Sergio "Kün" Agüero (Athlétic de Madrid and Manchester City), who was once married to Diego Maradona's daughter. These Argentine players are, each of them, engaged in literal and metaphysical movement: between places, Europe and Latin America, between Latin America and China,[13] between club commitments (which occupies by far the bulk of their professional lives) and national duty, each of which demands its own mode of being; of being in the world as a subject, and being in the world as a footballer, being in the world, more specifically, as a(n extremely) well remunerated world-class footballer. The difference, Messi's detractors allege, is that having left Argentina as a preadolescent, he has no grounding in, no standing within, the political memory of the nation's football fans. He has, they say, no base. Messi is, as it were, disconnected from who it is the nation demands that he be: rooted, unambiguously, within it, from the very moment of his senior playing career. The economic facts, such as they are, matter not. Other Argentine stars may play in Europe without having their "elective affinities" drawn into question.

Individually, and as a footballing collectivity, there is an unquestionable restlessness (*Ruhelosigkeit*, or *Rastlosigkeit*, a slightly more positive rendering) about Messi and his teammates, Messi in relation to his teammates. As Nancy remarks on the general condition, "Between us, nothing can be at rest, nothing is assured of presence or being—and we pass each other as much as each into others. Each with the others, each near the others: the *Near* of the absolute is nothing other than our *near* each other."[14] Despite the intensity with which Messi is labeled other ("El Catalàn"), or other-than-Argentine, he is bonded/bound to his teammates through what "passes" between them: the ball, through which they are (tenuously, interdependently) connected to each other; how they pass it to each other. Indeed, it is the ball that determines, defines, their "nearness." Through the ball, we might say, they "pass each into each other," to use the ball as an instance of Nancian 'penetration" (which can also be rendered as the deepening of thought) that also signals community (the team, the squad) and the intensely physical nature of intimacy that marks a football game. The players always "pass" closely by each other, that is, when they are not coming into direct (physical) contact with each other.

All this movement is organized around the ball and what Messi, Mascherano, Agüero—Barça–Barça/Hebei Fortune–Manchester City—can do with it; what they can do with it individually, what they do with it for each other, how they present it to each other, the speed, the accuracy, the invention, and the imagination that go into the pass, or the dribble (here Messi is the master), or the intensity and commitment that goes into the tackle (Mascherano is exemplary in this regard), how they care for it, care for each other, together.

The ball is the object of their relatedness as much as it objectifies (makes immanent) their relatedness. The ball proceeds along a line of interwoven threads from, say, Mascherano deep in his own half, to Messi, who has dropped deep (but not as deep as Mascherano) to collect it, who then proceeds to beat an opponent or three, before laying it off for Higuaín to take a shot that, so it is hoped, will result in a goal. The restless movement that is so key to passing means that passing to each other leads to the ball "passing into" the opposing net—a goal. Restless movement across continents, from Asia (China) to Latin America to Europe, among southern Europe (Catalunya, Italy), northern Europe (France), and the North Atlantic (England), out of this the (final) "passing into" is made possible.

The ball settles in the net.

In the process another matter, too, is settled, however temporarily. The goal, in its being scored, allows us to glimpse that in "being-with-one-another. We do not 'have' meaning anymore, because we ourselves are meaning—entirely, without reserve, infinitely, with no meaning other than 'us.'"[15] "Meaning" must be made. Or, schematically rendered, meaning is made out of Mascherano<>Messi<>di María<>Messi (<>goal/no goal, it matters, it matters not); passing, back and forth, between "us." (This schematic configuration is, needless to say, open to an infinite number of renderings, featuring any number of players; only the <>, connection, is irreplaceable.) The "us" that can be constituted only out of "being-with-one-another" that is the outcome, as it were, of the (first) "negation" of the self (Messi, Higuaín, again, it matters not) that creates the possibility of the "second negation": "us," unqualified "us," making meaning out of every fiber of the self's and the other's (teammate's) body. What is revealed through "negation" is not only "meaning" as such but the "self" coming most fully into its own being—*Sein*, as the football body, becomes *the* repository of all meaning. The football team is, in this sense, the craft—the work—of how to make meaning in order to achieve *Sein*. The team that can make meaning together, to play according to and then exceed the old football maxim that the "team that trains together, stays together," is the team—an exceptional team, it should be noted in advance—that can do no less than *be*. *Sein, Mitsein*, "achieved" in and through football.

*In Quito, on October 11, 2017, Ecuador opens the scoring in the first minute. Argentina responds. With three goals, all of them by Leo Messi. An international hat trick, when everything is on the line. The nation's chances of qualifying for the Copa Mundial balanced on a knife's edge. When it matters, Messi scores. The Argentine nation breathes a sigh of relief, steadies itself, and then gets ready for Russia. Argentina is grateful to Messi. But it does not love him. Argentina admires him, sometimes grudgingly, sometimes happily; Argentina respects Leo Messi. But it does not love him. In both Goethe's and the everyday romantic sense of the term, there is no "chemistry" here. Wahlverwandschaft is palpably absent here.*

However, let us descend from this heady philosophical excursion, having just scaled heights where the likes of Hegel and Heidegger dwell, and ground ourselves in the game of football as it is played on the field. Football, like all sports, depends not only on attack but also on defense, and so it is also important to recognize that what matters, in the matter of meaning-through-relatedness, is what the team does without the ball. (Coaches, players, fans, as I know from long experience, preach learning to play without the ball as fundamentally necessary for a team to be successful.) How do they support each other, how do they defend collectively, how do they react when a teammate loses the ball, when a teammate ignores the call for the ball (when the player calling for the ball is, as it were, passed up); all this is what "passes between them," the *Rastlosigkeit* of movement, integral to football, that always contains within it the possibility of restiveness; that is to say, a fracturing, a breaking up of, team. Or, as bad, the breaking up of team spirit.

As such, *Rastlosigkeit* can produce cohesion as easily as it can manifest itself as discontent and disruption, maybe even the destruction of the team. Under these conditions, to "pass into" marks nothing so much as the conflict that is always incipiently, autoimmunely, *entre-eux* (between-them). The team is a fragile sociopolitical unit. To extend this line of thinking idiomatically, we might say that *il y a de l'animosité entre eux* erupts—the dissolution of the "passing between" into "bad blood," "animosity." (And, as we well know, several teams—especially during the World Cup—descend into chaos when "bad blood" *entre-eux* flows.)[16]

There appears to be no "bad blood" between Messi and those whom he leads. But there is, as we have seen, "animosity" that is directed at him. What is presented, then, are two modes of "being-with-one-another" in relation to Argentine football. The team, the squad, which pivots on Messi, constitutes one mode of being, and then the amorphous but by no means anonymous, politically insignificant, or disenfranchised "we" that identifies Messi as "The Catalan," stands as the opposition-in-waiting (waiting for Argentina to fail because of Messi, because Argentina is not Messi's "elected affinity.")

*I encountered this "we" in the Recoleta in the immediate aftermath of the Peru game. I would encounter them the next day, a desultory Friday, a Friday made desultory by Thursday's result, after the disastrous draw in La Boca. They were still stewing on the streets around La Boca. In Buenos Aires, it would seem, this "we" was everywhere, inescapable.*

Between one "we" (Recoleta, Barrio Norte, La Boca) and the other (which constellates around Messi, a numerically much smaller "we") there is a separation, a breaking off of one from the other. One "we" fractures from the other precisely along the lines of Leo Messi. To be free in separation requires, as Nancy phrases it, "an upsurge in the course of the given, a rupture, nothing that could be posited as such. And each subject has to break off in its turn: each one is just such a rupture."[17] Messi's rupturing into his separateness, into his being-with-Barça, his "surging up" from within the "given" that enables him to "break off" (from the nation-state, from the city of his birth), marks for his "compatriots" a disarticulation from them (his decision—"electing to"— "disaffialiate" from the nation; there is only room for one—true—"affinity"), and, as such, Messi contains within himself the deconstitution of the "we" through his "negativity"; he is, as it were, the (anti-)national body of disaffiliation through negativity. (Rendered hyperbolically, we could say that Messi "negates" Argentina as a footballing nation.) No wonder he is such a target for Argentines, from Rosário to Buenos Aires to La Plata.

It is an animus that begins, as it properly must, at home. That is, in the city of his birth, Rosário, which is also, incidentally, di María's birthplace. "According to a report in *Business Insider*, football fans in Lionel Messi's hometown of Rosário are not among his more avid fans. In fact, many people from Lionel's home town are highly critical of the local boy-done-good."[18] The source of Rosarians' criticism apparently stems from the fact that Messi left the city for Barcelona and, in so doing, severed his relationship to one of the city's biggest clubs, Newell's Old Boys, more popularly known as "Old Boys." (Not surprisingly, fans of Newell's city rivals, Rosario Central, are even less enamored of Messi: "People from Rosario Central are waiting for Messi to fail."[19]) No matter that, as we well know, Messi left only because neither Newell's nor any of the wealthy Buenos Aires clubs was willing to foot the bill for his medical expenses. Exigency, and its standing as truth, the medical demands of the teenage male athletic body, is excised entirely from the thinking of the nation-state. In the wake of veracity's liquidation, excision—as the writing out of the truth and the writing out of the native son whose nativity is made a matter of no consequence; a further instance of Heidegger's *Sous rature* or thinking "under erasure"—is the only possible political outcome.

In the sympathetic phrasing of sports journalist Hernán Claus (who writes for the sports daily *Olé*), "Messi is right to feel maltreated because the criticism is not just about the way he plays for the national team. Instead, they've accused him of not knowing the national anthem, that he feels Spanish, that he doesn't love the shirt. . . . Instead of trying to help build a new idol, what we do is demolish him."[20] Messi is ascribed the identity of national nonbelonging through a strategy of insistent othering. His performances (reduced here almost to the status of incidental), "not just the way he plays for the national team," are critiqued through implication: the "way that he plays" is, explicitly, to state he is not playing as he should play for the national team; which is to say, that he should play for Argentina as he does for Barça. In addition, he is othered through his national "ignorance" (not "knowing the national anthem"), his nonidentity with the nation ("he feels Spanish"—an oddly antisovereign or anti-*autonomista* way to describe a putative Catalan), and, plain treachery ("he doesn't love the national shirt").

*In La Boca, in the shadow of the stadium, store after store sells football apparel. Argentine shirts; replica shirts for Boca Juniors and River Plate, their fiercest rivals; hats for kids in Argentine colors; and T-shirts for adults Some stores feature life-size figures of Messi and Diego Maradona, ragged imitations, both of them wearing the number 10 Argentine shirt. Tourists pose for pictures with their arms draped around the shoulders of both iconic players.*

In a word, Claus has constructed the Messi of the Argentine political imaginary as Lionel Messi, deconstituted, dis-affiliated, Argentine, a process that has its roots in the city of Rosário and has spread like an unstoppable political virus across the nation. In their various ways, their capacity to have joined forces against Messi has given the Newell's Old Boys–Rosario Central axis a political meaning that undermines their historic rivalry and animus for each other. In this instance, the singular football self (nonnational subject of the nation) born in Rosário has been made other not once but thrice by dint of that selfsame city's treatment of its greatest footballing son. Messi has been made other in relation to the club of his first affiliation, in relation to its age-old rivals, and this "maltreatment" and condemnation has extended itself into the entirety of the nation's football imaginary. This is an excommunication of Biblical proportions.

A FURTHER WORD, A BRIEF ONE, ON HIGUAÍN · The point, then, is not Messi's difference from his teammates, European-based or otherwise. Gonzalo Higuaín is, therefore, simply symptomatic, making him an unfortunate and undeserving point of comparison. (His dual citizenship speaks of either ambivalence [he does not want to belong only to the Argentine nation] or of a certain political expedience [he recognizes the value, in terms of the global political economy, of having a passport that allows him access to the European community and the rights of a European citizen].) He is the "Frenchman" who is not deemed a "Frenchman" who is, in truth, at least, partly, a Frenchman, and yet still indefatigably Argentine, unlike his "Catalan" captain.

Messi is, as such, made separate from the nation while his teammates are assured of their place in the Argentine football imaginary. What stands *entre-nous*, what stands between Messi and the nation-state, is one of the central preoccupations of this chapter, but it is a line of inquiry that has "near" to it, very "near" to it, the question of self. It is not simply a question of what stands between Messi and the nation-state; it is, rather, that there is something, some force, it could as easily be political as psychological, that stands *entre-moi-et-moi*, that stands between myself and I. Should the thinking about what constitutes the *entre* begin with the latter question rather than the former? Regardless, what Messi's singularity makes absolutely necessary is an address that seeks to understand the effect of both that which is *entre-nous* and that which is *entre-moi-et-moi*.

I pose these questions in advance of the answers while already knowing that one of the effects, perhaps the chief consequence, of what follows from Messi's separation—his distinct affiliation with Argentina, the distinctness within himself, *entre-moi-et-moi*—is that when the nation loses, it invariably follows that Messi is condemned. Or, to put the matter gently, "maltreated," or its harsher correlative, he is "demolished" by the nation's fans for his several culpabilities (betrayal and a lack of obvious investment in the nation not being among the least of them) in relation to the nation-state.

*At the far end of the La Boca district, a mime, who looks uncannily like Maradona, is soliciting tourists to pose for a picture with Diego. I hear it as, "Posar para una foto con Diego." My daughter, Andrea, who is traveling with me, and I decline, but we linger to watch his performance. Diego would be proud. A model of Messi, but no mime. In any case, what Argentine would want to be mistaken for Messi, especially today?*

Messi is condemned to be, unequally in the affective calculus—that is, according to those "instruments" that measure fidelity to the nation—of Argentina, in regular, restless movement between "birth" and "life." His simply being Messi is already transgression enough against the nation; in being Messi, he is, a priori, not of the nation, accommodated only because it is now too late to reject him or expunge him from itself. (In short, he is negation itself in that he is *not* the nation.) To be without a national fan base, a foundation, possessed of neither an a priori nor a preliminary integration into the nation, is, then, the equivalent of divesting Messi of "meaning" within the "us" of the Argentine team.

THE ENIGMA OF TINY TIM'S LOSS · So when one loses one is also faced with something enigmatic: something is hiding in the loss, something is lost within the recesses of loss. —— JUDITH BUTLER, *Precarious Life*

No wonder, then, that for all his brilliance as a footballer, there remains—in truth, we can say that there has always been—about Messi something of Dickens's Tiny Tim Cratchit. This is an odd evocation because his "physical" accomplishments make Messi a poor fit with Dickens's enfeebled character.

After all, he is no "lost child traveling in the snow," our Messi, because he always knows, on the football field, where he is going—or, at the very least, where he'd like to go and how he'd like to get there. Messi on the football field is, in this regard, a little like Miles Davis on the trumpet. As the jazz critic Nat Hentoff remarked of Davis's work on *Sketches of Spain*, "Miles *is* able to accomplish what he sets out to do, and even rarer among jazzmen, he's always clear as to what it is he does want."[21] Like Miles Davis, Messi is "always clear as to what it is he does want," and the Rosário native, too, always seems "able to accomplish what he sets out to do" on the football field. Dribble, shoot, pass, flick, feint, pirouette, all this Messi can do, with clear intent, even if that intent is discernible only after the fact.

For all this, however, even if Messi does not possess a "plaintive voice" (I know nothing of Messi's ability to hold a tune, although I suspect that Tiny Tim has the edge here), he nevertheless evinces an unmistakable precarity—in some measure, surely, the effect of being "maltreated and battered" by his fellow Argentines, as Claus puts it.[22] Claus's critique of the psychopolitical violence to which Messi is subjected is captured by Judith Butler in her terse, taut, thinking of post-9/11 life in America, *Precarious Life*. In the chapter "Violence, Mourning, Politics," which includes an almost poetic delineation of her notion of the (constitution of the) "we," Butler offers her insight in clipped, cryptic terms: "Let's face it. We're undone by each other. And if we're not, we're missing something."[23] It is impossible to know how it is that we will be "undone by each other," what exact form that undoing will take; or, as importantly, how we will respond to such an act of violence. (Indeed, the question might be whether or not we are able to survive such violence? Will we be, each of us, its victim?[24])

It is for this reason that what Claus's reflections on Messi's exposure to "maltreatment and battery" (shall we say?)[25] reveal is both the intensity of that violence and its non/domestic nature. (This is where Carl Schmitt's notion of "civil war" resonates.) This is a form of violence that emerges from within the most virulent strain of the national self (that articulation of the Argentine "we" that simultaneously excludes Messi and "suspends" judgment on him only if he performs in excelsis for the nation) and its effectivity derives directly from that source. Messi is the self denied his status as self, his right to national selfhood. (That is because as "conditional" or contingently enfranchised citizen, his commitment to the national—football—cause is always in doubt). Messi is the self made violently other by the punitive metric of selfhood that the vengeful "we" imposes upon those whom it suspects of less than absolute commitment to Argentina.

Phrased as a paradox, Messi is undone by the selfhood that is not his, but is, of course, his. It is his right as citizen (to stand as he chooses in relation to the nation), but it is not a right recognized by those who condemn him for his history, those Argentines who hold the history of his performances with FC Barcelona against him. The denial of selfhood (full citizenship, unambiguous citizenship, full affective belonging; or not, one should add, crucially) by the punitive, judgmental "we," confirms, as Butler argues, the standing of the self within the collectivity. "I cannot muster the 'we,'" Butler writes, "except by finding the way in which I am tied to 'you.'"[26] To reverse these terms, the "we" cannot constitute itself without accounting for the constitutive presence of the "I." The constitution of the "we" through a series of concatenated "I's" is what the "we" seeks to suppress through "battering" the "Messianic I" into exclusion. (What might be understood as the unrelenting pressure on the "I" to prove its fidelity all the time, in every game. Such an "I" is denied the right to have a bad game. To have a bad game, to make a mistake, to not perform at Barça levels is nothing less than betrayal of the nation. Di María is allowed to make a mistake, and Higuaín can, as he often does in crucial games, miss a golden opportunity. For them there is routine opprobrium; condemnation awaits Messi if he commits what has been elevated to the status of travesty and treason. Messi, Argenina's—lesser—Benedict Arnold.)

Paradoxically, however, every act of violence against this "I" by the "we" serves only to highlight the irrepressible presence of the indefatigable, immanently present "I." Lost within the "recesses of loss" is, ironically, the inability to lose this "I." It would be sentimental, but nonetheless salient, to suggest that one is confounded by what might motivate the "we's" desire for such a loss—sentimental because the subject of this violence is, after all, Leo Messi, the best Argentine player of his generation and, as I have suggested, possibly ever. (Once more, we encounter the specter of *Sous rature*, the Argentine body marked by the number 10.) However, the "we's" desire is explicable only as an unsustainable contradiction. The "we" wants nothing so much as Messi's fidelity (his love, not to put too fine a point on it), but since that love is neither forthcoming (in the "we's" terms) nor possible as a retroactive articulation (Messi's "love" cannot now be backdated, as it were; in the extreme—negative—rendering, he forswore Argentina for Barcelona that long ago, but by now not forgotten, infamous day that he left Rosario for his father's people; Messi, child of his father's land; one does not want to delve too deeply into that discourse), there is nothing to do but "endure" the greatest player in the game on the Argentine national team while simultaneously condemning him for his lack of love. What grounds this relation between the Messian "I" and the national "we" is the "we's" perception of its own loss, a love written "under erasure." An incalculable, always calculated loss, always calculated, as has been pointed out, according to an unmeasurable, nonspecific, perhaps nonspecifiable, metric. The "enigma" of the "we's" loss is that it believes that it incurred the first, constituting loss: the loss of Lionel Messi to Catalunya. Such is the political effect of loss to the fatherland: to lose the son to the fatherland. Its more discursively felicitous phrasing might be: *Den Sohn ans Vaterland verlieren*. That is the loss that is, at once, "hiding in the deepest recesses of the loss," and it is that (again, incalculable) "depth of loss" which constitutes (the) loss itself. A loss whose proper name is, as we have already learned, "treachery," or the nonpatriotic footballer-as-citizen who plays for but does not love the nation as he is presumed to love the *autonomista*. (Messi as nonpatriotic is best understood as a postnational Argentine subject who is not, however, "post" the desire for playing, displaying, his "elective affinity" for the *autonomista* that itself, of course, has deep and historic sovereign ambitions. Again, we confront the unavoidable charge: Catalunya is Messi's truth.) But these are by no means losses that are of the same order, particularly because the capacity of the "we"—as Claus implicitly notes—to inflict damage and harm, the capacity to commit violence against, is exponentially greater. But, as always, lurking there in the background somewhere, is the specter of love—the loss of love, love as an incalculable loss that the "we" must bear. Must bear in its love, in its bitterness and, yes, in its jealousy. Why, the unutterable question remains, would Messi love Catalunya? Love Catalunya more?

And so it is that we have to, as it were, discern "loss" in the facial expressions in a Dickensian fashion. The figure of Tiny Tim makes sure that we do not "miss" anything about the "losses" that Leo Messi is made to endure. Between the "we" and the "I" there is an unequal but mutually constituting "loss": "loss" is what separates the "we" from the "I." It is "loss" that is, above all and always, *entre-nous* Messi and Argentina; the "I" that immunized against the nationalist force that constitutes itself as the "we," that is constituted out of the thwarted love of the "we." And one is pressed to propose, what is *entre le moi-et-le-moi-même*: the "enigma of loss" begins with that is lost, to phrase this in Bob Marley's Rastafarian terms, between "I-and-I." And in the "recess" of that loss may reside the deepest, most profound loss of all. A loss that derives from the "rejection" that the "we" understands itself to be subject to; the "we" understands itself as not loved. Messi, in this calculation, *ama Catalunya y Barça pero no Argentina*.

From his facial bearing and his general physical demeanor, we can say that Messi sometimes carries himself as if the world contained within it an existential threat to his "bodily integrity and self-determination."[27] There is about him a sense of vulnerability whose raw power is ameliorated only by a certain wistfulness. The image of frailty that attends Messi may stem from his size. He is physically small, standing only 1.67 meters (five foot five), but many of the game's greatest exponents were of a comparable height. Pelé and the late Ferenc Puskás were both five foot eight, the late Eusébio was five foot nine, and his countryman (and bogeyman) Diego Maradona too was only five foot five. (Other greats, such as Johan Cruyff, five foot eleven, and Alfredo Di Stéfano, five foot ten, were slightly taller.) The perception of Messi as small, if not physically at risk, is intensified by the fact that he always appears to be hunched over, his body bent from the lower back, his head pointed toward the ground at thirty-degree angle. Even watching him play for Barcelona in early 2017, with his hair dyed blond and his recently cultivated shaggy reddish beard, it is a challenge not to think of him as little, although "Little Leo" will never gain any traction as a moniker.

That Messi seems constitutionally averse to the diminutive derives entirely from his command of the field. His size is inconsequential when he undertakes those characteristic quick Messi darts, those brief moments he lifts his head to rapidly scan the field of play, assessing his options. In those moments that may be named direct visual address, Messi looking at the world, even if he is only concentrating on the game, focused on planning his next move, the world appears to be, literally, at Leo Messi's feet. The "world at his feet" is, in one way, a physically inverted metaphor, an upside-down description of the source of Messi's abilities.

"The world at his feet" means that the world begins at the top end of Messi's body. It begins in his head. In that moment when Messi looks up, his act of visual stocktaking, the football world is entirely at the mercy of Messi's mind. In that instant, the world, the millions of fans watching him, await the outcome of Messi's decisions, his vision, his football imagination. In this regard, his feet—even his prodigiously talented left foot—are mere bodily appendages in the service of Messi's phenomenal football intelligence. Messi is, we can say, head and shoulders above the rest of the footballing world.

As such, the football world lies supplicant before the workings of Leo Messi's head, those rhizomatic "lines of flight," given to us by Gilles Deleuze and Félix Guattari, that are created in Leo Messi's head. Maybe for a moment we can imagine Leo Messi on the football field in the same way that Deleuze and Guattari identify a "burrow" as rhizomatic: "Burrows are [rhizomatic] too, in all of their functions of shelter, supply, movement, evasion, and breakout."[28] The ball finds "shelter" at the feet of Leo Messi; he is an infinite source of "supply" for his teammates; his skills are nothing if not about "evasion," making opponents miss, taking evasive action against those often crude tackles that are aimed at him; and he frequently "breaks out" of what seems like impossibly congested situations. One moment Messi is surrounded by two or three defenders, the next he has artfully escaped their attentions, off to create yet one more "line of flight." Messi on the football field: an entirely singular rendering of R ↔ ↔ S; separation, what separation; relation such as relation could not be imagined.

As one adoring fan writes online after viewing a Messi-in-action video, "All through the video, you can see him and his focus is just the ball and nothing else, everyone around him dives, everyone cries foul but this man never responds, he just keeps his eye on the ball and the goal and does what he does best, win the game and our hearts."²⁹ In such a moment, and Messi's career is marked by a plethora of such moments, it is possible to glimpse the "I" become more fully itself within the context of the "we." A "we," and on this there must be absolute clarity, that is never bounded—limited, restricted—by the colors of the number 10 jersey he is wearing. It is because this utter nondiscrimination that he, time and again, every exhibition of his talent a surprise, "wins our hearts." On these grounds it seems unjust that the national Argentine "we" will not, perhaps will never, take him fully to heart. Will not love him because they think him guilty of (national, for which read *autonomista*) infidelity. The heart wants what the heart wants. To be, alone and always, special, to hold an indisputable place in the heart of the beloved. The beloved is singular. No admission of singular plural is either possible, or, worse, permissible. It is an inflexible calculus: the nation wants, by itself, for itself, to be loved. It does not want to share its beloved son whom it will never admit to loving because it is denied, in its estimation, reciprocation. The nation-state wants to be first, not joint-first, among equals in the affections of the beloved. Alas, the nation, that most jealous, demanding and unforgiving of lovers. What a loss such a nation incurs, a loss entirely of its own making.

**THE FACE OF TINY TIM** · It seems as if every condemned man that ever occupied it was determined to leave his mark, here at least, if nowhere else. —— VICTOR HUGO, *Le Dernier jour d'un condamné* (The Last Day of a Condemned Man)

For all the salience of Messi's body on the football field, especially his feet and the ways in which he swivels his torso, it is in his face, in the looks that it betrays, that he most evokes Tiny Tim's sense of utter vulnerability. Messi appears "plaintive" in spirit before the world, his face bearing the weight of the title character of Hugo's *Le Dernier jour d'un condamné*. Leo Messi's face bears the inscription—the "marks" that fill the condemned man's prison cell, "marks" made by other, similarly helpless, ill-fated inhabitants—of condemnation. As it regards Messi, the mark of the "marks" is complicated by what occasions it.

The source of Messi's condemnation is, as know well by now, Argentina. Leo Messi is vulnerable before the force of affiliation to which the nation-state, his nation-state, condemns him. *Wahlverwandschaft*.

Messi is, by the logic of the World Cup, let's call it, condemned to represent the nation of his birth, an act that has, thus far, seemed to yield little but the invocation of the Dickensian variety.

To begin with, Messi's seems to be a face that only rarely allows itself pleasure, even when he is playing for Barça. Most often his face is wreathed in a grimace, of greater or lesser pain. Messi seldom smiles, and when he does it is fleeting. And yet, for all its brevity, it is at once memorable and difficult to recall. It seems possible to remember the profile of the smile, but it has nothing of Luis Suárez's unbridled enthusiasm. Suárez, of course, is Messi's teammate and comrade-in-arms up front for Barça. When Suárez smiles, it is all buck teeth and goofy joy. The other (former) member of the Barça front three, Neymar, the Brazilian, exudes his own kind of happiness—he emits, after scoring a goal, a radiance tempered with a soft reserve. But in the main, Neymar is happy and Suárez is over the moon. Meanwhile the trio's pivot, the player who used to hold these three divergent talents together (and now, as Barça captain, continues to hold the team together), always seems to hold himself in check, guarded, guarding against something (the "recesses of loss," surely, among other things), some force (malevolent?), accessible only to him. The inherent reticence of Messi's being might be what makes it so hard, as it were, to capture Messi's smile, so closed off from joy does it appear.

Not even Tiny Tim, who knows a thing or two about hardship, held himself so to himself all the time. On Christmas Day as the ultimate sign of his beneficence, Tiny Tim asks for a universal blessing, "God bless us, Everyone," even Ebenezer Scrooge. It may be, however, that it is in his withholding, in the immemorability of his smile, that Messi leaves the most indelible mark. His mark, like that of the condemned man, is unlike any other mark: it is the face of the condemned. That is what Messi makes us face when we look in his face and try to remember what the face of this great footballer looks like when it is smiling. Maybe the condemned do not know how to smile, maybe the condemned hold their smile from us. Maybe they do so because to be condemned is a condition that cannot be shared, its "truth" cannot be revealed to those who do not know a fate such as theirs. Condemnation is, so rendered, explicable only as the most disciplined act of affective withholding. It is, then, in these terms, both inexplicable and enigmatic—it will not admit of easy comprehension, and its nature is, as Deleuze and Guattari might have it, full of (natural) evasion, and yet presenting itself as an opening onto something fundamental.

The characteristic Messi look is thus exceptional precisely because it is so characteristic. It looks as though it is the only look he has. It is a look most often encountered in defeat, but there is something singular about its intensity and depth, perhaps better described as depthlessness, as though there were no end to it, as though we could never truly plumb the bottom of it. Messi's look suggests an ontological vulnerability well in excess of what is usual in defeat on the sport's field. There is no excessive handwringing, as is Cristiano Ronaldo's wont, or the histrionics (interspersed with moments of intense brilliance, of course) of John McEnroe on the tennis court in the 1980s. There is no show of exertion or public self-recrimination, matched only by the maximum effort that goes into every shot, that is Rafael Nadal's trademark. (Nadal and Messi are friends, supportive of each other; and they are both lefties.)

What there is can only be described as infinitely worse. What there is . . . is unbearable pain. It is etched unmistakably on Messi's face, palimpsest in its depthlessness, as though one could never be done with the work of unpeeling layer upon layer of pain. All that would be left to do would be to unpeel some more. Palimpsest beyond palimpsest. The real pain, however, is the determination with which Messi bears this pain. It is a pain that has no name, can possibly not know its own name, it is a pain that Messi seems to repress, with a real act of self-willing, into his very being, which makes it all the more legible, if not at first glance then certainly through our repeated encounter, three times, with it. Three times, as if Messi's face must first be approached exegetically. Appropriate, maybe, given that Messi is a devout Roman Catholic. *Sous rature.*

IN TIME, OUT OF JOINT: TEMPORAL JUXTAPOSITIONS · The juxtaposition of different temporal layers rather than the unmediated experience of an identity.
—— PAUL DE MANN, *Allegories of Reading*

It is perhaps because of the ambivalent stoicism with which Messi bears his pain that he cannot, properly, be understood as a tragic figure. ("Lord, let this cup of condemnation pass me by." "Lord, might I be spared the fate of nation-state affiliation.") There are, nonetheless, elements of, say, Shakespearean tragedy, such as being imposed with a historical burden that is crushing. But there is nothing, say, on the order of Hamlet—the prince who is doomed to know a life-destroying truth, in all its violence, political machination, and intrigue, producing effects that ultimately threaten to undo the entire state because of the truth, regicide and fratricide, that girds it. Messi, because he can bear what history demands of him, is not fated to die, like Hamlet; he is not doomed to madness, like Macbeth, who finds himself surrounded by an entirely different kind of familial and political intrigue. It may be that Messi is too successful, too elusive as a footballer and as a human being, for pure tragedy. Or it may be that condemnation is its own kind of tragedy, with its own kind of dramatic apparatus and effect.

Messi patently lacks the appetite for self-destruction of either the footballing or the literary type. He is not a wanton genius like George Best, the magnificently talented Northern Irishman who was drawn inexorably onward in the direction of his own undoing by that well-known trio of masculine vices—wine, women, and song. An apocryphal story about Best goes that, asked what he did with the fortune he made playing football, he replied: "I spent it all on wine, women and song. The rest I just wasted." Messi is not in the least like his countryman Diego Maradona, an audaciously gifted player who scored one of the greatest goals in World Cup history (against England in 1986, leaving five opponents lying haplessly in his wake), who transformed Italian side Napoli into a force in the Italian national scene through sheer dint of his skill and personality, but who was not above cheating on the world's biggest football stage (the infamous "La mano de Dios" "goal," also against England in that selfsame match) or drug use (for which he was banned during the 1994 World Cup) or madcap cantering along the sidelines during his tenure as Argentina's national coach (in the 2010 World Cup in South Africa). Maradona ran up and down the sideline, frantically gesturing, in part, one suspects, because he was a footballing genius—on the field—who lacked the requisite technical smarts to instill in his side a strategy for success.

*Walking around in La Boca with Andrea, I sense it. Maradona, for all his transgressions, is loved, remains loved. Messi is respected, his indisputable talent—his greatness, dare one say?—is recognized, but he is not presumed to be of this neighborhood. Maradona had two spells here, 1981–82 and 1995–97. Forgotten, it seems, is Maradona's own stint with Barça, brief but remarkable: twenty-two goals in thirty-six appearances. But neither Barça nor Napoli, much more consequential in Maradona's club career, ever held—lay unambiguous claim to—his heart. We are whom we love. Love of the nation is that singular which admits of no plurality. To not love singularly is to be condemned.*

It is, then, inevitable that Messi will be compared to Maradona. After all, this is Argentina, where memories of the 1978 and 1986 Copa Mundial triumphs live on, forever "marking" the nation's sense of self. It is unavoidable that Messi will be measured against Maradona; standing side by side as they do, replica to replica, on the streets of La Boca. And the only instrument of measure is, precisely that, the Copa Mundial. And, by that measure, Messi is condemned. Maradona won one, in 1986, no matter the *"Mano de Dios"* or the later drug use and the embarrassment it caused internationally, and Messi has, by this standard, failed to deliver. As such, he has failed the nation-state. As such, Messi is a footballer condemned by history. A footballer condemned by the tyranny of the nation-state. An Argentine-born footballer condemned by his predecessor, one whom in every other regard he has far surpassed.

*Martin Heidegger's distinction between "authentic" and "inauthentic" being might say everything about the difference between Messi and Maradona. Cryptically, anyway. "Authentic" being is that mode of being that "acknowledges" itself in the process of opening itself up to the world. "Inauthentic" being, on the other hand, never really fully understands itself and, as such, can never properly—or adequately—relate to itself. In critical ways, we can argue, the Argentine nation's adulation of Maradona is precisely what has rendered him an "inauthentic" being. Of course, I doubt very much that these Heideggerian distinctions mean anything to our Diego. They are sure to provide no solace to Messi.*

And therein lies the rub, and what a rub it is. It may, in fact, be more like a double specter: the specter of the other, Diego Maradona, intensified by the other's overidentification with Argentina as a nation. What we have, then, is the nation-identified Maradona (against whom Messi is designated other) functioning as the irrepressible foil for, in lieu of a more appropriate term, Messi (that self is itself other, "maltreated and battered"). Messi, who is, who has long been, disarticulated from the nation-state, who, through his playing, deconstitutes, in his very being, Argentina as a nation-state. Messi is capable of great destruction, at the level of the nation-state. Because of who and how he is in the world, he tears the nation apart. And yet, as long as he plays, he will never be able to (fully) tear himself away from the nation.

*Messi's "authenticity" flies in the face of Argentina's "inauthenticity."*

Such is the intense nature of what lies between Messi and Maradona that, on the eve of the 2010 Copa Mundial, when Maradona was managing the team, "conspiracy theorists suggested that he [Maradona] was sabotaging Messi's career to maintain his position as the greatest ever Argentine player."[50] The mischief of what is *entre-nous*. *Entre-eux*, between them, between Messi and Maradona, can be found a veritable witches brew of potential jealousy, intergenerational rivalry, a politics of suspicion, and, most importantly, entirely distinct modes of being; not only distinct modes of being a footballer. For all that, it is difficult to imagine Maradona, even as Messi's coach in 2010, being able to "sabotage Messi's career." On the field, Maradona could not reach Messi, however benign or ill intentioned his motivations may have been.

AN UNHOLY TRINITY OF DEFEATS · We must all be solidly indemnified. / Though all be worthy Victory which all bought, / We rulers sitting in this ancient spot / Would wrong our very selves if we forgot / The greatest glory will be theirs who fought, / Who kept this nation in integrity. —— WILFRED OWEN, "Smile, Smile, Smile"

Three, three in a row, three defeats in international finals, a hard pill to swallow for Argentina, a footballing nation that is so proud of itself, a nation that is so proud of its footballing history. Messi's loss to Germany, in Brazil in 2014, was, as Dickens puts it, the "Present" that foretold the "Future." Losing to Germany in Brazil was just the start of it. One, two, three, an unholy trinity of defeats: Germany, Chile, Chile, Father, Son, and Holy Ghost, to invoke a liturgical language well known to Messi, the Roman Catholic, and to his Argentine compatriots, most of them Catholic too. Three losses, was there no prospect of Resurrection? How was the nation to retain its faith in the face of such cruelty? Where was the mercy of the footballing gods? "My God, my God, why hast thou forsaken me?" Was Messi, and Argentina, to be sacrificed, like Isaac, on the altar that is the nation-state? Or not sacrificed but crucified on the cross marked "Argentina?"

And, to add ignominy to defeat, what bitter irony that it would all come to a head in the United States, a country with no footballing history of which to speak, or historic regard for the game, for that matter. One hundred years of the Copa America, and the final was to be held in a gridiron stadium—what is known in the United States, improperly, as "football." (Only rarely, is it ever noted, do ball and foot ever come into contact in this game administered by the National "Football" League. The NFL oversees a Fordist game with an intensely specific division of labor—"offense," "defense," "special teams"; "long snapper," "kicker," to name only a few.) Surely there were more fitting football venues for such a tragedy to reach its Biblical fulfillment. What about the Maracanã in Rio, in all its faded glory, because of all the faded glory that has accumulated there since the stadium opened in June 1950? Péle played there. And those other Brazilian greats, the genius of dribbling Garrincha (which translates as "the wren," so that he was also known as the "Little Bird"), and Zico, the "White Péle," and the hyperbolically named medical doctor Sócrates too. What of La Bombanera,[31] the "Chocolate Box," in the La Boca neighborhood in Buenos Aires that we have come to know a little? Daniel Passarella, "El Gran Capitán";[32] Mario Kempes, known, rather improbably, as both "El Toro" and "El Matador"; and Maradona? They all strutted their stuff in Boca Juniors' stadium. But no, the final was reserved for the most powerful nation-state in the world, in the shadow of arguably the most powerful city in the world, New York.

This is where we find Leo Messi at the end of the 2016 Copa América Centenario Final. He is at MetLife Stadium in East Rutherford, New Jersey, a venue that has now achieved, against all odds, a historic status in the history of football. Its status derives solely from the outcome of that game between Chile and Argentina, played on June 26, 2016. More specifically, MetLife Stadium's historicity owes everything to the look Lionel Messi bore when Chile triumphed 4–2 on penalties. When Chile's Francisco Silva converted his penalty against the Argentine goalkeeper, Sergio Romero, to give Chile an unassailable 4–2, the camera quickly panned the Chilean players who were streaming toward Silva, then trained its eye, in a sad lingering glance, on Messi.

What the camera found, what the international audience saw, was the look that had, by now, become tragically familiar. It was the same look that the world saw on July 4, 2015, at the Estadio Nacional in Santiago de Chile. It was that selfsame Messi look that was, it should be said, almost indistinguishable from the one a global audience had been witness to on July 13, 2014. These looks, one after the other, in three consecutive years, all in globally televised international finals, one look, it seemed, intensifying the other, thrice. Here was Messi, evoking Yeats's "Irish Airman," bearing the visage of man who "knew his fate."

On all three these occasions, 2014, 2015, and 2016, Messi's face bore the look of a condemned man. A condemned man who had not, in that tone of scathing pathos and indictment that only a Wilfred Owen, so deeply scarred by war, could master, "kept this nation in integrity." The dead soldiers of "Smile, Smile, Smile" do not, of course, live to enjoy the "greatest glory." That, and the "homes" that they will no longer need, "homes" built in preparation for the end of World War I, is reserved for those who live, those "solidly indemnified" by the dead, those for whom only the dead can vouch; those "homes" signed for in the blood of the dead.

When a footballer, or a soldier, cannot keep the "nation in integrity," then it is no wonder that something salient becomes visible. In such a moment what can be detected is an uncertain look that marks the footballer's face when he is on national duty. Something within the self has come between the self and the nation, a conspiratorial relation that will surely, at one point or another, result in violence against the self. (There is nothing mischievous about this look.) What that "interruptive"—disruptive—look reveals, of course, is its multifarious articulation. But, finally, it is nothing other than the self itself: that which is *entre-le-moi-et-le-moi-même*, that irruptive force that gestures at that which is hidden in the look, traces the "interruptive" forces that are borne in the face. *Sous rature.*

Such a look is etched, if not permanently, then always incipiently, at the edge of Messi's face whenever he wears the Los Albicelestes jersey, number 10. This is, of course, the same number 10 made famous by Maradona. Needless to say, Messi is entirely capable of exuding a real and infectious joy in his play. This joy seems especially evident when he is playing for Barça, and it seems particularly animated when, in possession of the ball, he cuts in from the right-hand side of the pitch, the ball attached to his feet (as if by some magical glue, a "substance," as it were, available only to him and the ball), swerving, jinking, stopping, turning, mesmerically weaving his way through defenders.

Watch Messi in those Barça moments, and you will see him smile, not a broad or rambunctious one but rather something poetic. It is an innocent smile, verging on, dare one say, the beatific. But winsome, too, and always overdetermined by the patina of sadness, the loss of something fundamental. You know, a little like the Mona Lisa's enigmatic smile but without the promise of seduction. You know, like that impossible-to-disguise look of pain and constitutive loss that can only be produced by domestic violence, the kind of smile that Charles Bukowski captures in "A Smile to Remember" when the poem's "Henry," the boy (son), remembers the violence his father inflicted upon his mother. Whatever violence Argentina has done, or has not done, to Messi, his remains the "saddest smile I ever saw."[33] It might be that Messi is the only figure who can insert poignancy, pain and, yes, the barest, slenderest hope for something else, something better, into so bleak and (domestically) violent a Bukowski poem.

**OF LOVE AND HATE** · I know that I shall meet my fate / Somewhere among the clouds above; / Those that I fight I do not hate / Those that I guard I do not love; —— W. B. YEATS, "An Irish Airman Foresees His Death"

The numinous rises up at every step and, conversely, every step of the numinous leaves a trace, engenders a memorial. —— JACQUES LACAN, *The Ethics of Psychoanalysis*

In signal ways, Yeats's critique of enforced conscription (which is both first cousin to and not the same as universal conscription) and the intense alienation from the nation (colonizing, in this instance) that it spawns, "Those that I fight I do not hate / Those that I guard I do not love," resonates with Messi's condition. It would require an immense leap of faith (or, *mala fides*, more precisely) to imagine Messi as capable of "hatred." While football, at the club and the international level, is often marked by intense animosity, Messi seems to play the game according to a different set of rules. He is not, I would argue, playing so much against his opponents as against the circumstances of the game, while always, it should be emphasized, remaining true to himself as a footballer. (Granted, these factors might very well overlap, but it is also possible to treat them as discrete phenomena.) That is, Messi confronts the kind of tactics that his opponents are employing as a conceptual challenge to be addressed. How is he being marked? By a single player assigned to follow him for the entire game? (This tactic is, as many opponents have found out, hardly a solution, because there is, needless to say, no one player who can stay with him for ten minutes, let alone the entire ninety.) Will his opponents try to close him down by overloading the right side or the center of the field? Will they defend deep, and in numbers, so that he has to break down a side that is stationing eight or nine players behind the ball? (This tactic is commonly known as "parking the bus.") How can he overcome this challenge? How can he pry open the game so that his skills, and those of his teammates, can flourish? What should be said, however, is that in seeking to "solve" these dilemmas, Messi is already flourishing, his mind and body exercised by the tactical challenges that lie before him.

It is always, then, to the set of on-field circumstances that Messi responds. But there is never any evidence of "hatred" as such. Those whom he opposes, he "does not hate": "Those whom I fight I do not hate" is Yeats's gentle declaration on the matter. The "Irish Airman" fights because he must, because he is instructed to do so, because during World War I Ireland was under British colonial rule. Here one might discern, given the context of Yeats's writing (and his politics), that critical title of that famous Wilfred Owen poem, a title that is at once mocking its source and deeply aggrieved at the violence sanctioned in the name of patriotism: *"Dulce et decorum est pro patria mori"* (It is good and sweet to die for one's country; sometimes "noble" is preferred to "sweet.") Crafting his lines as the "Great War" was claiming lives with an unprecedented violence (among them an entire generation of poets), Owen offers up his poem as a critique of the martial logic of war. With a title borrowed from one of the Roman poet Horace's odes, Owen at once makes his lines stand against those of his Roman counterpart and, in so doing, inserts the discourse of empire into the brutality of the "Great War," leaving us with a much bleaker critique of war as a(n in)human practice; without, we should say, throwing Yeats's partisanship for the Irish nationalist cause into anticolonial question.[34]

It might then be that it is precisely Messi's inability to "hate" that condemns him for Argentinians. "Hate," as it relates to the nation-state on the football field, can only function dialectically; that is, "hate" is always directly correlated to "love"; the "we" cannot but think itself in relation to, as constituted out of, as Nancy ("being-with-the-other") and Butler ("you are already of me") make clear, the "I";[35] *entre-nous* always there is something—that conspiracy of the dialectic that is compromised out of, among other elements, loss, love, hate, displaced animus, the effect of rejection, memory of that long-ago slight to local, regional, and national pride; remember Newell's and Rosario Central and . . . Between us, *entre-eux*. In order to "love" the nation-state demonstrably, it is necessary to harbor and display intense animus in relation to those who oppose the self's nation-state, on the football field, and elsewhere, obviously. Animus, on the football field and elsewhere, constitutes, in the *Zarathustra* chapter (entitled, appropriately, for our purposes) "On the Thousand Goals and One," "the tablet of its overcomings; behold, it is the voice of its will to power."³⁶ Messi, who does not play as if he has to impose Argentina's "will to power" (that most resonant of Nietzschean concepts),³⁷ which is to say he does play with "hate," cannot be said, by virtue of this ideological "deficiency," to "love" the nation-state.

Messi regards those lined up against him not indifferently nor without accounting for their particularities, first and only as opponents, not as his mortal enemies. He plays the game according to his own aesthetics. Messi's code, in this regard, can be described as immaculate close control, relentless, intricate movement, vision, the game played as though it were a thing of Keatsian poetics:

> When old age shall this generation waste,
> Thou shalt remain, in midst of other woe
> Than ours, a friend to man, to whom thou say'st
> "Beauty is truth, truth beauty,—that is all
> Ye know on earth, and all ye need to know."

Leo Messi is, above all, one of the great "friends" to/of the game of football, and lives by the mantra that football is nothing less than "beauty and truth." It is, in truth, all we "need to know" about football. That we know more, is, alas, our loss. For his part, Messi is the avatar of "Beauty" and, as such, he is not, and will never be, engaged in warfare. And because he is not given to "hate," those whom he is expected to "guard" when he wears the number 10 for Los Albicelestes suspect that he does not "love" them as they expect to be loved. That is, "love" as absolute fidelity to the violent defense of the nation; that is the condition of representing the nation-state as though it were nothing less than a metonym for the self; there is room for nothing other than, to invoke Nancy's critique of "fixity," the "absolute relation of finitude." That is, the view of the world that is hostile to the logic of negation, that will not abide the *Rastlosigkeit* of thought, a *Rastlosigkeit* that might very well be the wellspring of Messi's footballing being. Or, to phrase the matter poetically, it is Messi's *Rastlosigkeit* that produces a footballing imagination of such "beauty."

In its turn, Messi's *Rastlosigkeit* is met with suspicion by the "we." That is because anything less than absolute fidelity to the nation evokes condemnation of the order that *Webster's* lists first in its definition of "condemn": "to express an unfavorable or adverse judgment on."³⁸

NATION FIRST: MARADONA, HIGUAÍN, MASCHERANO · To focus, as we must, for a moment, on Diego Armando Maradona as we did earlier on Higuaín, Mascherano, and others. Let us revisit a logic with which we are now already familiar, one that demands a return to the comparison with Maradona because it so dominates the politics of Argentine football. Maradona, as we have established, may have played for Napoli in Italy's Serie A (1984–91), but the Argentine nation knew that his first loyalty was to them. He earned his keep in Serie A, playing more games for the southern Italians (188, scoring eighty-one goals) than he did for any other club, including his two spells with Boca Juniors (in his first stint, 1981–82, he scored twenty-eight goals in forty appearances, and then seven goals in thirty matches during his second tour, in 1995–97; an incredible scoring rate of a goal every second game) and a brief two seasons with Barcelona (1982–84, an uncanny twenty-two goals in only thirty-six appearances). But in his heart and in his soul Maradona was Argentine. He could be relied upon, to phrase the matter in idiomatic Argentine, *Levantarse a alguien (una mina / una piba / un chavón)*: "to lift someone up." That is, "to lift up" the nation through his play, through his absolute fidelity; to his absolute finitude. Maradona: who begins and ends with the Argentine nation; Maradona: Argentine to his core. Argentine at his very core, beyond question, such is the political upside of finitude: not to be drawn into question, to live in "fixity" not as a philosophical limit but as the buttressing of the subject in relation to the nation-state. (The nation-state is, in moments of triumph, burnished by an individual such as Maradona.) Such "fixity" makes the metonymy of Maradona eminently possible, serving as it does to render Messi as antinomy—or, finitude as opposed to infinitude, as Nancy might prefer. And *entre-nous* finitude and infinitude there is nothing less than *tout*—"everything." Or, more directly, "The absolute is between us."[39]

THE NUMEN · Maradona, Argentine before all else. In mapping the trajectory of Maradona's and Messi's careers, for all their unarguable differences, Maradona comes to figure as a kind Lacanian numen of the malevolent variety.[40] In coming (home) to Barça, in finding his home in Catalunya, Messi could also (already) detect the "traces" of the "numinous." It is Messi who is admired and who has "engendered the memorial," but, unlike Maradona,

Messi is not loved. In this way Maradona is the malevolent "divine spirit" that, as history would have it, "rises up at every (numinous) step" of Messi's career. There is no escaping the numen because it is there, "at the corner of every road, in grottoes, at the crossroads."[41]

So it is that Maradona rises up before Messi, wherever he turns, in whichever direction he turns, from Argentina to Barcelona, from Barcelona to Argentina, especially but not only, as we now see, in relation to the nation-state. In what is between them, there is an unbreakable bond; because of what is between them, they are bound together. Forever, it would seem. *Entre-nous* makes the world small. The conspiracy of *entre-nous*, the cruel mischief that emanates from it, is the force of restriction that it can enact. It is part of the secret, insofar as the secret is that which (in Derrida's terms) we already know, that animates what is *entre-nous* Messi and Maradona.

Wherever he turns, Messi might be said to encounter Maradona the numen. But mostly he confronts him unequally as a compatriot. After all, Maradona's greatest accomplishments (winning the Copa Mundial in 1986), as well as his greatest humiliations (being banned from the World Cup in 1994), were all achieved or endured in the cause of the nation. However, the nation may have been, in that moment, disgraced, as it was on July 1, 1994, when Maradona was removed from the World Cup in the United States because five variants of ephedrine, a banned stimulant, were found in one of his urine samples. In triumph and in failure, Maradona "loved" Argentina, loves it still, though he served it poorly in retirement and in his role as coach of the national team at the 2010 Copa Mundial. Maradona showed himself to be clueless as a tactician, and unable to guide his charges, Messi included, with any success. But his "love" for Argentina is such that it has had the benefit of "hiding," in full public view, his multitude of sins. It is, Maradona proves (despite or perhaps because of his transgressions), always better to love the nation-state than not.

In his most sublime moments such as his second goal against England in 1986, the one after the *"Mano de dios,"* Maradona did indeed demonstrate his appetite for beauty and otherworldly dribbling (he beat five Englishmen en route to that goal). I spoke with the great Liverpool and England winger John Barnes about this goal in March 2004. Barnes, who had come onto the field in that game as an England substitute, had a bird's-eye view of that Maradona goal, and he told me that it was all he could do to prevent himself from applauding the goal scored against his own team. In a Copa Mundial quarterfinal match, no less, such was the level of Maradona's skill in scoring that goal. (It is one of those goals that is worth a visit to YouTube.) Barnes proclaimed himself "proud" to have been on the Estadio Azteca pitch in Mexico City to witness that goal. It is not often that international opponents make such pronouncements, especially if they've lost the game in the most dubious ("unethical," Lacan might name it) of circumstances.

In moments such as these, Maradona showed his love for the game aplenty. But Maradona was just as capable of petulance, of niggling opponents, of foul play, and this, one imagines, is what passes for "hate" among the (Argentine) partisans. The public display of commitment through, as Lacan puts it, "the *jouissance* of transgression."[42] It may be that public "transgression," on and off the football field, does not so much give the nation pleasure as reassure it through lower-level (base) acts of,[43] if you will, *voyourism*; (that is, to render the concept of "etat voyou," the rogue state, in an individualist, mischievous register, a mode of transgression that always, for all its impish charm, verges on the unethical); to assume the role of the *voyou*, as Maradona does, with relish ("patriotism," fidelity to the nation) provides evidence, however unreliable, of the latent capacity for "hatred." Even if it is not "hatred" as such, it inclines that way. And for the partisans, that inclining will suffice.

For his part, Messi raises a more "ethical" prospect. That it is inconceivable that one can play without "beauty" or that one can play without love. What is more, he shows that it is entirely possible to play without "hatred." In aligning himself with Keatsian "beauty" and love, Messi brings fully into being Yeats's "Irish Airman": "Those that I guard I do not love." For Messi it is possible to play with love, to posit love as that mode of playing the game that refuses partisanship. In this way, we might ask, does love belong only to the Keatsian order? At the very least, we can be sure that love falls under the heading of Deleuzian "infinitude."

CATALUNYA, ARGENTINA · Or, does the suspicion of not "loving" those in whose name you play further plumb the "secretive" nature of *entre-nous*? As such, what *entre-nous* is may allow us to understand Messi's love as an entirely unsurprising question. While Messi may be bound to the Argentine nation, he is, by virtue of lineage (his father's ancestry, so that we can say Messi was, from birth, already predisposed to a place other than his geographical birthplace), his natural predilection (playing football the Barça way), and history (his long tenure in Catalunya), he is, in truth, Catalan in his soul? Rendered as such, it becomes possible to "complete" the joke about Messi and Barça. The joke takes the form of a riddle and it goes like this: if Barcelona without Messi is "Spain," as in the Spanish national team, then what is Messi without Barça? Lost? Cast adrift? Is he, this most prodigious of talents, rendered homeless as a footballer? Leo Messi, without Barça, a footballer sans home; or *sense ilar*, as they say in Catalan.

Or, does the "other" half of the joke bring us closer, at least in the second sense offered by *Webster's*, to understanding what it means for Messi to be condemned to perform for Argentina? According to *Webster's*, to condemn is "to pronounce to be guilty; sentence to punishment."[44] To play for Argentina is to interrupt the jouissance, the pleasure with which Messi plays, the pleasure his playing gives to us. The pleasure, however reticent that articulation might be for a subject such as Messi, is undeniable. Jouissance is, when all is said and done, what distinguishes Messi, the Catalan of the soul, *Catalá d'esprit* or *Catalá de mena* (both of which mean "*Catalá* to the core"), from Messi the Argentine national.[45] Messi the *Catalá de mena* is "sentenced" to Argentineness, the most palpable "punishment" issued by the nation-state against the footballing body. Is this his political crime, footballing infidelity (of the soul), of which Argentina, in its heart, finds Messi guilty? Is it, as Lacan argues in his lecture "Love of One's Neighbor," under these conditions that jouissance is "forbidden?"[46] Is the "punishment" that follows from this crime worse than being only putatively *sense ilar* because in his *ánima* (soul) he is *blaugrana* through and through? Is it possible for the soul to dissemble? Or, as we imagine Keats might insist, is the soul the very seat of truth? And, in Messi's case, footballing jouissance? Pleasure is truth, truth pleasure. No, it is more than that: truth is pure footballing pleasure.

> *I wonder if such a principle of pleasure is beyond Diego Maradona.*
>
> *Perhaps such a declaration is, in its own way, a condemnation of Maradona.*
>
> *A condemnation of Maradona borne out of love for Messi.*
>
> *Where does condemnation end and love begin?*

AUFHEBUNG I: ARGENTINA-BARCELONA · The primitive crime of the primordial law. —— JACQUES LACAN, *The Ethics of Psychoanalysis*

*Aufhebung*, i.e., the conservation of something destroyed at a different level. —— LACAN, *The Ethics of Psychoanalysis*

In Argentine victories, Messi's visage reveals, with the rare exception, very little. But in defeat, in "failing" the cause of the nation of his birth, the nation that he now captains, the truth of his "punishment" is more visible. It is in defeat that the nation in whose ranks, in whose colors, he performs, delivers a Yeatsian condemnation. For Argentina, he will always be an "Irish Airman," incapable of mustering either enough "hate" for the enemy or insufficient "love" for the partisans. (We could, of course, as easily say that he is to Argentina what Nietzsche's "Zarathustra" is to the various people he encounters upon leaving his cave.) "*His acts*," as *Webster's* phrases it, "*condemn him*" emphasis in original; *Webster's* uses this phrase, plainly, "*His acts condemn him*," as its example for its third definition of "condemn: "to give grounds or reasons for convicting or censuring."⁴⁷ More precisely, it is Messi's "failure" to act with "hatred" or to "love" those who demand it as their birthright—presumed to be the right that is inseparable from membership (citizenship) in the nation-state—that makes him subject to summary judgment, subject to the Law, as Lacan might have it. A damning judgment, of course, because Messi will not be, as *Webster's* puts it in its sixth definition, "forced into a specific state or activity."⁴⁸ While Messi can resist the "activities," as such, he cannot withstand the claim that the "specific state" of Argentina makes on him. Powerless, as a putative yet practicing citizen (dutiful, observant, but not enamored of the process), to resist the call of the nation. It is, however, in his Yeatsian propensities, because of his "Irish Airman" (and Zarathustran) proclivities, that it is possible to observe Messi situating himself at a remove from the nation.

*What is between Messi and the nation-state is everything.*

*There is no prophylactic that can protect Messi from the claims of the nation-state. That is why I turn, firstly, to Barça to watch his Truth and Beauty*

Messi stands at a distance from the nation while embodying and leading Argentina on the field, evoking that political location that Jonathan Culler identifies, in his work on the lyric, as "belonging without belonging."⁴⁹ Messi is, in that moment of the game, *in* the nation, but not *of* it. And that is a salient accomplishment. (Rendered in relation to *entre-nous* and to Butler's notion that "mustering" the "we" already presupposes—establishes the fact of—a "tie" to the "I," we might say that "belonging without belonging" bespeaks, before itself, the overwhelming political desire for location within; that is, a form of "belonging" not marked by the violence, the violent exclusion, that is extant. In the "recesses" of "belonging without belonging" one confronts nothing other than belonging as such—vulnerable, naked, open-faced, devoid of dissembling. The "I" stands exposed before the nation, awaiting its judgment. In that "recess" we can also identify the desire for something like the "we," whether we name that "political community" or, as Nancy and Butler, each in their own way do, the possibility of being "human.")

In a historic period in which the nation-state appears to be everywhere under threat but resilient, under attack from within and without but resourceful in its ability to posit itself as the only politically meaningful form of belonging, Messi has succeeded in making himself, as footballer, *in* but not *of* the nation. It is for this reason that we encounter something signal in Messi playing for Argentina. When Argentina loses there is something more at stake than the condemnatory effects of the nation-state and more than the articulation of Lacanian Law as it pertains to the footballer conscripted into the nation-state against his best instincts.

What we confront in Messi's ability to be in but not of is ("belonging without belonging," to keep the nation at a distance even as he wears the colors of Los Albicelestes), following Lacan, the condition of *Aufhebung*.[50] This, as it turns out, is a condition that Messi both exceeds and finds himself subject to; *Aufhebung* cuts both ways insofar as it enables Messi to achieve the "beyond" of Lacan's notion and to confront the reality what is "conserved" in the face of destruction at a "different level" that also demonstrates the persistence, if you will, of both the numen and Argentina itself. (The "sublation or upheaval of one by the other" that makes possible, through Messi, the "most serious penetration of thought" about football and the nation-state; about the nation-state and the ways in which it intrudes *entre le moi et le moi-même*—between myself and I; "I-and-I.")

When he plays for Argentina, it is possible, in moments, to see the "conservation" of Messi in Barça colors. Also explicable in these moments is the "upsurge" of Messi into that mode of being, that series of acts, where nothing stands between Messi and himself. Visible in those moments is Messi's ability to wrest, while playing with/despite the burden of condemnation, from this destructive ethos, the Messi who so routinely rises above this corrosive "level" and to put himself into the service of Argentina. In this way Messi can be said to "elevate" (or "liberate") himself to a higher level even as he plays—lives—in expectation of "censure" and "adverse judgment." Through Messi, Argentina is "raised" to the "level" of Barcelona, at least as it regards the Messian order of things. Barça is, then, "conserved" in Argentina through the person of Messi, in the way that Messi plays. However minimally, Argentina is made other to itself, and Messi is able to, as it were, preserve something elemental and vital about himself.

The national team, both as a playing unit and ethically (Lacan proffers psychoanalysis as a form of "ethics"; Nancy's "negativity"; Butler's argument for how the "human comes into being"), Argentina is "improved" through Messi.[51] If the Argentine nation might be said to be a "prisoner of [its] infatuation" with Maradona, and if Messi's relationship to the nation-state is filtered through and violenced by that "infatuation," then what Messi does in his Barça mode is interrupt Argentina's relationship to Maradona, whom Lacan might judge "an unmitigated scoundrel"; the relationship between Maradona and Argentina, we are free to speculate, contains elements that are decidedly pathological (we could confer the same honor on Suárez, that of "unmitigated scoundrel" or the "lovable rogue," a term I have used elsewhere in relation to another group of sports figures).[52] In his turn, Messi disrupts, commits his own kind of (ethical?) transgression against the Argentine nation-state by instituting a gap, maybe even a yawning chasm, between the nation and itself; he disarticulates the nation from remaining, without reflexivity, in keeping with itself.

Messi is the wedge that provides the possibility of an "ethical" Argentina, in Lacan's sense. As Lacan puts it, he is pursuing a "deeper dimension of analytical thought, work and technique that I am calling ethics," an approach that finds a very similar articulation in Nancy, the "most serious penetration of thought."[53] Messi can play for Argentina only in such a way that he "conserves" himself, which must also be understood as the "surging up" of the self into "negativity," which makes Messi signal. Messi is singular in that he is at once both the most un-Argentine Argentine footballer and the only international footballer who is not (fully) bound to the nation-state even as he incarnates it. Messi simultaneously, if reluctantly, affirms the nation-state and is the greatest threat to it; that is, his dispensation toward/for playing sans both "hate" and "love" makes him the only international player who can rise above the "destruction" of the nation-state because he is so patently not *of* it. In Messi, through and because of Messi, we can see how "being does not remain in itself; it liberates itself," it "surges up" furiously toward the world, so that we might, in a colloquial sense, negate that which is in order to achieve the "negation of the negation"—hyperbolically rendered, in such a way that we might see a Copa Mundial played according to Messi's terms, those which "negate" "love" and "hate," that which *always gives itself as something other than simply given.*"[54] We "surge upward" in the direction of that which refuses the "given," which seeks to make possible that which is "other than simply given." That is what thought must be given to, relentlessly; that is how *Rastlosigkeit* gives birth to the deepest "penetration of thought."

In this way, Messi posits the possibility of the footballer beyond the Lacanian principle of *Aufhebung*. Messi is circumscribed by the politics of the nation-state, but he cannot be fully held (restricted, overdetermined) by its paradigm. Messi, then, not only "conserves"—retains within himself what is ethical and valuable, what is worth keeping sacred, playing football in, shall we call it, a transcendent way—but he creates other possibilities for playing international football. How would a Copa Mundial be played without "hate" or "love?" We already have such a proposition, and its name is Leo Messi. We have embodied football without love or hate. Its name is Leo Messi. Let us observe the cost of playing ethically. To play with a "deeper dimension of analytical thought, work and technique" is to be, as Lacan so poetically phrases it, "a success of the night, a success of the damned."[55]

That is no small price to pay, but how else is Messi to "bear witness against" himself except by making himself vulnerable to the judgment of the nation-state, how else is he to bear that ironic moniker Lacan offers, the "success of the damned?"[56] Is the only way to play football to play as if one were, from the very outset, already, a priori, "damned?" Is "damnation," "condemnation," the only way to break the hold of "infatuation?" To be condemned is to be made to suffer "eternal punishment" or eternal exclusion ("belonging without belonging"), or, to remain felicitous to Lacan's intensely Christian and, in truth, intensely Roman Catholic register, is it to be an Argentine footballer who always risks the possibility of excommunication?[57] As such, Messi is the Argentine-Catalan or Catalan-Argentine, a designation that, despite the politics of the hyphen and its desire to complicate identity and belonging, demonstrates nothing so much as the hold of the nation-state as a political figuration for communal belonging, who stands—or, who plays—against the Law in its many iterations. The "unbearable" law of the nation-state, FIFA's law, which determines that national affiliation, is the only mode for competition between communal political entities, the Law of the Father (a fanciful designation for Maradona but, no matter, let us indulge it) who is "an unmitigated scoundrel" but is loved by the partisans. This is the compound of laws against which Messi positions himself, this is the "place where the battlefield of [his] experience is situated."[58] In this regard, what Messi manifests is akin to the way in which Nancy thinks "freedom," "independence," and "autonomy." It is possible to be free/d from the "'despotic ego,'" Nancy claims, only if we can envisage the law as that which "gives itself as precisely itself: it therefore gives itself the law to have no law, if it is itself, for itself, the law."[59] The law, the lawlessness of Messi, Messi, the "law that gives itself to have no law," is the possibility of freedom, the freedom of possibility, with which Messi confronts us. Messi might then be thought of as the idea in its "revelatory moment of manifestation."[60]

But Messi's law is constrained, for now (for how long? forever?), by the forces (laws) arrayed against him, and this is where Messi, in every international fixture that he plays, must work his Messi magic. This is where Messi, to borrow from Lacan's rendering of Marquis de Sade, must produce his own brand of "experimental literature [football]. The work of art in this case is an experiment that through its actions cuts the subject loose from its psychosocial moorings—or, to be more precise, from all psychosocial appreciation of the sublimation involved."[61] Every game, every attempted dribble, every pass, every goal (all of which, together, create the Messian mode of jouissance), is an "experiment" in which Messi seeks to conserve himself at the highest possible level, with the greatest amount of integrity. But, as Lacan makes clear, in order to succeed in his "experiment," Messi must, on a game-by-game basis, risk the possibility of "unmooring" himself from all that he knows (Barça would constitute the core of this "knowledge"). Nancy is, for his part, fully aware of this risk, because, as he says, "Each thought puts [all knowledge] of the self at stake."[62] And so Messi must think the very thoughts that would put him at risk, he must "stake" himself in order to "negate" what is, and all the while he must stipulate to the act of making himself vulnerable to the very forces that would restrain him back into the nation-state, back to that state where "hate" (the destruction and "fixity" of each one) and "love" (which must "manifest itself as a struggle" in order to bring about the "alteration of each one") reside with only the barest interrogation, he must do so without recourse to "sublimation": he must "unmoor" himself from his *Sein* and *Be* fully exposed to the very forces that have historically condemned him.[63]

This is a call to experimental arms that risks, as Lacan and Nancy, in their distinct ways, each knows, the very death of the subject. Isn't that, as Owen's poem reminds us, always the first expectation of pro patria? To be willing to die for the nation? To die in its name? Is Messi's on the order of a "primitive crime," one that can be met only with full force of the "primordial law?" Is Messi's greatest transgression his refusal to submit to the "primordial law" of "hate" and "love?" Is Messi's *Sein*, a radical reversal of roles, the promise—the articulate/d presence, *l'avenir*—of the numen that is (/not yet)? Is Messi the numen dribbling toward the "corner of every Argentine road" where football is played by boys, girls, women, men, *porteños y indios*? Will the "numinous" Messi be found in the "grottoes," taking up his position at those "crossroads" that dot the *muy buena* Argentine hinterland? There in La Plata, there in Rosário?

The threat of Messi as the numen who will either replace or supplement Maradona. What a twosome they would make, "Tiny Tim" and the "unmitigated scoundrel." Messi reminds us that the "numimous proliferates and intervenes on all sides in human experience . . . it is, moreover, so abundant that something in the end must be manifested through man; its power cannot be overcome."[64] Messi, like Maradona (before and with him; Maradona, against whom Messi stands and in relation to whom he will always be judged), is possessed in Lacanian terms of a power that cannot be transcended. Messi, like Maradona before him (and now with him), will "manifest" himself in the Argentine *Sein* (in the nation-state) and its "psychosocial" to such an extent that he will be, and now already might be, ineradicable to it. Messi may or may not be Argentina's future, but he is, without doubt, its (new) "numinous," its divining spirit. Whether or not he can "found a community based on his principles" is another matter entirely because he may just be such an unusual ("mysterious") being that who he is might surpass the understanding of Argentinians and the logic of the nation-state; he may incarnate a mode of playing football that is beyond the structure and ethos of the game as it is currently conceived. Nevertheless, out of those ethical possibilities that Messi posits in his play, he might continue to inscribe the law that "gives itself the law to have no law."[65]

AUFHEBUNG II: BARCELONA-ARGENTINA · Every statement splits the subject that produces it. Lacan is the last Cartesian. —— GILLES DELEUZE, "Dualism, Monism and Multiplicities" (Desire-Pleasure-Jouissance )

*Som mes que un club.* (More than a club.) —— FC Barcelona "motto"

In no way is the Barça Messi ever fully articulated when he plays for Los Albicelestes. Nor can he be. He is, after all, in his "every statement" the subject *entre le moi et le moi-même* and the subject *entre-nous*, the subject "split" into "I-and-I," the subject "split" between club and country. He is the subject who stands between the extant nation-state and its aspirational articulation a continent away. To begin with, when Messi dons the *blaugrana*, he consistently demonstrates, to misinterpret Lacan, his ability to perform at another, at his optimal level; that is where, for Argentine fans, his "upsurge" is most manifest, where, as Nancy says, Messi's "struggle" to play can be understood as the "phenomenon of the very thing whose reality is love."[65] For Barça, Messi always seems to perform in excelsis, always fully as and utterly in excess of himself; that is, as his true self. Messi performs for his club as though he is totally engaged in his "struggle for love." This is a different iteration of *Aufhebung*, one in which Messi achieves the Lacanian "beyond" as, we might suggest, as pure creativity. Playing for Barça, Messi plumbs the "deepest dimension of analytical thought," what Nancy presents as the "hollowing out of thought," exhausting the very limits of physical and "psychoathletic" possibility, and exhibits the most exquisite level of technical skill.

It should not surprise us, given Messi's national "belonging without belonging," that he is so overidentified with Barça. The Catalan club has always, from its very beginning, been receptive of immigrants. As one crosses into Catalunya, there must be a mythical sign somewhere that reads, *"Benvinguda,"* "Welcome," in Catalan. The club was founded by, among others, the Catalan Joan Kamper (formerly Hans Kamper) and the English brothers John and William Parsons; the first full-time manager, the Englishman Jack Greenwell, was hired by Kamper; during the successful 1920s, the club's star, Josep "Pep" Samitier, had tangos written in his honor by the French-born Argentine artist, Carlos Gardel, the most famous exponent of the genre. At the beginning of the Cold War, Barça welcomed into its ranks two Hungarians fleeing the repressive regime in Budapest, László Kubala and Sándor Kocsis. (Also, were it not for the dictator Franco's intervention, both another Hungarian, the greatest of the "1956" generation, Ferenc Puskás, and Di Stéfano would in all likelihood have been Barcelona players.) *"Benvinguda,"* indeed, because Catalunya has historically welcomed so many immigrants from Spain and the rest of the world. The effect of this hospitality has been to convert many of the immigrants to the politics of Catalanismo. Picasso, we might remember, was born in Málaga but identified as Catalan. Following in this venerable tradition, the most recent artist to give himself to Catalunya is, of course, Leo Messi.

If Messi is condemned to the prospect of eternal punishment at home, then he has found, like those who arrived before him, that Barça makes only one demand: that he commit himself fully to its cause, first, last and always. And so he has. And how he has. If Barça is, as I have argued elsewhere,[67] *Som mes que un club*, it remains—at least until such time as sovereignty is achieved through a break with Castilian Spain—less than a nation. What Barça makes possible for Messi, it can be argued, is the impossible: the not-yet (‹)nation makes belonging to that which is not yet possible a psychopolitical option for the subject who lives the condition of "belonging without belonging." Who lives, in other words, for the moment when what is between us, *entre-nous*, is no more. In the stands of Camp Nou, Barça's stadium, it is possible to hear the "beyond" iterated in those age-old chants, chants that have their origin in the long since demolished Le Corts stadium, that roar the team on, *Visca el Barça! Visca el cules!*[68]

If the examples of Gardel, Picasso, Kubala, Kocsis, and Messi are anything to go by, then FC Barcelona/Catalunya can be posited as that unique geopolitical space—let's designate it historical aspirational sovereignty, historical since the eighteenth century, to be specific—in which the exile, the artist, the itinerant laborer, and the condemned find a release from struggle and are offered a new lease on selfhood. Indeed, they are all offered an entirely new way of being in the world: *Sein* Catalan. The condition of historically aspirational sovereignty offers a reprieve from the nation-state's eternal punishment. In FC Barcelona resides, as Lacan frames it, the "most intimate part" of Messi. In this unique geopolitical formation there is the possibility of repositing and depositing the self, against all political odds. Catalunya makes it possible for Messi (and those like him) to strike a new pose in relation to an expanded political unit. Catalunya makes it possible to deposit, whether temporarily or not, that most intimate part of the self in a place where it might be, for a moment, possible to be—to be safe, to find shelter from the nationalist storm that rages up from Patagonia and sweeps across the Pampas to the foothills of the Andes. The self can be left *there*, that space that it could heretofore only have imagined or dreamed of. Or in Messi's case, it might have been transmitted through his blood.

He came by it honestly, he owes Jorge Messi a greater debt—the political fortunes of genealogy, as it were—than he could ever repay. There, but for the grace of God (in the person of the f/Father), who knows what might have become of that physically compromised ten-year-old. But for all his inclining toward Catalunya, for all the ways in which Catalunya has drawn him into itself, Argentina retains its own "numinousness." The spirit of the place of birth, for good or ill, cannot be excised.

As such, it might then be possible to argue, relying here on a term offered by Carole Slade in her critique of Saint Theresa of Avila, that Leo Messi is not able to—will never be able to—"find himself as a subject" in the Argentine nation-state.[69] However, even if he is not able to "find himself" as a citizen-subject within Argentina, every act of "representation"—playing for Los Albicelestes—reminds him of his impossible "belonging" *to* the nation-state; the force of Law [I use the capitalized L here, as elsewhere, to mark Lacan's rendering of the term], FIFA's rules, international law, sovereignty's mandate all, as such, restrict Messi's possibilities for national affiliation. The law of the father (Jorge) cannot overcome or circumvent the Law of the State; both these laws postpone, we know not for how long but it is always too long, the "law" that "gives itself the law."

*On Sunday, January 14, 2018, Messi scores on a masterful free kick against Villarreal. Taken some twenty-two meters from goal, Messi places the ball high and to the keeper's right, capping a 0–2 comeback. Suárez scores a brace. When Messi scores to secure a 4–2 victory, his face lights up so much that it seems to make his reddish beard shine.*

Even if Messi manifests through his "belonging without belonging," that he is, as Lacan says, himself as an "object necessarily in a state of independence" in his relation with Argentina, his every refusal, his every grimace, his inability to access jouissance on the international playing field, locates him directly within the logic of the nation-state, "split," *entre le moi et le moi-même*, again and again.[70] Even if the "object" Leo Messi is "taken" or appropriated by Argentina to work/play in its cause, the way in which he plays football can be read as a pyrrhic and not a Sisyphean "declaration of sovereignty." Messi, we are free to propose, incarnates the possibility of sovereignty through a Lacanian ethical; or he instantiates the peculiar alienation of the self-sovereign, the sovereign who resists, through how he plays the game, the overwhelming, overreaching sovereignty of the extant nation-state. In his struggle ("love") for "separation," Messi is, as Nancy phrases it, "what posits the distinct, and identifies it."[71] Messi inspires political possibility, he makes us think for [as: to think in the direction of] /of "separation" as such, because he models the "indestructible character of the Other," making Messi once more "enigmatic" in his "relation to the Law."[72] As such, Messi is, in this rendering of him as the manifestation of a philosophical/political "upsurge," engaged in the work of "opening the present, opening space and time, opening the world and 'I,' and throwing existence into restless exigency."[73] Messi is the object who will not be made part of the whole (nation-state) but who nonetheless finds himself, finds in himself, "something" he seeks to "destroy at a different level." As such, Messi demonstrates the indefatigability of *Aufhebung*: the difficult work of "transcending" the political purchase and ideological circumscription of the nation-state, the everyday (every game, club or country) effects of that intense division that Deleuze delineates, the need to produce that "upsurge" that Nancy so poetically urges. For Messi, and for the rest of us, the nation-state can be said to be "indestructible." We live, like Messi, with Messi, under the sign of *Aufhebung*, in all its iterations. And this sign is, as will be discussed in a later section, something approximating and approaching the sign of death, an iteration of death that locates Messi once more in relation to Maradona.

A MOMENT OF RESPITE · Once again / Do I behold these steep and lofty cliffs, / That on a wild secluded scene impress / Thoughts of more deep seclusion; and connect / The landscape with the quiet of the sky. / The day is come when I again repose / Here
—— William Wordsworth, "Tintern Abbey"

What kind of violence, against the other, "indestructible" or not, against the self, is condemnation, a word itself that bristles with violence, promising as it does the threat of "unfavorable judgment," "sentence," or "censure?" What could such a violence produce other than the "saddest smile" of a Leo Messi? What is revealed when the violence of condemnation is, for a moment or more, not enacted? Such moments of respite are inevitable because it is not possible to condemn, try as one might, without interruption. It takes time, firstly, to arrive at the decision to condemn, and then one must take a moment, however brief or peremptory, to deliver an "unfavorable judgment."

And so it is with Messi. In the interregnum between judgment and condemnation, it is possible to glimpse Messi in what those moments of respite might look like in a moment of "repose." In the semifinal victory over the Netherlands in the 2014 World Cup, via a penalty shootout, that look of anticipating, of bearing, the weight of judgment was absent. It had not quite been banished (one cannot banish the numen), but it seemed in temporary abeyance. It was held at bay by the prospect of the moment. After all, if Argentina prevailed against the Dutch, it would secure the nation its third appearance in a Copa Mundial final. And on the previous two occasions, 1978 and 1986, Argentina had prevailed.

In the company of his Los Albicelestes teammates, all huddled together on the halfway line as they watched the penalties being taken, as is customary when this is how the game is decided, Messi raised a rare smile. But it was only a fleeting departure from his customary shy demeanor. Messi appears in public as withdrawn. Even when he dyes his hair a dirty blond (beginning in the 2016–17 season; it has not survived in the present, mercifully) and when he grows a shaggy beard and shaves his hair around his ears (late in 2016, early in 2017, persisting into 2018, as though he were impersonating a Shoreditch hipster), it attracts no more attention to him than is usual. His hair, facial or otherwise, its color, dyed or no, fashionably shaved or not, is utterly extraneous to our understanding of his embodiment. Messi is the kind of footballer whom we watch for his "zones of distinction," to recalibrate Giorgio Agamben's phrase.[74]

We pay attention, intensely, to Messi's feet, in which magic resides; we watch his hips, which swivel like a tightly coiled rotating chair, capable of, in an instant, moving this way or that, throwing opponents off balance as he immaculately, against expectation, retains his. We watch his face and eyes, individually, separately, simultaneously, as if that were possible; we watch them because they provide us with a glimpse into his singular intelligence and vision. We are moved to "thoughts of more deep seclusion," and, as such, we watch in anticipation, in (vain, but inexhaustible) hope: that somehow, if only for a fleeting moment, we might see—fully conceptualize, imagine beyond our capacities—the football field, that world within a world, the ways in which the world appears to/for Messi; the *món* (*mundial*) Messi makes. Alas, poor Yorick, no such luck, but that is why we watch him, that such a view of the "steep and lofty cliffs" that he alone can scale might be afforded us.

Ours is the fan's futile exercise, but one nonetheless deeply rooted in poetic commitment. Ours is an act of fidelity to the spectacle, a pathos-filled homage to vistas unsightable, a "leap," Heidegger's term, of faith, of the most elevating football variety because it presents us with football as the purists would have it played ("we" purists, I should say, to make plain my allegiance). Messi-orchestrated football is the very stuff, we might suggest, of Keatsian (and Lacanian, and Wordsworthian) poetry because it is at once beyond us, beyond the ken of mere mortals, and yet still within the ambit, the outer reaches, of imaginings. Watching him we can at least see that such physical acts are possible on a football field and that we can—Messi makes this our responsibility—bear witness to it, even if it is so far removed from our own physical capabilities. (We have not skill enough for it, to say the least, although our old philosopher friend might disagree.)

It is a language that is foreign to us in athletic ability; and yet not, because as fans we have our own discourse, a discourse grounded in our unfulfillable desires. After all, without this discourse of ours, we would have no hermeneutic apparatus. (In truth, however, with Messi there are moments when it feels as though exegesis might be the more appropriate interpretative mechanism).

## *LA LENGUA DEL CAPITÁN*: THE LANGUAGE OF THE CAPTAIN · (5)

Since our acts are actions, we must always remember the distinction between producing effects or consequences which are intended or unintended; and, (i) when the speaker intends to produce an effect it may nevertheless not occur, and (ii) when he does not intend to produce it or intends not to produce it it may nevertheless occur. —— J. L. AUSTIN, *How to Do Things with Words*

On the football field, the brilliance of Leo Messi speaks Leo Messi, a language that has only one speaker. We can, if we try hard enough, discern its basic grammar—its physical building blocks, as I have just done in the previous section—but the finer points of the language, wherein lie its secrets, wherein lies its allure, those we can only incline toward; we can, as it were, only guess at, imagine, its syntax, its nuance, the intricacies of its technical structure.[75]

And so we must, against considerable odds, make our own language for Messi. We are faced with this project because, as regards his different linguistic "competencies," Leo Messi presents a difficult contradiction. Messi is a man of such prodigious footballing gifts (this is the football language that he speaks, one in which he is singularly articulate) and so very few words—the discursive apparatus, let us call it the "everyday language" that we have in common.

In August 2011, the new Argentine coach, Alejandro Sabella, appointed the twenty-four-year-old Messi national skipper. Messi is the very incarnation of the captain who leads by example, a description that is often invoked but all too frequently lacks substance, or truth, for that matter, about the manner—the style, if you will—of the player wearing the armband.

Messi's is a distinct mode of captaincy. With him there is no gesticulation, frantic or otherwise, and no loud exhortation. He does not berate teammates if they have made a mistake, and there is no desperate clapping of the hands when the team is trailing. Leo Messi does not trash-talk the opposition. He very rarely responds to the physical punishment that is so often handed out to him, something his teammate Suárez and former teammate Neymar, to say nothing players such as Ronaldo (Real Madrid and Portugal), who tends to flop at the first hint of contact, or Thomas Müller (Bayern Munich and Germany), who always seems to be trying to get opponents booked, are apt to do. Messi almost never quibbles with referees.

Leo Messi plays. With Messi it is the ball, the game, his love for just playing that is all he is attuned to. Messi, in the parlance of English football, "just gets on with it," with a kinetically measured relentlessness that reminds us time and again that he plays the game on terms identifiably his own. And yet, as we shall see, he is also bound by something that is perhaps incompatible, incommensurate with what we might name Messi's ontology—the very essence of Leo Messi.

In that moment when Argentina with Messi at the helm, fails, it is then that we come to know him as an ontologically condemned man.

Otherwise, however, captain Messi is always looking for the ball; he drops deep to collect it from his defense. Immediately, through a series of feints, dips of the shoulder (the left more than the right), he drives forward, not so much relieving the pressure on his defense as attacking from the back. In possession, there are few players in the history of the game who can be said to use the ball so intelligently. Messi understands the moment and exactly what it is the moment demands—he grasps what is appropriate to the time. However, and here his singularity is most immanent, it is not so much that he responds to the moment, but that he is simultaneously able to create the moment—he makes the game, again, if such a conception might be imagined—and can let himself to be absorbed into the "flow" (the rhythm, the tempo) of the game. (In this way, we can say that Messi "makes" time: he "opens" it up, bends it to his will. Leo Messi commands time. The only other player in the contemporary game who has a similar propensity of "making" time is Croatia's Luka Modrić.)

It is because of his array of skills that it is not possible to use the language of force in relation to Messi. One cannot say of Messi, as one would of other players who can command the game (Franz Beckenbauer, Zinedine Zidane, Steven Gerrard, Modrić), that he is "imposing himself on the game." (Of such players as Beckenbauer and Gerrard one would say, "He bosses a game," so affecting was their physical authority to the outcome of the match.) Messi operates, to render this speculatively, simultaneously at a higher level of abstraction and at an utterly mundane level. Philosophically, we can say that Messi makes the game: εξ' ἀρχῆς, the game begins with Messi; or εξ' ἀρχῆς λόγος, he is the first argument of the game, to "translate" Anaximander's first principles into Messianic terms. To "translate" a second time, and to play on the notion of "arche," Messi constructs the architecture of the game. Through his play, he "plans" the game—he is instrumental in dictating the game's intricate passing patterns, he determines the pace of the pass, he organizes, through his ability to command the ball, the spacing between teammates, critical for creating opportunities to score on offense and for "closing down" the amount of room available to opponents.

Possessed of a rare capacity for discrimination, Messi is a wonderful judge of the moment on offense. He knows when to shoot himself (either from close quarters or from distance), when to drive at opponents with pace (which, given his level of skill, causes them to back off, making him triply dangerous because now he can continue to drive, he can dribble, or he can shoot), when to dribble, when to draw back, and, critically, when to lay the ball off to a teammate who is well positioned to score. Messi seems to know, more often than not, exactly when to release a teammate into space; when, that is, to turn provider and creator.[76] When he is not in possession (the Barça way is to share the ball, not quite equally, but quite liberally, among all eleven players; the goalkeeper, as is increasing the trend in the contemporary game but which began at Barça, is expected to be good with the ball at his feet), Messi moves quickly to get into position to receive the ball. Always, it seems, Messi knows what he wants to do with the ball before he receives the ball, although, one suspects, he opens new possibilities even when he is not in possession of the ball. And, as such, he is in position to change his mind and adjust quickly to the new possibilities. This is, to invoke Wordsworth, what emerges from those "thoughts of deep seclusion."

In Austinian terms, Messi is himself the producer (the source) of much of the "intended" as well as the "unintended" "consequences." In Messi, it is possible to say, Austin's "distinction" between the "intended" and the "unintended" both holds, for a brief moment (when confronted with the unexpected, Messi must translate from the former to the latter), and dissolves. Messi is able to make the "unintended" his own; that is, he inscribes the "unintended" with a new "intention." Messi catalyzes the former into the latter, he translates the "unintended" into the idiom of Messi. Leo Messi is the first, and only, speaker in that language we know as "Messianic."

Moreover, there is something about Messi that cannot be fully explicated by Austin's "distinction." Austin's "distinction" that might, in a substantive way, be understood as a theory of contingency—that is, there is no guarantee that what is "intended" will produce the "effect" that governs, that drives, the "act." The "action" can as likely produce the desired "effect" as something entirely different—the always possible, even likely, "unintended."[77] Always, of course, cognizant of the possibility of the "act" fulfilling itself: "it may nevertheless occur."

Always lurking within the contingent, however, is the possibility of the event. So it is with Messi and not only because he knows what he wants to effect. He knows how he wants to *make* the game, he knows how to make the game in which he is playing speak the language of Messi. Messi can do this because he is an alchemist. He can transform the "unintended" (named "baseness" here, for the sake of argument) into an entirely new, previously, just a moment ago, "intended." An "intended" that he himself could not have imagined. Every time, therefore, that Messi is in possession of the ball, an event—*making the game in a distinctly new way*—becomes possible. Or, phrased as a proper noun, Lionel Messi on the football field is an event. Not an event in the sense that we expect it to happen (the predictability of the unpredictable) and yet are surprised when it does take place, but an event pure and simple: his every touch *makes* the game.

Messi is, in Heidegger's sense, the "disclosedness" of the event—*Ereignis*, the "event" or that which "comes into view." That is, what Messi does is "unconceal" (ἀλήθεια, *Aletheia*) the ways in which football, as such, can be played and contains within itself the event. Poetically phrased, Messi is the Being/ *Sein* of football: football-as-it-is. To be with Messi on the field is, in a necessarily amended Heideggerian sense, *Dasein*: there where the "being of football dwells".[78] Messi is the dwelling (in) which football is.[79] In Messi we can find football.

In this regard, Messi's accomplishment may be that he is able to achieve *Dasein* in an unselfish way, by integrating himself into the team while still maintaining fidelity to his language, to the language of (his/football's) Being. Messi is, of course, greatly advantaged by playing for Barça because Messi's and Catalan *fútbol* are compatible languages; they share a basic grammar, passing, preferably of short variety (*tiki-taka*, as it became known during former coach Pep Guardiola's tenure), intricate movement, creating and organizing space and time. To play for Barça also requires vision, not only identifying where teammates are but possessing a sense for recognizing what is happening in the entire field.[80] And so, Messi plus FC Barcelona is, to extend Heidegger's notion of Being to the collective, the event of *Mitsein*: of being-with; "being-with-the-other." Or, to exaggerate, *Mitsein* with *Sein* (both of which are unthinkable here without a fundamental grasp of and dependence upon *Dasein*)—being with Being, which might amount to same, of course, as Nancy and Butler's project; or beings with Being; or "we" or "being-with-the-other"—that is, to and through metaphysics and beyond.[81] *Mitsein* or no, in his number 10 Barça jersey there is no mistaking it. We can "see" Messi talk when he plays for Barça. We can see Messi talk irrespective of whether he is on the ball or not.

However, football is of course too "messy" a game, pun intended, for any player to produce, with any consistency, the effects he or she wants. That is because football operates in many registers, at once. Barça's mode of playing, or the *gegenpressing* that Jürgen Klopp's Liverpool play (and before that, Klopp's BVB Dortmund club), can be met with a number of footballing responses. Opponents might, *à la* José Mourinho's defensive strategy, "park the bus," that is, put as many defenders behind the ball in order to prevent their opponents from imposing their mode on the game; Italians, with their deep commitment to organization and defense (*calcio*), are equally adept at this strategy; or, although they make lack the personnel and/or the talent, the opposing team might decide to go toe-to-toe with Barça; or an intensely physical team could attempt to disrupt Barça's mode with fierce tackling; or opponents may try to attack directly, in no small measure by pumping a series of high balls, also known as "Route 1" football,[82] into the Barça penalty area in an attempt to unsettle the intricacies of the passing mode through sheer physical force. No matter which strategy or strategies are employed, any football game is always a struggle around, about, the language that is spoken. Could there be a more polyglot game?

THE CONDUCTOR · In this way Messi's football language—the *Dasein* that he inscribes—is precisely what enables him to play conductor to the massive talents of his Barça teammates, especially his attacking colleague Luis Suárez and, until the end of the 2016–17 season, in tandem with Neymar. As is needed, Messi draws everything together; he is the maestro who keeps "time" (the tempo at which the game is played, but also the *Zeit*, the time of all football as *Dasein* is kept, dwells, within him) as well ordering the spacing between the Barça players, whom he guides, the consequence of many years of playing together, into optimal positions.[83] In football terms, it is Messi (and Iniesta, and Xavi before him at Barça) who "pulls the strings" on the field for Barça. Defensively, he harries opponents on defense, often dispossessing them with a determined tackle and then emerging with the ball, under control, so that he is able to quickly begin a new attack.

As Argentine skipper, Messi possesses a quality that you want in any captain: that player who is always in control of himself and the game. Most importantly, Messi, like a LeBron James or Michael Jordan (basketball), a Gerrard (football), a Viv Richards (cricket), or a Wayne Shelford (rugby), makes everyone around them better.[84] Only very special players do that.

That smile at the halfway line, then, as the Argentine substitute Maxi Rodríguez beat the Dutch keeper Jasper Cillessen in the 2014 World Cup semifinal, was an aberration, out of the ordinary, something out of character. As such, this was a smile to be archived, marked as "exceptional"; this was a smile to remember but "not to be trusted," perhaps. If only because of its rareness, that 2014 smile was a moment to be savored. Messi, hands clenched into a low pumping fist, raced toward Rodríguez with his de facto vice-captain Mascherano on his left shoulder. Reaching the final meant everything to Leo. And he allowed us to witness it.

It was, however, but a moment. At the end of the very next game, Messi bore a look that was distinctly different.

THE CONDEMNED · Origins trouble the voyager much, those roots / That have sipped the waters of another continent —— ARTHUR NORTJE, "Waiting"

O ask me all but do not ask allegiance! —— ARTHUR NORTJE, "Song for a Passport"

Messi bore the look of a condemned man, already haunted even though the final whistle had just blown to signal the end of extra time in the World Cup final in Argentina's 1–0 loss to Germany.

In the 113th minute the first makings of that look could already be discerned. The camera turned to Messi immediately after Mario Götze scored what turned out to be the decisive goal in World Cup 2014. Messi looked not so much condemned, yet, as stunned, aghast that the Argentine defense had failed to pick up Götze, the lone German attacker. Messi's eyes betrayed just a hint of reproach, rare for him; in the main, his looked tended more toward incomprehension. The question was almost visible, "How did this happen?" Messi looked stunned because he knew the condemnation was imminent.

When the final whistle blew, Messi was condemned. He knew, that look said clearly, that he would have to bear the criticism of the international football community.

He, the greatest player of his generation, had failed to win the World Cup for Argentina. His name would forthwith belong with the likes of Johann Cruyff or the Mozambican-born Portuguese striker Eusébio, not with Pelé, Franz Beckenbauer, and Zinedine Zidane. Nor, most saliently, would his name be sung along with that of Diego Maradona. In the world's football imagination Pelé, Beckenbauer, and Zidane had not only won the World Cup, they had done so through spectacular individual performances.

Messi would be tied to Cruyff, another Barça great who had also fully embraced Catalunya. (Cruyff learned Catalan in order to fully immerse himself in the life of the city and the *autonomista*.)[85] Cruyff is renowned as the most brilliant exponent of "total football," a system designed by Rinus Michels, the Netherlands coach and formerly Cruyff's coach at his club Ajax. Total football was conceived in order to accentuate the skill of every individual and to blend each player's strengths into a free-flowing team. Michels had gathered together a supremely talented footballing ensemble in that 1974 Dutch team. Led by Cruyff, the Dutch lost 2–1 to West Germany in Munich, a game in which they were clearly the better team, in a tournament where they shone and won fans the world over with their way of playing.

Cruyff and Messi, bound by their relationship to FC Barcelona and their unwanted status: they are each the greatest player of his generation never to win a World Cup. Measured against his nemesis, Diego Maradona, Messi had been found wanting. The 1–0 loss in the final of the 2014 World Cup was the ultimate judgment.

Appropriately, then, the origin of the criticism would begin with the attacks from his fellow Argentines. He would have anticipated the onslaught; none of it would have come as a surprise to Messi. The raucous accusations, "He can't win the Big One"; the indictments, "He has been, apart from a moment or two, an underperformer at this Copa Mundial." His father had reportedly told all and sundry that Leo was tired. For the legions of his critics, only incredulity could follow such a declaration. Tired? What, tired on the eve of the Copa Mundial final? Such a proposition was impossible, unthinkable, no matter its veracity.

The only issue of consequence, however, was that Messi had missed his greatest opportunity to install himself in the pantheon of Argentine football greats.

Leo Messi is no Diego Maradona. That was not a whisper; it had the feel—the loud reverberation, not to mince words—of a strategic campaign against Messi. As the self-exiled South African poet Arthur Nortje knew well,[86] disenfranchisement comes in many forms, its modulations and tones unpredictable. Having left Argentina at the age of thirteen, as I said earlier, Messi had, in Nortje's phrasing, more than "sipped the waters of another continent." The popular perception, which holds not only in Argentina but more broadly, was that he had let the nation, in which his place has always been precarious, down. Messi was paying, once again, as he has been since he first came to prominence as a prodigy in Rosário, for his "voyages." Messi's diasporic tendencies, his "belonging without belonging," that which was *entre-eux*, to Argentina, had troubled him for his entire professional career.

I could discern it; Messi was condemned. Messi was condemned as surely as Nortje so tragically knew what it meant to live in exile, that the cost of exile is always bound to death. Nortje knew because living in apartheid South Africa was untenable, unbearable, and, when all was said and done, fatal. At the age of twenty-seven, like those 1960s icons Janis Joplin and Jimmy Hendrix (and Kurt Cobain, too, someone closer to our moment), Nortje committed suicide in faraway Oxford, his love for the country of his birth and a woman from Canada (although she too was born in South Africa) unrequited.

For his part, Messi committed a kind of professional and political suicide in performing so brilliantly for Barça. Messi's Barça excellence constituted, for Argentina, the equivalent of Lacan's "primordial crime": an unforgivable transgression against the nation-state: relegating it in the order of his performance—Catalunya before Argentina. Playing for Barça, leading it to the greatest heights in the club's history, enfolded Messi in the narrative of Catalan exceptionality: a hero in the cause of the aspirational rather than the de facto nation-state. Winning for Barça and not replicating that level of success for Argentina not only fed the notion that Messi was, as we now know so well, Catalan, first, and perhaps last and always, but it gave substance to the sense (suspicion) that he was Argentine only by the accident of birth. True for all of this accident, but fatally so for Messi.

Hence the look on Messi's face, registering, immediately, the anticipation of allegations that will not be stilled, that grew to an uproar in the wake of the defeat to Germany. Messi's true allegiances lie with Catalunya, with Barcelona, where he came of age and for whom he must, without a shadow of a doubt, feel greater affection. With Barça he almost never fails. There he scores goals aplenty and, frequently, with breathtaking brilliance. This is the force of *Aufhebung*, understood by Nortje as much as anyone. Indeed, "origins trouble the voyager much." How his origins trouble Leo Messi, how they are used as an instrument, a blunt one, in truth, against him.

The charge, unsustainable after his performance in the World Cup, is that Messi always reserves his best for Barcelona. He is, if not a traitor to the Argentine cause, indifferent to what winning the World Cup in Brazil, yes, Brazil, Argentina's archenemy, would have meant to Argentina. Messi does not understand, perhaps he cannot since he "belongs without belonging" (which carries for him the charge of betrayal), what winning the World Cup would have meant in Buenos Aires, the Paris of Latin America. Sticking one to the dastardly Brazilians, that is what it would have meant. Winning the Copa Mundial on their soil, winning it in their backyard—the Brazilians would never live that down. Messi didn't get that, apparently, because his origins do not mean enough to him.

The burden that Messi bore when the final whistle blew is merely (dare I even use this adverb? It seems to diminish what Messi must endure) the latest iteration of a burden he has borne all his professional life. But this may very well be the cost of achieving that "necessary state of independence," because Messi, like an epic hero, was made to carry the full weight of national expectation. With Messi the sole focus of national longing, it meant that the failings, technical and otherwise, of his teammates went unremarked upon. Who remembers the profligacy of Higuaín or the fact that Rodrigo Palacio just plain missed a gilt-edged chance? Even outlets sympathetic to Messi could not restrain themselves; the game was lost by Argentina because of the chance that Messi missed, somewhere around the hour mark of the 2014 Copa Mundial. In that moment, the "Argentina No. 10 ran clear down the left channel and saw his whipped shot beat Manuel Neuer only for the ball to also fly past the far post. Fine margins that some will have define a great career."[87] There is something at once tragic about this account, as though Messi were preordained to fail because the gods of football (fate/Fate) denied him that inch inside Manuel Neuer's far post, that is overwhelmed by its lachrymose quality, as though we are invited to shed tears, uncontrollably, at the tragedy. The failure to score once takes precedence over everything else that Messi made possible, not least of which was his ability to set up chances for his teammates; "being-with-the-other"—the pass that makes scoring possible.

So while Messi is condemned, it is not, apparently, very difficult to forgive a striker who, firstly, misses when through on goal (Higuaín) and, secondly, can't time his run to beat the offside trap of a static German defense (Higuaín). No, I can't decide if this is worse or better, if it is worth laying into an international substitute whose technical *nous*—just getting the ball under control often seemed a challenge to him throughout the World Cup—leaves much to be desired and who can't use his left foot to chip a goalkeeper when, again, clear through on goal (Palacio).

I suspect that somewhere in Argentina, watching the Copa Mundial final, Carlos Tevez was having a laugh. The maverick striker was left out of the 2014 Argentina World Cup squad because of the kind of problems a player as "temperamental" as he is could potentially cause. A man with a healthy self-regard for his goal-scoring abilities, Tevez did not take his exclusion well at all. However, for all the humiliation it heaped on him, Tevez must have known that, for all his reputation as a high-maintenance player, he is assuredly a more gifted striker than Palacio.

In his every appearance in the tournament, Palacio had the look of what he is: a thirty-two-year-old journeyman who just happened to have a career season for his club in Italy, Inter Milan. For his part, Tevez, who possesses wonderful close control and is not short of imagination, although he is sometimes—too often, his detractors allege—guilty of selfishness and poor decision making, scored freely in winning a Scudetto with Juventus. How Argentina could have used a player like Tevez to share the burden of scoring and creation with Messi and di María, injured for the final and unable to play even though he was on the bench. There is also the matter of aesthetics. Tevez is not encumbered by that rat's tail that dribbles sadly from somewhere on the back side of Palacio's balding head.

Nothing of these failings, because only the epic figure can bear the burden of overrepresentation: he is not only the One who must stand in for the Many, he is the One who performs for the Many in its entirety. The fate of the nation-state depends upon the epic figure, upon him in his exceptionality. For Messi the burden was, in that 2014 final, intensified because he was expected to perform in such a way as to overcome the fundamental lacks of those others wearing the colors of Los Albicelestes. He put Higuaín and Palacios through on goal with exquisite passes. If only he were on the other end to receive those selfsame passes from—who else?—himself. That would solve all Argentina's footballing problems in international competitions.

**MARIO GÖTZE AND THE ARGENTINE STRIKERS WHO COULD NOT MEET HIS STANDARD** · Higuaín and Palacio could have taken a leaf out of Mario Götze's book. When the chance came along, Götze, the cherubic son of a university professor (Dortmund Technische Universität), controlled a cross neatly on his chest (for his part, the out-of-his depth Palacio fumbled and stumbled in the penalty area when his opportunity presented itself). Taking the barest hint of a moment, Götze swiveled ever so slightly to his left, and sweetly smashed a volley past the Argentine goalkeeper Romero. It was not the narrowest of angles, but Götze hit it just so, giving Romero no chance. Game over and let's get ready to celebrate in Berlin and Dortmund and München. *Deutschland über alles.*

*Thanksgiving 2017. While visiting Dortmund, I take in a game at what used to be called the Westfalenstadion but has now adopted a corporate replacement—Signal Iduna Park, an insurance company. Borussia Dortmund ("BVB" to its fans) plays Tottenham Hotspur (Spurs) of England in the Champions League qualifying round match. "BVB" is dire. No imagination, absolutely no creativity, and everyone just seems to be going through the motions. Against the run of play, "BVB" goes up 1–0, courtesy of an opportunist goal by the Gabonese striker Pierre-Emerick Aubameyang. Spurs reply and eventually run out 2–1 winners. Disgusted, "BVB" fans leave as soon as Spurs score their second goal, wonder aloud when the oft-injured Götze will play for their club again.*

But Higuaín and Palacio were not the only Argentine strikers who failed to meet the standards of Götze, the German substitute. Sergio "Kun" Agüero seemed positively AWOL for the bulk of the tourney. Agüero, the much vaunted striker, struggled for fitness and looked sadly out of touch (in a word, he was woeful) even when he was supposed to be fully healthy. Desultory and unenthusiastic, Agüero showed himself devoid of the ability to release a teammate into space when Argentina had numbers on the German defense. Forgotten in Agüero's forgettable performance was his full-blooded commitment to the Manchester City cause. In the English Premier League season building up to the World Cup, the much beloved "Kun" played with abandon and was absolutely vital to Manchester City winning the English Premier League in the 2013–14 season.

And if the strikers were not up to the task, what can be said of the Argentine manager, Alejandro Sabella? His commitment to an attacking Argentina disappeared as soon as the group stages were complete, trusting everything to a stout defense that gave up only one goal after the final group stage win over Nigeria. That goal, history shows, was to one Mario Götze. With no real plan of attack, it was left Messi to shoulder the creative burden. The only help the Argentine captain received in this department was from di María and, to a lesser extent, Lavezzi. Now plying his trade in China (like Tevez), Lavezzi was then enjoying a good season with Paris Saint-Germain, and he played his part in the first half of the final. However, Lavezzi's particular aptitude is for picking up the ball deep and running hard down the inside right channel. It is hardly a talent to be sniffed at but he does not pose the same threat as a di María, let alone Messi.

The Argentine defense, for its part, was subject only to the tiniest indictment for Götze's goal. The central defenders, Martín Demichelis and Ezequiel Garay, between them lost Götze when the cross came over from the right flank (where Pablo Zabaleta failed to stop his man and Fernando Gago, who had himself come on as a substitute, gave the fullback no help whatsoever), giving the German striker more than enough time to settle the ball and pick his spot.

The Argentine defense left Sergio Romero, who had a superb tournament and was one of the two Argentine heroes against the Dutch, utterly exposed. (The second standout performer was that central midfielder we know well, Mascherano, who sprinted back, all out, for the better part of sixty meters to brilliantly intercept when a Dutch goal seemed assured. "Masch," as we Liverpool fans fondly used to call him, put in one yeoman shift after another in the tournament, covering acres of ground and bravely putting his body on the line for the Argentine cause. "Masch" is one of the key reasons the Argentine defense was so impregnable, until that fateful moment.) In the semifinal penalty shootout, Romero saved confidently from the Dutch central defender Ron Vlaar and brilliantly from the playmaker Wesley Sneijder to secure Argentina's 4–2 victory on penalties. But in the final, through no fault of his own, it must be said, Romero could do nothing to prevent Götze from scoring.

Those failures in the Argentine attack and defense, they're not so much forgiven as they are ignored. In fact, they are not even mentioned. They bear no reflection. They are not Leo Messi's failures. They belong to a lower order of transgression. As indictments, they do not bear the same sting. Appropriate, not so, because no indictment is possessed of the finality of condemnation.

THE CAMERA FOLLOWS · First, as the whistle sounded, the camera caught him, hands on his hips, his body turned toward a distant point on the horizon, his face a picture in pained containment. But his eyes gave away nothing. And it gave everything away. He knew what it meant, he knew what was coming; but his eyes always emit a fullness that is impregnable. They are hard to read. They are not meant to be read by us.

Leo Messi, as has been noted, almost never smiles on the football field. But that does not mean that he is incapable of communicating happiness.

Leo Messi smiles with his feet. He smiles most radiantly when he picks the ball up on the right flank or in the channel that old-fashioned center forwards such as his countryman Mario Kempes used to run with such relish. Messi's feet come alive as he drives the ball across from the right flank, preferring to cut inside, two, three defenders trailing him (Bastian Schweinsteiger drew that assignment in the final), trying to deny him a path toward goal. But he keeps driving, and soon his original markers cannot keep up. No matter, there are more of them, because by this time—it takes but a few moments—a whole new bank of defenders have materialized. Still he drives, feinting, showing his strength as he rides tackles, trying to pick out a teammate or, as he often but by no means always prefers, to find just the right moment and the tiniest fraction of space to hit a shot with that most educated of left feet. All the while, everyone on the opposing team is doing their damndest to stop him.

You can see Leo Messi think with his feet, you can see how singularly—no one else does it like him—he comes into himself with the ball at his feet. Messi and the ball, "being-with-the-other"; being, utterly, truly, with the self. Running at pace, he has opponents off balance, guessing, ganging up on this tiny maestro. Listed, as we said, at five foot seven, he seems at once physically bigger and smaller. Bigger because of the fear he so visibly installs in his opponents, smaller because he runs, powerfully, bent over, as if he were intent on doubling into himself, as if he could perform the same tricks with his own body as he does with the ball; as though he commands the power to transform himself utterly.

Even when he is running east-west (from one flank to the other), his opponents know that he could at any instant suddenly change direction, and change gears, and speed by them.

I watch Leo Messi with the ball at his feet because I am mesmerized, in awe, and because of his ability to concentrate on doing that for an entire game. He is frequently the target of tough tackles, brutal fouls, and double-, triple-, and god-knows-how-many teams.

In the 2014 World Cup, where Brazil's Neymar was anointed from the very beginning as the poster boy but showed himself as capable of incisive skill as in theatrics, where Arjen Robben of the Netherlands thrilled with his darting runs and his dramatic change of pace and appalled with his admission of cheating, where Suárez defeated himself with his bite when he had brilliance to spare, and where Germany's Thomas Müller (who has, it must be said, real gifts as a footballer) disgusts with his propensity for faking injury and working intensely to get opponents carded, Messi had truly been the tournament's singular star. According to statistics, he "created more chances than anybody at the 2014 World Cup" and "completed more dribbles than any other player with his tally of 46 taking him well clear of Robben's 29" (Bate).[88]

Neymar loves nothing so much as drawing attention to himself. From those rather horrendous haircuts to his theatrical gestures, Neymar has sought to replicate his ubiquity on the advertisers' billboards (across the media spectrum) with his centrality on the pitch. (And even before Neymar, Messi achieved a global ubiquity; a global presence that continues in our moment.) Neymar wants to be seen, he wants the camera on him. Even on the Brazil team, Neymar is not alone in this tendency—think, for example, David Luiz's ugly crowing over felled opponents in repeated outbursts of nationalist fervor. After Luiz fouled opponents, he would stand over them in a threatening fashion and then turn to the crowd for approval, the very epitome of the pro patria spirit that Wilfred Owen has done so much to educate us against. What do Christians facing lions in ancient Rome know of gunning up crowds compared to our shaggy-haired David? Luiz wanted to raise the home crowd to a fevered pitch so as to intimidate and make their opponents *indesejável* ("unwelcome") on the football field. The Brazilian nation, at least in response to Luiz's urgings, seemed all too game. "Hate," "love," how easily they are rallied.

The Dutchman Robben, for his part, is always complaining. It seems that in the course of his career, Robben, who had an excellent World Cup, can never be said to have lost a ball fairly. Every instance of him being dispossessed is the consequence of an opponent's transgression. Robben gesticulates with something approximating fury. He throws up his hands in anger, after which he barks at the referee with a snarl, his balding head presenting itself as a threatening pate. For good measure, he lets his opponents know it—and here it is not only the supposed culprit who is held to account; anyone in an opposing shirt is fair game. And when he cheats (as he did trying to win a penalty against Mexico in the round of 16), and boldly admits it, he declares himself the victim of a scurrilous attack. ("I dived," he said of his theatrical performance against Mexico, "but the penalty was real." Only in Robben's world does such logic compute.) Robben finds it impossible that he be held responsible for his transgressions. He is entirely free, Lacan might say, of the "deeper dimension of analytical thought." His clean-shaven head should make him more "receptive" to the penetration of "analytical thought" but, alas, he is the Teflon Don of ethics. He resists both ethics and thought with consummate ease. In terms of his skills, he may recall, but never equal, his ball playing compatriots, Cruyff, Rudi Krol, and the later generation of Dutch greats, Ruud Gullit, Marco van Basten, and Frank Rijkaard, but his conduct must surely bring them shame.

The German team that won the 2014 World Cup was unusual. It was, in truth, the culmination of a process that began at home in the 2006 World Cup under Jürgen Klinsmann and thrived in South Africa, falling short in the semifinal against eventual 2010 champions Spain. On the evidence of their 2014 performance, and their excellent outing at the 2016 Euros (they lost, but it matters not; they played with relish), Joachem "Jochi" Löw's team is the heir to that Spain side. They, too, in the fashion of the 2008–12 edition of Xavi, Iniesta, and Xabi Alonso, like the ball at their feet. "Jochi" Löw's boys pass with alacrity, and they are all, the hapless (and hopelessly slow) giraffe Per Mertesacker apart, delightfully quick on the ball. They hardly ever use the long ball. Not quite tiki-taka, but they are all exponents of the short-passing game. Bastian Schweinsteiger, now in decline and condemned to the life of unwanted squad player with Manchester United before being put out to pasture with Chicago Fire of the United States' Major League Soccer, came to life at just the right moment, commanding in central midfield as captain Philipp Lamm switched from the center of the park back to his customary right back position because Löw could no longer countenance Mertesacker's slowness of foot. It was the German team, not a single player, but the entire squad—like Götze coming off the bench after being consigned there for a good long while (he last played in the round of 16 game against Algeria before scoring the goal that won the World Cup)—that achieved this triumph. Literally, like the team's Adidas sponsor's motto, "All in or nothing," Löw assembled twenty-five players who were "all in."

However, if there was one player who detracted from this German victory, it was Müller. He is an entirely unlikable footballer and it is difficult to imagine a more picture-perfect definition of a cheap player. He is always up in the referee's face, always prone to simulation, always trying to get others in trouble; he frequently commits chippy fouls and then feigns innocence. If there is one player undeserving an honor denied to Messi, it is Müller. The way he plays leaves a bad taste in the football fan's mouth.

Messi, on the other hand, never complains, not even when he is hacked by opponents. He is not given to theatrics; he conducts himself with poise, with a dignity that seems to derive from the "deepest dimension" within him. An ontological dignity, if you will. After a bad decision by the referee in the final, when a free kick was incorrectly awarded to Germany after the goalkeeper Manuel Neuer hurtled in to Higuaín (leaving the striker crumpled on the ground), Messi quietly, in his capacity as captain, had a word with the assistant referee. No histrionics, no ugly gestures or animated gesticulating, no loud moaning.

It was a unique intervention that quiet word by Messi, if we can call it that, among both the stars and the average players (a misnomer, I grant you, but...) at the 2014 World Cup. In more ways than one, no one plays the game like Leo Messi. No one matches him in either ability or conduct; there is nothing between him and the game; this is "being-with," as such, the very manifestation of "being-with" in football. Through Messi, we have come to know—we know in every game he plays—the *DaSein* of football.

There may, however, be something more "primordial" at work in Messi being condemned. And it might have to do with, as Lacan would insist, about recognizing because of (and therefore it must reside in) Messi, for the Argentine nation-state, something on the order of the need for a primordial political violence. That is, were Messi to be proposed as the "Second Coming of Moses" his "arrival" as such would make imperative the political need to slay the Father, Maradona. And this putting the Father to death must be done not only for Messi's sake but for that of the nation-state itself.

If Maradona is beloved for his willingness to put the nation first, then in order for Messi to be anointed as the "true heir," Maradona must be put to death, as it were, because if Messi wins then Argentina can be redeemed through the figure who "belongs without belonging." If Messi wins, then Maradona and all his missteps, to phrase the matter euphemistically, can be obliterated—killed, put to death, and, yes, condemned to the past. Only Messi, in (and, again because of who he is) this political tableau, can restore Argentina to the ethical. (It is, of course, a work that we might say Messi is already, has long since already, been undertaking by himself, from his singular position.) And not only Maradona and the entire matter of *"Mano de Dios"* and the drugs and the international embarrassments he has caused, but also the "bad spirits" of the *guerra sucia* and the tainted history of that 1978 Copa Mundial victory on home soil.

It may be that Messi alone can consign the brutal violence of the Videla regime and that tainted 1978 triumph by Passarella and his team to history. In this way, Messi lends himself (with some ease) to the mosaic, if something well short of the messianic, for which we must be grateful. It is out of Messi alone, out of and precisely because of his being condemned, that the Argentine nation-state can be deformed and reconstituted. Messi alone can redeem Argentine football, the Argentine nation-state, for the ethical, for "analytical thought"—or, we might simply name it "philosophy." It seems, under these circumstances, safe to assume separation as the first demand of a Nancian philosophy.

*Jorge Luis Borges, as we well know, refused to watch the 1978 Copa Mundial final because of his opposition to the generalissimos and their Guerra Sucia. I would wager that Borges would want to watch Messi. Only Messi could match Borges's economy of words—no story longer than fifteen pages, so the common wisdom goes—with his own economy of words. And, they are equals in the matter of their magnificent Geists. But, alas, I fear, it is high time that I "aufgeben"— that I give up that ghost (called political hope).*

Lacan makes a memorable promise in this regard. Once the "murder of the father" has been successfully undertaken, the "return of love" is "accomplished."[89] (Or, at the very least, Borges can once more watch the Argentine national team in good conscience, shall we say.) Lacan's promise of 'love" here is of the order of his ethics. It is entirely free of the justified suspicion that Yeats's poem advocates. A Messi victory, as such, promises nothing less than "love." A love that "comes from the other to unseal the consistency of self" and so makes the self itself open to the other in the act of having been opened up by, and in response to the other.[90] Love is the negation of the self that is made possible by the "nearness" to the other. Love, as such, is the most intense mode of "being-with-the-other," of being-through-the-other. *DaSein*, then, as the being-there, the very dwelling, of love; love lives in and through *DaSein*.

**THE CAMERA FOLLOWS, AGAIN** · Misfortune insists, tearing the ground apart. —JEAN-LUC NANCY, *Hegel*

After cutting to the jubilant Germans, the camera returned to Messi. This time he was on his haunches, facing away from us; the deep disappointment that he was experiencing, however, could not be denied. His body was coiled in the bitter pose of defeat. He knew what losing meant; he felt it more keenly, and privately (in full public view), than any one of his teammates.

In a touching gesture, the Germans, first Götze, followed by a substitute still clad in his tracksuit (I do not remember who it was), came across to console him. Messi, with a silent gracefulness, accepted their condolences, but he never once looked his opponents in the face. He could not be consoled. It was, that inconsolability, the Nancian political moment par excellence. Our "world," says Nancy, "needs truth, not consolation."[91] There could be no truer word that could, in that moment, have applied to Messi in his truth.

Nor could the man he replaced as captain, Mascherano, the hard man who gave up his days as a marauding central midfielder for Liverpool to slot in, with relative ease and confidence, as a central defender for Barça.

How Masch gave everything this tournament. Indeed, if there is "player of the tournament," I'd give my vote to Masch. He tackled with venom; he ran until every fiber of his being was exhausted. He intercepted German pass after German pass; he cleared with sure headers, on the half volley and occasionally with pure hacks. Along with Romero, it is Masch who saved Argentina in the semifinal against the Dutch. Late, very late, into extra time, Robben made a swerving, twisting run into the Argentine penalty area. Masch, who seemed entirely out of the play, scampered back in that determined, characteristic tiny-footstep, jackrabbit style of his. As Robben passed what he assumed was the last Argentine defender, Masch appeared on his right shoulder and, just as Robben seemed destined to score, there was—not so much Masch as—Masch's right boot, deflecting the ball to the right of Romero's goal. Game saved.

Like Messi, Masch was beyond reach after the loss in the final.

> *Alas, in a moment such as this, the overman's bridge leads to that place we might name not solitude (which Zarathustra enjoys and advises as a necessary withdrawal to his disciples) but "aloneness." That place where only those who know "belonging without belonging" know, where they alone must take refuge.*

For the first time I realized how much losing meant to Leo Messi.

For the first time I felt immense anger at those who question him. It is not that they question his loyalty to Argentina; it is a more precise anger: those who doubt him do not understand that he plays the game, in every single aspect, with utter integrity. He gives everything, all the time. Love, openness to the other (to render Nancy in a Levinasian register); love, "being-with-the-other" from the first whistle to the last; that is love, that is the love of Messi. It does not matter if he is wearing the *blaugrana* of Barça or the blue and white strips of Argentina, Leo Messi is a player of absolute integrity, possessed of a Nancian truth. This truth is what separates him from every player of his standing. The extravagant public displays of bad behavior, that is the reserve of Luis Suárez; the petulance and grandstanding, that is for the likes of Robben and Müller.

It is not only the sheer magnitude of his talent, the keenness of his vision, the brilliance of his ball striking, or the mesmeric quality of his dribbling that sets him apart from others. It is how true to the game, in the very best sense, Leo Messi always is; he seeks truth in the game, and most certainly through how he plays the game.

He has no World Cup winner's medal to show for his considerable effort during the 2014 World Cup. Müller has.

But Messi stands alone as not only the greatest player in the world but the truest exponent of the game.

Perhaps, on these terms alone, it is proper that he is denied canonization in Argentina. That would put him alongside Diego Maradona and, World Cup winner though he be, Diego Maradona is no Lionel Messi.

Alfredo Di Stéfano, whom Maradona recognizes, with good reason, as the greatest footballer the game has ever known, died—in Madrid—six days before the 2014 final. An Argentine who is not held much in reverence in his native land (he represented, we recall, first Argentina, then Colombia, and finally his adopted Spain on the football field), it strikes me that the best Argentine players are those whom the nation does not hold to its bosom.

Under these circumstances, the very best thing that Lionel Messi can endure, in the name of Argentina, is to be condemned by it.

In trying to explain why the Marquis de Sade is an exceptional writer ("different in character from those who offer us these entertaining little stories"), Lacan argues that it is because "we see emerge in him in the distance the idea of eternal punishment."[52] This movement toward "eternal punishment" is overlaid by what might be named a desire for secrecy or withdrawal from the public eye. What Lacan finds in Sade is an extreme response, one that verges on self-obliteration—death, suicide, the extinction of self. Lacan apprehends Sade as that "writer who wants nothing of himself to survive, who doesn't even want any part of the site of his tomb to remain accessible to men, but wants it instead to be covered with bracken. Doesn't that indicate that he locates in the fantasm the content of the most intimate part of himself?"[93] *Messi, Sade, Nietzsche: "eternal return of the same."*

It is indeed ironic that Messi, that most intensely private of public individuals (after all, everyone can "see" what he is doing, can "see" him whenever they want in whatever media they so choose), has revealed fully his "fantasm." He has achieved the remarkable feat of revealing, fully, the source and the content of his "fantasm," what it means to be condemned, without once so much as offering a single word on the subject. The force and effect of Messi's condemnation is, again ironically, that it compels us to offer a language for it, demands that we "account" for it, and provokes us to think about what is, his face, his body, the "psychosocial" depth that is contained in the act of hanging his head or not making eye contact with magnanimous opponents in the wake of defeat. It is what is not hidden, ironically, that makes the most severe political requests of us. Or perhaps it is fitting that we should think about what it is we imagine ourselves to know but, in truth, know nothing of.

And the first articulation of that request might very well be that in order to, as it were, speak Messi, we must begin by learning the discourse of condemnation. (Or, condemnation as the failure of love, condemnation as the failure of negation.) Failing that, everything else, all other languages, all other reflections, might amount to little more than, as Scrooge would certainly phrase it, "Humbug." Or, as Lacan might say, it would signal the triumph of the Father over love. No wonder then that Lacan demands of the other an "indestructible character." It is only out of such a "character" that the nation-state can be disarticulated into its Messianic promise.

As such, there must be something to this adjectival rendering of Messi, something that we hear when we speak or write his name, "Messi," something that is obvious to us when we watch him play. It is something, this condition of making us think what it means to be condemned, that fits him for the task. Let us be playful, and yet not. Let us muse on, let us contemplate such a formulation: only (a) Messi(ah) can undertake the "deepest dimension" of "analytical thought."

If Lacan is the "last Cartesian" psychoanalyst, then it is very possible, given the ways in which Messi presents the nation-state with such an array of difficulties, the ways in which he animates and "stylizes" its "splits," that he is, as the player who articulates the greatest tension between club and country, between extant nation and aspirational one, the first schizophrenic Cartesian footballer. I play for Barça therefore I am; I play for Barça therefore I am not Argentine. In so doing, I ensure that only "I" can stand *entre le moi et le moi-même*, and as such I submit to "ordeal, misery, or *Rastlosigkeit* and the task of thought."[94]

Messi has, in truth, lived the "ordeal" of the finitude of the nation-state; he has endured "misery" in its name. Or, more precisely, because he had been made miserable he will not submit to the "ordeal" of the nation-state. This "ordeal," this "misery," it has, however, allowed Messi to embrace the very restlessness that is the "task of thought." In *Rastlosigkeit* or through the "thought" that he makes necessary, Messi enables us to make new sense of the world, in no small part because he evinces for us the absolute value of "negativity."

# INTERLUDE

## "*Nog Lansur!*"

> The accumulation of details... —— JACQUES LACAN,
> "The *Jouissance* of Transgression"

> Serenely let us move to distant places / And let no sentiments
> of home detain us. / The Cosmic Spirit seeks not to restrain us /
> But lifts us stage by stage to wider spaces. / If we accept a home
> of our own making, / Familiar habit makes for indolence. / We
> must prepare for parting and leave-taking / Or else remain the
> slave of permanence. —— HERMAN HESSE, "Stages"

I left Cape Town, South Africa, on August 4, 1989, for graduate school in New York. I boarded the plane at what was then still D. F. Malan airport. It has since been renamed Cape Town International, a designation that is geopolitically specific but altogether soulless—devoid of either poetry or history, which at least "D. F. Malan" had going for it, even if it was ideologically anachronistic and, yes, politically objectionable. On August 4, 1989, Nelson Mandela was still imprisoned; the major black political organizations, the African National Congress (ANC) and the Pan-African Congress (PAC), were still banned. For my part, I was leaving the land of apartheid. I was leaving for good, it turned out, even though I could never have envisaged then the finality of that long ago embarkation.

In truth, however, I had long since left. I suspect that I left at the very moment that I first learned to read. Reading, more than writing, was what allowed me to "get out." Except, of course, that I would never leave. Not fully, anyway. Nor did I want to, much as I wanted to. "Some of us make it out," is how Coates phrases it.¹ "Some of us" know, long before we know, that such an option is never available to us. That's never how it works. The choice is never "get out" or "stay in." Even when you're out, you're in. And even when you're in, you're never really all in. *Entre-nous*: to live in relation, to live always negotiating, always thinking, always asking yourself if you're in or out, always aware that to be in relation is . . . always to be both in and out, to be neither, to always be bound by conflicting relations, by relations that conflict, relations that cause a merciless to and fro in you. Between you and the world, stands, first, this world, then that one, both of them unstinting in their demands, both of them asking nothing less than absolute fidelity, both—or all three or . . .—of these worlds knowing, in advance, that such fealty, that such a pledge is beyond your capabilities. Is beyond your ken. You have no idea as to how to commit to this series of endless relations. This, I suspect, is what Coates is arcing toward when he reflects on the process of "learning to live in the disquiet . . . in the mess of my mind."² A "mess," yes, but what a glorious, intellectually fecund, politically provocative "mess." Besides, no one ever said that "living in disquiet" is a bad way to be in the world, especially for a thinking, sentient being.

The (Southern Hemisphere) winter of 1989 marked the closing of a decade in which apartheid had been subjected to severe pressure, economically (the divestment campaign), politically (sanctions at international bodies such as the UN), and culturally (countries placed a ban on performers visiting South Africa), both internally and internationally. Since the early 1980s, first president P. W. Botha's and then F. W. de Klerk's National Party (NP) government had been engaged in a daily struggle against the ANC-led campaign to "make South Africa ungovernable." Protests, marches, strikes, and antistate violence were all part of the antiapartheid insurgency that could be, in truth, traced back to the Soweto school protests of June 1976.

I started at Livingstone High School in January 1976, so I was literally present at the birth of a political moment—it could as easily be called a movement—that would play a defining role in the next epoch in South African history. Nevertheless, as someone who lived through that moment, I still find it difficult to determine now, more than forty years later, if I belonged to a generation that participated in a high- or a low-level insurgency. All I can say with certainty is that Soweto 1976 constituted an event, in the way that events rupture the present and change the course of history.

Leaving Cape Town in 1989, I was under no illusions that South Africa was a country on the brink. On the brink of something momentous, it turns out, but I had no way of knowing that in August 1989. Few people outside the highest levels of government did, I would venture. Still, I was glad to have the chance to pursue graduate life in a faraway land. There were certainly "sentiments of home" that occupied me that August day, but none of them strong enough to "detain" me. After all, graduate school promised some respite from the increasing violence that marked black life in the townships such as those in which I had grown up. South Africa felt like a country in an unwinnable state of war with itself. Neither the white minority, with its superior armaments, nor the black majority, by sheer dint of numbers, could triumph. A good moment to "get out."

Publicly, at least, de Klerk's government seemed intent on maintaining white privilege, and they had the machinery of repression to do so; but late-1980s South Africa was not a *machine à habiter*, a place in which one could live. So great was the disparity between the state's arsenal and the disenfranchised's lack of weaponry (stones, bottles, a Molotov cocktail or three) that no one could have predicted that within six short months it would all be over. Certainly not me. I had every intention of returning. It would have been impossible. I returned, I continue to return, every year. My stays, on the whole, are shorter, sometimes just a few days. Until about fifteen years ago, I'd stay for a month or two, sometimes as many as three. Now I rarely stay more than a week. Still and all, except for 2016, every year I land at what remains in my political imaginary "D. F. Malan" airport and cast my glance once more at the majesty that is Table Mountain. As I did every day until August 5, 1989.

On Friday, February 9, 1990, de Klerk announced at the opening of parliament that the government would be releasing Nelson Mandela, and all the other political prisoners, and that the ANC and the PAC would be unbanned. He also made it clear that negotiations for the transition from white-minority rule to universal democracy would begin forthwith. On Sunday, February 11, to great international fanfare, Mandela walked out of prison. Shortly thereafter, he addressed an adoring throng on Cape Town's Grand Parade. In that moment, no matter that the details of black majority rule had yet to be worked out, apartheid was, for all intents and purposes, condemned to history.

The older of my two sisters had called me early on that Friday morning from her home in Cape Town to inform me of the momentous event. On that Sunday, my daughter, Andrea, just three days before her first birthday, and I watched on TV as Mandela, full of joy, addressed those many thousands gathered on the Grand Parade, a place I knew well. Even from the wintry cold that gripped the world outside our Morningside, New York, apartment, it was impossible not to feel the sense of elation emanating from Cape Town—a city that did not, in that moment, feel very far away. Even if I was in the first "stage" of opening myself to Herman Hesse's "Cosmic Spirit," on that Sunday in February 1990, I would suspect that my "Spirit" strained toward Cape Town's Grand Parade. On that Sunday, the last thing I wanted was to "get out."

In August 1989, I had left South Africa a disenfranchised black man. I would return, in August 1990 a citizen. What a difference a year makes.

MOVEMENT · Thought is the accumulation of things and the ordeal of this separation. But thought is thus itself the separation of things from thought—judgments, conceptions, significations . . . as relation itself and, better, as the restlessness of relation, as its restless love. —— JEAN-LUC NANCY, *Hegel: The Restlessness of the Negative*

I would return, as I said, to Cape Town every year for my "summer vacation" from graduate school, first Columbia University, where I did my master's, and then Princeton University, where I completed my PhD.

It was, as I mentioned, winter in the Southern Hemisphere, so I had the unfortunate experience of going, in both directions, from spring to autumn. And every year, until 1992, I returned to the working-class Cape Flats township of Hanover Park, where I grew up and where my mother still lived, to play football for Lansur United Amateur Football Club (AFC). This meant that every year, whether I was in New York or New Jersey, I packed my boots ("cleats," in the American vernacular) and my training kit (sweats, football jerseys, socks, rain gear; Cape Town winters are renowned for being damp, wet, and windy), ready to join my teammates at Lansur about midseason.

I kept fit while in the United States by playing for the Princeton graduate student team in the local Mercer County league. Our team was composed of, naturally, graduate students, with varying degrees of technical proficiency, again, naturally. Three players stand out in my memory of that team, two of whom were named Dave. The Daves were our skill players. One Dave, a talented midfielder, was a Brown University undergraduate and of Cuban extraction, enrolled in a PhD in philosophy, and the other was a quick, tricky winger, getting his PhD in computer science. The other player who made an impression was a towering striker, a Dutchman whom I dubbed "Groot Man" ("Big Man") and whom I remember especially for the very fancy red Acura coupe that he drove. (Only a graduate student in the sciences could afford such a snazzy car.) The Dutchman and I communicated in a compromised language: he spoke Dutch, I responded in Afrikaans, a "lesser" version of his language. It was fun to watch our teammates' and the opponents' befuddlement at our exchanges. I used to take the free kicks for Princeton United, and before I delivered the ball, aimed at him, I'd shout "Groot Man!" I have no idea what he made of it, being so hailed, in a language vaguely his own (at least, derived from his, colonial/apartheid baggage and all), on the football field. It also reminded me of my Lansur teammates, all of whom spoke Afrikaans as a first language.

All, except me.

This "return" to Hanover Park, to my Lansur teammates, constituted an inevitable recursion into my primary football mode of "being-with," on the "wrong" side of the Atlantic, as it were. But I would have to say it provided a small measure of footballing and psychic comfort.

Speaking this "two-part" language on random New Jersey football fields reduced the "spacing" between my worlds; it drew one, so far away, closer into the other. Their differences remained, but there was the possibility, every Sunday, of drawing them into each other. In this way it is always possible to assert that, in Jean-Luc Nancy's terms, "Language says things, it does not say itself, or language itself . . . that is, the universal relay of differences whereby language speaks."[3] As such, "Groot Man" says something, it is a reaching out, a reaching into, the deep, unspoken, and "unknown" (to the Dutch self) history of relation (the Netherlands to South Africa, a relation that goes back to Jan van Riebeeck, who in 1652 founded a colonial outpost in what is today Cape Town; a relation that "culminated" in the founding of the apartheid state in 1948 by some of those who proudly traced their lineage back to the Netherlands) that is spoken as the "universal relay of differences." All of this is historically resonant, if not necessarily audible, in the single shouting out of one graduate school teammate to another. "Groot Man!" cannot simply be understood as a hailing. Language, as such, "does not say itself." It manifests all—in this case, two unrelated languages, Dutch and Afrikaans; the history of Dutch colonization; apartheid; a "secret" football language—that which is located in the history of universal relays, from, within, one language to another.

Playing for Princeton United provided a pleasant diversion on the weekends. But it was only a placeholder, an unequal bidirectional form of restless relation, so to speak. I was, as it were, always between seasons, always, it seemed, on my way to play elsewhere, to leave one place only to return to it. My football loyalties were with Lansur, my intellectual life was organized around the university, as it had been in Cape Town. Princeton was an extension of the separateness I had known as the only Lansur player on the 1985 team to pursue a college degree. I played for Lansur while studying at the (then-racially segregated) University of the Western Cape (UWC).[4] Before that, I was the only Lansur player who had attended high school outside of the township of Hanover Park. All my teammates went to high school locally, either Hanover Park High (later renamed "Crystal High School") or Mountview High (which opened later), the latter of which was situated on the very same street where my family lived. It was less than eight hundred meters from our front door.

Because there were no schools at all in Hanover Park when we moved in (there were, as yet, no paved roads, either), September 1970, my mother was able to enroll first me and then my three younger siblings at Portia Primary, a middle-class grade ("primary," in local terms) school. There was also an infallible logic on my mother's side. At the time that we moved in, having been deracinated from a racially mixed neighborhood in what was then called Black River and now goes by the altogether more respectable name of Rondebosch East, not only were there no schools, but the ones that were later built, all the primary schools as well as Crystal, were Afrikaans-medium (Afrikaans was the main language of instruction). My family spoke English, so my mother could legitimately look to the middle-class coloured townships just to the west of Hanover Park for her children's education. I now understand that the act (no matter that it was less a choice, as such, than a decision imposed by historical circumstance) was decisive. From that moment, my—and my family's—relationship to Hanover Park would always be marked by the politics of *entre-nous*: there would always be something between the township and my family, something, language, educational aspiration, early arrival in an as yet materially unstructured Hanover Park, that intervened between the township and me, my teammates and me as a footballer. It might very well have been that very same thing that bound me to my teammates.

I understand it now; I imagine that I knew it instinctively then. How could I not? It was there, in this language that I brought into the township with me;

it was this language that set me on a different path. I could not have known, however, that its passage would lead, inter alia, through the halls of academe, esteemed and venerable halls such as those at Columbia University ("Philosophy Hall") and Princeton University ("McCosh Hall"). And later, as a faculty member, in the literature program at Duke University (the old "Art Museum" now renamed the "Friedl Building"), and Cornell University, where I currently teach.

No matter, the die was cast. Once my siblings and I were in a middle-class grade school, we were on track to attend a middle-class high school outside of the township. My Lansur United teammates all walked to school. I took the bus or I hitched a ride to Livingstone High, where English was the lingua franca and my teachers read and recommended to students such as me Karl Marx, C. L. R. James, Raymond Williams, and, most beloved of all, Leon Trotsky.

The movement between: wake up in a working-class house, go to school in a middle-class neighborhood, return to our working-class home; play football for my middle-class school during the week, the act of being-with my middle-class teammates constituting one iteration of my "singular plural," while practicing (in the evenings, normally Tuesday and Thursday) and playing for my working-class club on the weekend, out of which a quite different iteration of *DaSein* (is dwelling possible under such conditions? Surely I aspired to it, aspire to it still) being-with, and "being singular plural," is made manifest. This is what it means to live the condition of "constantly renewing rupture"; this is what it means to be with the other (middle-class schoolmates/teammates), and then to be with the other (working-class teammates), so much so that the very concept of "other" is thrown into question, in a rather dizzying fashion, to say nothing of the turmoil to which the notions of "being-with" and "being-oneself" are subjected.[5] Who, in all this to-ing and fro-ing, is *really* the *other*? Does the concept even really hold as much as it retains its psychopolitical effects?

At stake here is not only how the self thinks "separation" but also how the self attends to the "judgments, conceptions and significations" that "surge up" so rapidly, one might even say "furiously," in rapid succession, one after the other after the other. What the self undergoes, time and again, is a series of "judgments" that, per force, verge—it could not be otherwise—on self-indictment. What does my "being-with" "here," as opposed to "there" (the first meaning of Heidegger's *DaSein*), signify? Why am I "here" rather than 'there"? What are the effects of my attending "this" and not "that" school? How does the self conceive of itself in the hic et nunc? After all, this is not simply the "restlessness of relation" but its intensification into both *Ruhelosigkeit* as a more neutral phrasing, and *Rastlosigkeit* as might be understood more positively, as the kind of restlessness that can lead to "negativity" and not simply the "negation" of one language by another. Nor, for that matter, should it be understood as a simple matter of substitution; that is, the "negation" of "this" team in favor of "that" one. What lies *entre-nous* Lansur United–Princeton United cannot, under any circumstances, be reduced to the names because, as Nancy makes clear, in "every given unity . . . [there is] something derived, deposited—a moment, unstable like every instant, in the movement that gives relation, in which relation gives itself."[6] What relation is it that the "Lansur-Princeton" "relation gives itself?" The relation whose "conception and signification" exceed, out of pure restlessness and necessity, the name?

Important, then, that *Rastlosigkeit* is understood as that mode of being that recognizes the subtlety and difficulty that constitutes *entre-nous* as that condition which cannot be reduced to a difference in the level of education, "access" to the world (a great deal more than just geographical distance lies between Hanover Park and, say, Morningside Heights, New York), without taking into account the effect of these differences. That is, in the midst of all forms of restlessness, regardless of what can be achieved by thinking them, *Rastlosigkeit/Ruhelosigkeit* loses all philosophical efficacy if it does not, cannot, or will not acknowledge the desire for the other, for its—necessarily dialectical—other: to be, if only for a moment, at rest.[7] Don't we all need to be, if only for the briefest moment, just now and then, at rest, separate from—separate/d from, relieved of the intense demands of—restlessness, as it were, in order to think?[8] To simply be? To think separation, *Rastlosigkeit*, and what this thinking entails, as much as anything else. In order to think restlessness it is necessary to break into, to bring to a momentary standstill, to cease the "ceaseless movement that leaves nothing at rest."[9]

Advocating for such a moment of rest, a rest from *Rastlosigkeit*, as it were, without undermining the value of thinking in and because of *Rastlosigkeit*, would make it possible to think relation through separation as something other than a ceaseless chain of relation. Thinking about relation in this way is exhausting. Thinking about relation in this way is exhilarating. It gives life, strangely, exquisitely, all the while exacting an unpayable cost.

Of course, all relation is through separation, but not every relation that emerges out of separation marks a return to the relation that was. Instead, it is important to stipulate the difference between the relation through separation that emerges out of the separation into relation. Schematically, in order to distinguish every one relation through separation from every other one, it is necessary to identify relation ↔ separation as different from separation ↔ relation. So rendered, it becomes possible to understand how the relation that emerges out of separation into a new relation is, from the very beginning, connected to but still distinct from that relation ↔ separation out of which it emerged. Every relation marks a new possibility for separation, every separation "founds" a new relation that is itself constitutively open to separation. Relation ↔ separation, separation ↔ relation, and so on, infinitely. That is to say, every Lansur ↔ Princeton separation produced a new Princeton ↔ Lansur relation. No relation is ever the same as the relation that preceded it or the one that will follow it; similarly, while there may be similarities that mark the different separations, they are never equivalent, they are constitutively other-than each other.

ENTRE LE MOI ET LE MOI-MÊME · With my Princeton United teammates I shared an educational affinity, but they were no match, in terms of pure football skill and in terms of the depth of my affiliation, for the guys at Lansur. Princeton United was a team of transients, a bunch of footballers, from various parts of the United States and around the world, just passing through. We were all young men in the business of preparing for careers. For their part, my Lansur teammates were holding down, sometimes struggling to hold down, a variety of jobs, few of which rose above the level of menial labor. Playing for Princeton United, our commitments were in the moment, of the moment, and for the moment only. No wonder I remember less than a handful of names.

In turn, I was separated from my Lansur teammates by the life I was living "*in die States*" (in the United States), as they reminded me from time to time—sometimes more subtly than others. (I was, as we've already seen, and will encounter again later, separated by more than just that.) I had, as it were, "gotten out," gotten very far out, farther than any of us had ever dreamed possible (I no less than any of them) when we were playing those endless football games as schoolboys on the asphalt tennis court of Summit Primary, just opposite the Duncans' home and mine.

My living separate/d from them was a reality made more manifest with every trans-Atlantic flight I took, and it assumed a different manifestation, relation ↔ separation, separation ↔ relation, with every departure and every return. They knew, as did I, that *entre-nous* was of no small consequence, but it was, nevertheless, not enough to undo the ties that bound us together; our "being-with" was the consequence of a shared passage located in a much longer history. That is, the relation that emerges out of separation alters the relation, but it cannot obliterate or disfigure it beyond the point of recognition. Relation is, in some way or other, always recognizable as relation; it is not the same, but it possesses, in this instance, what we might name a resilient constitutive core.

However, as I said, I was separated from them, as I had long known I was, even before I left, but now the professional, professorial future I was crafting in New Jersey made that separation inarguable. What had been only incipiently *entre-vous*, different schools, distinct relationships to the township, the different languages we inhabited, now made itself palpably, viscerally present. As we know, what was *entre-nous* could neither be attributed to Princeton nor named incipient. It was simply a matter of the difficulty of relation making itself, in Nancy's terms, "accessible": "'coming to presence, but presence itself is dis-position, the spacing of singularities.'"[10]

I am now able to recognize that the extended process of "coming to presence" had in fact long been constitutive of my relation to, as this "Interlude" has already in part explicated, my Lansur United teammates. The "spacing of singularities" between my teammates and I, that which was *entre-nous*, as well as that which was *entre le moi et le moi-même*, had emerged long before I ever set foot on American soil. Such an acknowledgement, even these several decades later, constitutes nothing less than an "ordeal," because the "spacing of singularities" necessarily demands an accounting. There are, as it were, questions to answer, new questions that emerge out of the original questions, constituencies to be addressed.

Above all else there is, not to put too fine a point on it, a sense of loss that always reaches, as Judith Butler teaches us, into the deepest "recesses of our loss." It is always something, this "being-*oneself*," the decision that we make to be "self," that finds us unprepared for the effects of the decision, for how it acts on us; it is always difficult, and, yes, painful, to confront those effects, to live with them, to know them as life-constituting, as life-deforming. Because of what is *entre-nous*, because of what we have inserted between the self and the other, we have passed from one mode of being-with to an entirely different one: "being-self" in ways that one was not before. Relation ↔ separation, separation ↔ relation.

To be "spaced" from the other when the logic of the team dictates the primacy of "being-with" stipulates to a mode of being in the world whose "passage" is a complicated, psychically distorting one. This "passage" runs through the football joys of "being-with" as much as it marks, indelibly, incontrovertibly, that "spacing," within the team itself (my teammates, as will be recounted later, were by no means like "each other"—a few of them, me included, did not like every other player on the team); that "spacing" can also be named "being-oneself," in Nancy's sense of the everyday "being oneself"—that which posits the "everyday" as in itself, a priori, already distinct, discrete, and separate.

This is very much a recognition of the infrahuman (internal differences; differences within the self) in the sense that it marked each member of the team. That marks us still, I should say, perhaps more evidently now. This is why, as Nancy insists, how we understand the everyday matters because it is in the everyday that the constitutive difference-within manifests itself. For Nancy it is at the level of the everyday that we encounter, and must explicate, the infrahuman. As he writes, the *"everyday* is already by itself: each day, each time, day to day . . . each time singular."[11] While recognizing our various (multiple) infrahumanities, for the team to be successful, as a team, what was both *entre le moi et le moi-même* and *entre-nous* has to be disciplined in order for us to achieve our optimal *Mitsein*. Although ours was a small squad, twelve in all, or, perhaps because there were only twelve of us, we learned (as all squads do) that it is not easy to "be-with" as a team of players over the course of a season. To "be-with" through preseason runs that hurt the body back into football shape, through technical practice sessions that begin in February sunshine so that teams can be ready to face the season's April kickoff, and, more importantly, be fit enough to play through the rain and the cold that can make up the Cape Town winter, June through September. To "be-with" through the long slog that is a test of a team's stamina and its capacity to "be-with" each other, four or five times a week, every week, for somewhere between twenty-five and thirty weeks. By the time October rolls round, the sun is out, temperatures are on the rise, and the season's about to wrap up. If you're lucky, come October, you're relieved to be rid of each other, if only for a little while. However, what you do in February—the amount of road work you put it, the intensity of the training sessions, the strategies that are devised, all of this and more—is what enables the team to compete in the tough winter months and be involved in meaningful games in late September and early October. The 1985 edition of the Lansur United team, as I will recount momentarily, was able to do exactly this.

And that is why, if we take Judith Butler's point that the recesses of loss serve only as passageway to a still deeper loss, it is possible to present the other face of loss. Beyond the commitments that make "being-with" possible, there is a yet more profound and lasting set of ties that bind. In the very depth of "being-with," as I discovered in December 2015, one finds bonds that are the true source of "being-with." The ties that are sustained over the course of a season (that sustained us in 1985), are ties that, I found, sustain us, one and all, still. They have sustained us over the course of thirty years, to say nothing of the years that preceded the coming together of that 1985 team. Those ties, alloyed by the passing of the years, buffed to a shine by memory, so vivid and animated in the sheer pleasure of unadulterated recollection, have a proper name. It is a name that the twelve players who constituted the 1985 Lansur United team would have eschewed as, well, "unmanly." Its name is, as we well know from our casting of the event of *Mitsein*, love, and love, as such, is testament to the "singular plural of the origin of 'community' itself."[12] The "singular plural origin" of the team—the "plural origins," we all came to Hanover Park, to this one nexus within a single township, from a plethora of origins, not all of them compatible, consonant, or commensurate, but out of that "plurality' was produced a "singularity," Lansur United AFC, that itself marked a "singular plural origin." A "singular plural" shared, in the name of love.

Ironically, much as we were too full of braggadocio (we ran on testosterone) to admit the depth of relation to each other, each to the other, we had a ritual that entirely undermined the brazen masculinity of our discourse. Before every game, we would huddle in the dressing room ("change room," in American parlance) and sing, beginning with our goalkeeper, Errol Aalee Cupido, and ending with our one (and only) substitute, "Nontjies": "We love you, Aalee, we do, O 'Aalee,' we love you. . . . We love you, Nontjies, we do, 'O Nontjies,' we love you." We were then, as I am able to say now, a team bound in love, by love. Lansur 1985 constitutes the "being-with" of love, love through the act—the many football languages—of "being-with." Rendered as such, it is impossible to gainsay the event of (Lansur United's) *Mitsein* as love. However awkward, maudlin, or trite it may have sounded to those outside our circle, there was an unarguable veracity in our song. Some of us, me included, may have felt slightly embarrassed about it. No matter, we gave voice, I now know, to our *Mitsein*.

Love, that is the name, the name the "given unity" must be given so that it can know itself, so that the 1985 team can speak its name. It is the name that we can now extend from the ritual into life, into the "unity" of our lives together. That love, "deposited" in the "unstable instant" that was Tuesday practice, a Sunday game, or the various intra- and infrahuman struggles and tensions that marked our season. Those tensions and difficulties that, in truth, helped to make our signature season, has moved toward the relation such that the relation can now be fully known in its "singular plurality," known as the "singular plural origin" of a "community"—or, "team," more precisely phrased. One can say here, as one might of Leo Messi, that "singularities is the discreet passage of *other origins of the world*."[13] This is not to suggest an equivalence between the movement that marks the "spacing" that is Rosário and Catalunya, on the one hand, and township football in apartheid South Africa. It is, rather, to recognize that, although operating on a much-reduced scale, everyone came to Hanover Park (a political structure imagined by the apartheid state as the enforcement of separation) produced, out of "being-with-one-another," a singularity of the order that was open, not always entirely, rarely in the same way, inconsistently, to "other origins of the world." Again, regardless of whether we think this "singular plural" in terms of Jacques Derrida's notion of "infinite hospitality" (radical openness to the other), Emmanuel Levinas's commitment to "welcoming the stranger," or Nancy's insistence on the constitutive presence of the plural in the singular, what is unarguable is that in some way or other, every address to the other, as other, is bound—firmly or loosely, happily or under protest—to love. Is love.

It can be said that what it takes to make a team is that love, that force, that marks the "opening [of] the present, opening space and time, opening the world and 'I,' and throwing existence into restless exigency."[14] Through love the "present," our 2015 reunion, which occasioned (provoked) the writing of this "Interlude," "opens" up the past. More importantly, however, the "present opens" the present as the articulation of that—love, the deep recesses of "being-with"—that was already present then. As such, the "present opens" our "world," the one we made, the one we shared (through and because of football), to us in such ways as to make of it an entirely new world, at once recognizable and entirely unfamiliar. Such is the "rupturous" force of the present that it makes all time cohere in it, come together as one because of it: *Sein und Zeit*. In one way or another, we have all left the world of 1985 that we made. I went furthest away, and yet not. And we were all, whether we knew it in the present or not, prepared to return to it as an utterly disruptive—but "undisturbed"—present. Nothing is the same; materially, all of our lives have been transformed, some more radically—for good and, as we shall see, ill—than others. And yet, in our coming together again, in what we presented as footballing terms but was so much more, everything is as it always was. In some ways, with the benefit of time, some things—victories, goals scored, tackles made—are even better.

BACK FOR (PART OF) THE SEASON · Everything is at the same time separated in relation, everything is only separated and in relation. —— JEAN-LUC NANCY, *Hegel*

The South African football season would have begun in April, like clockwork, on the first Saturday after Easter. I would play for Lansur from late May or early June until early September. My teammates took care of the business of registering me because they knew that, without fail, one wintry Tuesday or Thursday evening, I'd pitch up at training. Tuesdays and Thursdays were the nights when Lansur practiced, and one of these evenings there I'd be, welcomed, greeted, in Afrikaans, with a "'Hoe's it my, broer?,' 'Jy, jy's 'trug'"—"How are you, my brother?" "Hey, you're back." I was more than ready to reconnect and compete for my place on the team. I looked forward to getting back into the routine of training and playing because I'd grown up with the guys on Lansur, and I was eager to practice, keen to play with them again on the weekend and in the occasional Monday night game. If we had a Monday game, it was a big deal for us, because it was one of the rare occasions when we got to play a night game, under the lights and all.

However, the transition from graduate student to township footballer was, if not difficult or onerous, hardly seamless. These were two different worlds, two distinct modes of "being-with." One of these worlds, the one in which I was becoming ever more immersed, the one that would preoccupy my future, turned, broadly speaking, on reading and writing, and the other on playing. These were two distinct worlds, neither of which I could ever fully or with any comfort, inhabit. I was, in different ways, in different measures, out of place in both yet also made out of both these worlds; the world of books, shall we call it (high school pupil, undergraduate, graduate student, professor), and the world of amateur footballer (combative central midfielder, sometime defender, of two decades' standing). These were worlds in which I was entirely immersed and, to phrase the matter poorly, worlds that demanded that I translate myself into and out of, again and again. I have never been able to fully reconcile these worlds, nor do I ever wish to make them commensurate. In this regard Nancy's thinking on separation—"Everything is at the same time separated in relation, everything is only separated and in relation"—is apropos. "In relation," I was "separated" from my Lansur teammates, much as it was only in my "separation"—in what was *entre-nous*—that I was "in relation" to them.

It is what "separated" us that needed to be thought and, as such, it was through thinking (our) "separation" that our being in relation was not only established but explicated and brought to light, if not fully, then certainly as fully as possible. "Everything" in my relation, then, was entirely derived from and provoked by the "separation" that bound us. (My relationship to my Princeton United teammates never rose to such a level of thought. With them, the nexus between separation and relation was much more on the surface, much more easily explained; still, it left, as I articulate it, resonances, even if only ones that draw their thinking from comparison to a team they did not know and, in all probability, lay beyond their imaginary.)

That is why, I know now, I have always found pleasure, as well as a series of political explanations, in thinking relation and separation simultaneously and not, as Nancy advises us not to, followed the impulse to keep them apart. It is for this reason that I neither could undertake an attempt at "reconciliation" between these distinct (but related) worlds nor have I any desire to do so. That would constitute an infelicitous act. The truth might be, when all the Sturm und Drang has dissipated, remarkably simple, if revealing. I had begun the work of movement, at once, within (the infrahuman, this is what it makes possible) and between the world of books (the University of the Western Cape, Columbia, Princeton) and the world of the playing field (Lansur) long before I ever grasped what translation as such entailed.

TRANSLATION · When I played for Princeton United, of course, no translation was necessary; we understood the order of things; football was a weekend activity. For my Lansur teammates and I, football represented something very different. Football constituted the ontological of our lives. As young men in a working-class apartheid township, football was—at that stage in our lives—our raison d'être.

The impossible work of return, the son of the township who never ever belonged (only) to the township but who never sought to write it out of his life, was made more stark by disparities that marked the (material, political, psychosocial) realities of moving annually between Hanover Park and Princeton. Those disparities that distinguished the township from an extremely privileged bastion of higher education. More than anything, the impossible, necessarily "messy" work of thinking return is not a negotiable. It is what the diasporic subject, the exile, the displaced person, the refugee, must do; voluntarily or not. There is no other way to be. And so thinking relation–return–the impossibility of return is the conceptual, affective and political difficulty that this "Interlude," with no small amount of trepidation and with little expectation of success, undertakes.

The greatest difficulty, and this is revealed in the different registers employed in this writing, might very well reside in producing—it is not a matter of "finding"—a genre that can accommodate the disparate and yet overlapping demands of sport's history, political philosophy, and sport's writing, all of which have a significant role to play in this "Interlude." A difficulty made all the more complicated by the inaugural presence of the poorly constituted, insufficiently iterated "I." Such is the difficulty of writing that begins with the "I's" constitutive "distance from," to euphemize Marx's alienation, the Lansur United football team that is at the core of this "Interlude." The reality of that "distance from" fights against the writing, fights from within the writing, fights as the writing, to make itself audible, struggles to make the particularities of its voice heard; no wonder at the intensity of the struggle, because the political and psychological costs of such an acknowledgement are, unsurprisingly, considerable. What is more, the "distance from" anteriorizes, amplifies, and adds layers of philosophical complexity to the struggle that goes by the name of "return"; which is, of course, always linked to thinking relation. And, as such, the impossibility of return; or, more truthfully, the recognition that the impossibility of return was long since written into the a priori condition of/ as "distance from." That impossibility that is only partially captured in the concept of *entre-nous* and yet which requires the possibilities and especially the nuances and subtleties of *entre-nous* in order to approach the work of writing that which is between, that which is related through—and in—separation.

These are political conditions distinguished by the force of *entre-nous*, by the psychosocial forces that coagulate within what is between, and the various forces of repression operative because of the force of the infrahuman. That is why it is so difficult to give everything, all those forces, that is and constitutes *entre-nous*, what they above all want, voice. That is to say, they demand their (own) writing; that they be written, even if only under the threat of erasure—that is, for everything they say, they leave several things unsaid; that is to say, even as they are subjected to the force of *Sous rature*—even if they remain in plain sight despite the determination to write them out. The need, then, is, to write knowing how the "length of silence shapes lives," how the relation that is shaped by and formed in separation struggles against silence, against—in the spirit of impossibility—its own conceptual inadequacy.

WRITING · It is only in my work, in my writing, most especially, that I have struggled toward a language in which the township footballer and the diasporic graduate student, long since a diasporic professor, could confront each other. No wonder; these were not worlds that had a great deal in common, so they faced each other uneasily. Or I faced them uneasily and, again in the spirit of the governing concept, with a certain mischievousness. All of which makes it difficult to produce a language that can bear the weight of that which is *entre-nous*. That is, to understand that the act of making a language is nothing but the commitment to producing an articulation adequate to the task of thinking that which is at stake. A project that always, in one way or another, in one form or another, articulates to, articulates as, the self, a self that is here engaged in the difficulty of movement, a self that is, from the very beginning, constituted through movement, the movement that relates self to other and the language that marks, punctuates, disrupts, animates, enervates relation through separation. Out of these infrahuman contestations is the grammar of relation struggles to emerge, struggles to impose itself on the unruliness that governs what is between relation and separation.

The movement in language that transforms the hailing of a teammate, "Groot Man!" into a palimpsest of thought, a hailing that is (historically) multiple in its singularity. It is a hailing that echoes beyond the confines of Mercer County, New Jersey, where its enunciation begins—where its enunciation shows the force of the "accident of history" made inevitable by language.

When a blond Dutch striker and a historically disenfranchised South African midfielder become teammates, there is already, well before them, something *entre-nous*. A certain historical irony. In late-twentieth-century America the scion of seventeenth-century imperialist adventure is being interpellated by a teammate from the "Cape of Good Hope" (as the Dutch named their colony although the crews on their sailing vessels often knew it as the "Cape of Storms") in a language resonant in its familiarity. A little historical mischief and political naughtiness no doubt inflected the name I called my Dutch teammate. A small cry across the centuries that established a relation made uncanny by the site of enunciation. Seventeenth-century imperialism echoing across the oceans to southern Africa and to the European low countries; seventeenth-century imperialism being made to look obsolete, quaint, and old-fashioned in the age of American empire.

How different and at once hauntingly similar, then, when an educated township midfielder speaks English to his predominantly Afrikaans-speaking teammates. Then again, everything is already ready to be "relayed" through language because of what is already *entre-nous*, constitutively between them, what simultaneously and by turns unites and divides them. In this way, every language, every speaking of a language, marks the struggle within and against that selfsame language or languages, as in the case of greeting a teammate as "Groot Man" or being welcomed back, "Wat sê jy?" (What do you say?). Indeed, what does one say? And how does one say it?

In the 1990s, the grim, increasingly violent but nevertheless vibrant township was a long way from the intensity of New York City or the rarified, bucolic environs of New Jersey, and so it remains to this day. But returning as a graduate student and a still-active footballer, I had the cushion of familiarity to "break the fall," metaphorically speaking. I knew my teammates, we shared a passion for football. Moreover, we were Lansur partisans through and through, veterans of many a football skirmish.

Still, returning required me to master at least two forms of translation. Firstly, I had to transition from a strictly academic setting to one where almost no one (else) had a high school diploma, to say nothing of a master's or a PhD. I literally had to "learn"—to learn again, to think carefully about my vocabulary, the range of my references, to fit (my) language to the purpose at hand—to speak in a linguistic register appropriate to my context. I had to, if not abandon, then momentarily hold in abeyance, my "usual" mode of reading and responding to the world in terms derived from and confluent with the cultural studies texts or postcolonial theory that were my Columbia or Princeton linguistic stock-in-trade.

In order to "return," I had to find the language, the set of rhetorical tools, that would allow me to reacquaint myself with Lansur's training regimen, prematch banter, or postmatch analysis of Lansur's most recent game. Of course, I had these in my linguistic arsenal, but some effort was necessary in order to reactivate it. It is not quite so easy to go from reading Antonio Gramsci's *Prison Notebooks* to deciding how to counter the opponent's tricky winger. Still, I enjoyed having to work at this particular mode of translation because it reminded me of the demands of transition, of how separation and relation were related. It also reminded me that I lived in more than one world; or rather, that I was copresent in a world that had two distinct modes of authorship. And I had to acknowledge that such a disjunctive mode of being was invariably overdetermined by attendant difficulties as well as pleasures—among which numbered the privilege of moving between, as in my case, the township football club and the Ivy League lecture hall.

Secondly, I literally had to change languages. I had to go from speaking English, the lingua franca of graduate school, to conversing in township Afrikaans. Growing up, English was my first language. (My father and his brothers sometimes, but not always, spoke Afrikaans to each other; English only to us. My maternal grandparents might address each in Afrikaans, but they too only rarely strayed into that language with my siblings and I.) While this was hardly unusual among the residents of Hanover Park, it was by no means common. To speak English and not township Afrikaans, and to speak English in a mode now inflected by years of graduate study, an English now supplemented by the other languages, the smattering of French, Spanish, German, graduate school introduced me to, was, for better or worse, to bear—to speak—the mark of difference, the mark of separation through other relations; speaking English almost made measurable the difference between my teammates and I. Thankfully, and for this I am grateful beyond words, that difference never rose to the level of alienation. The hedge against alienation was not only a shared love of football but our shared commitment to Lansur. However, the effect of difference, its "costs," Michel Foucault might say, cannot but intensify the nature of the relation to the other. It will be thought. It wills itself, Nietzsche might say (or, Heidegger might say Nietzsche would say), to be thought. There is no other way to live, unbearable or pleasurable as it might sometimes be, except in relation through separation.

Township Afrikaans is a hybrid tongue, the greater part of which is based in standard (or, "formal," if you wish) Afrikaans but is supplemented by English and a number of terms that are invented, whose origins may lie in languages from Asia (courtesy of indentured laborers brought to South Africa by the British and the Dutch in the nineteenth century from their Asian colonies, most notably the Raj and Indonesia, respectively) or be derived and adapted from American movies or from English football. Growing up as an English-speaking kid in the township, I'd been engaged in this kind of translation all my life, so it required little adjustment. Township Afrikaans is a language in which I was fluent and comfortable as a child, and I remain so to this day. It was a familiarity that mitigated and ameliorated (my) difference. However, as we shall see later in this "Interlude," the effect of speaking English is—was—never, could never be, fully ameliorated. It returns, as it must, such is its history. It returned as a gentle haunting more than twenty years after I'd last pulled on a Lansur shirt.

When I returned in 1993, after having retired from the game in September 1992, Lansur was in decline. It was also, sadly, the club's last season. By 1994 it died a quiet, unspectacular death. Like many clubs from the coloured ("mixed-race," in American parlance) townships, Lansur fell victim to factors such as a lack of money, loss of infrastructure, and movement of players away from Hanover Park. Add to this the simple fact of players of my generation getting older, their prime years behind them, and it all seemed rather inevitable now, even if it seemed avoidable, and was certainly experienced by the stalwarts of my generation as a sociopolitical tragedy. With the end of apartheid, South African sport, at all levels, had to be integrated. Football, the most popular sport among the historically disenfranchised, faced particular economic and logistical problems. There had been more than one governing body among the disenfranchised, and only one controlling white football, to say nothing of the discrepancy in resources between the white leagues and those of the disenfranchised.[15] In this way, the end of apartheid was a kind of violence against township football.

That is because what it finally meant was that, very simply, for a club such as Lansur, or any other Hanover Park club for that matter, a new demand arose— the need to travel to play games outside of the township—for which the club was not particularly well equipped. Once the secure environs of township football, for so long a bulwark against the world, as well as the effect of apartheid's statutory inequities, had been breached by the end of apartheid, there was nothing to do but adapt or die. A few clubs, the better-organized and -resourced ones, adapted. Lansur and those like it mostly did not.

THE END OF APARTHEID, THE DEATH OF A CLUB · Under the auspices of the South African Council on Sport (SACOS), which administered nonracial sport, clubs such as Lansur played by far the vast majority of their games in their home township, normally at a central venue. This was a venue that normally consisted of four, five, or six fields, where all the clubs from the township congregated on the weekend to do battle. Lansur United played in Hanover Park, on an open, sprawling ground on the southwestern edge of the township. On a clear day, there in the west, was the magnificence of Table Mountain. On a rainy, blustery day, the wind swept up from the Atlantic Ocean (southwest) or the Indian Ocean (north) and made footballing life difficult. On such a day, you hoped your captain won the toss so that you could play, as we said, "into the wind" in the first half so that you could have the benefit of the wind at your back in the second. Windy days made for a miserable, utilitarian quality of football. Hoof and hope, more or less.

At the Hanover Park field the grounds, known as Die Veld (The Field), were unfenced, and there were certainly no stands for spectator seating. This left the spectators to take their places right at the touchline. On more than one occasion, a spectator intruded onto the football pitches, which were divided into the A, B, C, and D fields, and caused mild havoc. But it made for an intimate—and intense—football setting, spectators pressed close in, so close you could hear their running commentary. You certainly heard when they booed you and, of course, when they cheered you on. Players, spectators, coaches, and referees from all the teams walked to the games. For the Lansur players and faithful it was a leisurely stroll, ten minutes or so, from most of our homes to Die Veld.

After the end of apartheid, traveling to the white suburbs on the fringes of Cape Town's city center, or to teams—white, black, or colored—in far-flung areas around the Cape Peninsula or the nearby Boland region, taxed the resources of township clubs. Few, I expect, survived. Lansur, as I said, did not. The irony is that the end of apartheid, as is historically true of such seismic events, condemned clubs such as Lansur to die.

We could not, we were in no way prepared, to deal with the new demands history was making of us. There is a cruelty in that. Postapartheid South Africa was the condition (that facilitated) for the death of one of the key political institutions that sustained antiapartheid coloured life. With the end of apartheid, with the franchise universalized, the average amateur township club was condemned to die. It is a recognition that will not, even these three decades later, let go of me. Much as I cannot forgive the ANC for the decreased level of healthcare, the decimation of the schools, the unchecked spread of drugs, and the increased violence that has wracked Hanover Park (to say nothing of the rampant kleptomania and corruption that marks its rule), that has left many of its residents hopeless, undereducated and entirely unfitted to live as citizens in this devastated postapartheid landscape.

There were, of course, the other factors I listed that precipitated Lansur's demise. As the players got older, got married, started families or increased the size of their families, gained a little socioeconomic mobility and a foothold on the lower rungs of the middle-class ladder, more than a few left Hanover Park. I went furthest afield, but I was by no means the only player to leave the township. Teammates such as the Duncan brothers, Hamat, Aarie, and Wakes, all moved into modest middle-class homes in Mitchells Plain, a gigantic collection of suburbs built for the aspirant coloured middle-class. (The various homes that the Duncan brothers moved into were, unquestionably, an upgrade on the houses we'd all grown up in.) As a result, it became more difficult for everyone to attend training if not the games themselves; and, less discernible but by no means less true, was the loss of team cohesion that followed from our dispersal. We went from encountering each other on a daily basis, from being neighbors, from buying meat at the same butcher, to seeing each other only at practice or at the game.

There was, furthermore, a final—fatal, in more senses than one—factor in Lansur's undoing. Four months, four months almost to the day before I left for the United States, on April 3, 1989, our chairman, Henry Dirks, passed away. "Mr. Dirks" or "Die Ou" (The Old Man) or "Die Don" (a term that I doubt requires translation, although I'm sure he would have preferred to be known by his full title, *padrone*), had been Lansur's chief benefactor. He was also a surrogate father to many a player and our most inveterate booster. Henry Dirks was Mr. Lansur himself.

I don't think that we, as a group of players, as a club that had been centered at his house, 40 Lansur Road, Hanover Park, ever recovered from losing him.

AN EMAIL, A REUNION · All these thoughts, these recollections, pleasurable, painful, filled with memories of a moment that was, that was massively significant in the lives of all Lansur players, are with me as my wife, Jane, and our then-seven-year-old son, Ezra, drive to the Lansur reunion in Mitchells Plain, organized by Hamat and his wife, Shaheeda, Henry Dirks's daughter.

The idea for a reunion began about two months earlier, when, out of the blue, an email arrived in my inbox. The subject line read *"Nog Lansur."* It was from "Shaheeda Duncan," and it inquired if I was 'that Grant Farred who had played for her father's club." I was a little taken aback, so much so that I showed the email to Jane, subjecting her to a quick history lesson on Lansur United AFC.

So began a correspondence that culminated, when I told Shaheeda that I'd be back in Cape Town with my family for the Christmas holidays, in the thirtieth-anniversary Lansur reunion. Planned, I was touched, in my honor. It was psychologically disconcerting, the prospect of going back after all these years, decades, in fact, but exciting all the same.

And that is how I found myself, in December 2015, more than twenty-six years after leaving Cape Town, on my way to the Lansur United AFC reunion.

THE REUNION · All told, there must be, players and supporters alike, about forty people in the hall where the event is being held. Jane, Ezra and I walk in. We are all uneasy. Ezra's an energetic kid, but he's shy around strangers; Jane's American, from small-town Iowa, and she has nothing in her experiential repertoire to prepare for this—the coloured working-class reuniting. Quite frankly, I'm not much better equipped, but I am keen to see the old faces.

Nevertheless, these many years later, I'm a little nervous about my place in this place so many years after leaving. This reunion unsettles and excites me, despite the fact that I've never been to this part of Mitchell's Plain called Rocklands. I hope that the name does not foreshadow some form of desolation. That would be a pity, because I haven't seen most of my teammates since the last game I played in 1992.

It's 2015, apartheid is long dead, although its effects are still palpable, and nowhere more viscerally for me, as I said before, than in Hanover Park. My community, I think—and it is mine, I have a proprietary relationship to the

> **YOU ARE INVITED TO THE**
> **LANSUR REUNION DISCO PARTY**
>
> SATURDAY 19TH DECEMBER 2015
> @
> CEDAR HIGH SCHOOL
> TIME : 7PM
> BRING YOUR OWN PLATTER&DRINKS
> REMEMBER ITS **FREE FREE**....NOG LANSUR EN NOG LANSUR EN WEER LANSUR
> KOM EN GENIET DIE AAND SAAM MET GRANT FARED EN SY FAMILY ALL THE WAY FROM THE USA
> PUT ON YOUR DANCING SHOES NIE JOU SOCCER BOOTS NIE

FIGURE INTER.1 Invitation to Lansur United AFC reunion, December 2015.

Hanover Park of my childhood and my football years—is worse off now than under apartheid. Yes, it's relation through separation, I grant that, but the affective pull, the memories of growing up, playing football, cricket, tennis with wooden bats, of hanging out with friends on corners and in the shadow of hulking, three-story council flats (apartment blocks, of the kind that would be equivalent to a project in an American innercity). In this township where we came of age, this place in the world that was our place, our world, however circumscribed by apartheid it might have been. It is all of these factors, these conflicting, concatenating sentiments that, I know, makes this relation through separation a horse of an entirely different color.

When I go back to Hanover Park now, as I do every time I visit Cape Town (religiously, as I said, with only one exception, 2016, since 1989), I find that its residents are less safe, that many live in fear. Gangs are rampant, violence commonplace. The youth of Hanover Park are more prone to drug addiction, and those belonging to the generation after the end of apartheid (known as the "born frees") see little in terms of social affiliation that is not gang-related. Everybody seems poorer, and I check this with my friends, our old neighbors, just to make sure that I am neither romanticizing my past nor imposing my judgment from afar. (I may, of course, be guilty of both.) In postapartheid South Africa, I wonder how this can be. How is it possible that postapartheid has failed this Cape Flats township? For just a moment (it must, I admit, have a much longer history, but it manifests itself as memory, on this occasion), I understand Bruce Springsteen when he talks about his loyalty to the people of Freehold, New Jersey, with whom he grew up. "I began to ask myself new questions," Springsteen writes in his autobiography, the personae who inspired his album *Born to Run* (a title, of course, in which movement, fear of the past, the impossible desire to be free of that past, overwhelms everything else), "I felt accountable to the people I'd grown up alongside of and I needed to address that feeling."[16] I know just what you mean, Boss, I know just what you mean. *Entre-nous*, between us, let me whisper it quietly.[17] This is my secret because I am doing what Springsteen did: "addressing that feeling," writing an account of postapartheid "accountability," of a sort. "Accountability" to Hanover Park, to Lansur United, to eleven teammates.

So it is here, walking around my old neighborhood, where I feel most angry, most alienated, most connected through memory, vivid memory, most angry about the state of my community, that it has come to this. Garbage strewn everywhere, the roads blackened by marks that can only come from fires that were set, in the middle of the street, no less. The fences to Summit Primary, the school opposite where we lived, built in 1971 with prison labor, is trodden down, everywhere; the windows are broken. I am angry at this violence done to this particular neck of the Hanover Park woods; this is where I grew up, no matter that I moved out of Hanover Park in 1986 or that I now travel on a US passport. What is *entre-nous*, this township and me? Between my teammates, all but one of whom have left Hanover Park, and me? Everything? What is *entre-nous*? Nothing, nothing can dissolve the ties that bind; nothing can repair the bonds that have frayed over more than twenty years. This is the effect, this restlessness, this rapid to-ing and fro-ing among critique, judgment, regret, sadness, loss, the smile of memory, and fidelity (to what was and what is no more but remains indestructible), that now inhabits me as I come back to Hanover Park. I know, and I know that I know, what it means to live the relation through separation, I know what it means to live both at the same time. Everything I am is, in this moment, *entre le moi et le moi-même*; nothing is *entre le moi et le moi-même*. I am, for a moment, through the relation that is separation, entirely myself, for myself, entirely of this place.

In a strange way, however, my anger at the conditions that obtain in Hanover Park reorients my thinking. I now know, beyond question, what I am doing at the reunion: I am paying homage to what was. Not nostalgically, but I am paying tribute to a mode of life that was, a mode of being made possible by, among other things, playing football, by playing for Lansur. (Perversely, one could say, I am paying homage to having played football for Lansur United AFC under apartheid. A perverse gratitude to apartheid.) Given that, how can I not be here, this occasion that is being held in my honor? How could I not have made the trek from Cape Town's southern suburbs, where we are staying with my sister and her family, to Rocklands, driving along the eastern and southern fringes of Hanover Park to get to the reunion?

Upon entry, my fears are quickly allayed. I find myself being warmly greeted, in Afrikaans, as though we were all back at practice in, say, 1988 or 1991. We all overcome our various hesitations. Jane and Ezra are introduced, and we find a place to sit. There is food, drinks, the courtesy of our hosts. All this means that after the initial act of seeing each other, in the flesh after so long, the conversation flows freely. Among us players there is, as one might expect, a certain jocularity, laddish jokes about someone's weight (one or two guys have added a few pounds), and real pleasure at seeing one another again.

This is the spirit in which we greet each other. First Shaheeda, then Hamat and then "Aalee." This is the tenor that governs our exchanges. We have a lot of catching up to do, and set to it with gusto. Still, and we know this even though it remains unspoken, there is a great deal we cannot say. It has been a long time. Our lives have followed divergent paths. We are men in our middle years, the flush of footballing youth has long since passed. But, as we discover, there are unbreakable bonds. The bond is football, and the life we made together through it. To honor the life that was in the presence of the living, to bring that life into its own language, that is the prophylactic against nostalgia, against maudlin recollection.

Knowing this, I understand how playing for Lansur enabled me to learn some of the most important antiapartheid lessons of my life. I belong to a generation of disenfranchised South Africans who, regardless of their level of education, learned politics through sport, football, in my case. Playing township football under the auspices of the South African Council on Sport taught me politics, politics as a form of community—albeit an often combative community—that was fully engaged in both the everyday politics of South Africa (resisting apartheid, being rendered powerless by it) and in the routine matters of football (winning, losing, crappy referees, great goals, silly mistakes, that kind of thing).[18] Playing township football in the 1980s had the benefit of making antiapartheid politics an enjoyable and sometimes unforgettable experience. Politics so constructed was simultaneously the foundation of our lives and, in our best football moments, reduced to mere afterthought. Winning a big match at Die Veld had the power to, if only momentarily, make nothing of the strictures of apartheid. A good goal, a well-timed tackle, an acrobatic save (Aalee made several of those) allowed us to transcend—to be, just for a moment, footballers, purely footballers.

In December 2015, we incline, unknowingly or not, toward the transcendent.

And, as such, it is predictable that at the first opportunity the conversation turns to old matches. For the most part, we steer clear of the losses and intraclub rivalries and disputes, not all of which have faded from memory. We're especially careful to avoid thorny topics such as which guys didn't get along, unless, that is, we can make a joke about it. We are complimentary toward each other as we reenact our performances in key matches. There is a lot of standing up and pantomiming someone's signature trick, our bodies heavier but our spirits still light, glad that we can meet and talk again. It's not as good as being in the dressing room ("locker room") before a big match or after a tough loss, but this is good enough. It is good enough because it takes us back to the training ground or Die Veld. It will have to do, we make do with it. We laugh, both at the things we did on the playing field as well as those silly pranks we pulled off the pitch—the guys who smoked weed before a game, the guys who were hungover, the pettiness of the squabbles between teammates and infelicities of other kinds.

A TIME FOR SADNESS · There are moments of sadness too. About players who passed on, the two Appels boys come quickly to mind. John and Ivan Appels lived at 5 Etosha Court, a stolid block of council flats about sixty meters southwest of my family's house. John, the eldest, was also the smallest Appels brother (all four of them, including the younger two, Willie and Clive, good footballers), and a nifty left back. He, like Ivan (a dancing left winger, tall, always possessed of a ready, mischievous smile), the second eldest, dropped out of the game too early; a victim, like many others, of the drug culture that was already then causing havoc with township lives. (This devastation intensified after the end of apartheid, when more lethal, and cheaper, kinds of drugs began to flood the townships, and, it should be added, infiltrated many wealthier communities as well.) I see the third eldest, Willie, doing menial labor around the Cape Flats when I'm back, and he has a smile like Ivan's, and his face shows evidence of a hard life. But, unlike John and Ivan, he is still alive.

At the reunion our focus is less on the deceased Appels brothers and more on the passing of our former striker, Perry, who moved in the same circles, loosely speaking, as Ivan. We used to call Perry "Bags," I don't know why, because, unlike others, I was never close to him. We reminisce about what a good goal scorer he was. Bags, part of a Rasta collective, was a soft-spoken central striker who combined pace and silky moves with a sure eye for the net. How sad that he is gone. I can still see him in action, going—as he always preferred—right at defenders, his head aimed directly at the goal. Bags could score. Moreover, unlike most strikers, he would say almost nothing after he'd put the ball in the net. He'd just quietly make his way to the halfway line and get ready for his next run at goal.

But our deepest regret is for our pencil-thin, highly skilled midfielder, "Cavalla" (so nicknamed after a brand of cigarettes), who joined Lansur in 1987. "Cavakes," as he was sometimes also known, is gone, a victim of ill health. (His given name was Rudolph, but he was always just Cavakes to us.) All of us remember his trickery, his hunger for the ball, and his smile.

Cavakes seemed to smile most broadly when he had the ball at his feet. He was that kind of footballer whom every teammate loves because you could give him the ball anywhere on the pitch. If you were surrounded by opponents, just slip him the ball and he'd wriggle his way past defenders. Cavakes could make anyone look good. But, we note, he was also given to pouting and could be downright peevish when he didn't get the ball when he thought he should. And he almost always thought you should pass the ball to him; when you did, he performed pirouettes and little bits of magic that were marvelous to behold. Just slide Cavalla the ball, from anywhere on the pitch, and in an instant defense was converted into attack. He was particularly fond of dragging the ball along the touchline, sometimes even going out of bounds, shimmying past defenders, smiling; the stealthy kind of smile that is about to break into infectious laughter. Whether you were playing with or against him, he seemed to draw you into the joke. *Entre nous*, the joke, between Cavalla and us. At Lansur we knew this well because we used to do battle with Cavakes before he joined us.

He came to us from a team called Young Pirates, where he formed a very effective partnership with a tall striker named Chris "Gunny" Lewis. They were difficult to play against, but fun, because Cavakes and Gunny were all about trickery; they loved nothing so much, Cavakes more than Gunny, as beating their man. However, in the cauldron that was Hanover Park football, where the battles were often personal, Cavakes was one of those rare opponents whom one enjoyed playing against. Lansur United never lost to Pirates,[19] but I know that I liked to watch him at work. Of course, I liked it more when he was wearing Lansur's maroon-and-white strip, as opposed to the black-and-white of Pirates, but as a player Cavakes always caught your eye because he reminded you of how joyful football could be.

No surprise then, that there, just at the edge of our conversation, just beneath the surface of our animated conversation about Cavakes, is the kind of sadness and loss that can't find its proper register. It is not only that we are brought up short, gathered here as we are to celebrate, reminded of our mortality, but that with a passing such as Cavalla's, the truth of an irredeemable loss ghosts among us. We're at the outer fringes of Judith Butler country, at the edge of the deep recesses where the loss within the loss resides. This is no easy place to be, but it is, given that we are thirty years removed from our physical pomp, an unavoidable psychic location. As W. H. Auden phrases it, this is what it means to face "our uneliminated decline."[20] "Uneliminatable," there, before us, in the ghostly shiftiness of a Cavalla swivel. There, 'uneliminated," within us.

As that line by Dylan Thomas goes, "These are the boys of summer in their ruin."[21] We're not ruined yet, but we can see it coming. What's worse, maybe, is that the vibrant physicality of 1985, or 1989, is assuredly behind us now, recuperable only in our shared company. Together, through our poignantly boisterous conversation, we each hold up a metaphorical mirror of our early adulthood for the other, sans Cavalla. And so we know that things are decidedly different. As Roland Gift of the Fine Young Cannibals puts it, we are not, a one of us, "The man we used to be."[22] Certainly not as footballers, and that makes us, all of us, just a little "crazy."

HOMELESSNESS · However, death is not the only loss we've suffered. Gerhard "Gert" Fortuin remarks that our former defender, Mike Cupido, is homeless. No one imagined such a fate would ever befall Mike, one of two high school graduates on our 1985 team. (I was the other; Mike was a high school senior in 1985). Poised on the field and off, possessed of a wry, understated humor, and confident in that quiet way that only really good footballers can be, Mike was a guy who seemed to have it all together. How could he possibly have come to such an end?

I liked playing with Mike. I liked to interchange passes with him, central midfielder and central defender, respectively. He was erudite in the pass, and tackled with a silky steeliness, combining seemingly incommensurable qualities through his particular art of defending. Mike's tackles were never rough or crude, but they were undertaken with a decisive, never excessive, force. He could make tackling look an art form of sorts, such was his ability to gussy it up as skillful dispossession. Mike could control the game from the back. We could always trust Mike. Moreover, in a team where there were two or three guys (Gietzman, Hamat, and me) given to exuberant outbursts, Mike was a player who could command the pitch without shouting.

Mike's homelessness is not an easy proposition to digest. As I write, almost three years after hearing about his fate, the prospect continues to haunt me. Mike on the streets; a life vulnerable to vagaries of poverty, hunger, and the violence of the postapartheid South African streets. That is not an image commensurate with our elegant central defender, the five-foot-ten guy with that subtle smile and that neatly coiffed mini Afro. How can this be the same guy who is now wandering the streets of the Cape Flat pushing a supermarket trolley that holds all his worldly possessions?

Here Dylan Thomas's words assume a hard, unforgiving edge: "These are the boys of summer, in their ruin."

"Ruin," it has come to Mike. Goddamn, goddamn.

We are not sure if this is true, no one can verify it, but we are all, for a moment, stilled into silence. But it is not, I recognize as we sit quietly for a moment, the same kind of silence that reverberated when we mourned Cavakes. (Of course, for me it is a posthumous mourning because I didn't learn of Cavalla's death until that very evening. Rudolph died of ill health; Mike is enduring a very different, and, for me, more sociologically arresting fate.) So our silence around Mike is, as it should be, a manifestly political silence. As a group of working-class guys, as boys who grew up around adults working menial, yes, dead-end jobs, as guys who grew up in Hanover Park during apartheid, we knew want. We saw the effects of alcoholism almost daily; we witnessed drug use, recreational and of the addictive variety; we regarded violence as a normative township experience. There were knife fights, a few gunshots, and the occasional running battles between gangs called "The Americans," "The Backstreets," "The Cisco Yakkies." The police either came too late or did not bother to come at all. (Protecting our community was hardly their priority.) Or, worse, they were wholly ineffective when they did come punctually. We knew families (some of them our own) whose electricity had been disconnected because the bills weren't paid, and we knew lots of families who struggled to make ends meet. Ours were not lives lived in innocence.

But in our playing days, even though only two of us were high school graduates, we never imagined that homelessness would befall one of our own. Sons of the coloured township, almost all of us are at least lower-middle-class now. Everyone but one of us (Pung) owns their own home, everyone has (again, with that one exception), in his own way, "made good."

Most of us have steady jobs. We are parents to the first generation of South African kids who did not have to endure apartheid either at all or past their teenage years—Hamat, Aarie, Wakes, and Pung had kids early, so their children had at least a passing familiarity with that system. Nevertheless, everyone has, in one way or another, made something of their lives. Mike is the object lesson: there but for the grace of God go I. It's not the kind of thing one wants to be reminded of at a reunion, but how could one possibly avoid it? The precariousness of our lives, the fate that did not befall us, but in whose shadow we know we live. Suddenly, without speaking to each other or acknowledging it, we find ourselves right back in our darkest moments in Hanover Park. This is loss within the deepest recesses of loss.

However, neither such serious contemplations nor the silence lasts very long. After all, we are here to catch up, to celebrate, to remember our exploits, to enjoy each other's company. Before you know it, we're off again, recounting another game, regaling each other with tackles that were made, goals that were scored. There is always one more set of opponents whom we bested. Someone offers a version of an incident, someone else contests it, yet another offers a further correction. And so it goes. This is how one reunites with old teammates and supporters. Pleasure, joy, within the deepest recesses of loss; the deepest recesses of loss lead back to joy, to the "singular plural community." A community that now reaches into ghostly territory. Like Marcellus in Shakespeare's *Hamlet*, we are able to speak to the ghost because we are now, all of us, "scholars of life." This is what it means, in Derrida's gently evocative phrase, to "learn to live, finally," to "learn to live" (*apprendre à vivre enfin*) because we are able to find, in almost every moment, the "trace of life."[23] "*Apprendre à vivre*," says Derrida, "means to mature, but also to educate: to teach someone else and especially yourself."[24] And so we have reunited after thirty years to teach each other, and ourselves, about how to live the lives we have, the lives we have made, and how to recognize the value of the lives we lived, the lives that are still, each in his own "singular plural," with us. Thirty years of *entre-nous*, reduced to a life, elevated through how we apprehend the death of the other. The other with whom we were together, the memory that is "being-with."

1985 · Politically, the mid-1980s in the coloured townships of the Cape Flats, as was true of most disenfranchised communities in South Africa, was turbulent, much of it the result of the ANC's campaign to make South Africa "ungovernable." School and economic boycotts, conflict with the apartheid state's security apparatuses, were so frequent as to have become the very stuff of township life by 1985.

This was a moment in which running battles between township youth and police officers in their canary yellow vans and their armored vehicles, named "Casspirs," were commonplace. We vented our anger by hurling objects, stones, sticks, glass bottles, anything that came to hand, at the cops. They chased us through the streets. In our turn, we dodged them by ducking into the narrow alleyways we knew so well, losing them in the back streets—which explains the name of one of the gangs—of the township.

It goes without saying that this affected us as footballers. A few of us were active in the protests; some of us were involved in community organizations,

FIGURE INTER.2 Lansur United AFC, 1985. Back row (left to right): Stan "Sailor" Van Wyk, "Hamat" Duncan, Michael Cupido, Grant Farred, Jeremiah Shiri, Norman Terblanche ("manager"); middle row: "Wakes" Duncan, "Aarie" Duncan, Julian "Brother" Dirks, Shahied "Pung" Arendse; front row: Lyndon van Heerden, Errol "Aalee" Cupido, Anthony Gietzman.

one or two of us spoke at public rallies. Sometimes, when tensions were really high or when police brutality became unbearable (too many casualties, too many funerals, rising levels of community anger), our practices were cancelled or our games were postponed. It was not an unusual occurrence for us to be practicing and then a Casspir would come rumbling by and we'd immediately switch modes. We'd put away our balls and join the street battle that had just erupted. Our football activities did not so much accommodate our antiapartheid politics as they were woven from the same political fabric. One moment you're running a wind sprint, the next you're "taking up arms," with the nearest stone to hand being your only weapon.

In the midst of all this, we were Lansur United of Hanover Park.

And, as Lansur, we played; we played football, a skillful brand of it, at that. We were led in this regard by our mercurial number 10, Shahied "Pung" Arendse. In the second half of that memorable 1985 season, we were the dominant team in Hanover Park Football Association (HPFA). We beat everyone, with the odd draw here and there.

1 THROUGH 11 · The 1985 Lansur United AFC side was a settled team

1. In goal we had Errol "Aalee" Cupido. Aalee was as agile and sure-handed a goalkeeper as you could wish for, and by far the best keeper in HPFA in our day. Aalee was a confident shot stopper who also commanded the air from set pieces. Standing an inch or three over six feet, Aalee was hunched of shoulder and sharp of chin; all this capped with an impish but tightly drawn smile, which hid the gap left by four missing front teeth. Aalee was languid, funny, and the rock upon which our team was built. In all the years I played with him, I only remember a single mistake.

    As our captain, he was not given to verbosity. Instead, he saw his role as being limited to taking the toss and then letting us get on with it. As captain, Aalee trusted us, and in our turn, we had complete faith in him as the last line of defense. Our faith was well placed, because we knew that it would take a shot of some power to beat him. Between 1985 and 1988, when he left Lansur, Aalee was not only the best goalkeeper in Hanover Park but ranked among the elite on the Cape Flats. Leaving Lansur proved a mistake, because he never again displayed the form he'd had with us. A pity. He deserved more.

2. Mike, who, like Aalee, bore the last name Cupido (they are not related), was the right back on our team. The next season, 1986, he would move to his natural position, central defense, but for starters he was our right flanking defender. As I have remarked, Mike was among the most elegant defenders Hanover Park has ever produced. Time on the ball, Mike always had time on the ball. I hardly recall him making a hurried clearance. Mike joined Lansur partway through the season, and his presence stabilized a back four that had been, until his arrival, promising but, without a regular right back, a little unsettled.

    Mike calmed everything down, in no small part because his quickness of mind meant that he was always a step ahead of the game. As such he could cover for our central defensive pairing, neither of whom was blessed with pace. Together with Aalee, Mike was the glue that held our defense together.

3   Mike was partnered on the left flank by Anthony Gietzman, a manic, erratic, but tough tackling defender whose trademark was his socks. Pung called him "Malles," an affectionate rendering of the Afrikaans word for "mad" (*mal*). The rest of us just called him "German," for reasons unknown to most of us but most likely because he played as though he were a World War II Panzer tank—intent on brute, destructive force. Gietzman pulled his socks, our maroon-and-white hoops up all the way over his knees. Don't ask me why. Now that I can command a smidgeon of Spanish, I think of Gietzman as "El Loco," the "Crazy One." He was fast and strong, like the rugby player he sometimes was, but he was entirely undisciplined. Wild, maniacally confident, he was always upbeat and, from my point of view, infuriating because you never knew what you were going to get from him. However, his speed made him a danger—to our opponents, to us, to himself, I sometimes thought—and, with Mike's smarts on the other flank, we compensated nicely for the lack thereof in our center backs. Gietzman's greatest attribute was his infectious optimism—he was always making some god-awful joke, he was always laughing, a crazy smile on his lips, no matter circumstances. He drove me to distraction.

4   In the center of our defense, Hamat Duncan and Julian "Brother" Dirks were not the kind of players who were going to win a footrace. However, brothers-in-law that they were (and remain), they worked together uncannily well with a keen understanding of each other's strength and weaknesses. Hamat, tall, lanky, hair shaved close to his head, was sure in the air and deft of foot, always a danger at corner kicks—in fact, at set pieces in general. Moreover, he had—a fact to which he readily admits—the biggest mouth on the team. Hamat was always, good naturedly, trash-talking someone. Mostly with a smile, because for all his talk he abjured contact and preferred deftness and his ability to read the game to the unnecessary hard stuff; he was a cultured player, a threat to score with his head, and, in truth, a man who would rather juggle his way out of defensive trouble than aimlessly boot the ball clear. This too had the effect of sometimes throwing me into a panic because I played ahead of him, so if he lost the

ball, I'd have to cover for his indulgence. Thankfully, it didn't happen very often. At the reunion, we laughed about it. However, I could only laugh because I no longer had to worry about racing back to cover Aalee.

Hamat was the oldest of three brothers on the team, and also our oldest player on the team. Nonetheless, he would rather play than lead, except when, according to him, the match had reached a crucial point, and then he would make his desires known. Plainly. Mainly, however, he was a happy, smiling, opinionated guy. The Duncans and my family were neighbors, so I saw a lot of him, and he is, courtesy of his wife, Shaheeda (with whom I email), the Lansur player with whom I have the most contact, vicarious though it be, since I don't think Hamat writes his own emails. We even spoke via WhatsApp once.

5   Julian Dirks, Shaheeda's older sibling, was known to all as "Brother." Now retired from his job, "Brother" attended Hanover Park High and later obtained the equivalent of a GED. (In South African terms, this is called getting your "matric certificate" through "night school.") Brother held an administrative position at the University of Cape Town (UCT) and had a keen interest in trade union politics. He lived, as such, between two worlds. During his working hours, he was exposed to the rarefied environs of Africa's best university and ranked now as one of the world's finest institutions, a sense of possibility that he fully embraced during his days at the then-predominantly white university up on the hill. He returned in the evenings and on weekends to the geographically removed realities of Hanover Park, to the bustling, sometimes grimy, littered streets of the Cape Flats; a far cry from the neatly manicured environs of UCT.

Brother had a keen eye trained on the world, and when I heard that he left Hanover Park for a place in the suburbs close to the center of Cape Town, it did not surprise me. He was, for all his camaraderie with Hamat and his closeness to a player such as Pung, a man not entirely at ease in Hanover Park. His view of the world was by no means restricted to Hanover Park. He lived there, played his football there, but it was not the limit of his horizons.

Brother was stout of build and, possessed of such a physique, knew how to crowd out the opposition. He could, in his day, read the game, and that made him adept at intercepting through balls. Our team was set up in such a way that Hamat played "last man," with Brother sweeping ahead of him.

Their understanding did not start out assured in 1985, but as the season went along they adapted to one another, with a clear division of labor. Brother did not like heading the ball (he laughed about this at the reunion), and Hamat wasn't too keen on robust physical contact, so they learned to complement one another in a Jack Sprat kind of way, if one were to substitute the willingness to either seek or retreat from physical contact as analogies for "fat" and "lean." Our center backs communicated easily, and at the end of the 1985 season they were a partnership we could depend upon. Brother drifted out of football soon after, but he remains—to this day—among Lansur's most loyal members.

8  Arawaan "Aarie" Duncan, Hamat's brother, and the middle of the three Duncan boys on the team, played right half, and he was as sweet a passer and accurate a corner taker as Hanover Park knew in the mid- to late-1980s. Unlike his self-confident older brother, Hamat, and his garrulous younger sibling, Wakes, Aarie was quiet, erudite, and remarkably self-possessed. For a man who played with his head seemingly pointed down all the time, he had remarkable vision and had no trouble picking out just the pass the moment demanded. To this day I could not tell you if Aarie was fast or slow. He almost seemed to ghost into place, always taking up the right position.

It was easy to play with Aarie because he was always mutely steadfast in support. He never called for the ball, but he always took up position so that he presented himself, unselfishly, as the most logical outlet. He was the kind of teammate who was just there, in the right place, when you most needed him. He didn't score often, in fact I can't remember him notching a goal, but he encouraged all of us to get forward.

One Saturday afternoon we played a team called, improbably, Celtic Spurs, and I nicked the ball off their defender and it ricocheted off the Spurs player into the net, fortuitously. That goal made the score 5–2, and when I failed to claim the goal, Aarie corrected me: "It's yours," he said in Afrikaans, "and that's your hat trick." (*Is joune; en daai's jou hat trick.*) How could one not enjoy playing with such a teammate?

Aarie is the kind of wide man who holds a team together with neat passes and sure defending. He and Mike could be relied on to keep us tight on that right flank; together they snuffed out opposition attacks, and it was a pleasure to watch them interchange, one making space and creating attacking opportunity for the other. Our right flank had two candidates for a Trappist monastery.

6 Playing opposite Aarie was Stan "Sailor" Van Wyk. Sailor was a *voyou*, a lovable rogue if there ever was one. He was always involved in one dubious undertaking or another, and, like every good rogue, he had a smile that seemed to stretch well beyond his face. For all that, Sailor was the consummate team player. He was a naturally right-footed player who had enough skill and touch to play on the left. Moreover, Stan could do so without compromising his effectiveness as a dribbler and a playmaker at all. And, boy, did Stan like to dribble, did he love just running at opponents and jinking his way past them.

However, even if Sailor's first instinct was to take on his opponent, he was disciplined enough to rein in that tendency. What is more, as we'll see in a moment, he scored the best goal I've ever seen hit the back of the net in Hanover Park football history. Like Aarie, Sailor was willing to track back and help out the defenders.

7 With our skill players out wide in the midfield, I was the anchor. On a team of ball players, I made the small passes, I kept things, as they say, "ticking over," I covered for Hamat and Brother, I loved to put in the crunching tackle, I sprinted forward to get into the opposition box, and I took our penalties. Above all, however, I drove myself to make sure that we won. I hated losing.

Playing in the center of the midfield, my job was also to spread the ball to Stan or Aarie. Or I would try to put our strikers in behind the opposing defense. My passing, my uncompromising tackling and high work rate were my signal contributions.

11 Up front we played a strange formation. We played a 4–3–1–1–1 formation. In Lyndon "Lynnie" van Heerden, the smallest player on our team and the fastest by just a fraction (over Wakes), we had a conventional right wing. Lynnie had only moderate close control, but he was savvy, and he knew just how and when to take on his opponents and beat them for sheer pace.

He would just push and go, leaving defenders flailing behind him, with Wakes, Pung, and I scurrying to make up ground to help him in attack.

Lynnie sort of drifted into Lansur with Aalee. They lived in the same neighborhood, a notorious collection of apartment blocks nicknamed "*die backstreets*," which gave, as I said, one of the local gangs their name. In "*die backstreets*" it was not uncommon to hear gunshots being fired and to see people scurrying for the safety of their homes.

Lynnie used to joke about coming from "*die backstreets*," whereas Aalee only rarely did. Lynnie liked adopting a faux macho stance well out of alignment with his gentle disposition. But for all that, and what with his cool Afro and a penchant for loud colored trousers, a pumpkin pair that stands out to this day, Lynnie was one tough hombre, and he was, to my mind, the most pleasant and easygoing member of the team.

9   The lavishly named Abdulwazi Duncan, "Wakes" to his family and all of us, was our lone ranging striker. He was skinny, with the littlest Afro and a ready smile. Salient about Wakes, and something opponents (many of whom played against him for years) never quite cottoned on to was how quick of mind and swift of foot he was; Wakes was just a skinny blur. Unlike most strikers, Wakes never possessed a cracking shot. He was very good at creating goals for others, and he was, again by the standards of strikers, not in the least greedy. He would as happily play in Pung, Lynnie, or me as score himself.

In fact, in the fifteen years we played together (from 1977, when we were barely teenagers, to 1992, when I retired; Wakes had stopped being serious about the game a year or so before I gave it up), I do not remember Wakes ever scoring a spectacular goal, like Sailor, nor could he beat two or three defenders, as Pung had little trouble doing. No, Wakes Duncan "stole" goals. In the parlance of the Cape Flats, he was a *skelm*—a thief, as impish and light of touch as a pickpocket. With Wakes's goals it was always a nick here, a nudge there, a well-placed header (it always seemed to come off his head softly) or a breakaway achieved because of his speed. With just the goalie to beat, Wakes would just flick the ball around the keeper. I never saw him power the ball past the keeper. No, my best mate on the team was too canny for that.

Wakes Duncan had no problem scoring goals. That, I used to muse, is what Abdulwazi Duncan was born to do. And, as I have remarked, he was generous in creating them. From a corner or a set piece he'd head the ball down to me for a shot (I played directly behind him in central midfield) or he'd lay on a lovely through pass to set Lynnie or Pung free. Because he could head the ball well, Wakes was a real asset defending corners, and he man-marked better than any forward I've played alongside.

Wakes Duncan was my favorite player on our team. I loved playing with him, and if I had to choose one player to do battle with in a single game, no matter the stakes, I'd pick Wakes. We had little in common. Wakes quit school without completing ninth grade; he was a real social animal, but he had everything I wanted in a teammate: he was tough, he was unselfish, he was versatile, and he loved playing for Lansur.

10  I played football in Hanover Park, from kick-arounds in the schoolyard opposite our house to first team games for Lansur (and a couple of years in the Western Province Super League for Premier United) from the early 1970s to September 1992, and in that time I can say with absolute confidence that Shahied "Pung" Arendse is the best player ever to emerge out of our township.

Physically strong, he had thighs the size of a tree trunk. He possessed wonderful skills. He loved nothing so much as the ball at his feet, and he was always finding new ways to dribble by opponents. At practice, he'd take a ball, juggle it, run the ball off his back, twirl it, control it with both feet, seeking to invent yet one more trick. Naturally right-footed, he had absolute confidence in his left, and he was no mean header of the ball. Best of all, when he was in the mood (and he always seemed in the mood), he'd just power by players as if they weren't there, cutting inside, his eye trained on goal. He single-handedly won more than a few games for us.

He was the first footballer from Hanover Park to achieve the highest honor available to those of us who played as amateurs in the apartheid era. At the end of the 1988 season, Pung was chosen to represent Western Province, the equivalent of, say, representing the state of New Jersey or Maryland, a feat that confirmed his elevated status among all the footballers of Hanover Park. No one was more proud of him, now attired in his gray slacks, his white shirt, and his navy blue Western Province blazer, than us, those Lansur players who had so long valued him as a teammate and friend.

For my part, what I admired most about Pung was how much he hated losing. If you saw him among us off the field, you'd recognize him as the first guy to laugh at a joke, to compliment a teammate when talk turned to footfall. That bonhomie, however, could never hide his fierce competitiveness. Only I, a much lesser player, hated losing more than him. Around that we bonded.

However, his real friends on the team were those who had admired him from the first, those who—because they were a few years older than him—watched him grow up. Pung lived opposite Brother on Lansur Road. He lives there still. Hamat and Brother were tight, and they were a trio, with Pung as lord of the Lansur manor.

At that reunion in 2015, when I sung Pung's praises, Hamat murmured his assent. In our distinct ways, each of us appreciated how good Pung had been.

Whenever I go back to Cape Town, I visit my old haunts in Hanover Park, a little stretch that runs east from Etosha Court and 59 Athwood Road, where the Duncan boys grew up (my family lived, as I said, next door, at number 61 Athwood Road), south to 40 Lansur Road, where our club was based. I look Pung up. (What used to be our clubhouse is opposite where Pung still makes his home.) We hug; I inquire after teammates; he updates me. I ask about his son (a central midfielder, of all things), and he speaks with a father's pride and footballer's knowledge about his boy, now a man who is the same age we were then.

I loved talking football with Pung, discussing tactics, going over training regimens, rating opponents, imagining ways in which Lansur could improve. Shahied Arendse was born to play football. Had he come into the world a generation later, I have no doubt that he'd have played professionally. What is more, he would have acquitted himself well, too, make no mistake.

There is a further irony that links us. Pung's son, Nathaniel, whom I knew only as a toddler, and then from a distance, has, according to talk in the Hanover Park football community, become a central midfielder of some local standing; the goal-scoring, dribbling father has produced a tough tackling midfielder who, word has it, wears number 7. My son, Ezra, has ambitions about becoming a goal-scoring number 10. Across the miles, despite the years, it is good to know that Pung and I are still, in some small way, conversing with each other.

Pung has given up his carefully rounded Afro. His hair is shaved close to his head now. He is almost completely gray, but when I look at him, I never fail to see that amazing talent. There he is, we're playing, I don't know, Melchester Rovers on the C in the 3.30 p.m. game on Saturday, and he has his chest out, his thighs are bristling, his feet are moving quickly, and, there I spy it, there it is, as always, that twinkle in his eye, a sure sign that he is planning some mischief to undo an opponent. He played with joy, our Pung, with joy. Now when we talk about those days, his smile breaks wide, and once more the joy is there for all to see. Just for a moment, it's 1985 all over again. We could beat anybody. And in that 1985 season, we pretty much did.

NUMBER 12 · Our invincibility was our chairman's dream. Henry Dirks was a portly man who chain-smoked. Between cigarettes, he wheezed and coughed. Wearing his customary suit and tie, he would lean over the railings of his home, 40 Lansur Road, and make small talk with all and sundry who passed by. I would like to say that football was his passion, but it wasn't. Lansur United AFC was. The man was an extreme partisan, a condition that was only partially offset by an innate friendliness. He gathered Lansur United footballers together like an apostle casting for souls, hailing us off the street, recruits to the Lansur cause. He used his son, Brother, his son-in-law Hamat, and his opposite neighbor, Pung, as bait. To some extent or other, we were all willing to sign our football souls over to him. In one way or another, he recruited us all. In order to do so, he smooth-talked us all with the prospect of Lord knows what promise about our footballing greatness.

In truth, Lansur United's axis was 40 Lansur Road and 59/61 Athwood Road. Only eighty meters or so separated the three houses where the Dirks family, the Duncan family, and my family lived. Put together the three Duncan boys, Brother, Pung, and me, and you had the playing and administrative core of the club. (Gietzman lived just a few houses south of the Dirks on Lansur Road.) I was, as the permanent student, club secretary. I was, as befitted my talents, responsible for keeping records and club correspondence. Mike was assistant secretary.

It was fitting that Pung, our best player, was our coach, and Hamat helped with team selection. As club chairman, Mr. Dirks oversaw everything. Hamat called him "Die Ou," which translates roughly as "The Old Guy" but is probably best understood as "The Man."

Appropriately, then, P_ng dubbed him "Die Don," a titular that requires only the merest linguistic gloss. Henry Dirks was our "Don": chief administrator, wheeler, and dealer. Our meetings took place in his living room every Monday of the season at 8 p.m. At the back of the brick structure that was 40 Lansur Road was our clubhouse. It was a rudimentary wood-and-iron structure in which we had team talks, played pool, drank, smoked (something more proscribed than cigarettes, in some cases), and just got together to talk. Talk football, of course, and not only on meeting night or on game days but as often as we wanted. Either there or on the front porch ("stoep" was our term for it), there was always some collection of Lansur players to be found; in the presence of The Don, a man who was happiest when holding court, surrounded by his players.

On the day that Henry Dirks died, April 3, 1989, we gathered there in silence. We just stood around, all of us a little lost. It was three months almost to the day before I was scheduled to leave for New York City, August 4, which was Henry Dirks's birthday. It's Barack Obama's, too.

If his life revolved around Lansur United, ours, in so many ways, revolved around him.

No one, not a player, not a fan, was prouder of our accomplishments, worked harder for it administratively, funded more of it, than Henry Dirks. No one believed more in Lansur than he did. No one would have been more distraught at the dissolution of his beloved Lansur, as happened at the end of the 1993 season. By the late-1980s, as I said, the Lansur players had started to disperse. The three Duncan boys had moved; Aalee and Mike had moved to other clubs; I was in graduate school in the United States, only a part-time player. Wakes was only sporadically active; Aarie had long since flown the coop; and Lynnie had moved to a western outpost of the Cape Peninsula. By the end of 1992, Lansur was barely holding on.

Hamat assumed The Don's role, but not only had someone vital, irreplaceable, been lost, but ours was now a postapartheid society. Hanover Park clubs now plied their trade not only in our township but all over, to far-flung parts of the Cape Peninsula. We still loved football, but we could see, in the midst of a political sea change, that the time for small, locally based clubs was coming to an end; Lansur was about to become an anachronism. By 1993, it was all over.

IN HONOR OF "DIE DON" · I am glad that Henry Dirks did not live to see the demise of Lansur United AFC. It would have destroyed him.

In our first game of the 1989 season, we wore black armbands in his honor. We won that game, 3–0. Our striker, Mark Petersen, got two, and I scored one of the two best goals of my career.

It was a pure accident. I should never have been there in the first place. At the start of the 1989 season I'd decided to switch to right back, swapping my favorite number 7 for number 2, Mike's old jersey. I was four months away from leaving for graduate school in New York, and I wanted to try a new position. I started the game at right back, but our left back, Clive Daniels (more on him in a second), was getting scorched by our opponents' right wing. In his infinite wisdom, Hamat had me switch flanks to keep tabs on their jackrabbit winger (who'd started on the left wing, playing opposite me, but moved from left to right wing in order to escape me). That is how I found myself in the unusual position of left back.

We were awarded a free kick about forty meters out, on the left flank of the A ground, just inside our opponents' half. I took the free kick with my right foot, giving me a natural right-to-left bend. Still, my intention was to hit Hamat, who was positioned to the right of the penalty spot, but I had too much bend on it, or so I thought. I hit the ball high, aiming wide of the far post. And then it began to curl toward goal. It just kept curling and dipping, from right to left (the natural curve of a right-footer's shot, as I said), until it hit the net at the junction of the left upright and the crossbar. The opposing keeper had no chance. The moment I knew I'd scored I pointed my right index finger skyward. "This one's for you, Mr. Dirks," I whispered underneath my breath.

In truth, however, I was paying homage to both Die Don and the best goal ever scored by a Lansur player.

And that goal, scored some three and a half years before mine, saw Henry Dirks lift his first trophy as chairman of Lansur United AFC.

I never saw him prouder than the evening when he put his hands on that trophy.

"SAILOR'S GOAL" · The 1985 Lansur United team had the smallest possible squad. In fact, we had our regular starting eleven and a single sub; and that sub hardly ever saw playing time. For a while a promising young midfielder,

Clive "Kai" Daniels, was our number 12, but he quickly tired of not getting a game and became a second-team stalwart. Eventually Nontjies, sometime Christian fundamentalist, sometime Rasta, full-time irascible, took the role of substitute, and he thrived on it, now and then coming off the bench to save us with a goal. With Nontjies—I swear, it took me years to remember that his proper name is Jeremiah Shiri—you never got just a goal. Instead, Nontjies would give you a spectacular slaloming effort, opposition defenders sprawling in his wake. In retrospect, we should have used him more—or that might have blunted his effectiveness; I'm not sure which. He never seemed entirely happy on the bench, but neither was he too keen to start. A hard man to figure; what I remember most about him was that he was really close to Bags.

The 1985 Lansur team took on all comers; and, more often than not, we beat them. One weekend, within twenty-four hours, we mauled (as recounted earlier) Spurs 5–2 on Saturday and then beat high-flying Premier United 2–0. That Premier game—it was on a Sunday in August—is probably the best game that Lansur played in that season.

In fact, it may be the best game any Lansur team I've been on ever played. It was one of those days. No, it was possibly *the* day. We were just on. Our passing was crisp, our defending sure as Aarie, Sailor, and I protected the defense, which looked impregnable. Between the midfield and the defense, with Wakes and Lynnie putting in a real shift upfront, we kept the Premier attackers firmly under wraps. I do not recall Aalee having a save to make all day.

Such was our mood. Like a good team in its pomp, we took our chances clinically. Aarie worked the ball wide, crossed it, and it required only a nudge from the perfectly positioned (as always) Wakes to direct one past the Premier keeper. That typical Wakes goal and a driving finish from Pung, a right-footed shot executed with authority following a strong run, sealed a game that had never been in doubt.

Throughout that game between the top two teams in Hanover Park, we held our shape, and our discipline was impeccable. In hindsight, that may have been our peak. It is undoubtedly one of the two best team performances of my career. The way we played that day, we could have beaten whoever lined up against us. However, what stands out most for me about that game, these many years later, is how calm we were. We were absolutely in control of both the game and of ourselves. In my experience, such calm, discipline, and control are rare. For some teams, and I've played on a few of those, it never happens. I played in the Western Province's Virginia Super League (where the elite sides played) with Premier United (also of Hanover Park) for two seasons, and only once, and that in defeat, did I even come close to experiencing anything like that August 1985 Lansur moment. That Premier game was against the middle-class Thornhill United, and we battled hard that night under the lights at Athlone Stadium before succumbing to a 1–0 defeat. (Athlone Stadium, massively improved, was one of the Cape Town stadia used in 2010 when South Africa hosted the World Cup. None of us could have imagined such a thing in our playing days.)

LANSUR'S FIRST TRACKSUITS · Between June and October 1985, I can recall us losing only two games. Of those two games, only one was of consequence. It was a cup final loss on the first Sunday in October to Leeds United. It was one of those games that we lost despite having bossed the game. We were a little profligate. Aalee missed a penalty; I hit the bar with a strong header. Worse, I did poorly with the rebound, aiming a weak short straight at the keeper. And, to be perfectly honest, we were a little cocky (and just a little spent) after having beaten that same Leeds team just twenty-four hours earlier, in another cup final.

In the opening twenty minutes of that Saturday "Knockout Final," the first in Lansur United history, we were just slightly off the pace. It was a big deal for the club, that final. In honor of that final, we'd raised funds to buy new tracksuits with the club's name emblazoned across the back—"Lansur United A.F.C."—and our names were stitched on the front left chest. What's more, we got to choose exactly how we wanted our names represented. Shahied's read "Pung," Wakes preferred "Wazi," and I opted for "G.F."

On the Friday evening before the final, we met at the clubhouse to try on our maroon-and-white tracksuits. For a club in its infancy, for a bunch of working-class boys who took such pride in their club, it was a moving moment, one to be treasured. We were, proudly, the only club in HPFA to date to have our own personalized sweats. Things like that don't happen every day.

Of that 1985 team, only Mike and I were students. Everyone else worked, mainly engaged in "manual labor," as the contemporary phrasing would have had it. Wakes and Hamat worked at one of the local hospitals (Groote Schuur), following in their father Abraham Duncan's footsteps. Wakes was a porter, and Hamat worked in the machine shop, as did Sailor, maintaining hospital equipment. Pung worked as a panel beater's assistant; Aalee was a delivery driver; Lynnie was employed in a factory near to downtown Cape Town; and for the life of me I had no idea what line of work Gietzman was in. (Nor did I make much effort to find out.) Brother and Aarie had clerical jobs at UCT, though I am sure Brother's was of a more technically advanced nature than Aarie's.

In terms of the work most township footballers did, we were little different from our parents. Hanover Park was a working-class township and as such most of its residents performed jobs in the menial sector of the economy in and around the area. The men among them our fathers, brothers, uncles, nephews, almost all our friends (all my friends), worked in "manual labor." They worked construction jobs (known as the "building industry"), and they worked in factories, as did many of the women, who were employed in the garment, linen, or shoe industries. At the northwestern fringes of Hanover Park, in an area called Lansdowne Industrial, was a cluster of factories where these women, and some men, worked. In the morning you would see the women on their way to work, and in the evenings you watched them tread, weary, back home. Except for Fridays, payday and the last day of the working week—then they had a pep in their step and smiles on their faces. Some women, such as my mother, worked in clerical jobs downtown, or they worked as cashiers at supermarkets in Cape Town or in one of Cape Town's southern suburbs, the predominantly white southern suburbs with names such as Claremont, Wynberg, and Mowbray.

Many of the older generation of men in the "building industry" were assistants to (mainly but by no means exclusively) white artisans. They did the backbreaking work for qualified carpenters, bricklayers, electricians, mechanics, roofers, and the like. Some guys from the townships worked as messengers (they were called, regardless of their age, "messenger boys"), delivering mail to the post office in Cape Town, or delivering packages from one company in Cape Town to another. One or two players, I remember one from Leeds distinctly (a guy called "Aapie," a talented winger), worked as a garbage collector. His nickname, known to all in the township, was a mildly derisive one: he was called "Brommer," after a breed of fly that is notorious for being big and nasty and is to be found only around garbage. There were, of course, a fair number of unemployed in our ranks, guys who just stood around the small shops, the equivalent of bodegas, shooting the breeze for the better part of the day and hoping for a break. A few guys worked in the informal sector, selling fruit and vegetables, and some dealt weed and drugs or sold liquor illegally.

People held on to these menial jobs, the only ones available to township residents who hadn't graduated from high school. It was the norm, the prospects of transcending out of these ranks almost nonexistent. Very few of us dreamed of careers, which required higher education, professional training, and appointments holding out the prospect of advancement. For that, we looked around and saw few people with jobs in the post office, and sprinkled in here and there were a few teachers. They, however, were the exception. I understand those exceptions better now.

No matter. The discrepancies in our educational achievements, our employment opportunities or lack thereof, notwithstanding, regardless of what language you spoke, on the football field everyone was equal. What is more, anyone with pretenses to imagining themselves even a little superior was treated roughly, cut down to size ruthlessly—if not by your teammates then certainly by the opposition. On the football field there was only one currency. Either you could play or you couldn't; there it didn't matter what language you spoke. If you couldn't play, whatever language you spoke or whatever degree of education you had wasn't worth a stitch; if you could play, you could speak whatever language you wanted. I made sure I earned the right to speak English.

**LANSUR'S FIRST TROPHY** · On the day of the "Knockout Final," Lansur, for all the sparkling form with which we had come into the game, lacked our usual rhythm and poise. We started slowly, finding ourselves trailing 1–0, deservedly, after about twenty minutes to a hard, uncompromising Leeds team. Our passes were, uncharacteristically, going astray, the midfield wasn't clicking, and we were a little careless at the back. Uncharacteristically, Wakes was just a step late up front, Lynnie let a ball or two get away from him, and Pung was not dominating the defense. Into this mise-en-scène stepped Sailor. He did something that far exceeded changing the outcome of the game, as important as that was to us. He did something I will never forget. In so doing, Sailor etched himself into my consciousness forever.

Sailor proceeded to score the best goal ever in the history of Hanover Park football. I have no trouble asserting this despite having not played or watched football in the township since 1993. However, as you will see, I have good historical reason for my confidence.

It was cup final day, and there were plenty of spectators in attendance to watch the last weekend of football for the 1985 season. This was the culmination of the season's play, the first team game (every club also had a second team, but that game had little status, except for the players and clubs involved, of course) that pitted newly constituted Lansur United (from the west end of the township) against one of Hanover Park's more established clubs, Leeds (from the southeast end of the township). Our styles were distinctly different. They were, like their English namesake, a rugged bunch, with plenty of experience, to say nothing of their strength (their center forward, John, was a handful) and speed up front (in both their left winger, "Leiman," and their right winger, Aapie) could turn on the jets, but we had Mike and Gietzman to counter them.

We were young, we were a passing team, and we were a tightly knit unit. We'd reached that point in the season when we were not quite telepathic in our anticipating each other's moves, but we had a very good idea of what each of us was inclined to do. Except we just couldn't find our groove, and Leeds wasn't giving an inch.

With Leeds leading, Sailor, by turns a flashy player and committed team man, picked up the ball on the left flank, a few meters inside the touchline, some forty meters out, at about a thirty-degree angle to the Leeds goal. The crowd, pressed tight to the touchline, watched carefully, but without any sense of the momentous goal to come. Sailor jinked inside his defender, leaving him about five meters in from the touchline. Sailor had done this a few times that season, so no one was either surprised or unduly impressed. Little did we know what was about to transpire. I wonder if Sailor did. In any case, he was in the mood, and he sensed an opening as he switched the ball from his left foot to his stronger right one.

Once the ball was on his right foot, Sailor had no hesitation. He hit a screamer of a shot. The ball struck, thunderously, the underside of the Leeds crossbar and just crashed into the net. I recall the reverberations from the collision between ball and woodwork. It was, literally, a matter of seconds from the moment Sailor picked up the ball on the left to when it nestled in the back of the net. In that brief interlude, the Leeds goalkeeper had not moved an inch. Sailor left him mesmerized. We, the Lansur players and spectators, we were ecstatic. The Leeds players looked on in disbelief. I can't say I blamed them.

We all raced toward Sailor, amazed at the goal he'd just scored. Even Aalee, who had to run almost eighty meters from his goal to where Sailor now stood enveloped by all the outfield players, embraced him wildly. This was the absolute euphoria of "being-with," of "being-together-with-one-another." It is entirely possible that only sport and politics can provide such moments in which the intensity of 'being-with" overwhelms everything else.

For my part, I'd had a bird's-eye view, positioned right next to Sailor as I was in the center of the park. I'd been able, no, privileged, to watch it unfold.

At our thirtieth reunion, I told the story of that goal, and all of us who were there became, for a minute, a little misty-eyed. Rightly so; it was a special goal, one for the ages, one that stood the test of time—thirty years and counting.

In fact, in the glorious moment of the actual goal, Sailor transported me to another time, another place, a place I'd, as yet, never seen, but one I'd read about and watched on film. That is because, if only for an instant, I thought, when the ball went into the net, "Sailor's done a Geoff Hurst," recalling the England striker's famous—and controversial, in Germany's account, anyway—second goal in the 1966 World Cup final at Wembley Stadium in London. Hurst got a hat trick in that final, the last two coming in extra time after England and Germany were level at 2–2 at the end of time. On July 30, 1966, there was a lot of talk about whether or not Hurst's shot, which first hit the underside of the crossbar (like Sailor's), had crossed the line after beating the German keeper, Hans Tikowski. The linesman, Tofiq Bahramov (from Azerbaijan, then still part of the USSR), and the referee, Gottfried Dienst (Switzerland), did not speak a common language, and so it took a moment before Bahramov signaled "goal" to Gottfried.[25] The Germans protested, to no avail, and Hurst, who scored his third in the final minute of extra time, became the first footballer to score a hat trick in a World Cup final. (A feat only emulated in 2015, when the United States' Carli Lloyd scored a hat trick in the women's World Cup final in Canada.)

So now, I hope, the reason for my confidence is evident. When you make like Geoff Hurst did in a World Cup final, you're pretty much guaranteed the best damn goal ever in the history of Hanover Park football. When you make like Geoff Hurst, you reduce to nothing what is, what should be, *entre-nous* between a World Cup final hat trick and a spectacular goal in the Hanover Park Football Association Knockout final. There is so much that stands between these two moments, the magnitude and international import and reverberation of one, and the infinitesimal significance of the other. So much is *entre-nous,* but for a moment, in one player's mind, it is nothing, nothing, *niks, nada,* stands between. In that moment, nothing can disarticulate Wembley 1966 from Hanover Park 1985. For one moment, football makes it possible to "be-with" in the most expansive, incorporative historic sense.

Sailor's goal won the game for us, 3–1. You don't come back from a goal like that, and Leeds had no chance. We knew it, they knew it. I was playing opposite Gunny (not to be confused with Chris Lewis, of Young Pirates fame), their central midfielder, and when Sailor scored that goal, Gunny's face just dropped. He put his hands on his hips and trudged wearily back to their side of the field to resume the match. It was game over. All the time that remained on the clock—and there was plenty—the result was a mere formality.

"NOG LANSUR! NOG LANSUR!" · It took our fans a moment to realize what had happened. And then they erupted: *"Nog Lansur!" "Nog Lansur!"* The chant echoed around the A field of the HPFA ground. *"Nog Lansur!" "Nog Sailor!"* our fans cried. A player or two might have done the same. That, I regret to say, I can neither confirm nor deny. Now I wish that I'd been paying attention.

*"Nog Lansur!"* It is a difficult phrase to translate. It is difficult to translate it not only from Afrikaans into English, but into—as—Afrikaans itself. Technically, it means, very simply, "More Lansur!" (As well as, in this case, a salute to the goal scorer: "More Sailor!") However, being thus rendered in English denudes the phrase of its local resonance, so much so that any translation does the phrase no justice. Better to leave it as it is and to settle for a description of it. The phrase is, to be as precise as I possibly can be, at once an injunction, a cajoling, and an exhortation. This makes it, all in all, a tribal shout in the way that football fans align themselves with a club. As in, say, the way that Liverpool FC fans regard our anthem "You'll Never Walk Alone" or chant *"Allez, Allez, Allez."* *"Nog Lansur!"* means, by turns, "We are Lansur!," a mark of pride; it means, "C'mon Lansur!" encouraging the players to improve their performance, to score a desperately needed goal, to relieve defensive pressure; it means "Great goal, Sailor!"; it means "Lansur has done it one more time!" It means, quite simply, when its very definition, its resonances, are anything but simple: "We are Lansur."

Through this chant, our fans, mainly women (a collected assortment of wives headed by Shaheeda, girlfriends, neighbors, and friends) and a few guys (friends, the odd younger or older brother, uncles, neighbors) were saying to our opponents (and their fans): Look at us, in our maroon and white strip. Look at us, we (the royal "we," fans and players alike, because, among ourselves, in the changing room, at practice, on the field, "*Nog Lansur!*" was often our rallying call) are Lansur: fear us. I doubt we inspired fear in our opponents. Most of the players on the various teams lived near one another, knew each other, and were generally friendly with one another, so no one was too intimidated by anyone else.

Mostly, what "*Nog Lansur!*" did inspire was a sense of solidarity and, I must add, joy. It was fun to play football for Lansur with such dedicated and raucous backing from the sidelines, to hear our opponents' being barracked by our merry band of loyalists. As a player you'd sometimes hear an especially sharp quip or witty putdown from our fans. Then there was nothing to do but smile and enjoy the moment. The mischief of what is *entre-nous*.

So intensely identified with our club did the phrase become that eventually we players would greet each other with it, or we'd use it on the pitch when we needed a kick up the pants or when we just wanted to support each other. Aalee might say to Aarie, "*Nog Lansur!, my broer* [brother], *Nog Lansur!*" As a phrase, it's a much more poetic way of saying "C'mon!" to a teammate. "*Nog Lansur!*" became, in the most public and poetic way, our most public private code. It was our pledge of loyalty to each other.

However, it was also, in a township dominated by sameness (same jobs, same prospects, same outlooks on life; all of the married players on our team married women from Hanover Park; all the single guys dated women who lived in the streets around them; and so on), our preferred *Nog* was more than a form of greeting. It was a linguistic ("tribal") means of marking difference. We were staking a claim, albeit a precarious one, to our singularity, marking ourselves off from everybody else; if only for the duration of the game, if only in our regular encounters with players from other teams, we had produced—coined a phrase, trademarked a greeting, patented a form of exchange—that was ours, exclusively ours. "*Nog Lansur!*" encoded a language that worked to instill solidarity among us. It was a language sui generis. It was, and it remains, I learned thirty years later, a language that spoke of a commitment that bound us to each other. That, I have learned many times over, binds us still. It is what it means for us to be-with each other; to be bound, from that moment to this, and beyond, to each other. To be bound across the Atlantic, across the various divides, social, educational, to each other. In, and through, the phrase *"Nog Lansur!"* it is possible to discern the "singular plurality" of our "community." Furthermore, I would insist that it is about the "community" as such, the community that is constituted of players, the team, as such, administrative officials, spectators, family members. *Nog*: more than the team; *Nog*, all of us, together. Not, of course, by any means on the order of FC Barcelona's *"Som més que un Club"* (More than a club),[26] but produced out of very much the same sociopolitical sentiment. No one, least of all me, wants to "get out" of such an entangled set of relations.

    I recognized the veracity of this bond over the years. During my annual visits to Hanover Park, I grasped, however tentatively, the expansive and incorporative nature of Lansur United as a "singular plural being." When I drop in to see Pung now, we will say to each other, without fail, half in jest, half in absolute seriousness, *"Nog Lansur, my broer. Nog Lansur."* However, I felt the full communal effect of that bond, of its sustenance, the power of its resonance, and its affective force only when I addressed my teammates and our supporters at that thirtieth reunion. I knew then what *"Nog Lansur!"* meant. It had shaped all of us, me no less than others, and had created an unbreakable union among us. I know this because of how it survived in me, whole, intensified, alive, more than twenty years after I'd last seen all my teammates, almost twenty-five years after we'd played our final game together.

    *"Nog Lansur!"* has survived my deracination because it is, in the most constitutive, sustaining sense, what is *entre-nous*. Full of life, marked by the desire for a "plural singularity," and always inflected with a soupçon of mischief. It had altered hardly at all despite my graduate education, my professorial appointments in the United States. Only a language grounded in footballing truth has that kind of staying power, possesses the stamina and resonance to reanimate itself without fail, without prompting, after more than two decades. Through *"Nog Lansur!"* it becomes possible to always return, refuting, if only for a single instance, the logic of the diaspora that insists that return is, as I have argued elsewhere, impossible. It is also an object lesson in the politics of *entre-nous*: never underestimate the sustaining power of what is between you, what constitutes—again, and again, through relation separation, separation relation—the truth of "being singular plural."

THIRTY YEARS LATER, AN EMAIL · *Ce qui ne cesse pas de nepas s'écrire.*
(What doesn't stop being written.) —— JACQUES LACAN

One morning in October 2015, as I said, there was a message in the inbox of my email account. I did a double take, but, yes, I was not misreading the words in the subject line. It read: *"Nog Lansur."* Hard as it was to believe, after decades, here was this call to me. (I played my last game for Lansur in September 1992, and not even at Die Veld, I regret to say, but at the Vygieskraal Ground, about four miles from Hanover Park. I do remember that we won, 2–1, and I played at right back, wearing, uncharacteristically, the number 13 shirt. I practiced with the club only in the early months of 1993 before returning to New York to work on my dissertation.) Here was this call to me: addressed directly to me, to the footballer I'd once been. Within moments, it seemed, everything—the games, the goals, the camaraderie, those long ago Tuesday and Thursday night training sessions in the cold and wet of a Cape Flats winter—came rushing back at me.

All the names, all those players I'd taken the field with while playing for Lansur, were once more real, immanent, transporting me across the miles and years, taking me some eight thousand miles from my study in upstate New York back to Hanover Park. Entirely different worlds, apartheid South Africa, circa 1985, and Ithaca, a bucolic American college town in 2015, brought together by that phrase that had lived so full a life in me, a life I was not even fully aware I was incubating and nurturing, for decades, it turns out. Again, nothing, for a moment, stands *entre-nous*.

A lifetime ago I wore number 7 for Lansur United of Hanover Park.

Turns out it wasn't quite so long ago. I replied to Shaheeda, recapitulating what seemed to me like Lansur's entire history. I asked after Wakes, Mike, Aalee, Aarie, and Pung. (Wakes and Aarie are her brothers-in-law.)

Turns out Jane, my wife, and Ezra, our seven-year-old, were planning to go to Cape Town for the Christmas holidays. Keep me informed, Shaheeda insists, so that we can have a reunion. I muse on this prospect, smile, but never imagine that it can become a reality.

My study is a predictable space. There are books, pictures of our kids, pictures of my nieces and nephews, a few pieces of art, and there, in front of me just to my right, is a framed picture from my playing days. Three photographs from when I was with Premier United, and, at the top, two—one in black-and-white, the other in color—of that 1985 team.

When I show Ezra the Lansur photographs, he can't pick me out. I realize then that thirty years makes you unrecognizable, even to your own kid. We were young then, in those photographs. Occasionally while I am working, I glance at that picture and I smile. I remember. How I remember. How often I've wondered where my teammates are. My life and theirs, how the years have separated us, how those photographs bind us. Bind me. That is what strikes me when I look at those photos after I've written Shaheeda. Somewhere, in my head, maybe many, many times, I've written that email, I've made Lacan's point. For me Lansur is "what doesn't stop being written." I return through writing. Through writing, I am alive. *Entre-nous*. I remain at a distance through writing, writing that cannot be characterized as memoir because it is too fragmentary for that. Nor is it social history, because it is too episodic, partisan, and epigrammatic, too personal, too much Lansur, for that. It is not political philosophy, because it is too interspersed with cultural recounting, too sustained and founded upon the discourse of football, for that.

It may be that, as Springsteen says, it is a form of dialectic address: "I didn't want out. I wanted in. I didn't want to erase, escape, forget or reject. I wanted to understand."[27] There is truth in Springsteen's declaration, his writing to Freehold, New Jersey: in the determination to write in order to understand, no one genre is sufficient. To "get in," you have to write through all these genres, from memoir to social history to political philosophy. To write, then, as Foucault says of philosophy, as the "struggle for truth." Diamond hard, unadorned, truth in all its difficulty, angst, pain, and, indeed, joy—the unadulterated joy of memory.

It is for this reason that what emerges here, in this "Interlude," situated awkwardly, improperly, even, between Messi and Luis Suárez/Óscar Washington Tabárez, is the connective tissue that is *écriture*. What is *entre-nous* is what holds (the self, the deep need to be-with-the-other, with-one-another) us together, is what holds this project together. It is a writing about three figures from two adjoining countries, Argentina and Uruguay, held together by the writing of a faraway amateur football team in which, through which, because of which the world was opened up. It is the refusal of identity (South African, coloured, Argentine, Catalan, and so on) as a political limit. This is what it means, as Coates phrases it in one moment of direct address to his son (Samori), to be a "conscious citizen of this terrible and beautiful world."[28] Between the (black US) citizen and the world, everything; between the disenfranchised (noncitizen) of apartheid and the world, everything, and then some; between the citizen, the noncitizen, and the world, nothing, absolutely nothing.

As such, to refuse (apartheid's legal strictures and its geopolitical limits) and to stake a claim, however tentatively, for "global citizenship," this "Interlude" constitutes an attempt to mobilize a provisional, dialectical (local/diasporic; national/global; apartheid/postapartheid; South Africa/America), sense of self. The "Interlude" offers such a dialectical self as that force operative within the community and within the self that seeks, above all, not to limit the self to itself. This "Interlude" is a writing against limit, a writing that will abide any strictures. It is a blanket rejection of (apartheid; diasporic) limit. It writes instead as fidelity to the experience of "being-with" as, a priori, already containable within itself. It follows, in this way, Nancy's argument that "existence can only be grasped in the paradoxical simultaneity of togetherness (anonymous, confused, and indeed massive) and disseminated singularity."[29] The "singularity" of a Messi, a Suárez, or a Tabárez is indeed precisely that: infinitely singular. However, the ability, and the need (to "understand," as Springsteen rightly reminds us) that "singularity" bears the traces of a multiplicity that begins, for *Entre-Nous*, in a place, Hanover Park, where such "plurality," where the prospect of such a "disseminated singularity," was forbidden by law.

*Entre-nous*, as such, marks the determination to make of the space between a place for thinking from that which is, on the face of it, the World Cup. That is, a major sports tournament featuring professional footballers who could be admired only from a battered but vibrant township on the Cape Flats; the World Cup as negation, then, in that it marks the denial of the possibility of "being singular plural" for amateur footballers from Hanover Park. *Entre-Nous* writes from the desire to "be-with" from that place where the prospect of "being-with-the-other" is most stringently denied. *Entre-Nous* seeks to understand what it might be like to "be-with." As such, *Entre-Nous* is a letter crafted in love that is addressed to Messi, to Suárez, and to Tabárez. It inscribes, this letter, a love that is entirely indistinct from their love for this game. Such a writing can, if only for a moment, make naught of what is *entre-nous*. That is because there is now, for a moment, nothing *entre-nous*, it becomes possible to forge a bond between the amateur township footballer and the international superstar, because we can now draw an affective line between a ragtag collection of coloured young men, Lansur United AFC circa 1985, and Lionel Messi, possibly the very best player that the game has ever known. As such, *Entre-Nous* is an introduction to the love that is within, *entre le moi et le moi-même*, within every player. Even those players, maybe especially those aging (former) amateur footballers, who can now only recount faded glories. It is, above all else, to "think football," to "say within language what language does not say."[30] To think what is "written" *Sous rature*.

That address to language, to think language into "saying what it does not say," began, I realize, long before that email from Shaheeda arrived over the transom, to use the language of techne. Having replied to Shaheeda, I notice that I signed my email, as I sign all my other emails (except to my daughter, there I use "Dad"), "gf." Small letters, but still, recognizable as/in the "G.F." that adorned my tracksuit jacket in October 1985. I recognize in my signature a certain "stability," a marker of self that makes me eternally legible to Shaheeda and to all my old teammates. I remain legible, in part, of course, because of technology, but also because I have retained my identifying mark, have remained true to it. A truth, as it were, grounded in a place distinctly different from the one from which I respond to Shaheeda. I am so easy to find, it requires little, for those who played football with me, or watched me play football, to find me, no matter where I am in the world. No matter where I am in the world I will heed the call of *"Nog Lansur!"*

Is this the sign, the address that is also a clarion call that is untranslatable, that mediates, that ameliorates, the psychopolitical tension between return and remove? Is this the sign to which the diasporized always write? Is this how love survives? Is this the direction in which all diasporic writing inclines, in the direction of *entre-nous*?

INVITATION TO THE REUNION · On the morning of Friday, December 18, I drive my mother to Hanover Park so that she can collect her medication at the local "day hospital" (a satellite medical facility built during apartheid to service the disenfranchised communities). After I drop her, I visit our old neighborhood. Opposite Etosha Court there is garbage, burnt, black, strewn all over the place, papers and plastic bags fluttering in the early summer breeze, broken glass, people evincing nothing so much as a "quiet desperation," in Billy Joel's phrasing. (The opening lines of Joel's "Everybody has a dream" goes, "While in these days of quiet desperation / As I wander through the world in which I live."³¹) The end of apartheid came more than twenty years ago, but here, in Hanover Park, life seems no better. I notice that there are no kids playing on a sandy patch where we contested many a fierce battle. The Summit Primary asphalt that was our old pitch has long since been torn up. Of it, nothing remains. This is the community where I grew up, and as such I cannot fathom the deterioration in the neighborhood's physical structure. It has the feel of a community that is, if not abandoned, then certainly beaten down by postapartheid life. I am forced to acknowledge, if only to myself, that it is markedly worse than when I lived and played here.

There are still teams active in Hanover Park, but the organizing structure, HPFA, I am told by old Lansur players, Charlie Theunis (a fleet-footed right back) and Steven "Scarra" Swartz (a talented midfielder who had bad luck with injuries), no longer exists. Much like Lansur United, too, no longer exists, except in our spirit and in our memory. No, it is alive — in glorious fragments, in shattered wholes — in our very beings, collective and individual.

I check in on the Duncans and cast a quick glance at our old house, number 61 Athwood Road. Scarra and his family bought the house from mine almost twenty years ago (in 1998), and the Swartzes have spruced it up nicely. 61 Athwood Road is, mercifully, I tell myself, unrecognizable.

However, everywhere around it, with few exceptions, there is squalor and, friends such as Scarra tell me, violence, gangs, drugs. Things have come to such a point, Scarra remarks sadly, that his own son is now, in his words, a "gangster." *"Ek het hom uit gesit,"* "I put him out of the house," Scarra tells me, his voice a mix of regret and determination — this was not an easy decision for him as a father, but he sees no other option.

On a previous visit I had parked outside the Duncans, and when Scarra appears to greet me he won't let me walk alone from his house to Charlie's in Etosha Court, a distance of less than a hundred meters. Scarra goes with me and we lament what has become of our neighborhood.

Later in the afternoon of the 18th I return to Hanover Park to pick up my mother.

I stop by Lansur Road, in front of "Pung's" house, out of habit. I see a group of guys hanging out there and I ask if Pung is home. No, they say. Then one of them recognizes me, and I know, after a minute's hesitation (it feels longer), who it is. It's Saleem Amerdien. Saleem, Wakes, Aarie, Hamat, and I grew up together. Like many a decent township footballer, Saleem got waylaid — drugs, which led to a stint in prison; he is unemployed now, thin, no doubt a consequence of his lifestyle. The Amerdiens lived at 67 Athwood Road, just three houses down from my family's.

Then, the strangest thing, the damn strangest thing, I tell you. In his hand Saleem has a whole stack of invitations to the Lansur United "Reunion Disco Party." And then the denouement: "The reunion's for you," he says. To prove it, he points to the invitation and there it is, in a blend of Afrikaans and English: *"Kom geniet die aand saam met Grant Fared [sic] en sy family all the way from the USA."* ("Come and enjoy the evening with . . .") I am moved. I don't know what to say, so I just listen to Saleem give me directions to the event that is being held in my honor.

THE REUNION · Three decades later, we are gathered here in Rocklands, in the hall of the school where Shaheeda now teaches kids how to use computers and Hamat, parked outside the school gates, sells school supplies, fruit, and assorted snacks to the schoolkids and passersby. As Jane, Ezra, and I walk in, I immediately see Aalee and Hamat talking together, flanked by Shaheeda; there in a corner is Brother. There are a few supporters. I introduce Jane and Ezra, hug folks, and then the talk immediately turns to football. 1985 could have been yesterday.

We're the only four of the '85 team that is in attendance, me included. The spine of the team, I tell myself: goalkeeper, central defenders, central midfielder.

Within a few minutes, however, other players, their families, and supporters drift in.

About half an hour into the event, Shaheed "Puppets" Arendse, no relation to Pung, Aalee and I find ourselves in a cluster. Jane and Ezra—who has his face buried in his iPad—sit next to me. Puppets, who married, had two kids, and who now lives in a middle-class neighborhood, looks at Jane, reprimands everyone else (in Afrikaans) for not engaging her, and then begins to talk to her in English. I am touched.

Most of the Lansur folks here tonight do not, for reasons that I outlined earlier, speak English. In fact, on the '85 I am the only one who spoke English as a first language. (Mike and Brother had a more than passing command of the language, but it was by no means their preferred tongue. I was the minority, more than happy to switch linguistic codes.) Puppets is proficient, and he makes conversation with Jane. I am grateful for how solicitous he is. We always got along well, he and I. In fact, it was Puppets and not Hamat who called me to tell me of Mr. Dirks's passing.

Seeing Puppets draw Jane out, I am reminded of how close Puppet and Cavakes were, old Pirates boys both. They were both at home with Lansur, but they came together from somewhere else, and that bond has endured, has endured death. Puppets takes the lead in our reminiscences about Cavakes, and he speaks of his old friend with a gentle dignity. It feels right to come to Cavakes through Puppets. He knew him not only longest but best.

After Jane and Ezra have left, the talk among Puppets, Aalee, and I turns to the issue of speaking English in the home. Both of them have moved out of Hanover Park and married women who speak, irony of ironies, English as a first language. As a result, both of them (they each have two kids) find themselves in a household where their kids were raised to speak English. Now, as Aalee says, *"Ek is die einigste een in die familie wat Afrikaans praat"* ("I am the only one in the family who speaks Afrikaans") *"Ek oek"* ("Me too"), says Puppets. I laugh quietly.

In all the time I played for Lansur, I was teased incessantly, and mostly good naturedly, for speaking English, for being the only one to speak English as a first language. English, it was the language of education, the language of the educated. I knew then that I was marked by it, and it is only now, these decades later, that I am fully comfortable with it. My moniker used to be "Die Engelsman" ("The Englishman"). As such, I now understand that language is not, following Nancy, about "speaking about itself, but penetrating in itself."[32] We have, in our discursive turn to language, "penetrated" to a truth, "penetrated" to this truth through a passage that runs, to my quiet delight and surprise (history has thrown "Die Engelsman" a linguistic bone) through the language that once marked my separation. English assumes, under the realities of our lives, a new status. What once separated us, kept our singularities singular, has now mutated into a relation built on the grounds of what previously separated us. Now, although we do not say it, or maybe do not realize, but we are now—Aalee, Puppets, and I—forging a new relation through separation; our apartness is grounded in what was once singular but is now shared, the singular (English) that has made a plurality of us. We arrived separated, we leave separated, but not, no longer, from each other; at least not as it pertains to the ways in which language has made a new relation among us possible. We have become Hegelian beings insofar as we are "capable of containing and enduring [our] own contradictions as subjects"; we are "constituting our own finitude," a finitude whose proper name is the (plural) singularity of English as a lingua franca.[33] As such, we give life to Nancy's notion that the "self that negates itself, instead of coming back to itself, throws itself into the other, and wills itself as the other."[34] Aalee and Puppets have indeed been made to "will themselves as the other," willing themselves into the other—wife, son, daughter—through the negation that is their first, their familiar, their ontological, language. Afrikaans has been negated, and then spoken as a negation to that self who was once "other" and has now been made, by love, marriage, fatherhood, 'other' to itself.

This is how history works, making my teammates other, making of them minorities, linguistic outsiders, in their own homes. A part of me takes just a little pleasure in their discomfiture. However, I can tell, they're also proud of the fact that their kids speak English rather than Afrikaans. They know, they understand, it is the lingua franca of the present, and the future. If their kids are proficient in a language they once made fun of, then they will, in the hurly-burly that is postapartheid life, stand a better chance of surviving, maybe even thriving, economically, socially . . . English gives them the best shot at a better life. Aalee and Puppets both want that for their kids. We have, every one one of us here at the reunion, made our way in the world. We've all grown up, had to grow up, had to adjust to new realities. Puppets and Aalee have done it best, far as I can see. I am proud of my teammates, proud of how they are now in the world.

Finally, it seems, through the thicket of language, because of our struggles with language, we have moved beyond our past as footballers. For this I am grateful. I wonder now if they were too, in that moment?

For them, that their children are fluent in English, speak it as their first language, dream in it, signifies as a mark of progress. They have, as we all have, left something of Hanover Park behind. Tonight, we are able to recall our past without being held hostage to it. It is possible to talk, as friends, and not just as teammates. Lansur made this possible, yes, but we are also refusing the limits that it might have imposed on us. It is probably time to recognize that we were held together by something other than, more than, football. There is something in that, something worth taking the trouble to understand. *Entre-nous*: it demands a declarative: between-us is not only football. Between us was not only mischief and insouciance, football triumphs and defeats, training sessions and dreams of an impossible footballing glory. Such an insight can be gained only postfootball, after all the football has been played, as it were.

For Aalee and Puppets, the language in which their children live is, for them, an accomplishment to be savored, and as such it is something to be shared with me in the act of catching up. We're all Hanover Park boys, here to celebrate our time in the township, but we are also here to note what we've done with our lives. A new thread of connection has been forged among us. Now there is something else within, *entre le moi et le moi-même*, and among, *entre-nous*, the three of us.

Through this thread of connection we have made it possible to understand that we are no longer held hostage by language, that we are not condemned by the languages of our past. The pluralities of our various singularities make themselves manifest. It is good to know that we are not condemned, and I mean this in the best possible sense, to be *only* Lansur United players. However, I then recognize that we are able to produce this post–*"Nog Lansur!"* language, this more than Lansur language, only because we are Lansur United players. Through Lansur, moving through and because of *"Nog Lansur!,"* we are no longer condemned—contained, restrained, held back, held hostage to, held within, held by—the language(s) that once defined us, the languages we once "gave" to each other.

The work of "getting out" is discrimination. That is, recognizing that an absolute disconnection from the place in question—the place of origin, Hanover Park, West Baltimore, Chicago's South Side, and so on—is an impossibility. What remains to be done then is to discern, fully cognizant that all decisions made in this regard are a fraught business (that regret might follow as easily as relief), just how much of this place, how much of this time in one's life, is constitutive, and can under no circumstances be eschewed or sloughed off. Equally important, however, is the ability to understand what it is that can be, however provisional and painful (or, painless, as the case might be), left behind. That is, what it is that one is no longer condemned to be subject to, what it is that one is now free to leave in that place and time. That is, to recognize that while "getting out," in toto, is not possible, it matters just as much that one "get out" from under other stuff. To do otherwise is an act of indulgence, self-flagellation, and speaks of nothing so much as intellectual neglect. That is, the self has not done due diligence to the work of thinking its relations, all its relations, in sequence and in their singularity. The work of "getting out" depends entirely upon the veracity of the self's decision-making process. That is, undertaking properly the work of thinking relation.

Understood as such, relation stands as a bulwark against being condemned. All of us, no matter our language, our level of education, our aspirations or the lack thereof, were, a priori, condemned by apartheid to a certain future, a future that promised little and was intent on delivering less. That our futures negated those expectations, that it put a lie to the effects of apartheid's best efforts at destruction, is precisely what enabled Puppets, Aalee, and I (perhaps all of us gathered together, reunited) to have a heretofore unimaginable conversation.

It is because each of us have thought our "getting out" that we were able to make, if only for this evening, if only for this reunion, a language in which, through which, we can live as "more than" Lansur. Perhaps this is what it means, as Lacan says in his mischievous rendering of Freud's understanding of jouissance (as the "security of the rich") and sublimation (the "transformation of the sexual instinct into a work"), to have made a "success of the night, a success of the damned."[35] (In reading Freud, Lacan is using him to get a better grip on Sade's work.) Indeed, under the cover of night we have found something resuscitating, life-making, in our having been "damned." To have achieved such (a) "success" strikes me as no mean feat, to have made a language ("success") under the cover of night and to have found an unexpected pleasure (jouissance) in the language of the "damned."

In returning to each other in this reunion, in what has been a "successful night," we have also managed to turn toward something else, something that our playing together obscured. We were, none of us, ever *only* Lansur United footballers. In truth, it may be that it was in the pleasure of the "damned," out of the buried depths of the pleasure of the "damned" that we unearthed this new language, this new, direct, deeply saturated with the languages of our past, mode of address. Or it may be that finally, we are able to address each other in a more or less common language. And that, as Lacan says of Sade, is a wonderfully "scandalous" thing—we have just initiated an entirely surprising encounter with the limits and possibilities of our now shared, however unevenly, language; we are celebrants of our new relationship to the English language.[36]

It may be that only the night can make such a celebration possible, only under the cover of night, the night as the time of reunion, can such a language be forged. As footballers, as only footballers, we were too much creatures of the day and, as such, we were not free to create this bond among ourselves through the English language.

As such, our greatest debt is to the night. Such is the effect of, I am happy to report, the "accumulation of details." Still, in order to achieve this language, we needed to "transgress" our past, the only selves we (then, in the past) made available, articulable, to each other. In truth, what we needed to "transgress" for this new language—this English that now sits differently with us, that has now untied our tongues in relation to each other—to be born, was nothing other, nothing less than, our selves. The time of language moves, as it were, at its own pace. That is, we wonder about how many years (some three decades, it turns out) it takes to make, to attempt, a "transgression" of so intensely personal a nature. In agreeing to "transgress," we have made of ourselves language-forming creatures of the night; our "being-with" has assumed, has taken the form made possible by, another, a different temporality. Outside of our natural milieu, the football pitch or the practice ground, temporally out of joint (in the sense of Shakespeare's *Hamlet*), a more direct and linguistically honest, dare one say "authentic," bond has been forged. Out of a reunion, the precarious, precious, unity of the night, is produced a language that is shared, a language that holds its speakers in its thrall, in an intense relationship to each other, to the past, to the intensity of the present. This is what emerges out of the "accumulation of details." This, the nocturnal language of love; after all, do we not associate love more with the night than the day? Language itself is only possible, in this moment, when the "subject is cut loose from his psychosocial moorings."[37]

We have to be untethered into language, unmoored by language into the truth of *entre-nous*. We have to be made utterly vulnerable by our families, within the very bosom of our families; we have to remember our violent relationship to a language, how we used it as a weapon and a shield, and we have to relinquish that now in order for a sustainable, communicable, language to emerge into and as itself. Only then, only then. Only then a language that can bear truth.

MY OMISSION · Midway through the evening, Shaheeda calls for silence and recounts how the reunion came about. She asks me to say something. I thank her. I acknowledge our fans, who more than match the number of players in attendance. I offer a roll call of the 1985 team. I tell stories, some of them funnier than others, about that team.

However, in an important regard, I fail my audience. I am so overwhelmed by my memory of that 1985 team that I do not pay tribute to all the other Lansur players who are there. To Kai (Clive Daniels), whom I first coached as an under-sixteen player before we became teammates; to Charlie Theunis, the local fix-it man and the fastest forty-year-old right back I've ever seen, and as steady and consistent a teammate as one could hope for; to Puppets, a player so versatile he could play any position on the left—defense, midfield, attack. Or "Scarra"; I've sometimes wondered how his career might have unfolded had he not suffered those injuries. Or "Boeta" Marcus, a bullish central defender-cum-central midfielder. Or "Gert," whom I played with at Premier and who is every bit as versatile as Puppets, with a roguish streak to boot.

This is what I failed to say to them. As entrenched in my memory as that 1985 team is, Lansur United is the only club I've played for where everyone went out of their way to make a place for everyone else, both players and supporters. A township kid like me who loved football but spoke English was accommodated (and, yes, made fun of), a township kid like me who grew up with everyone and then moved away, far, far away, is welcomed back in the name of everyone else. Or whose name is invoked to bring everyone else back together, for one evening, in spirit if not in actuality. Lansur, as I learned in December 2015, was—and is—so much more than just that one team, a single iteration, that I so venerate. It is, indeed, more than just 1985, more than just those 1991 or 1992 sides I played on.

It might very well be that I have, by accident, hit upon the core meaning of "*Nog Lansur!*" It is more than—"*nog*"—than any single team. It is more than any single collection of players. The quality of "more than" speaks to unique ability of a working-class football club to have accommodated, made a place, for all of us. Me, I am very glad to say, included. It is in this way that I now understand how both our supporters' chant and Shaheeda's email was addressed to me: as part of the "more than."

"*Nog Lansur!*" Everything of political consequence, everything upon which the self turns, through which the self configures, reconfigures itself, which allows the self to be and to position itself in the world, is that which can understood through the relation that is separation. "*Nog Lansur!*" is, to fall prey to a contorted syntax so that a truth might be borne, might be written, everything out of which that which is *entre-nous* is made.

## CHAPTER TWO

### The Shame of Loving the Condemned | *The Philosophy of Óscar Washington Tabárez*

> To indulge for a moment, in any attempt at *thought*, is to be inevitably lost; for reflection but urges us to forbear, and *therefore* it is, I say, that we *cannot*. If there be no friendly arm to check us, or if we fail in a sudden effort to prostrate ourselves backward from the abyss, we plunge, and are destroyed.
> —— EDGAR ALLAN POE, "The Imp of the Perverse"

On Friday, June 27, 2014, the unthinkable became inevitable. It was inevitable that Óscar Washington Tabárez, the then-seventy-six-year-old coach of the Uruguay national team, would disappoint those of us who have admired him as that football man given to thought. In football, Tabárez is what Søren Kierkegaard names a "single individual," given to thinking in ways that far exceed his skill as a strategist, as a coach—*el técnico*—who plans for his team's victory. However, I hasten to add, he possesses a sharp, inventive, and, quite frankly, a liberating football mind. Like all exceptional coaches, Tabárez has achieved for himself a remarkable freedom. This former Uruguayan primary schoolteacher sees the game, and asks his players to perform, in a way that is unshackled from expectation without demeaning or ridiculing those who conform; he has nary a bad thing to say about his colleagues who bow to the pressure of expectation.

Like many successful coaches, Tabárez can boast only of an entirely unremarkable playing career, marked by peripatetic movement among Uruguay, Argentina, and a stint in Mexico. In the modern game, it is the retired player,

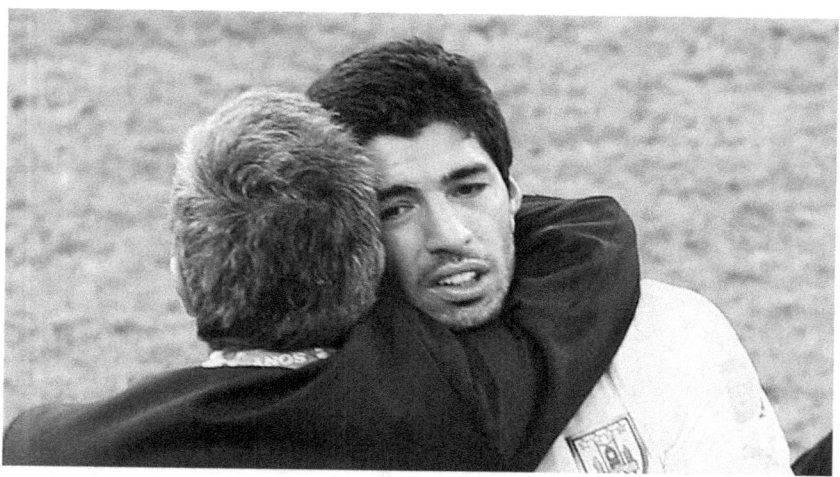

FIGURE 2.1 Suárez with Tabárez. Image source: Julian Finney/Getty Images.

who has only a modest CV, who has transitioned best to the manager's seat, such as Jürgen Klopp (Dortmund and Liverpool), a manager who is refreshingly ironic about his talents as a player in Germany's second tier—"I had the mind of a *Bundesliga* [Germany's top tier] player and the talent of fourth division player," an apochryphal story about Klopp goes, "so it was only right that I played in the second division." Other managers in the modern game, such as José Mourinho (who has led Porto, Chelsea, Inter Milan, and Real Madrid to notable success), began as an interpreter (for Bobby Robson, then the coach at Barcelona). Today the exceptional player who makes the switch to coach is limited to the likes of a Josep "Pep" Guardiola, who has, in fact, succeeded as a coach (at his native Barcelona, Bayern Munich, and a truly thrilling Manchester City side in the English Premier League) in ways that exceed his wonderful playing career.[1] The *tiki-taka* (short passing, pass-and-move, ball-to-the-feet, immaculate close control) style that has become so closely associated with Barça is attributed largely to Guardiola and his fidelity to the club's commitment to playing exquisite football. Leo Messi, of course, and a succession of teammates, not least of which includes the native Catalans Xavi Hernández and Andrés Iniesta, was at once integral to that philosophy of playing and the beneficiaries of it.

As a defender of extremely modest talents, Tabárez played for Sud América, Montevideo Wanderers (a club he would later manage), Fénix, and Bella Vista (Uruguay). He also played for Sportivo Italiano (Argentina) and Puebla (Mexico). One is reminded here of the famous "Author's Confession" with which Eduardo Galeano prefaces *Football in Sun and Shadow*: "Like all Uruguayan children, I wanted to be a football player. I played quite well, in fact I was terrific, but only at night when I was asleep."[2] Tabárez was, we can safely conclude, a much better player than his countryman the renowned author. Galeano's oeuvre covers at least three genres: fiction, *Memoria del fuego* (the *Memory of Fire* trilogy); political critique, *Las viernas abiertas de América Latina* (*The Open Sore of a Continent*), and his unique brand of football writing of which *Football in Sun and Shadow* is his pièce de résistance. But Eduardo Galeano was no Óscar Washington Tabárez, at least not on the football pitch.

But then again, that's not saying very much. A year after retiring from his last club, Bella Vista, Tabárez became their coach (1980–83), which led to his appointment as the very successful coach of the Uruguayan under-twenty team.[3]

While embarking on his coaching career, the Montevideo-born Tabárez taught in the city's poorer neighborhoods. He also worked in adult literacy as well as championing the cause of the visually impaired. For his efforts, Tabárez was appointed as an Honorary and Goodwill Ambassador for UNESCO, a recognition, it has to be said, of his pedagogical politics—there is something of Paolo Freire's *Pedagogy of the Oppressed* (*Pedagogia do oprimido*, published in Portuguese in 1968), a foundational text in the radical tradition known as "critical pedagogy," a discourse that has much in common with the "liberation theology" movement that was sweeping Latin America in the 1960s and 1970s about Tabárez as a teacher—and for his ability to translate that into a philosophy of football.

All coaches and players, Tabárez knows, are subject to the pressures of expectation. (As a coach who has been fired more than a few times, sometimes dispatched with in unseemly haste, Tabárez knows this all too well as a fact of his professional life.[4]) Notwithstanding this, Tabárez coaches his teams to answer to nothing but its own truth. We recognize him then, immediately, as a man of thought. Óscar Tabárez is a philosopher in football, a philosopher of football. There is no way to avoid such a designation for Tabárez, neither is there the desire to resist such a nomenklatura.

FOOTBALL AND PHILOSOPHY · Sacrifice. If one LOOKS carefully, one can find the place of sacrifice in all political philosophy (or rather, one will find the challenge of the *abstract*, which makes a sacrifice of concrete singularity). —— JEAN-LUC NANCY, *Being Singular Plural* (emphasis in original)

It is possible, in one thinking of "sacrifice," to understand it provisionally. That is, as separated from, without abandoning that tradition for more than a moment, its Judeo-Christian articulations. Preeminence in this tradition, of course, belongs, as we well know, to the figure of Jesus-the-Christ—the Son of God whose life must be given up in order to save all humanity. This tradition, of course, exacts the most unimaginable cost, the Crucifixion of the Son in order to secure the Resurrection and Eternal Life of All. As such, of course, "sacrifice" is well suited to political discourse insofar as it asks its adherents, the partisans, to willingly give up something, sometimes as much as the very life of the self, so that the cause—justice, liberation, freedom, sovereignty, the nation-state—might be advanced or achieved. This narrative ends, as we are well familiar, with grandiose, bloody, iconic martyrdom—the glorious death of the revolutionary leader; only rarely does it culminate in joy. In fact, it probably never does. It is no simple coincidence, then, that revolutionary figures such as Che Guevara, Patrice Lumumba, and Fidel Castro, especially Guevara and Lumumba, have about them, in their taut physical minimalism, the aura of Christlike sacrifice. Lives dedicated to struggle that end in gory violence, enveloped by shrouds of mystery (which serves only to add to the mystique of death, and the factors that brought about this death) and romance, all of which makes the sacrificial death the stuff of political legend. This, in its turn, feeds the logic—the narrative—of sacrifice. (Recall, in this regard, the ways in which Bob Marley, himself an iconic revolutionary figure with a nigh-emaciated physique, invokes an ambiguous discourse of accountability in "Redemption Song": "How long will they kill our prophets, / while we stand aside and look. / Some say it's just a part of it, / we've got to fulfill the Book."[5]) Frequently, it is this logic, this calling on the partisan to do more than "look on" from the political sidelines, that becomes the ultimate litmus test of political fealty.

Nancy engages "sacrifice" in his thinking of what he names the "philosophico-political horizon," particularly in relation to community ("community of essence"), considered within the context of "first philosophy."[6] (In essence, what emerges out of "first philosophy" is the study, one close to the heart of Heidegger, of the "being of being.") Nancy seeks to undo philosophy and politics as we know it in order that the auto-generative/auto-*Destruktion* forces within philosophy and politics might present us with new ways to think both. "Philosophy," he advises, "needs to recommence, to restart itself from in itself against itself, against political philosophy and philosophical politics. In order to do this, philosophy needs to think in principle about how we are 'us' among us, that is, how the consistency of our Being is in being-in-common, and how this consists precisely in the 'in' or in the 'between' of its spacing."[7]

For Nancy it is important to "restart" in order to not only regain—or retrieve—what is already incipiently, historically, philosophical and political about politics and philosophy, but because such a "recommencement" makes possible the "first" responsibility of the "philosophico-political": to think our "being-in-common." To think "how we are 'us' among us," to think, that is, the very first articulation of our Being: what it means to be together-with-the-other.

To be with-the-other means understanding how to "find the place of sacrifice" insofar as it puts the self in relation to the other. And to recognize at what point the "rupture" of self from other occurs. Such philosophical "itinerizing" demands that we grasp, no matter how imperfectly, "sacrifice"—in its full political articulation, with all its "abstraction" made manifest—as the concretization of our relation to the other's "singularity." The other, constitutively, is not the self, not us, bound together as we are through our being-with, our "being-in-common." What distinguishes the self from the other is that which "consists precisely the 'in' or in the 'between' of its spacing." The "spacing" is that which marks, that which inhabits the "in" and defines, at once, and in turn, the R in its relation (its constitutive force) to the S, the R which surges up, sometimes more violently and unexpectedly than others, out of the constituent forces lodged (and struggling against each other) with-in the space of its "spacing." At work in the "spacing" as such is always the internal combustibility—anything, as easily as nothing, can erupt out of the multiplicity that is "housed" in the "'in'"—and the plurality that separates self from other, that is at the source, the core, of what makes "being-with" at all possible.

What emerges out of "being-with" is, saliently, the recognition that in order to apprehend the other as other it is necessary to attend to the spacing that is *entre-nous* (or, *entre-eux*) self and other. It requires, as Nancy points out, a thinking beyond the philosophical and political insufficiency of seeing that the "other pure and simple, the other merely juxtaposed to the other as well as to the same, is not yet an *other*; it is an in-itself next to an in-itself, just alike."⁸ It is not so much that the "other" must be made, or must be made "other," or that the capitalization of the term ("Other") is designation enough of the other's non-"alikeness," to phrase the matter awkwardly. It is, rather, to understand the other in its singular plural, as its own singular plural. The other as individuated, the self made individual; that is, the self making of itself a singular plural self. This understanding of the other always begins with the premise that the other can never be presented as that which is "not-I" but is still recognizable enough, familiar enough (to "me") as "I." The "origins," as Nancy properly insists, of the other's singular plurality is what must be attended to; the spacing between self and other is constituted, firstly, out of the (base) material that can be named, if only for the purpose of initial thinking, "origins." In "hollowing out" the "origins" of the other, what becomes clear is that the other is not in the least "just alike." All this, however, must still be thought within the difficulty of "being-with" that has, in its turn, its "origins" in the shared "access" to the singular plural. The other in R to self as "affirmative negation"; the other "affirming" itself through negation, if a certain philosophical playfulness with Nancy's terms might be permitted.⁹

This means, then, that when we speak of "sacrifice," we understand, a priori, that we are committing to a political R to the other: we stand with the other in our (mutual, mutually constitutive) apartness from the other. The other, with whom I am undertaking this political act, is conceived fully as other; this act is not to redact (the impossibility of *Sous rature*, once more) the other's "origins." The other is, as such, other because it has been spaced from the self through the singular force of its "origins." It is always advisable to anticipate the other's "origins" as an event. Phrased in Nancy's terms, it is best to anticipate the "surging up" of the other's origins in the enunciation of its (of itself as) "origins." It is in the encounter with the other's "origins," in that moment that the force of the "origins" makes itself manifest in, manifest as, the full singularity of its plurality. In that encounter what is singular about the other is most easily recognized in how it gives voice to its "origins," that is, what makes the other other, or what makes the other self to itself; or what makes the other not-"like" the hyperindividuated self.

This leads us to a paradox, a paradox that is intensely "philosophico-political," a paradox that frames (reiterates) the importance of the singular plurality of "origins." What is it that resides with-in that disposes us toward sacrifice?¹⁰ That disposes the self toward, to proffer a rudimentary definition, but one freighted with political intention (and, history, as such), the decision to "give up" the self, and, of course, what matters to the self, in the cause of the other? So that the other might not, we could stipulate (however speculatively), be injured, harmed, imprisoned, or subjected to violence? In short, the self decides to "appropriate" (to take upon itself), insofar as such an "appropriation" is possible, the vulnerability intended for the other.¹¹ The self stands where the other is meant to be "sacrificed, as it were. Standing in the place of the other, the self absorbs into itself the degradation, humiliation, vilification that is intended for and targeted at the other. What is, rendered as such, *entre-nous*, *entre-eux*, is, in Nancy's terms, "sacrifice." The discourse of sacrifice is saturated with vulnerability and innocence, most familiar in Christian doctrine as the "sacrificial lamb." The Biblical "lamb" is that "being" given up in its innocence, in order to achieve and to recognize, one imagines after Abraham and Isaac, the achievement of a greater good. The lamb is "sacrificed" because Abraham has, by turning his face from his community and to God only, demonstrated absolute fidelity to God above and before all else. (It is a memorable lesson, of course, because God will show himself willing to sacrifice his own Son, whereas Isaac was spared because of this father's truth. The cup, God decides, will not "pass his Son by.")¹²

Every notion of sacrifice, then, is replete with the possibility, or, we might say, the demand, of death as a political outcome. Death, we can say, is at once the absolute and the minimum political requirement of sacrifice. No politics without sacrifice, no sacrifice without (the possibility of) death. Sacrifice is the test that Abraham passes with unflinching fidelity. But death is the demand God makes of his Son. Death is what distinguishes God the Father from Abraham the father. Isaac is spared, almost unknowing, of the fate that awaited him, allowed to live despite his father's willingness, in the act of loving God, to condemn him to death. Jesus-the-Christ is not so spared, although, of course, he is resurrected in the name of universal love—so that all might be saved by the grace of God because the One (the Son of God) was sacrificed. Nietzsche, in a phrase that Derrida designates, perhaps a little unfairly, as "sacrificial *hubris*,"¹³ names this the "stroke of genius on the part of Christianity."¹⁴ Nietzsche then bitingly expounds, "God himself sacrifices himself for the guilt of mankind. God makes payment to himself. . . . the creditor sacrifices himself for his debtos, out of *love* (can one credit that?), out of love for his debtor!"¹⁵ Following

Nietzsche, that famous verse from the Gospel of John achieves a new (philosophical) difficulty and, it must be said, with it a new moral force: "For God so loved the world that He gave his Only Begotten Son." (John 3:16) God, cast here by Nietzsche as both creditor and debtor is forced—or, acts out of grace, will not default on his own loans. God will not default on his own loans to Himself.

LOVE · At our slightest attempt to solicit the thinking of love, we are invited to an extreme reticence. —— JEAN-LUC NANCY, *The Inoperative Community*

There can be no doubt that the Abrahamic tradition establishes, most notably of course in the work of Søren Kierkegaard (*Frygt og Bæven—Fear and Trembling*), the act of sacrifice as a central component of what, in that way that Derrida names "ir-responsiblity,"[16] follows from it: love. Nancy, with his frequent invocation of "trembling," is Kierkegaardian in his rendering of love, in no small measure because it is through sacrifice that we are able to be "in touch with *ourselves* and in touch with the rest of beings."[17] Sacrifice is among the first openings of the self to love and, as such, it marks among the first (there is no reason to believe that it is not the first) rupture(s) to the other. The other, we might say, enters us in the name of love. The other enters us in that moment when love becomes a condition of being; in turn, this opening to, this desire (all desire, in Nancy's terms, is desire for the other) allows us to enter the other through love so that we are always compelled to think about love as that act of "breaking into," of "breaking open," the self. Love makes the self responsible to the other before the self and, as such, "ir-responsible" to it-self.

To be responsible to the other is nothing less than, as it were, to know the Abrahamic tradition and to understand Kierkegaard metonymically. That is, to grasp in one's very being the philosophical import of *Fear and Trembling*. On this matter Nancy could not be clearer: "I cannot stop trembling before the other, and even further, at being in myself the trembling that the other stirs up. And thought cannot penetrate the thing without trembling."[18] Before all else, Nancy confronts us, confronts himself, we might say, with the utter physicality of love, thinking, the other, and the physical rupturousness that the other "stirs up" in the self. Thinking, so rendered, must be known, forthwith, as that which surges up out of us ecstatically. The body is made rapturous by a thinking born out of Kierkegaardian "fear." In turn, our "trembling" is the manifestation of our love, of our thinking. That is, we tremble most violently, which is to say, rapturously, when our love of thinking manifests itself in what we call, perhaps erroneously but still in good faith, "trembling." The passage to love, to thinking, to sacrifice, to the love of thinking, must pass through Kierkegaard, must know—and be fully "in"—why it is we tremble before the other. Love begins in trembling. We can only claim to be thinking, to have given ourselves to thought, when the trembling that our bodies endure "penetrates" to the very Being of our being.[19]

Nancy phrases the matter as nothing other than risking, in the most intimate terms, the self in R to the other. The "other self subsisting outside me," Nancy writes, "imperils my subsistence, this being-all-to-myself that I thus know can only be affirmed in risking it."[20] There is no "being-all-to-myself" that is sufficient in itself. In order to be-all-to-myself, the self (the political "I") must risk thinking—"voiding," "invalidating," "obliterating," if possible, to use a vocabulary that may be entirely unsuited for demarcating the spacing that is S—the other as an articulation of the self, part of the self's plural singularity, that must establish R with the other that is located as constitutive, as politically integral to, and not as "outside me." The other, who is not the self, who must remain the not-self, who must be understood as relentlessly individual (and, as such, individuated), must, regardless of the spacing, of the force of the between, be understood as "being-with." The other, so conceived, can be apprehended as the other who is simultaneously unequal to (), indistinct from, the self. The constitutive "/" marks, at once and in turn, turning again and again, relentlessly, without end, R S. And if love is the apogee of being-with, then sacrifice in the name of the other is also the act of fidelity to self that always opens the possibility of love.

To love is to begin from the decision to "imperil" the self's "subsistence" and, as such, it is to posit love as that act constitutively not premised on the guarantee of reciprocation. (Love, then, in terms we derive from Marcel Mauss, as nothing other than the gift of self. The gift is that act of giving that refuses, as its first condition of being, an economy of exchange. The gift is only a gift if it begins from the promise of neither expecting nor desiring anything in exchange for what the self gives the other. The gift, Nietzsche might insist, acidly, that reveals fully—once more—the "genius of Christianity.")[21] In these terms, sacrifice stands first of all as a political risk for which every known calculus is necessarily insufficient. Love begins, then, in the name of the other, in the act of showing our love for the other by showing a self that refuses to engage in political accounting. There is nothing to do then, when giving love, but to declare our love and to act upon our love for the other and to give everything in order—and still with no expectation—that there may be a "coappearance," crafted in love, of self and other; in love, self and other are, in Carl Schmitt's terms, "instantaneously copresent."[22] Love is that relation that intervenes most rupturously (and, rapturously) *entre moi et moi-même*: between-myself-and-I there, in the "in" and in the "spacing between," there is love. Love is what happens, what we make possible, when we give ourselves up to love, when we stipulate to love as the "very first figure, this relation to the other, and, more precisely, this being self-through-the-other."[23] Love as the inclining toward grace, not love as Nietzschean "genius."

But it is also about, to extend Nancy's argument in the direction of the rupturousness of love, more than "being self-through-the-other." Love is the passage to (infinite) possibility, a passage made possible as the gift from the other, what is given by the other as the gift of "disruption" to the self; it raises the possibility of self and other being "immediately copresent" to and with each other. Love is "what comes from the other to unseal the consistency of the self."[24] So conceived, love possessed the power of "dissolution" and to love is, as such, that act that marks the self's willingness to (let it-self) "come apart." Love is the other's capacity to "unglue" the bonds that hold the self together; love is the undoing of the cohesive elements that bond the self into a consistency (into a consistent "whole," as it were); love pries those elements apart, allowing the passage—or passages—through which the other, the other's love, the other as love (itself) might inveigle itself in the self and in so doing unravel the self. (Love is what makes us vulnerable before self and other. Or, in Judith Butler's terms, love is the most affirming mark of our "precarity.")[25] In the place of that earlier "consistency" of self, a new series of bonds, filled with ("precarious") room for the passages of love, the passages that facilitate and encourage the movement of love, might be forged. If love has the power to undo, to unmake, then what its undoing forges is the making of a self as something radically other than itself. The name of this new bond is, needless to say, nothing other than love. It is love as that force within that "unseals" the self and makes something other than itself, something other than how it used to be, possible.

Love is a force that is, as will be argued shortly, especially important for Tabárez in the act of loving, and showing himself open to, committed to, sacrificing for, Luis Suárez. Love, Nancy concludes in a Shakespearean tone, apropos of Tabárez and Suárez, is the "alteration of each one."[26] (Nancy's "alteration" brings to mind that most bitingly ironic opening lines of Sonnet 116: "Let me not to the marriage of true minds / Admit impediments. Love is not love / which alters when it alteration finds, / Or bends with the remover to remove." It is also, however, this—arguably—most famous of Shakespeare's sonnets, an unflinching commitment to love, as the sonnet's last four lines make clear: "Love alters not with his brief hours and weeks, / But bears it out even to the edge of doom. / If this be error and upon me proved, / I never writ, nor no man ever loved." Even if the sonnet ends as it begins: on a note of irony. Albeit, the rhyming couplet, a moment of "scientific hubris.") Where these passages, the passage of love, as we will see momentarily, might culminate, is, possibly, to extend the logic of "unsealing" to its logical end, is, surprisingly, in the "final" unsealing—death. As such, Nancy must be thought in R to Heidegger's notion that "all being is being toward death." As such Nancy draws us once more in the direction of Nietzsche's skepticism, where "man's guilt" is paid for "out of love for the debtor." Nietzsche's is, however, a skepticism that recognizes the self-sacrificial generosity of God the "creditor." Derrida's "hubris," then, is nothing other than Nietzsche's head shaking incomprehension at God's grace; at God's unthinkable capacity for love, beyond love.

The thinking of love in philosophy, and here Nancy is especially critical of Heidegger, "forms the limit of a thinking that carries itself to the limit of philosophy. Until thinking extricates itself, it will not be able to reach love. But what this thinking, at its limit, lets emerge could be this: that one never *reaches* love, even though love is always happening to us. Or rather, love is always offered to us. Or yet again, we are always in our Being—and in us Being is—exposed to love."[27] It is salient, and perhaps even surprising, although it should not be, that it is possible to write sport as "love" precisely because it is—if we accept sport, as the act of participation, as fandom, as, in short, a mode of being—that which is "always happening to us." As players, fans, and as thinkers of sport (let us call such figures "philosophers" for now), in and through these subjects, "Being is expose to love," on a daily basis, certainly with an unquestionable regularity. In the very Being of the athlete or the fan, "love is not only exposed," as such, but the Being is the passage through which love passes, and, as such, is renewed. The athlete or the philosopher of sport is always "reaching" for love, straining in the direction of love, in search of the object of love, always committed to, in its many iterations, love itself. There is no limit to which the fan, especially, in the act of fidelity, will not exceed, or will not seek to breach in order to express, to make manifest, love, the love that the fan has for her team, or for his teammates.

> We love you, Lansur, we do
> O Lansur, we love you.
> We love you, Luis Suárez, we do.

Similarly, there is no philosophy that the philosopher of sport will leave unturned in order to declare, in a language that always bears within it the singular plurality of that love, that love, to seek a new way to articulate self in relation to the object, which is unfailingly intimate to, coextensive with, the self. Love, to make the self (permanently) precarious in relation to the other. Love, thought in relation to sport, is the very Being of sport. It is the willing exposure, a being open that is always fraught with risk (loss, defeat, disappointment) of the self to love so that love can assume a range of names, none of them necessarily recognizable, at first, as love, but known to the player or the fan as the very inextricability of the self from love. There is, as it were, no possible limit that can be imposed on love as the fan knows it. Love is, in this regard, fueled and not limited by what Nancy critiques as "every excess and every exactitude."[28] If there is a limit to the way in which love can be expressed, and it is very likely that this might be the case, then it is experienced by the fan, by the philosopher, not as an inhibition but rather as an invitation to revitalize, to find new names for love. (That is, the self is ever willing to extend itself even further—to extend itself beyond what is known, always in the direction of what might be unknowable, even daunting, but will never be beyond the reach of the fan or the player. Love as the very refusal of—its own—finitude.) There are new players to adore, new heroes to be identified, meaning that there are always new names to chant, with love.

Love, as such, finds in sport that space for expression where the love of love, as a limitless relationship to the other, can always be renewed and find new articulation. In fact, love as manifested in and through sport is infinitely creative. The fan, the player, the philosopher of sport responds to all "solicitation" about the "thinking of love" not, never, with reticence, but always with exuberance, animated, made alive by the sense of possibility, keen to produce that turn of phrase that can negate the cliché, the aphorism, the rote expression. All this (work, this thinking) in order to make love live again. To make the player's love alive again, to give it new life; the philosopher and the fan (who must be thought as the "same," who co-appear in a writing such as this) seek to craft a language fit for their love. All these figures (or these different constituencies, we might prefer to call them) are determined to dredge from the very core of their Being precisely the language worthy of their love.

"Reticence" is nowhere to be found when it comes to the love of sport. In sport, "reticence" meets its match, early and decisively, and love is free to flower, free to seek a passage beyond limits. To love is to live the singular plural of being, to know the other as being-with-me in my Being, to know my Being as "indissociable" from the other's being so that love marks the plural origin, in Nancy's terms, of my singular (plural) being. In my Being, through my Being, I am with-the-other in being. Through Being, I am in the world as the singular plural of being.

SACRIFICE · The truth was obscure, too profound and too pure / To live it you have to explode / In that last hour of need, we entirely agreed / Sacrifice was the code of the road —— BOB DYLAN, "Where Are You Tonight? (Journey through Dark Heat)"

Sacrifice makes possible our being-with-the-other under conditions that are, generally speaking, trying, difficult, and where the decision to act risks the self, as much as, if not more than, the other. Framed as such, we reach, we are "in touch" with, we, to raise the conjuncture of love and self as an autoeroticism, "touch" ourselves and the other through sacrifice. Love, so presented, is that political act that can only begin (putatively, reductively grasped) outside ourselves because its deepest, most profound political and philosophical core is what is most constitutive of the self's inside. We act with love toward the other because our act in the name of the other marks the extent to which the self is already, before itself, with the other, of, made in part by the other, made of the other, and therein inheres the being of Being, or the Being of being. Acting on, or in, the terms of sacrifice, adhering to sacrifice as a political modality, means committing to an extant political code, Dylan's "code of the road," a commitment grounded in truth where the risk of self-destruction is a very real prospect. "To live it you have to explode," suggests that self-destruction is almost the precondition for sacrifice, making of sacrifice a pact that must hold under extreme conditions, under extreme conditions more than anything else, in fact. Such is the need of the "last hour of need," such is the need for agreeing to the sacrificial terms of the pact.

The terms in which Nancy presents "being-with-the-other" as the ground for acting politically, and because of the ways in which the discourse of sacrifice is intimate with, intimately connected to, and is indeed constitutive of, death, it is possible to suggest that Nancy restores a certain political veracity, the absolute truth of being-with, to Heidegger's notion that all being is being-toward-death. There are implications for this argument in Nancy's (Kierkegaardian) claims about "negativity" (that it "makes all determinateness tremble") that present the possibility for extending "being-with" as "applicable" in death. That is, it may be possible to assert that if we can "penetrate" "being-with" fully, we can be with the other in death; that is, the self can be with the other, possibly even take the place of the other as the self in sacrificing the self when it is the expectation (it is the law, the law's expectation, when the law of the law demands) that the other be sacrificed. Understood politically, Nancy's "penetration" into "being-with" as that which we can manifest fully, provides—contra Derrida's reading of Heidegger in *The Gift of Death*, where Derrida argues that there can be "no gift of self"[29]—the opening into the death of the other. While it still remains impossible to die as the other, through being-with we dispose (or, expose) ourselves to that death as "being-self-through-other." We can, therefore, know death as that which is, at once, our own demise, politically speaking, and death which is the experience of "being-through." We can come to know death as that which is not intended for us but to which our decision—sacrifice—gives us a mediated access—"access" understood in its Nancian iteration. The death of the other is that which we can, as a political end, dispose ourselves to know; a disposition and a (/the) knowledge of death is established along the road that is politics. A road whose cartography bears the inscription of itself, as the patience that is inherent to, that is demanded by, thinking. As Nancy writes, extending his contemplation on "reticence," love and thinking, "Thought therefore essentially takes place in the reticence that lets the singular moments of experience offer and arrange themselves."[30] Along the road of sacrifice, given how long it takes to make this journey, time presents itself as a vital component of thought. In "reticence," in offering the declarative that is its own negation (to say "I love you" is to say that I am unable to properly phrase what it is I am toward you), it becomes possible to take the time (appropriate time, for the sake of this argument) to confront what is on "offer."—And what is on "offer" is the self, the other, R, S, thought, as such. Out of that confrontation, which is another name for thinking what is before us, it becomes possible to "arrange" our thoughts, to organize our thinking, to set ourselves to thinking. To thinking love, especially, such as we have never thought it before. But such as we will surely be called on to think it again.

Through love it becomes possible to gain a firmer hold on the terms of sacrifice, terms that will demand, in the moment of record, that no one be found wanting, or missing, when the Dylanesque question "Where are you tonight?" is raised. That Dylanesque question that itself appears to be an account of a love that seems somewhat unsteady, a love that is itself in question. In that moment, the code demands that all answer the call, no matter the profundity or purity, inanity or transience, of the "truth," no matter how rocky the road of love has been. "Where are you?" in R to me? Or, to cast Dylan's question in the disco register (and the high falsetto of the Bee Gees) that his 1978 LP *Street Legal* seems so obstinately immune to, "How deep is your love?"[31] (The soundtrack to the movie *Saturday Night Fever* [1977], probably the high water mark of disco, was released in the same era as *Street Legal*, by which time disco was already firmly established as a mode of—cultural—being.) In truth, the Bee Gees' demand for depth may stand as a sharper request for sacrifice, solidarity, and love than Dylan's.[32] Between Dylan and the Brothers Gibb it was a good year for questions about the politics of sacrifice and love. As the Bee Gees warn, if we do not mine love for all that it is worth, "We'll be living in a world of fools, breaking us down."[33] Love will not permit of such destruction. Instead, it is love that will keep the fools at bay. That is because love knows its intimacy to sacrifice, the sacrifice that makes love possible. The sacrifice that is love, the kind of sacrifice constitutive of what is *entre-nous* Tabárez and Suárez, the kind of sacrifice unthinkable, inconceivable without love, without understanding the intimacy that is between player and coach, the kind of relation that throws R and S into flux.

**ETHICS THROUGH *AUFHEBUNG*, OR, THE ETHICS OF *AUFHEBUNG*** · Sacrifice is one of the discourses that is at the core of what is *entre-nous* Tabárez and Suárez. The other key discourse, to which we will attend shortly, is shame. Sacrifice proceeds from what is *entre-nous*. It must begin with what is between self and other. In the case of Tabárez and Suárez, however, this is a freighted question largely because what is *entre-nous*, that which is so forceful and considerable, must be set here against the way—the philosophical ways—in which Tabárez thinks. That is, how Tabárez thinks about the world, how he thinks about football in R to the world, how football constitutes a world. This is especially consequential for Tabárez because for *el técnico* the possibility of being in the world ethically—that which, as Lacan argues, commits to a "deeper dimension of analytical thought, work and technique"—is critically important.[34]

It is also, in this regard, worth thinking Lacan's ethics against the grain here, for a moment, by locating it in relation to *Aufhebung*. To forge this relation in order to produce a potentially keener insight into the philosophical difficulties—the difficulty presented by how the self, Tabárez, thinks (of) itself/himself in R to the world—presented by this intense and committed relationship to the other: Tabárez →← Suárez. The difficulties, that is, presented by what is broadly understood to be the transgression of the other, a transgression that extends even so far as to constitute an act against the self, that self (Tabárez) who has historically been supportive of the other (the other self, as it were, Suárez). It is in this regard that figuring the ethical through *Aufhebung* allows for the emergence—possibly even the "upsurge"—of another, a different, way of understanding how the self situates, thinks, itself in relation to the other. If *Aufhebung* is understood as a conception with which we are now well familiar, the "conservation of something destroyed at a different level," then ethics as the "deeper dimension of thought" (that is, thinking that is relentlessly, and restlessly, felicitous to itself) makes possible the "extraction" of that which is the very crucible of *entre-nous*.[35]

What is revealed in and through the transgressive act is nothing less than the absolute truth of what binds self to other, that truth that stretches S to its very limits. (It might break R into nothingness, not possible, we know, but to raise this as the threat of transgression is to possibly achieve a sense of how vulnerable R can become in light of the event; the event as that which threatens, beyond any imagining what is *entre-nous* self and other.) Or, to think it in Lacan's terms, the event distills the truth into its own truth, distills truth into the finest grain(s) of truth. Truth as nothing but truth, entirely unembellished, true. The code of the road named "sacrifice" is then nothing other than truth. Through what *Aufhebung* makes visible, makes immanent, the ethical emerges, tried and tested, (finally) able to come into its own out of the "upheaval" that is, as Nancy frames it, the "most serious penetration of thought."[36] (What emerges, when all is said and done, is that what is *entre-nous* is "just a couple of men trying to carry a project through."[37] Just, we might say, a coach and his player trying to understand how the "project" that is the Uruguayan national team might be made, in the aftermath of the event, anew, considering R that is S that has been made vulnerable to the force of the event.)

However, in order to achieve the "most serious penetration of thought," it might be useful to begin with a basic etymological account of the ethical. Precisely, to approach the ethical as that which compels us to distinguish—and to act in and on the terms of—what conduct is right and what is wrong, a standard dictionary definition.[38] It is possible, in more than one way, to posit Tabárez as just such an ethical figure: the coach committed to playing the game of football, win or lose (or, to borrow a philosophical principle from Galeano's opening "Confession," "when good football happens, I give thanks for the miracle and I don't give a damn which team or country performs it"[39]), according to a set of principles (playing "good football"), the "right way." That is, the coach whose mode of being begins in the world, of football, of education, of politics, and for whom in all cases the principles are the same. For Tabárez, it is always about working in the cause of the good and just. Equal access to education, no (massive) inequality in wealth, equal regard and political standing for all people, beginning in his native Uruguay. Tabárez is, so conceived, a man of his principles—a man of principle. The world as made in football is the world he strives to make immanent in general, a world where justice and equality are the universal order of the day. A world where his principles are operative every day. But there may be more to Tabárez's ethicality than that, an ambition that Derrida "touches on' parenthetically in his work *On Touching—Jean-Luc Nancy*. The ethical world, the world as ethical (place), Derrida suggests, can be understood as the one offered to us in the oeuvre of Emmanuel Levinas. For Levinas, Derrida writes, '(peace itself is the ethical for Levinas)."[40]

There can be no just argument that can be mounted against the kind of principles that Tabárez espouses. (As Derrida so poetically delineates for us in *On Touching*, no defensible argument can be proffered, so of a "just piece/peace" are Nancy and Tabárez's commitments.) However, what does it then mean to surrender, if not the self, but then that for which the self is presumed to stand, to incarnate, that set of principles which the self has preached, and, most certainly, practiced? What is the ethical subject to do in the face of the event, in view of the fact that Suárez has bitten Giorgio Chiellini? What then? What kind of thinking, what kind of sacrifice, we might (hasten to) ask, is required in the face of the event? How does the self establish an R to itself after so rupturous an S? What kind of R can emerge out of the event in which the self is made, not to put too fine a point on it, vulnerable to itself? (Is this the violent, ethical truth of what Butler understands as "precarity?") What, as it were, is "conserved" out of destruction at a "different level," "conserved," we might speculate, to a "higher," more clearly enunciated level? What does the event of the bite (the bite that is, that cannot but be, concatenated to the preceding two biting incidents in Suárez's career) allow to surge up into clarity, into that which can be thought at "deeper dimension of analytical thought?"

THE BITE OF RESIGNATION · We have to insist on it—that the intuitionistic-continuistic logic of immediacy shows itself to be as irrepressible as desire itself, as intractable as language constraints, grammatical violence, and all that we spoke of as shared-out faith a moment ago; it can always happen, it has always to be able to happen that the power of this law regularly allows some symptoms to crop up. —— JACQUES DERRIDA, *On Touching*

The passage from self to other, from self to self, lies in the "plural singularity of the Being of being." We reach it to the extent that we understand self: "*Self* is precisely without return to self; *self* does not become what it already is: becoming is outside of self—but such that this outside, this ex-position, is the very being of the subject."⁴¹ The "very being of the subject" Tabárez was at stake, on display, at least, in the aftermath of Suárez's bite of Chiellini in Uruguay's match against Italy on June, 24, 2014. Two days after the Suárez event, Tabárez used the press conference before the round of 16 match between Uruguay and Colombia to announce that he was quitting his FIFA positions, nominal though they were.

He went on to denounce the English-speaking media for the unprecedented ban imposed on Suárez. Tabárez may have been especially aggrieved because the Mexican referee, Marco Antonio Rodríguez—known, ironically, or appropriately, depending on your point of view, as Dracula in his homeland—did not see the incident, and so the FIFA ban was entirely technological and retrospective. (Retrospective punishment is permissible, in fact, only if, as in this case, the referee is "unsighted," and makes no call on the incident. If the referee rules on the incident during the course of a match, it is more difficult—but not impossible—to impose punishment retrospectively.) As soon as the Suárez bite had occurred, however, it was broadcast again and again, first in several TV replays, after which it went viral, compelling FIFA to act.

After an investigation, FIFA did act, banning Suárez from all "football-related activities" for four months. FIFA subsequently saw fit to amend that decision, allowing Suárez to have a medical examination that allowed a transfer from his then-club, England's Liverpool FC, to FC Barcelona, to take place before he was actually eligible to return to the field of play, or, for that matter, to set foot in any football stadium. So even before his ban was properly in effect, Suárez was already on the move to Catalunya, to join Messi and the Brazilian Neymar in an electric front three known as "S-M-N." (The deal, which took Suárez from Liverpool to Barça, was rumored to be in the region of £75.5.)

In his press conference on June 26, however, Tabárez was faced with a difficult decision. He could accept what Suárez had done, as Suárez himself has subsequently done (after steadfastly denying that he had bitten Chiellini),[42] which would have meant—more or less—condemning a player for whom he has great affection and a bond that is closer to, in some idealized logic, that of father-son rather than that of coach-player. In defending himself, Suárez complained of being treated like a delinquent and a criminal, the very language—a point that will be revisited later—that is at the core of the narrative of his ascent in the world of football. That is, the narrative that condemns him. It is this account of himself that Suárez echoes: "Me trataron peor que un delincuente, destacó el delantero" (They treated me worse than a delinquent), he said.[43] Suárez explains his bite not as the premeditated act of violence but as "instinct," "instinct" that just "takes over in the moment": "Son instintos que te salen en el momento."[44] It is difficult to discern an apology as such, so much so that the closest we get to a Suárez mea culpa is his regret at having let his teammates down: "De lo que me arrepiento es de haber dejado a los compañeros de la forma que los dejé."[45] Although he does not mention Tabárez, it seems clear that the coach is first among *los compañeros*.

It is worth pointing out, however, that the bond between player and coach follows its own set of rules, and that they are difficult to predict not only because every coach is different, but because the bond, within the same team, between player and coach is distinct. (Even, as we know, between the coach and this player as opposed to the coach and that player.) The paternal metaphor is relied upon because it posits either the most politically recognizable or idealized version of what the bond between father and son should be, but also because the figurative repertoire of sport has not yet been able to craft a new metaphor, a nonfamilial image (a nondomesticated image) that obtains with the same resonance. Such paternal invocations, for better and for worse, abound in sport. It runs the gamut, from sports such as boxing, say, where Cus D'Amato and Mike Tyson formed a very close bond, to football, where the friendly hand of the manager on a player's shoulder after a bad game, for which managers such as Ron Greenwood and Bobby Robson were famous. In basketball, Phil Jackson's most notable relationships were not so much with his star performers, Michael Jordan, Shaquille O'Neal, but his trusted "role players," the Craig Hodges' of the Zen meister's world; those constituted that the pivotal R for Jackson. We need look no further than Tabárez to prove this point. The paternal metaphor applies, in toto, to the R that binds Tabárez and Suárez: "Tabárez's affection for the players he has helped nurture is obvious. Indeed, when he speaks of Suárez—the kid from Salto who became a superstar—his tone becomes more that of a concerned parent than a football manager."[46] In the press conference on June 27, 2014,[47] before the Colombia game, Tabárez addressed the FIFA ban. Loyal to a fault, the coach promised that Suárez would "never be alone."

The Liverpool FC anthem, borrowed from the Mersey band, Gerry and Pacemakers, is "You'll Never Walk Alone." At the time of the Chiellini bite, Suárez was a Liverpool player and that famous Scouser (as Liverpool natives are known) anthem can be heard to reverberate from Liverpool to Montevideo to Rio:

When you walk through the storm
Hold your head up high
And don't be afraid of the dark . . .

In Brazil, at the 2014 World Cup, echoes of the Liverpool anthem. That famous football song now links Tabárez to Liverpool to Suárez. Political triangulation.

Don't be afraid of FIFA.

Even now, years after the fact, I find it impossible to watch Tabárez speaking at this press conference and not be struck by his thoughtfulness, his love for

Suárez, and the political care with which he mounts his defense. It is not necessary to agree with Tabárez in order to be "touched" by him, as Derrida says of Nancy. It is a heartfelt promise from *el técnico* to player who is sometimes known as "El Pistolero" ("The Gunman" or "The Shooter") for his accuracy as a marksman. Tabárez is explicit: his striker will always have his support, especially in moments such as this, when difficulty is all around.

When you walk through the storm . . .

It is, in truth, Tabárez's lyrical rhetorical act—full of pathos, haunted by Suárez, characterized by the coach's attacks on officialdom. It is the classical tactic: circling the wagons when under threat from outside. At the very end of the conference Tabárez signs off with a "Muchas gracias." A smattering of applause, from the journalists, can be heard.[48] The journalists registering their support, however modestly, are, I presume either Uruguayan or Latin American. But I could be wrong. A part of me hopes I am.

> As a Liverpool fan and a Suárez admirer, even after he left us, I do not want him to have to "walk alone." No matter that I recoiled when I saw him lean into Chiellini. I knew, as did scores of other Liverpool and Uruguayan fans, I'm sure, what Suárez had done.

> Again. No matter. Love.
> "At the end of the storm
> There's a golden sun
> And the sweet silver song
> Of the lark."

What surges up out of the event is, in Nancy's terms, a "self" that is "ex-posed," thrown out of its (old) position, expelled from itself (thrown into the world against its wishes, against its inclinations and proclivities), into a self that must be reconstituted through the act of "becoming outside of itself." What surges up is, as Derrida phrases it in delectably Nancian terms, "apartness in contact," the "outside in the inside of contact."[49] What we are made privy to through the event is nothing other than the "ex-position" of what is (putatively) external, the "outside," but which is, in reality, possessed of the most searing intimacy: the "outside" as it is encountered in the act of "seeing" it from the "inside" when it comes into "contact" with, shall we say, another body. What does the "outside" look like "inside" in the event of contact? When it comes up against, to phrase it confrontationally, something, some force or object, other than itself? In such an encounter or confrontation something—both Nancy and Derrida insist, each in his own way—of the "outside's" "inside" is shown to us. After that "ex-position," that act of having been made visible, we can no longer, and must, indeed, no longer, approach, consider, or think the "outside" in the same way. Something, through the act—deliberate measure—or the accident—the act that produces unintended consequences—of contact, something of substance is revealed. The self, as such, can no longer return to itself (by which we really mean "retreat," as in beating back a path to). The self can never be, especially true in light of the event, "what it was."[50]

And so it was with Tabárez. The Suárez event compelled the self (Tabárez) to confront itself in the process—El Proceso of a philosophical order—of reaching for something other than that self, the self made self through the event of the other; the event that "ex-posed" the self to a no longer tenable self; the self confronting the self that has been made redundant; the self ex-communicated from itself. This is what Hardt and Mezzadra name the "highest power of the event," but in a distinctly Nancian way: how the event of Suárez's bite exposes negation as the "highest power of the event."[51]

There was, of course, for Tabárez, as there would be for any coach in his position, the recognition of how central Suárez is to Tabárez's plans for keeping tiny Uruguay competitive (population inching just above 3.5 million) within Latin American and international football. In truth, Tabárez was in a barely tenable position. Any critique the coach would have offered, and let there be no doubt that such a critique was surely roiling within his philosophical self (he must have been doing everything in his power to prevent it from surging up), would have meant betraying Suárez and undermining the rugged defense mounted by his Uruguayan team of their condemned striker.

The Uruguayan captain, Diego Lugano, led the charge. Lugano suggested, rather improbably, that Suárez was being made a victim and that Chiellini was "not a man" for responding so demonstratively to Suárez's bite. When he is bitten, Lugano more or less suggested, a man must simply grin and bear it, but never show, the marks of so intimate—so intimately public—an encounter. When one man marks the body of the other, of another, those marks must be kept between the combatants. Such an injury belongs, in Lugano's logic, strictly within the confines of the game, mano-a-mano. Biting on the football pitch is between men and, as such, must be kept private. Any other response was surely little short of "unmanly."

Chiellini, for his part, demurred, rather loudly. From the very beginning, the Italian center-back showed himself immune to the discourse of "private masculinity." Chiellini sought instead to be publicly intimate, with the world, the world of the TV camera and the distribution network that is the internet. As such, Chiellini shared his mark, his battle scars, with the world, as quickly and expansively as possible. Contra Lugano, Chiellini wanted everyone to see how he had been unjustly wounded. He bared his body as well as his football soul for all the world to see. And to hear, because Chiellini wanted not only justice for his pain and suffering, but condemnation for his Uruguayan foe.

THE PHILOSOPHY OF THE MANAGER · To have publicly declared Suárez wrong would have constituted an unprecedented act by a football manager. It is the rare manager (I have yet to meet one) who speaks poorly of his charges, no matter the nature or severity of the transgression. Tabárez, as has been established, chose the managerial path well-trodden. His "small country" was being treated unfairly, the coach insisted, but no one outside of Uruguay believed him. There could be no argument about what Suárez had done. The evidence was clear for all to see.

Uruguay has a population of around three and a half million, making it the smallest country to have won the World Cup. Twice, no less. The first time, in the inaugural tournament in 1930,[52] came at the expense of their neighbors, Argentina, in Montevideo, making Uruguay the very first country to lift the trophy;[53] as Galeano mischievously tells it, the "two nations of the River Plate insulted Europe by showing the world where the best football was played."[54] The second time, at the Maracanã, against Brazil, in 1950, was achieved against considerable odds, such overwhelming favorites were the hosts. Brazil led through a goal by Friaça, to which Uruguay, led by its legendary captain, Obdulio Varela, responded with goals by Schiaffino and the winner by Ghiggia. The Brazilians, to a person, were stunned, prompting national commentators to proclaim the defeat the "worst tragedy in Brazil's history."[55] It is highly unlikely, what with its history of dictatorships, unparalleled economic inequity, and a seemingly willful rush to destroy its greatest natural asset, the rain forest, but the hyperbole certainly gives a sense of the affective impact of the defeat on the Brazilian national psyche.

The ban, Tabárez complained, was excessive. By raising the length of the ban as an issue, something critical seemed to escape Tabárez: such a contestation amounted to an admission of his striker's guilt. Tabárez went on to suggest that Suárez's punishment by FIFA was the result of the British media's vendetta against the then-Liverpool striker. On this score, it is possible to exhibit the smallest amount of sympathy for Tabárez. (This, after all, constituted a third offence for the same crime; the first was committed against Otman Bakkal in the Netherlands in 2011, and the second against Branislav Ivanović while playing for Liverpool in 2013.) While Suárez was handed a historic ban, Arjen Robben, who publicly admits cheating (he simulated a dive in the match in the round of 16 game against Mexico, an act for which he has expressed no regret) and has a long history of such behavior, escaped without punishment.

There is, in the disparate ways in which transgressions were treated, or ignored, to present the matter properly, a certain undertone to FIFA's actions—or lack thereof, again. While the self-proclaimed Dutch cheat is free to continue in his dishonest ways, having informed the world of his intentions, the Latin American who bites is severely punished. One could ask if this has anything to do with the underlying structure of world football, where certain stereotypes about the "character" of Latin Americans (and Africans, or black European footballers) still obtains, stereotypes that bear within them the long history of colonialism, discrimination, and the exploitation of underresourced nations. (Under-resourced, structurally speaking, if not in terms of the talent nurtured in Latin America and, increasingly, Africa, Asia and the Middle East.) In significant ways, given his past, his reputation as a *voyou* and his refusal to buckle under the threat of censure in no way helped Suárez's cause.

Still, this discrepancy elicits only a minimum of sympathy, in part because these are very different orders of transgressions. Repeated simulation, however much it contravenes the spirit of the game, is not the same as repeated biting.

If any manager or coach in the contemporary game was capable (or "is," I must struggle to say, to continue to say) of breaking with managerial tradition (defend your players at all costs; deflect the blame; implicitly impugn others— the referee, opponents, FIFA), there is good reason to have always imagined

Tabárez as that coach. After all, this is a man who runs his team(s) on that famed Che Guevara principle "One must toughen oneself without ever losing tenderness." Tabárez, it can be said, has never shown any sign of "ever losing his tenderness," such is the nature in which he approaches his task, such is the way in which he instills in his team the commitment to playing with joy while remaining resilient and uncompromising on defense. Here the defenders, Lugano (West Bromwich Albion), Diego Godín (Atlético de Madrid), and Martín Cáceres (Juventus) exhibit the toughness that Tabárez prides himself on. Then there is Arévalo Ríos ("El Cacha," which means "the handle of the knife"; he played for Peñarol, among a host of other clubs), the aging central midfielder (he was thirty-two at the 2014 Copa Mundial), who is the epitome of what the Uruguayans call *garra*, "fighting spirit." Ríos is imbued with a spirit of combativeness, refusing to lose, competing intensely for every ball, fighting until the final whistle. Uruguay under El Maestro also has about it a kind of streetwiseness, a quality that his "star player," Suárez, possesses by the bucketload. This is what Tabárez has instilled in the Uruguayan national team: toughness, an appetite for the delightful touch, relentless running, and *garra*.

If there is one player on the Uruguayan team in whom all these qualities come together, it is Suárez. The man from Salto is a mercurial striker who can as easily "nutmeg" an opponent (pushing the ball through an opponent's legs, arguably the most embarrassing way to beat an opponent, especially a defender; to "nutmeg" an opponent is little short of humiliating her or him; the equivalent in ice hockey would be beating the goaltender between his pads, beating him through the "five-hole," as they say) as he will race back eighty meters to help out his left back. (The other term for "nutmeg," the one I know best from my playing days, is "dummy": as in, to "sell your opponent a dummy.") As a Liverpool fan who watched Suárez for too brief a time with us, I would constantly marvel at what I would have named, in typical English fashion, his "work rate," but now I know that *garra* gets closer to what I admire, and admire still, about him: Luis Suárez plays football with his soul.

That Suárez thinks football with, and from, his heart, is a poor transcription of what it means to a Liverpool fan to see a player give his all, in every game, and to do so with that buck-toothed grin that bespeaks absolute joy. Suárez plays football with the kind of abandonment that can only emanate from love for the game. He plays as though he remains, at his core and at his extremities, that same "kid from Salto" who found a home, for a season or three, up on Merseyside, an English city renowned for producing its own brand of streetwiseness. "Scousers," as Liverpudlians are known, have a reputation for their offbeat humor, their edginess, and their capacity to "put one over on you." Scousers are worldly folks, not above a trick or two, like Suárez—who has always known when to throw a stealthy elbow, how to nudge an opponent or pull his shirt without drawing the referee's attention. All of this was always carefully calculated, calibrated for maximum effect. Suárez plays to win, so there is always great deal of thought, to say nothing of imagination, in every Suárez football move—successful or not.

This propensity for thinking about the game is an attribute Suárez shares with Tabárez. The Uruguayan coach is, unlike Poe's murderous narrator in "The Imp of the Perverse," neither afraid to "prostrate" himself in the direction of the "abyss," thought, nor is he afraid of being "destroyed" by thought. This understanding of Tabárez as a (football) man of thought arises from the sense of universality that Tabárez possesses. El Maestro is, after all, a man who is philosophical by nature—Tabárez says of Suárez's "litany of controversies," which "cannot dilute Tabárez's affection for his star player. I think, through the years, he has matured. . . . He's learnt a lot from the thing he's been through and now he sums up the philosophy that I've brought here.'"[56]

Tabárez is a coach who ascribes to a set of transcendent principles, principles that are in every important political way connected to being in the world as subject with inalienable rights. It is the work of football, or, more precisely, Tabárez sees it as his responsibility to work toward securing those rights through his role as coach, as a coach who draws on his philosophical thinking—or, his philosophy, which is already, a priori, a commitment to thinking—in order to be with his players in the world. On this score Tabárez is categorical, putting me in mind of an equivocal Bill Shankly (the most legendary manager in the history of Liverpool; Shankly's most famous pronouncement is, "Football is not a matter of life or death, it's much more important than that." Whereas Shankly assigned ontological essence to football, Tabárez is more interested in what can be accomplished politically through football.) "'I'm a football man,' he begins, "'but I understand that there are more important things than football. But there are things that football can help. Sport can contribute greatly to health and education, which are the two measures we use of development, not just of wealth.'"[57] And then Tabárez moves into full Che/Paolo Freire mode: "Football should help marginalized people into society, to contribute to equal opportunity, for government policies to encourage its use as an uplifting activity, to combat idleness."[58] In terms reserved strictly for the politics of the body, burnished with the patina of Shankly, we can say with Tabárez that "football is good for you." It is a deterrent against "idleness" because it promotes healthy physical activity, lending Tabárez's philosophy a decidedly Calvinist bent (glossed with all the hallmarks of nineteenth colonialism); after all, the elect are known for their industriousness.

Football is also politically instrumental in that it can contribute to the "health and education" of the Uruguayan people, an index of "development" that ranks higher—arguably—for Tabárez than wealth as such, wealth as capital and capital only. On the axis that is football, through the thinking of Tabárez, what is at stake in playing, promoting, football, in nurturing footballers from all walks of life, is nothing other than the nation's understanding of itself. The nation, to phrase this hyperbolically, can best be grasped in how football figures in its political imaginary. How football is regarded, how it is funded, tells us much about what kind of nation it (Uruguay, metonymically) is. By your football will you be known; football, as both elemental and alimentary to the health of the nation.

As such, the focus of Tabárez's vision of football is strictly political. It is through football, and here the figure of Suárez is at once towering and symptomatic, that the other (the "marginalized") can be made part, integrally, as equal, as full citizens of a democratic soceity, of the national fabric. It is through football that the other enters the body of the nation, so much so that, as in the case of Suárez, it becomes the body from which the nation, in moments of triumph and embarrassment, cannot be disarticulated. It comes to stand as the nation before the world, the other's body becomes synonymous with the nation. And, as Tabárez insists, it is the responsibility of the structure of the nation, "government policies," to make this possibility available as a political principle. The government is responsible to football because football is the measure of its responsibility to its citizenry. The more stars there are from locales such as Salto or the poorer neighborhoods of Montevideo, the more the nation can be said to have made it possible for the other to publicly constitute, as full citizens, the nation.

*I find it impossible not to be absolutely taken with Tabárez.*

SHAME · Shame breaks the connection. We have to care about something or someone to feel ashamed when that care and connection—our interest—is not reciprocated.
—— ELSPETH PROBYN, *Blush*

Examine these and similar actions as we will, we shall find them resulting solely from the spirit of the *Perverse*. We perpetrate them merely because we feel that we should *not*. Beyond or behind this, there is no intelligible principle. —— POE, "The Imp of the Perverse"

Tactically astute, captivatingly reticent in his pronouncements, almost taut in his conduct, Tabárez has about him an endearing wisdom that he wears easily, as though he were everybody's really smart uncle.

His intelligence is worn without ostentation.

He knows how to give himself to thought because, unlike Poe's protagonist, he has nothing to hide, and less to fear. Poe's narrator struggles against thought because it would remind him of his guilt. In vain, it turns out, because thought—or, "conscience"—cannot be escaped, and it is finally, emerging out of a resounding, haunting silence, what indicts him. Or what compels Poe's narrator to indict himself. Tabárez walks the path of thought with an engaging self-assurance, which makes his response to Suárez's bite at the 2014 World Cup all the more salient. Tabárez has set himself up so that we have of him expectations, so that, when intervening in the event, a certain level of the ethical must be manifest. Failing that, Tabárez opens himself up, not fatally, of course, but to the kind of philosophical examination that other managers, those in charge of their national or club teams, would not be subject.

One asks the kind of philosophical questions, questions that go to the heart of the ethical, or the moral (in the *Webster's* sense), of Tabárez because his thinking of the world demands that he, a man who stands so publicly for justice, equality, he who stands on the side of the marginalized and makes them the body of the nation, be addressed in the terms that are so constitutive of his being. If one takes one's political cues from Che, and advocates for the writings of Galeano, a different mode of (football) being is long since in play; the being of football, of the football manager, points to a distinct passage.

It was a moment, then—Suárez's bite and the reactions that ensued (both before and after FIFA issued its decision)—that called for reflection, contemplation, and instruction. Lugano, reduced to the role (until late in the match against Italy) of nonplaying captain, was presented an opening, and he threw himself with all his might into the cause of defending Suárez. His pent-up energy had found its outlet. No matter. Lugano and his teammates were entitled to their response. Lugano and his colleagues did what teammates do: they come out vigorously in support of their own, they impugn the world, they decry injustice. Lugano was first to proclaim, loudly and frequently, Suárez's innocence.

The frothing at the mouth of the Uruguayan media was little short of unseemly. In this moment, the journalist Luis Roux was the single—notable—exception. Roux, it is worth remarking, offered his critique of the Uruguayan nation's full-throated defense of Suárez in recognizably Tabárez—and Galeanoesque—terms: "These are difficult times for those who wish to stop and think."[59] Roux clearly understands the psyche of his compatriots ("The entire nation feels aggrieved, wounded, humiliated."), but he will not succumb to the hysteria. Instead, he pauses and calls for "thinking."[60] With Tabárez failing to be (true to) Tabárez, it was left to Roux to play the role of Tabárez, philosophical interlocutor, calm critic.

And a good thing, too. While Roux was gently calling his fellow Uruguayans to account, the nation's president, José "Pepe" Mujica, offered, in colorful language, impassioned denunciations of FIFA. It is quite a spectacle to see the president of a country so comfortable in everyday, masculinist profanity.

> *But then again, what am I saying, given that citizens of the United States are familiar with first a presidential candidate and now a president proposing what amounts to, politely phrased, sexual groping, a tawdry affair with an adult entertainment star named "Stormy," dubiously created LLCs in the state of Delaware, and, last but by no means least, is given to denouncing an entire continent as either a "shithole" or a "shithouse." Take your pick of expletives and decide whether the excrement that is African countries more closely resembles a "hole" or a "house." The latter term at least has the benefit of affording Africans modern domestic structures, unlike Nigerian immigrants to America, who are fleeing their "huts." The "hut," as every Nigerian knows, is the preferred abode in Lagos, Ibadan, Port Harcourt, and the university town that is Ife, where a few of my friends and colleagues acquired degrees. Against such a backdrop, Mujica's vulgar raving seems preferable, if for no reason other than it is borne out of deep political conviction. Suárez's act may have been indefensible, but going to bat for a footballer wins out any*

*day in the profanity stakes over racism, the defense of neo-Nazi rallies, and the condemnation of all Haitian immigrants as being infected with "AIDS."*

For his part, Mujica was hysterical—by which I mean both funny and a little *loco*—in his onslaught against FIFA's "fascist ban." Not for a moment, it would seem, did Mujica pause to contemplate that his was an entirely questionable political defense. After all, Uruguayan politics after the mid-1960s is marked by, firstly, the sidelining (president Óscar Diego Gestido) and then the outright banning of Left and Communist movements (president Jorge Pacheco Areco banned the Tupamaro National Liberation Movement) before descending into an outright dictatorship. Consistent with the Cold War logic of Operación Cóndor, which sought to attack all Leftist movements in the Southern Cone region (Chile and Argentina perhaps foremost among them), Uruguay experienced military dictatorship, restrictions upon civil liberties (the right to political organization, free speech, the right to protest, and so on), and some of its population was "disappeared." Although Uruguay had far fewer *desaparecidos* than neighboring Argentina, the repressive "civic-military" regimes led by the likes of Juan María Bordaberry and Alberto Demicheli, among others, the violation of human rights, and the rule of "JOG" (Junta de Oficiales Generales) left its mark on Uruguayan life. During the dictatorship, almost 20 percent of the population was imprisoned, giving Uruguay the highest per capita ratio of political prisoners. During this era, almost 10 percent of the population, seeking to escape repression, emigrated. Even when democracy was restored in 1984–85 with the presidency of Julio María Sanguinetti, the new democratic incumbent did not press for tribunals to try and punish those who had committed the atrocities. Instead, Sanguinetti opted for Ley de Amnistía, which, in essence, granted immunity to the perpetrators who had tortured and "disappeared" "dissident" Uruguayans. Considering Uruguay's checkered recent political history, history replete with its cast of characters from the *generalissimo* handbook, Mujica would have been well advised to refrain from casting about the term "fascist" so freely. Nonetheless, the president's rote defenses meant little, in no small measure because we do not expect much from a political figure such as Mujica.

*Not so with Tabárez.*

*Not so with Tabárez because . . . when he was asked a question about his relationship with Miguel Zuluaga, Tabárez balked at the inquiry. Since 2000,*

Zuluaga has been in charge of the security team for Uruguay's selection committee. Whose head is, of course, Tabárez. During the dictatorship Zuluaga was the deputy commissioner of the National Intelligence and Information Directorate. Zuluaga's name has come up from time to time in the testimony of political prisoners. Zuluaga, it turns out, was involved in meting out punishment to these prisoners. So much so that in 2011, Zuluaga was named in a case before el Juzgado Penal de 17° Turno (17th Shift Criminal Court).

Confronted with questions about Zuluaga, Tabárez responded,

"Pero al finalizar la entrevista, las periodistas de Brecha le hicieron una pregunta que molesto al entrenador de Uruguay" (At the end of the interview, the Uruguayan coach was annoyed by the question).[61]

Not "amused":

"Entonces, no pretenda. . . . No me hace mucha gracia que se acerquen a mí para poner en."

In a press conference or two, Tabárez can proclaim himself indignant, he can skirt the question, he can prevaricate.

But for those of us who admire Tabárez, who find Galeanoesque comfort and confirmation in the way his teams play, and recognize in him the possibility of a thinking coach who transcends the game, his refusal to denounce Zuluaga—to even entertain the question, amounts to more than disappointment. It opens onto a concatenation of questions, beginning with "Que?" "Porque?" "Why, why?"

And then, inevitably, what else is there to be found out? Possibly, nothing, "nada," but . . . "pero" . . .

Twice now, we can say, in the moment of record, love or no, Tabárez has given us cause for pause.

That it were not so. That it is so troubles, unsettles.

Uruguay remains haunted by "Operation Condor." It traces legible in the inner circle of "El Proceso."

That it were not so.

It is so. History is unforgiving. The work of history is to haunt us.

The work of history is to cast a shadow over our philosophical inheritance. The footballer philosopher, in two moments at least, fails us.

Once more we can assert that philosophy begins in the question. It begins when the question—"una pregunta"—is encountered as the refusal of the question.

*In such a moment, the philosopher's indignation doubles as self-indictment.*
*Who knows the full extent of the crime?*
*Are they friends now, Zuluaga and Tabárez?*
*It matters, because if they are friends, then we know how friendship can soften historical antagonism. We know that friendship makes forgiveness possible, even in the face of the most horrendous historical violence.*
*Perhaps it is again in love that we find the "key" to any thinking of Tabárez. Love as absolute loyalty to the other.*
*Love as the refusal to condemn the other. Love as the refusal to abandon or condemn the friend, no matter how much the other's acts go counter to the self's better angels.*
*Love precludes condemnation. Love indemnifies the other against condemnation.*

It is El Maestro who preoccupies us because it is to him that we look when the event is Uruguayan football. One could, as I have already acknowledged, imagine his predicament as a manager. Yes, and all, but we all knew that what the moment called for was judgment in the Kantian sense; that is, where one thinks one's pronouncements, where discrimination—the ability to distinguish right from wrong, good from bad, simplistically rendered, to think the event in its complexity and yet retain the power of discernment—obtains. The truth is never an impossible position (Until it is, that is.) This, we imagined, is a philosophical skill in which Tabárez is well versed. A politics, judgment as such, in which Tabárez is more than adequately schooled.

And here one believed there was historical reason to trust Tabárez because he understood what is at stake. We trusted that he, if no one else among Uruguayan public figures (besides Roux, that is), grasped that which was proper to the moment. Kipling, that most intriguing—and complex—of colonialists authors, says that we must treat the "impostors," victory or defeat, the same. Rendered in the terms of the event Suárez, what was clearest was that sharp (by which I mean incisive, not punitive, as such) judgment was the order of the day. That is not to say that such judgment did not have to account for the difficulties that emerge out of R, that deep bond, we can call it love, between self and other, between Tabárez, the institutionalization of thought in football, thought through football, football as thought itself, and Suárez, who instantiates the surging up of the "marginalized" into national prominence.

Not so Tabárez, not in the case of événement *Suárez*.

Instead, disappointment awaited.

Although the brouhaha activated by Suárez began immediately after the Italy game, it was only at the press conference before the upcoming game against Colombia that it can be alleged Tabárez came fully into his own. Or failed to come into his own.

*How one frames it, as failure of one order or another, determines the magnitude of the failure. What is most true, however, is that as an admirer of Tabárez one is never prepared for such a disappointment. For such a failure, no matter the order or magnitude of that failure.*

At that press conference, it could be said, Tabárez was not so much obstinate as almost myopic (willfully myopic? dare one say "self-blinded?") in his defense: "Primero tengo que decir que yo no la he visto. Tendría que revisar la jugada. Y si sucedió, el árbitro tampoco la vio" ("First I have to say that I did not see the play. I would have to check the play. And if it happened, the referee did not see it either").[62] He did, of course, "review the play," "take another look at it"—*Tendría que revisar la jugada*—but this did not cause him to revise his position. Instead, he committed himself, as reported (in the language of fatality), to Suárez, until the death: "El técnico de la selección uruguaya, Óscar Washington Tabárez defendió a muerte a Luis Suárez cuando los periodistas le preguntaron en rueda de prensa por su mordida a Giorgio Chiellini."[63] In short, *defendió a muerte*: Tabárez would defend Suárez "to the death." A resoluteness in keeping with Uruguay's national motto: "Libertad o muerte:" "Liberty or death." No amount of Uruguayan defiance could free Suárez from FIFA's sentence, but Tabárez, Lugano and Mujica did everything in their power to ensure that he was not condemned to professional death. There is loyalty aplenty in their commitment to Suárez, but there can be escaping the depth of their—that is, the nation's collective—rationalization.

If the discourse of shame is operative here, and there is every reason to believe it was, because Tabárez's face was a contortion—taut, defiant, set against what was before him (sometimes love means having to say you're sorry)—that spoke a lack of conviction, then it worked to (1) either efface the break, or (2) to intensify the connection (love) in face of the condemnation heaped upon Suárez. Let us call the second "rationalization," that is, playing fast and loose with the truth. (All of it, of course, born out of love.) Or the break was located in the denunciation, in the unsustainable defense of Suárez: that is where the shame is located, that is where (the) shame (of Tabárez) showed, as it were, its face. In the refusal to name "shame" as shame; and such a refusal, of course, makes the shame more, not less, visible; the degree of shame, we might say, is directly proportional to the intensity of the unsustainable defense.

THE ROAD TO BRAZIL · But before we turn our attention fully to the event, let us start with Tabárez's response to the Uruguayan achievements in the 2010 Copa Mundial and the qualifying campaign for the 2014 tournament in Brazil.

To begin with, as a general principle, Tabárez declared victory to be more or less his enemy. He cast Uruguay's successful qualification in the language of an overly cautious dentist when complimented on that accomplishment. "Winning is the sweet that rots the tooth," he offered, making one wonder what the effects of defeat might be. Defeat, if we are to follow the analogy to its periodontological end, breeds healthy dental hygiene. Defeat is what inspires footballers (in Tabárez's charge) to brush twice a day and to floss daily. As such, defeat produces a sound team structure. Or maybe Tabárez was speaking only hypothetically and using the analogy of bad dental hygiene to keep his players on their toes. In truth, it is difficult to posit "winning" as the ultimate goal when El Proceso could easily stand as its own objective, victory or defeat notwithstanding, victory or defeat be damned.

*All athletes know the coach's mantra: "It's not the ones you make, it's the ones you miss." Yes, we learn more from defeat than victory. Yes, defeat provides a unique form of motivation. Defeat is a painful lesson for an athlete and, as such, a very good teacher. But, again, this is not to undermine the pedagogical and political value of defeat, but let us allow ourselves a moment of unvarnished truth, there is no fun—no joy—in losing. I don't recommend it, certainly not with regularity. Not as a player, and certainly not as a fan.*

Tabárez was, of course, not advocating defeat, but he was alert to the increased expectations and how those could adversely affect his team. It turns out that he was right.

Uruguay struggled in the qualifying rounds for Brazil 2014. It took a late run to get them into a playoff—against Jordan—to qualify for Brazil. And, although they beat both England and Italy to qualify second to Costa Rica, who defeated them in the opening group game (when Suárez did not play), this team lacked the verve of their 2010 predecessors.

The quarterfinal loss to Colombia, with Suárez already back in Montevideo, was a mere formality. At that press conference before the game, Tabárez conducted himself in a most un-Tabárez fashion. He spoke like a man without conviction. He spoke like a coach who could master victory and defeat, but not, not this, this "spirit of the perverse," for which he could discern "no intelligible principle." In truth, such unintelligibility may be the story of Suárez as well.

This poses Elspeth Probyn's assertion of the work of shame as an interrogative for Tabárez. For Probyn, shame is always cast affirmatively. Shame is good because it demonstrates, in her terms, "interest." Shame provides "evidence": that there is an investment in—shall we say?—the other, in what the other is undergoing and in what the other has experienced. Probyn's work often turns, insightfully, to the relationship between white Australians and Aboriginals. (On this account Probyn advocates for how it is that shame could, and has, function in relation to national discussions about addressing—through government apology—white transgression in the Australian political sphere: "We must use shame to re-evaluate how we are positioned in relation to the past and to rethink how we wish to live in proximity to others.")[64] It is a good thing, in Probyn's terms, if white Australians feel shame about their history of violence against the Aboriginals, because, in her estimation, this means that something "productive" can emerge out of their feeling of shame. Most notably, one can easily deduce from Probyn's argument, the "rethinking" of nothing less than Australian being. That is, how to "live in proximity" to the other, the other whom "we" have acted against with a violence that borders on, if it is not in fact, the genocidal, if it has not already in fact transitioned from settler colonial violence to genocide.[65] Because white Australians feel shame, it is possible for them to do something about their shame. White Australians have an interest in addressing it, in, best case scenario, doing something about the violence they have committed. White Australians are moved to respond, decades later, to the violence done in their name, the violence (expropriation of land, the "stolen generation," Aboriginal children wrenched from their families and placed with white ones, the denigration of Aboriginal culture, and so on) and its ongoing effects. (Among these effects are the disproportionately high rates of alcoholism in Aboriginal communities, violence within the family, lower educational achievements, etcetera.) Shame provides—and here the Levinasian ethics of the political effect of coming face to face with the other resonates—at the very least evidence of that "care and affection" we have for the other.

> *Is Tabárez ashamed of what Zuluaga did during the dictatorship?*
> *Is he ashamed of Suárez's bite?*
> *Its political effects aside, what kind of inner turmoil does shame provoke?*

In being shamed, we are called upon to account for why it is we "care" that we have done violence to the other. Shame demands, as the introspective effect of what our face registers, shame makes us "blush," that we produce a philosophical response to our physiological "outburst"—the involuntary reddening of the face. We have to think our shame, we have explain to ourselves and the world why we are ashamed and how we intend to address why it is we did what we did to cause us shame.

It is, and this is the pivot of Probyn's argument, when we encounter the complete absence of shame that the prospect for a "productive politics" is diminished, if not quite eliminated. The absence of shame is what mitigates against, say, campaigning for the return of Aboriginal land, sacred cultural sites, such as returning Ayres Rock to its Aboriginal name, Uluru, or designating greater resources to Aboriginal communities for healthcare, education, housing, drug and alcohol recovery programs, and so on.

Shame provokes us to do something, to act politically, to address the effects of the event that caused the shame, and, in so doing, if not to undo the shame—impossible, of course—but to acknowledge and to act in its name, to act in the knowledge of shame. And shame, as Probyn frames it and has just been iterated, is unarguable—it is the only unarguable affect—because it is, literally, visible. Our face, that with which we face the world, shows shame. Our face changes color, shame is the only biologically marked affect and, effect, as such. Shame shows, shows itself to the world and, no less important, shows us ashamed—how ashamed we are. Shame shows our shame to the world. In shame the depth, "hollowed out" fully, is on display all for the world to see, for the world to make determinations—to judge—about who we are and how we are in the world.

Politically, the primary effect of shame may be, as Probyn says, that "sometimes shame makes us reflect on who we are—individually and collectively."[66] And how the self stands in relation to the collectivity, or how, as in Tabárez's case, how the self enunciates itself in relation to the "collective," that "collective" for which the self is understood—has presented itself as—an articulate, thoughtful metonym.

> How, in Tabárez's case, the self stands in relation to the living and the dead. To that euphemistic political moment (1973–1985) and mode known as Uruguay's "Civil Dictatorship," the movement in which Zuluaga had a role. Starring or not, it matters not. At the very least, he bore witness to violence against the other.

> As much as any other affect, shame bears within it inexpungible traces of the dead. Our shame is haunted so that it can always be said to extend beyond the moment of shaming itself. It extends to 1977, to 1981 ... and much farther beyond. As Nancy reminds us so powerfully at the end of his essay "Being Singular Plural": "Our understanding (of the meaning of Being) is an understanding that we share understanding between us and, at the same time, because we share understanding between us: between us all, simultaneously—all the dead and the living, and all beings."[67]

What is exposed, as such, is nothing other than the political, public constitution (and ex-position) of what Nancy frames as "our just-between-us [entrée-nous], the just-between-us of our manifestation, our becoming, and our desire."[68] Everything that is *entre-nous* is now no longer only *entre-nous* but is now shared with everyone else. What is *entre-nous* has now been made, for all time, public. It belongs to the world now. In order to "become," it is necessary to achieve the truth of that which is *entre-nous*. In order to "reveal" such a truth, it is necessary to recognize that what is "just-between-us" can no longer tolerate or admit of restriction unto itself. That which is "just-between-us" must now be the passage through which self and other, in the fullness of its R, "exits" into the world.

> Suárez's bite. Whatever transactions, political, personal, professional, took place between Tabárez and Zuluaga now belong in one place and one place only: exposed, fully, to the world. What is "between" is now between the world y el técnico. It has escaped any pretense at containment. It is the secret that belongs fully to, and fully in, the world. Sous rature.

It is for this reason that the way in which shame "breaks the connection" presents itself as a philosophical supplement to thinking *entre-nous*. Shame, at least as Probyn argues for it, is intent on "hollowing out" what is constitutive of *entre-nous*. As such, S ↔ o (self ↔ other), T ↔ S, R as it constitutes that relation, must, after the event, be rethought. That is, the tie that binds, let us call it "interest" (although we can, as we have, as easily name it "love"), Tabárez and Suárez may not have been "broken" as such. However, at the very least, the love that they share has been interrupted. And having had to endure such a rupture, no matter how big or small, that love has now been tested, been put to the test.

The self, in this case, has been put in the position in which it must "assume," take on, the effect of the other's shame; the shame that the other has caused has now become, because of the political and affective force of R, the self's shame.

*Surely this does not mean that Tabárez must take on Suárez's shame? Or does it?*

*Surely this does not mean that Tabárez must now take on Zuluaga's shame? Is that his shame to assume? What would "free" Tabárez to assume such a dastardly, brutal, violent shame? Friendship? Love? Collegiality? What a burden friendship threatens to become.*

*Confronted with Zuluaga's atrocities, does Tabárez wish that he could say, after Aristotle, "O my friend, there is no friend?" Can he betray the friend, like an ethical Judas? Can we even conceive of such a figure, an ethical Judas? Or is too much of a contradiction in ethical terms?*

Love is that mode of being that bears the other's shame as its own. (This means that as we think the effects of love-shame there is a third conceptual element, sacrifice at work, which we must keep in mind. This conceptual element must find its voice, in either a loud or a more subdued register. This conceptual element must be accounted for in our thinking of this R. Foremost among these questions might be: What difficulties reside *entre-nous* shame and sacrifice? Does shame demand the demonstration of sacrifice, sacrificing the self in the cause of the other? And so on. For our part, and for now, these questions resonate but are operative only in a lower register.)

Love is nothing less than truth, for Tabárez, the most proximate, fact-to-face encounter with the truth of R as it stands between him and Suárez: "My truth is to become for myself in my other. To be for self, to exit simple being-other."[69] Shame, as understood in R that is T ↔ S, should be liberating. (That it was not in the Suárez instance was entirely down to Tabárez's intransigence, as we know from his press conference. In a press conference following the event, Tabárez was obstinate in his defense: "Primero tengo que decir que yo no la he visto. Tendría que revisar la jugada. Y si sucedió, el árbitro tampoco la vio.")

*Intransigence. Zuluaga.*

Or, phrased in its Nancian vocabulary, shame is the passage of thought that opens up from "simple being-other" to the truth of "becoming for myself in my other." Instead, what is being named here, the shame of the bite, is the event that may, at least in schematic terms, compel us to dispense with the figuration T ↔ S (R as we know it, as we have presented and thought it) in the direction, in search of, some other, more fitting of the condition of having "exited self-other." We might propose, tentatively, a simple rendering, T ∴ S, with the ∴ marking at once, with its "solidity," the constitutive dots that form the "broken," interrupted, but still legible and discernible angled "line." ∴ marks the porousness that stands between self and other. ∴ identifies those spacings, that "gap" between self and other that announces self as self and other as other and yet achieves the being of being-together as self-other.

The other is no longer, as Nancy warns us, the "other pure and simple," the other who is "just alike," but other-in-being-self. That is, the "meaning" of "'Self' being unto the ordeal the event of shame of being" is made possible by the event. ∴ marks the entrée into "being" as such. The self is not other, the other is not self; the self is in ∴ to other. As such, through what is instantiated by ∴ the critique can no longer be made that "being-one-with-the-other can only provisionally pass for a unity" because the presumption of "unity" as understood in that formulation has been rent. In its place stands ∴, the porous solidity of the true R of self and other. ∴ is how self and other, the being of self and other, is liberated into absolute freedom.

∴ is the "concretization of negation": self ∴ other. It is difficult to achieve ∴ precisely because the truth of love resides in the recognition that "struggle is also the phenomenon of the very thing," ∴, "whose reality is love."[70] Whose goal, as Nancy phrases it, is to know that "freedom is freedom-with or it is nothing"; ∴, as such, is the sign of nothing less than "freedom-with," the "freedom-with" that surges up out of thinking through and because of the event of shame.[71]

TRUTH · However, without diminishing the insights made present—made available—by the event, it is possible that there is something even more important that emerged from Suárez's bite.

And here we limit ourselves to Suárez, haunted as we are by what transpired between Tabárez and Zuluaga.

What may be transpiring between them still.

It is the possibility that the manifestation of "truth comes back to us. It finds us or happens upon itself *as us*, and it is *to us* that it is entrusted."⁷² The "truth," then, was "entrusted" to Tabárez and Suárez from the start. But the truth, as such, in order to trust to the truth, to trust to the possibility of making the truth accessible, requires something specific and blatantly obvious of us: we must understand and account for why Tabárez's defense of Suárez rang hollow from the start.

To begin with, under no circumstances could Suárez's bite be rationalized. This, one can have little doubt, Tabárez knew, knew in the moment of its having happened. He could inveigh against the treatment handed out to Suárez, but he could not, under any circumstances, defend it. He left it to deputies such as the Luganos of the world, aided in no small measure by the partisans in the Uruguayan media and those unthinking zealots who occupy high office. Tabárez's not speaking directly to the event speaks of his ∴. But even so we can say that Tabárez belongs, beyond question (which is in itself an act of judgment against him, in abstentia), to that part of the "collective self" that stands before the world indicted on the counts of love, sacrifice, fidelity, and being-with.

In his dissembling, rationalization, and prevarication Tabárez showed us that he was incapable of showing his true face to the public. Or show his true colors (to show the true colors of his—a true—face in public), as those given to the Anglophone expression are wont to say. Tabárez would not dare to show his face to the public. "What makes shame remarkable," Probyn writes, "is that it reveals with precision our values, hopes, and aspirations, beyond the generalities of good manners and cultural norms."⁷³ If what (and who, too, of course) is dearest to us is precisely that which (and those who) cannot be circumscribed—or disguised as, or by—"good manners and cultural norms," then it must stand as truth. More narrowly presented, it must stand as the truth of what is most truthful—the kernel of truth—that is contained in but not restricted by that which is named "values, hopes, and aspirations." Truth, as such, is that which is impatient with societal norms, it is that which, and this matters in the case of Tabárez, flies in the face of convention. That is to say, the "break in the connection" is not only between self and other. (At least potentially, an issue that will be complicated shortly.) Moreover, it marks a radical break. That is, the break that demarcates truth from everything else.

Love, we might say, marks the entry into that mode of being that breaks, that ruptures, truth (philosophy) from sophistry.

> *That ruptures truth from the refusal to answer a direct question. The refusal to answer the question directly.*

How we love in the moment of record, that is, in the event, is where the truth of our thinking can be found. In Probyn's lyrical rendering, "Shame reminds us of the promises we keep to ourselves."[74] And, we might add in the case of Tabárez, the intense difficulty of "keeping that promise" to himself. A difficulty, of course, that arises directly from the ways in which that promise is complicated by his love for Suárez, by his recognition of the nature of the (unarguable, unarticulated, but not unacknowledged) transgression. (What is more, of the pattern of that transgression, the way in which it became a seemingly regular if not exactly routine occurrence.) Surely, Tabárez knew the (untruthful) nature of the sacrifice that was now, made necessary by the event, expected of him. The promise, as such, derives its worth proportionately: the promise is worth keeping only if there is something of value at stake in the promise itself. Trenchantly phrased, the promise only has worth if the cost of not keeping the promise exacts a cost from the self who underwrote the agreement between self and other. However, it is only through something like the promise that we can live, in an ethical fashion, in proximity to each other, with each other, live being-with; live with the "all the dead and the living, and with all beings." How, that is, we face each other, face-to-face, every day, self to other, self-other.

> *But how do you keep a promise to the dead? To those put to death at the hand, at the behest, of the friend? Nancy's "Being" comes back to haunt us, as we knew it would.*

> *As much as anything, as we well know, entre-nous marks a relationship of mischief, a relationship in which mischief plays an important role. A constitutive one, even. But what happens when, as in the Zuluaga instance, the mischief is of an entirely different order? When the order of mischief is fatal? What happens when death itself constitutes the core of what is entre-nous? How does one live with those who were put-to-death (by or) in the presence of the friend?*

It is for this reason that Probyn's argument for shame resonates with Tabárez. If we acknowledge shame (as a preliminary political gesture or commitment, as in Australian prime minister Kevin Rudd's address to the Aboriginal people), then it becomes possible to establish R in the wake of S, painful as the effects of S might—and, should, properly speaking—be. What shame does, Probyn points out, is "promise a return of interest, joy, and connection. This is why shame matters to individuals."[75] If the shame-producing event is subjected to thinking, then R is established, in the aftermath of S, as a new point of "interest, joy and connection." However, all is conditional on shame being confronted in order that Tabárez-Suárez might produce, out of the ethical difficulty that is the event, a "connection" that accounts for and incorporates the effects of the event. The event, reductively phrased, is valuable only insofar as it reconstitutes the relationship, insofar as it recalibrates the various, and variously troubled, points of "connection."

**THE FACE** · The face, in an instance such as the Suárez event, "betrays" us. Generally speaking, our face shows who we are because on our faces is registered the truth of our thinking: our thinking as nothing other than the truth of our being.[76] My face, then, was like every other face—or, I should be precise, the face of every other Luis Suárez fan, the face of every other Suárez admirer who was also a Liverpool fan—watching the Uruguay-Italy match in the summer of 2014.

Because of my "interest," I know now, as I did then, that the vacuity of Suárez's defense and that of his proxies was immediately evident. The unsustainable arguments that it was an "accident," that he was not at fault because he had "fallen" into Chiellini, that he was being targeted by the media, with the British contingent especially culpable for the poor treatment Suárez was made subject to. I knew with certainty because, as I have admitted, I am an admirer of Luis Suárez's prodigious gifts as a footballer. I remain, to this day, enamored of his ability as a footballer, of the boyish enthusiasm with which he plays the game. Buck-toothed and all, as I have said.

Since he scored his first goal for Liverpool, my club for almost fifty years (forty-eight at the time of writing), against Stoke City on his Premier League debut (coming on as a substitute), I have pinned my hopes on him and marveled at this technical ability, at the infectious way in which he plays the game, exhibiting the enthusiasm of a schoolboy released early from class.

> *In its own way, it's a classic Luis Suárez goal. He is entirely capable of scoring spectacular ones, but more often he dinks his way past defenders, sialoms through traffic, and nudges the ball home. So it was on February 2, 2011. Coming on late as a substitute for Fábio Aurélio, Suárez stationed himself on the halfway line.*
>
> *From a gritty Dirk Kuyt pass, Suárez sped away, taking the ball in the direction of Stoke's left-hand post. At pace, he left Stoke's Bosnian keeper, Asmir Begović, for dead. He rounded Begović before scuffing his left-footed shot. Andy Wilkinson, the Stoke defender, tried valiantly to cut off the goal-bound shot but succeeded only in slipping and putting the ball into his own net.*
>
> *Suárez was not one bit bothered by the technicalities of Wilkinson's effort. It was his goal, and he claimed it.*
>
> *He broke out into that goofy smile, kissed his right wrist (in honor, first, of his eldest child, a daughter, and then of his son), and wheeled away into the waiting arms of the Dutchman Kuyt.*
>
> *Us Liverpool fans would see many more such goals.*
>
> *How we thrilled at his exploits.*
>
> *How shamed we were at his shenanigans.*
>
> *Still we loved him.*

And so, like every Liverpool fan and every Uruguayan partisan, I was filled with dread when I saw the encounter between Suárez and Chiellini.

This was a place I'd been before. This was all too familiar. There was nothing to do but succumb to that sinking feeling in the pit of my stomach. At first I thought that "Lou," as the former-Liverpool manager Brendan Rodgers refers to him, had head-butted Chiellini. However, it quickly became apparent that Suárez was back to his trademark behavior. Chiellini, self-pronounced hard man who proved himself adept at playing the victim, was eager to show the world his battle wounds (wags in the Uruguayan media intimated that the Italian was trying to show his "bra"); in any case, incisors tend to leave a mark on human flesh. The body, as Probyn argues, following Pierre Bourdieu, is its own "habitus"; the body is how we "embody history."[77] The body is, in Probyn's estimation, a "repository for the social and cultural rules that, consciously or not, we take on."[78] In Suárez's body we encounter a "repository" that resists those "rules," and so makes of his a body of transgression. Of course, all footballers, in the course of a game, certainly over the course of a career, transgress, but Suárez, as was alluded to in the introduction, has a history of transgression that is more substantial than most. However, what marks his transgressions as so singular is that they seem to erupt out of nothing—that is, they are always an event because they always catch onlookers (fans, commentators, his teammates, his coaches, and so on) off guard. It is of course entirely valid that the logic of the event is such that one lives in expectation of it and still one is surprised when it happens, but this still does not provide any solace to those who admire Suárez as a footballer. In other words, the question "Why?" persists, however persuasive the logic of the event might be.[79]

> *Why did you do that, "Lou?" Why, in the good Lord's name would you do such a thing?*
>
> *Not once but thrice.*

It is, as Probyn argues, in this way that shame is "productive": "It is productive in how it makes us think about bodies, societies, and human interaction. That shame is both universal and particular."[80] We can hear in this critique something of Probyn's address to the problematic of indigeneity in Australia, but we can also derive from it, for the purposes of thinking T.·'S, how the act of the body determines "human interactions" from others who are R to that body. In the event, the intense social interactions of the individual body are made manifest. Every other body ("societies"), to phrase the matter hubristically, must determine how it stands R to the transgressive body. Every other body, beginning of course with Tabárez. It is in this way that the "singular plural origins" of the social, of "human interaction," as such emerge—once more—as the mode with/through which to think *entre-nous*.

The mark left on the other is what haunts those who admire Suárez. (Indeed, we might speculate that it haunts him, too. But that is entirely a different matter.) More importantly, however, is that because of his proclivity for biting, it is now possible to allege that the bite is how Suárez marks his "habitus." His propensity for biting is the threat that his body brings to the "habitus" that is the football field; across continents, from Europe to Latin America, from the Netherlands to England to Brazil.

THE FAN · You only love / when you love in vain. ——MIROSLAV HOLUB, "Ode to Joy"

I felt sick. My mouth was dry. Embarrassed as a Liverpool fan, once again, shocked that Suárez could have done this, again. He was coming off his best season as a player, reaping awards for his spectacular goals—a Premier League–leading thirty-one—and his brilliant performances, proclaimed by all to be the best player in England.

My immediate response was twofold. I could not defend Suárez; I would not defend him. I neither could nor would do what Tabárez would later do. But neither did denunciation offer itself as the apropos response; not thoughtful enough, perhaps. That is because, much more troublingly and painfully, I wondered then as I wonder now, if anything, and anyone, beginning with Tabárez (that is, Tabárez ∴ Suárez), can in the future prevent Suárez from repeating this behavior. (So far, since he joined Barça in 2014, and seemingly happy to be among a gaggle of Latin American stars, Messi foremost among them, and before that Neymar and 'Masch," he has shown no evidence of recidivism. There is, then, reason to be hopeful.)

However, in the moment of the event, this was not the thought—a fourth or a fifth bite—to which I wanted to admit, nor do I want to admit to the possibility of it now. My reluctance is born in large measure out my resistance to feeding the narrative that pathologizes the "kid from Salto"—the kid from the streets, the street fighter, the kid from the ghetto, as they say in the United States, a discourse that is inherently racialized and not a little racist. With Suárez, however, it is a mode of figuring the other that is rooted in class, poverty, and the shared (with African American athletes, in the popular media,[81] in government policy—the infamous Moynihan Report of the late 1960s,[82] and so on) experience of being raised by a single mother. That narrative should always provide cause for discomfort, its objective truth notwithstanding. Here Holub's verse rings true, more true than one wants it to be, true because it reeks of melancholy: "You only love / when you love in vain."[83] Or in "pain." What a love it is of which Holub speaks.

And, within the context of *Entre-Nous*, some of that discomfort, that "pain," is present, present to us in this project's opening figure, Leo Messi, to whom we will return, if only for a moment.

A MOMENT: MESSI AND SUÁREZ · As we of course recognize immediately, the narrative that lends itself so easily to Suárez is not the kind of discourse that presents itself, it certainly does not "surge up" à la Nancy, in relation to Messi. Their "singular plural origins," in this regard, leave room only to accentuate the difference in their "plural origins." Messi, the young boy from a solid (at least) lower-middle-class background, a two-parent household, who, even when faced with a potentially crippling medical condition, could summon up (that is, his family could; their "singular plural origins" gave them access to Europe, directly, through patrilineage) the requisite resources. The force of the "singular plural origin" obtains, for Messi, at the superstructural level—reductively speaking, it operates at the level of the nation-state in its "conflict," as produced by the figure, in the body, of Messi, with the *autonomista*. There are, as we know, less than two hundred miles that separate Salto, Uruguay, from Rosário, Argentina, but what is *entre-nous* Messi and Suárez is, at least in terms of their being-in-the-world of their "origins," that the distance between them is exponentially greater. They came, these star footballers of the class of 1987, into the world—football—from singularly distinct worlds. It is only in Catalunya that their singular pluralities find articulation, one in the other.

If Messi is, in terms of the discourse of *entre-nous*, the enunciation of the superstructure, then Suárez is, without question, its socioeconomic opposite. Suárez is the rogue from the "street." Suárez is, in Marxist terms, just a part (exceptional, indeed, but only insofar as the exception proves the rule) of the indistinguishable base. The nine-year-old street sweeper that the boy Suárez was belongs, there but for his talents as a footballer (such are the ways of "grace," one is tempted to suggest), to the lumpenproletariat. The lumpenproletariat is that part of the economic base that is, as Marx cautioned, so abject as to be potentially beyond organization (made into a trade union) and, as such, of questionable revolutionary value. Or, more appropriately, the boy from the barrio, that boy so romanticized and celebrated in popular culture—in literature, in film, in the lyrics of a Carlos Santana song ("Maria, Maria," accompanied by Wyclef Jean)—is not the boy from Rosário, no matter how "marginalized" that native son may be by his original club, Newell's Old Boys, or their bitter rivals, Rosario Central. What is *entre-nous* Messi and Suárez is substantial, even as it is dissolved (almost) entirely in their playing together for Barça. What is between-them is not always between-them; or it is not always between-them because something else, such as being-with for Barça is, for a moment, all that is *entre-nous*. We have to be alert to what constitutes the changing dynamic of what is *entre-nous* in order to keep what constitutes the between-them in view.

Because what is *entre-nous* is fluid, then, it is always subject to thinking. It is in R to itself, S within itself, possibly even S itself.

ILL AT EASE · Since joining Barça, Suárez has put us at ease, for the moment, but we—by which I mean me—remain on edge. As Suárez fans, we—again, I might be invoking the royal "we" out of pure trepidation and political fear—live with history. "We" live with his history, the one we know only too well. Part of the reason for concern is that, as Poe recognizes, with Suárez there are always precautions to be taken. Poe writes, as if to simultaneously demand that we retain our caution and reckon with the infectious impishness, the capacity for delightful mischief (just watch him nutmeg an opponent and see if you are able to contain your glee), that pervades Suárez, "Examine these and similar actions as we will, we shall find them resulting solely from the spirit of the *Perverse*. We perpetrate them merely because we feel that we should *not*. Beyond or behind this, there is no intelligible principle." Poe has put his finger on it; this is who Lou is: the imp of the perverse.[84] A truly world-class footballer, at the very top of his game, overcome by the "spirit of the perverse": bent on an inexplicable path to (repeated; "eternal recurrence of the same") transgression. Suárez has a proclivity for transgression that puts one always in mind of the prospect of self-destruction. Sometimes it seems inevitable, at others Suárez appears to negotiate difficulty with ease, but the specter of self-destruction always threatens to manifest itself. 'Alas, poor Yorick." Suárez, as such, raises the specter of a professional punishment that will be visited upon him. Yet once more. And what will the length of the sentence be this time?

*So it is with love. So it is with love for a fan such as I. Suárez has long since left Liverpool, but I continue to be concerned for him.*

*One is never done with love. With the one who is loved.*

Every time it happens, Suárez is punished. Every time it happens, he promises—to his team, teammates, now, in the latest incident, to his children (what sins they are being asked to bear)—that it will not happen again. Suárez knows what he should not do—Tabárez knows this, too—but neither of them is master of the "inexplicable principle."

*Luis Suárez, one of football's profane mysteries.*

I understand the inherent political danger I am raising in this articulation. I do not mean to either excuse or pathologize Suárez; I do not mean to suggest that there is something innately unhealthy and abnormal about his behavior. I mean only to suggest that he is, for reasons inexplicable (to me, and possibly even to him—*profane mysteries*), given to doing things—things that he "feels he should not"—that will cause destruction to him. I wonder for how long he can curb his tendencies; I wonder what will happen when his skills decline, as they surely will. I wonder, writing on the eve of his thirty-second birthday (January 24), about what happens then. But this I know: Liverpool misses him; we miss his mesmerizing talent, the joy with which he plays the game. I still have delightful visions of him tricking opponents, pickpocketing the ball off defenders, dancing in my head. But mostly I just want the Chiellini event to be the last act in that particular Suárez drama. An unholy trinity. *Basta*. That is my fervent hope. My hope is that for once, just once, I do not want to "love in vain."

*Let this cup pass me by.*

This hope is, naturally, constitutively insufficient but I have nothing else to offer.

This may be why I turn to Poe. His narrator grasps, if only perversely (that is, entirely unlike Tabárez), the unintelligibility of tragedy and the tragedy of tragedy. It is difficult to explain tragedy, all the more so when the tragic figure is so revered; revered, as Suárez is, because of his immense talents. When he bit Chiellini, the full force of the tragedy became evident. Suárez is a footballer who has such greatness in him, who has given us ample evidence of his brilliance, but who is subject to a fatal flaw: his ability to undo himself, to reduce his gifts to mere ashes.

*Sackcloth and ashes. Tragedy. Autoimmunity. It is precisely what makes Suárez so wonderful a player, all those skills, all the unbridled love for the game, and contained within that is the germ of his capacity—or, is it his appetite?—for self-destruction.*

*Long before he can let us, his fans, his coach, his teammates, down, he is already on the brink of a fate far more invidious: he is about to disappoint Luis Suárez.*

This is, as Poe says, the promise of perversity. In the end, it will bring everything crashing down. That is, for Poe's narrator, the perpetrator who is also, in his own perverse way, his own hero, the effect of perversity: it is destructive. It never spares the self. It spares the self least of all. This, if the poetry is to be believed, and I see no reason not to believe it, is the fate that awaits Suárez.

*Will there be one more bite? Am I tempting fate?*

*When his talent wanes, who will be there to speak in his name? To protect him?*

*Who will love Lou Suárez then?*

TABÁREZ AND HIS PROTÉGÉ · After Uruguay had beaten Italy and before FIFA handed down its verdict, Suárez trained on his own, apart from his Uruguayan colleagues. I watched the footage of the press conference: Suárez, dressed in a white Uruguayan polo shirt, his eyes downcast, his usually ebullient face held tightly, as though he was refusing to let his face betray him. It already had, of course, but he was battling to stay within himself, to maintain something of himself in the midst of the event that he had made.

I watched that footage. Suárez's face bore the look of a condemned man. Only in part a man condemned by others, in large measure a man who looked as though he could not, ever, help himself in the moment of consequence, in the three moments of consequence. Suárez's face bore a look of overwhelming sadness. It pained me, because I knew, with the certainty of a fan and lifelong Liverpool FC supporter, that our support could not sustain him. Suárez was, in that moment, for me, lost to Uruguay, to Liverpool, and to himself. I sought (metaphoric) help by leafing through my catalogue of tragic literary figures.

Not Hamlet, not Othello, not Lear, not Don Quixote (a figure Tabárez would surely have no truck with) could help me—none bore a resemblance to Suárez, although the Moor came closest. However, unlike Suárez, Othello could find no one (within his inner circle) to trust, a harsh loneliness that began with his own judgment. He did not trust Desdemona's love, and so he fell, long before he knew it, victim to the Iago-inspired whispers of intrigue and plotting. His tragic end began with his own self-doubt. For his part, Suárez has Tabárez and Steven Gerrard, who was soon to be his ex-Liverpool skipper as Suárez departed for Catalunya. He and Gerrard share a deep affection and respect for each other, a respect that outlasted Suárez's departure from Liverpool. They continue to speak highly of each other.

For a moment (although the mischief-maker in me wonders what he made of it), Suárez was also the beneficiary of the public support of one Diego Maradona, and, as well as we know, that of, perversely, Chiellini.[85]

Nevertheless, in that moment, Suárez stood, literally and for all figurative intents and purposes, alone. His smile, so illuminating when he is on his game, was reduced to a series of muscles clenched for the camera; muscles tensed in the struggle to keep himself true to himself, determinedly trying to maintain who he was in the face of that which had surged up out of him. That force that had surged up out of his face, out of his mouth, to be exact. It is precisely because his better self lay strewn on the turf of Estádio das Dunas in Natal, Brazil, that he could not hide his pain.

I missed Suárez already. I missed him before he was gone. I could see no good coming of his staying at Anfield. His leaving Liverpool would, as it did, pain me. It pains me still.

Because I will miss him, I cannot wish him ill—unlike, I suspect, many other Reds fans. He made us proud, he thrilled us, he shamed us, not once, but thrice, as though he were our very own Saint Peter, wearing not the garb of a simple fisherman but a liver bird on his chest as he denied us our uninterrupted adulation of him. Fittingly, the third bite was the final act. An unholy trinity of transgressions. But now, faced with the prospect of saying goodbye, I balked. I watch him play for Barça, and I miss him still, although it is a complicated sort of loss, as it should be. There is a great deal *entre-nous* Suárez and me.

Still, I hold my memories of him fast but not too close. Still, he is tethered in my Liverpool iconography to the lineage that is the great line of Liverpool number 7s.

Lou was the worthy heir to the Liverpool greats, that lineage that stretched from Kevin Keegan in the 1970s to "King" Kenny Dalglish in the late 1970s through early 1980s to Beardsley in the late 1980s. After that, not a single player wore Liverpool's number 7 jersey with distinction. And then along came the "kid from Salto." With his impishness, his propensity for mischief, and the unbridled joy with which he played the game, I am more or less convinced that Salto is best understood as the Scouser equivalent of Uruguay.

But the event made manifest its effects, and among those effects was the surging up of a range of questions. Among them, was my cherished memories of him tarnished? Wasn't it always so? After all, he arrived from Ajax with one bite and one infamous handball to his credit, if "credit" is the correct term.

I would like to say that I have finally faced these questions, but the truth is harsher. To this day, the matter is not resolved for me. And so, provisionally, I acknowledge that I have been left bereft, saddened, and only so sure of his place in my affections. I remain caught between, on the one hand, the beauty, joy, and effervescence of his play and, on the other, his tragic tendencies.

*Entre-nous: what is between.*

Of this I am certain: I will always be haunted by Luis Suárez. I will never forget his buck-toothed grin, whether I recall that in pleasure or pain. I can see him now. I will see him many long years from now. I suspect I will not be alone in the ranks of the haunted. I will always, when it comes to him, as is true for me of Keegan, Dalglish, the midfield hard man Graeme Souness, the black winger John Barnes (my favorite Liverpool player of all time; Gerrard comes next), and Gerrard, have perfect recall. It is a necessary thing, as a fan, to be haunted, is it not?

I wonder if Tabárez, who knows Suárez better than any of his coaches, who nurtured him and nurtures him still, gave him support when others doubted his talents, will not share my sense of being haunted. What Suárez demons does Tabárez wrestle with? Which brand of philosophy, if any, provides him with solace? I would like to ask him. I wonder at his possible answer. Would he offer, "There is so much *entre-nous* Luis Suárez and I"? "There is nothing *entre-nous* Luis Suárez and I that cannot be explained."

*Por favor, El Maestro, speak to us on this matter as you alone can.*

**GRACE** · My grace is sufficient for thee: for my strength is made perfect in weakness.
——2 Corinthians 12:9

However, more than anything, Suárez moves me to reappraise my own putative disappointment (although it was not in the least experienced as "putative"), or whatever inclination toward disappointment I might harbor, in Óscar Tabárez. It is not simply that Tabárez was loyal to his charge. It is, rather, that for Tabárez fidelity to the other—to the player he had nurtured and so would not abandon—demands something in excess of the suspension of judgment. It demands grace. That is, grace as love beyond love, grace as inextricably bound to mercy. Grace as the Nietzschean "genius of Christianity." Without the philosopher's skepticism. Grace is God's withholding of judgment, even though—as Nietzsche is only to happy to tell us—it is entirely undeserved on our part. Grace is the "strength" of God made manifest—"made perfect in weakness": God's mercy, of course, is the mark of God's strength, strength that he names "weakness." Conceiving of grace and mercy as different sides of the same theological coin is a staple of the Apostle Paul's letters. This is a subject that Paul takes up in Romans, Ephesians and, of course, Corinthians. In Corinthians the Apostle testifies, "But by the grace of God I am what I am: and his grace which was bestowed upon me was not in vain; but I labored more abundantly than they all: yet not I, but the grace of God which was with me."[86] In this testimony Paul acknowledges, with humility ("by the Grace of God I am what I am"—humility, it should be noted, is hardly Paul's signature mode). But this is a humility that is, as is customary with Paul, never without at least a hint of self-aggrandizement. As such, it is through Paul, and not us (as Corinthians reminds us), to begin with, that God works: "the grace of God was with me." Nonetheless, it is through Paul that we are privy to the unimaginable depth of God's love (grace, undeserved, unmerited love beyond love; a love we can only know, however partially, because of the death of the Son) and made aware of our responsibility to that grace.

Understood in its Pauline articulation in relation to Suárez, it becomes necessary to conceive of grace as the commitment to love (by Tabárez). As such, Tabárez's "grace" (his love) stands as the commitment to love in the face of—that is, because of, the other's—Suárez's propensities—his transgressions, as it were—for making the event. It is Tabárez's "grace" that enables him to love and to live with the other; Tabárez commits himself to loving Suárez whether or not it is precisely out of Suárez's transgressions that the event arises, that, in Shakespeare's terms, the tragedy is made. Or perhaps an event that does not quite rise to the level of tragedy. If a certain grandiosity might be permitted, it is in Suárez's "weakness" that Tabárez's "strength," his love, his willingness to "labor abundantly" in his love for the other, becomes manifest. More so than, it is possible to assert with confidence, in his relationship to and with any other player. "Father" (Tabárez)-' Son" (Suárez)-"Holy Ghost" (the event).

Unlike Abraham, who was willing to sacrifice his son Isaac in order to obey God, Tabárez would not sacrifice this perverse, this impish, this massively talented, occasionally wayward son of his. He would not "love in vain" (although his love was surely tried), and so he was true to Suárez, true to the very end—which is not yet. He would not condemn Suárez for the loss to Colombia; he has not condemned him since. To make love manifest in the face of tragedy (the event) is the true strength of his love. Tabárez's strength is the strength of his "strength." Abraham was willing to sacrifice Isaac not because he did not love him. He was willing to put him to death because he loved God.

Tabárez, it is safe to assume, would refuse God were such an Abrahamic request made of him, were God to issue such a command to him. In terms of the Trinity, we can say that Tabárez privileges the Son over the Father. God, especially, knows this as love itself, and while it is unlikely that God would approve of Tabárez's fatherly fidelity, He would find Tabárez to belong to an order of faith that does not rise to the level of Abraham's. But God surely would see in Tabárez a being open to the possibility of grace, or a being capable of practicing grace because of the expansive capacity of his (Tabárez's) love.

In such a scenario, we can, with confidence (a confidence that is in no way assured, except in its pronouncement of itself), assert that what is *entre-nous* Suárez and Tabárez is "love beyond love": grace. As such, grace is the highest achievement of ∴; grace is where it is possible to encounter, beyond question, love as the "strength" of God.

In the face of international condemnation, Tabárez offered truculent critique that was, in truth, dissembling in the cause of loyalty. Tabárez's fidelity, moreover, should be understood not as the suspension of his judgment but as his pained recognition of the futility of judgment in the face of the larger force that is tragedy-cum-grace. It might be that we achieve grace only through tragedy. (The Resurrection would support such a conclusion.) It is the tragic event, the event as tragedy, that provides beings with the passage toward grace.

*If grace is God's love, God as love, then it is when love is given, when forgiveness is given, that God's love becomes manifest.*

Tabárez's fidelity is a mark not of his rationalization but of his inability to publicly pronounce his helplessness. In the face of tragedy (real, imagined, impending, averted), Tabárez offered Suárez something that can only be cast as a coach and mentor's grace (since only God is capable of grace—love beyond love): love beyond judgment. Here God and Tabárez are on the same side. And, we might add, Che Guevara, too. At its core, Che's "tenderness" is indistinguishable from love but it is (also) a love that surges up out of the struggle (the "toughness") to which Guevara dedicated—and in whose name he sacrificed—his life. Out of the struggle, for liberation, justice, the transition of the other into a sovereign selfhood (Third World independence, the end to the subjugation of the other, from Latin America to the Caribbean to central Africa), would emerge the preservation of the "tenderness" of the subject.[87] The struggle for the self is the struggle for love, so that love, understood in strictly political terms, contains within itself some mode of being-with (the self, with the self-as-other) that a priori is set toward exceeding itself.

As such, "tenderness" is the passage that opens the path to, the possibility for, grace—for a love that cannot be restricted to love as such. Grace, then, is what emerges from struggle, which means that grace, per se, the force that is grace, begins in, begins with, the other—whether that be the other as such or the (subjugated) self-as-other. Grace is what is, in one way or another, given to us. ("It is the gift of God"; it is nothing less than the "gift of God," a gift too overwhelming to be properly conceived; it is "the love that passeth all understanding," beginning with ours, certainly.) Given to us, grace then "passages" its way into and, this is surely the ultimate intention, it passes its way through us and into the world.[88] Grace, then, as a "sacred mystery" that all beings can, in a moment such as the event, find within themselves. Find within themselves because of R to the other.

Suárez, in this rendering of love, of struggle, of grace, must know himself to be the recipient of Tabárez's grace. His face, bearing shame as it does, seems to acknowledge as much. It is a love that is unyielding, deeply reflective and intense in its complexity. Above, it is a love that has been given him. That Suárez knows it we detect, appropriately, inevitably, from his face. It is etched in the pain he showed, before the world, both at his final training session with his national team in Brazil (2014), and bearing his son on his arm, his daughter looking on, upon his return to Montevideo after his suspension from the World Cup. Suárez knows that Tabárez knows his helplessness. That is Tabárez's wisdom. That is his love. Suárez, made the gift of that love, must now love his children, who have him as their father as he did not have one. Suárez must love his children (his daughter, Delfina, born 2010, and son, Benjamin, born in 2013), for whom he kisses his wrist every time he scores a goal, as Tabárez has loved him. That is the one promise he must keep, the one promise he, unfailingly, must be strong enough to keep.

So it is in the best Socratic tradition that El Maestro is a teacher. Through his actions, he poses questions, of himself and of us. In the face of a loved one's violence, he offers grace. He knows the proper place of judgment because he knows when his judgment would be out of place, when judgment must bow to the force of tragedy. When it is clear, we must remember, that the force of tragedy has not yet exhausted itself. It is this recognition that might be Tabárez's, and Suárez's greatest fear. That might be what the helplessness in Suárez's eyes betrays.

Nevertheless, Suárez is a man fortunate in his tragedy. He has in his corner a coach whom he can disappoint but who will never be disappointed in him. After all, Tabárez values defeat. Tabárez has respect for the pedagogical and philosophical insights afforded by moments of difficulty; he possesses strength enough to withstand the "slings and arrows" aimed at him. In his "worst" public displays, Tabárez reveals not his limitations but the full range of his philosophical complexity. In his refusal to condemn there is not the suspension of judgment nor indulgence or rationalization. *Entre-nous* Tabárez and Suárez is grace, the "strength" of love; the love that is *entre-nous* is the measure of their strength, of the strength of the bonds that hold them together, that bind self to other. It is, then, entirely appropriate (in Pauline terms, at least) that the strength of Tabárez's thought should become most manifest in the event of Suárez's "weakness," in the moment of his greatest professional vulnerability, in response to the act of his dissembling (denial, reluctant acknowledgement of his transgression).

For all this, under no circumstances is it possible to suggest that Suárez is excused. *Au contraire*. There is, instead, a far more potent, thought-provoking response. Tabárez offers an unqualified, but carefully considered, grace for the condemned, alongside whom he takes his place—as condemned, as subjected to critique, as exposed to himself, to what he believes in, publicly, and in these pages, no less. Perhaps, always, with the specter of Zuluaga and the violence that the former deputy commissioner did (bore witness to, did nothing to prevent; guilt through commission as well as guilt through omission) haunting El Maestro.

If Lionel Messi and Luis Suárez have shown us, in how *Entre-Nous* thinks them, that what is *entre-nous* the Copa Mundial and us is, in one form or another, in one iteration or another, nothing other than pain, then in his turn, Óscar Washington Tabárez shows us, wittingly or not, the face of grace. That is perfectly intelligible, that is perfectly visible, a "strength" that is truly singular plural in its origin, drawing as it does from Che's, Galeano's, and Tabárez's own ethics, as well as leading us to think about him in, broadly speaking, Pauline terms.

And for that reason, it is entirely necessary, to say nothing of it being appropriate (in light of the press conference of June 27, 2014,) to acknowledge that thinking Tabárez *entre-nous*, demands, in its conclusion, precisely the same salutation.

It is in this spirit that we offer our thanks for what Tabárez offers us. *Gracias, El Maestro, gracias.*

# POSTSCRIPT

> From the moment he begins to use words like colors in a painting, a writer can begin to see how wondrous and surprising the world is, and he breaks the bones of language to find his own voice. —— ORHAN PAMUK, *Other Colors: Essays and a Story*

I watched the 2018 World Cup ethnographically. That is, I mainly, if by no means exclusively, wanted to observe how things turned out for Lionel Messi and Luis Suárez. I wanted to record Argentina and Uruguay's fate in order to make this book as current as it possibly could be. I wanted to put on paper the words: "At the time of writing..." What is more, in the cause of full disclosure, I hoped, against my better instincts, that things would go well for both of them, especially for Messi. I wanted Leo to win. An impossibility, I was well aware, but objective reality—the severe limits of the Argentine squad, for starters—is never an insurmountable obstacle for the partisan. The facts of the matter do not, as it were, really matter; obstacles, mere obstacles.

As we know now, I was put out of my misery early. First, Argentina, in the round of 16, and then Uruguay, in the quarterfinals, lost to France. Messi's team went down 4–3, and Suárez's, 2–0. Neither game was particularly close, no matter that Argentina briefly led 2–1.

Another way to look at it: I got an early start on my misery.

Either way, the task that awaited me was to write an account of Messi, to bring things up to date, if not to a close. I watched the 2018 World Cup in Russia in search of something more than an accurate depiction of Leo Messi's fate. Watching the World Cup, I realized that above all I wanted to give language to Lionel Messi. I wanted to craft a language worthy of Lionel Messi; worthy of how it is he plays the game—intelligently, beautifully, and always without complaint. A language that would have to be found, a language that would have to emerge out of the "bones" of the linguistic skills I had at my disposal, capable of doing justice to such a mode of playing football.

As Orhan Pamuk puts it, I wanted to "break the bones of language." However, I wanted to do something with language not in order to "find my own voice," or so I convince myself, but rather to "find" Messi's "voice." However, such a pursuit would of necessity demand a rummaging through the "bones" of my own language.

Fool's gold, it turns out. It simply cannot be done. Leo Messi's voice belongs, as it were, exclusively to Leo Messi.

However, the advantage of a Pamukian ethnography—Pamuk is, after all, the best ethnographer of a European city since James Joyce. Pamuk does for his native Istanbul what Joyce does for Dublin—is that dedicated observation reveals not only the writer's limitation but, against all expectations, also brings to light a sharper truth. Sometimes a writer's ambition inadvertently leads him in a most fruitful direction.

When the final whistle blew to bring the curtain down on Uruguay's 2018 Russian adventure, Luis Suárez cut a dejected figure. Still, Suárez was recognizable. Hands on his knees, head bent down, he seemed to accept defeat, no matter how much it pained him. There was no anger to be detected in his look. Suárez was simply exhausted. Defeat was hardly a surprise, even though it surely stung. Suárez is not a player who enjoys defeat. However, there was no petulance, his demeanor was free of bitterness; in fact, he appeared resigned. It was over. He had perhaps played his last World Cup game. But it's Lou Suárez, so you never know. Don't bet against him being back in 2022.

Messi, on the other hand, surprised me. In Argentina's group stage defeat, 3–0, to Croatia, he offered perfunctory handshakes to his opponents before striding down the tunnel, disappearing from view, quickly. It was if he had decided to immediately put the loss behind him in order to concentrate on the next game to ensure that Argentina advanced out of the group stages. In this undertaking, he was successful, but it proved, as I've noted, a pyrrhic victory. It merely postponed the inevitable. There would be no Argentine triumph for Messi.

Not so with the loss to France.

For an initial moment he looked totally spent, the truth of defeat overwhelming his face.

Then, however, he did the unexpected. With his hands on his hips, he looked around—it was as if he had decided to stop, to take not just a moment but all the time he needed to take in everything around him.

He looked around, from one corner of the stadium to another, pausing however long he felt he needed.

I had expected that I would need to "break the bones of my language" in order to render Lionel Messi.

Instead, and perhaps I should have known this all along, Messi has long since possessed his very own language for the moment. Whatever language, it seems fair to acknowledge, Messi understands that moment to demand.

In a strange way, Lionel Messi turned the tables on me. It was not I, the would-be ethnographer, who was watching Messi. In what might, like Suárez, be his World Cup swan song, Lionel Messi was watching us.

It was Messi who was recording, for his very own purposes (and I would really like to know what those purposes might be), us. Or maybe he was recording not only us, not only the materiality of the stadium and mood of the crowd, but he wanted to absorb this moment, to take it into his consciousness. He wanted to understand, on his terms, the entirety of the moment.

In that moment, Lionel Messi seemed anything but a tragic figure. Instead, he appeared preternaturally calm, utterly in possession of himself, and, most importantly, in command of time itself.

However history, however football partisans may depict his defeats for his national team (they will hardly linger over his victories for Argentina), it seemed to me that Messi was detailing, with the precision, unerring accuracy, and sureness of a Messi dribble, the moment itself. It was, this defeat, being catalogued, filed away, if not for immediate use, then perhaps, later, in order to subject it to forensic study.

In looking at us, Messi rendered ethnographers such as me superfluous. He was capturing the veracity of the moment, and, in so doing, he allowed us to witness something remarkable.

Lionel Messi "broke the bones" of our language and, in its place, there, there it was, audible, the silent power of Lionel Messi's voice. If we observed him, there was no need to strain in his direction to hear the quiet force of that voice. If we listened to him, we would hear the voice of a man who has always known his own voice.

It was the voice of a man whose stream of consciousness was insulated against us. In all our raucousness, in our interrogative insistence, and certainly the various iterations of condemnation ("failed," once more, at the World Cup), unfavorable comparisons (to Maradona, reduced to a clownish presence in various Russian stadia), our voices could not penetrate the stream of Lionel Messi's consciousness.

Lionel Messi, in that moment, made Orhan Pamuk's desire for his own singularity—this act of literary and linguistic violence, "breaking bones," and all that—seem rather quaint. Pamuk attempted to craft a literary, political, and geographical vocabulary that spoke his own language, that spoke specifically of Pamuk's Istanbul. Messi made such a project seem indulgent, possessed of a certain affectation. However, perhaps I am being unfair to Pamuk. In comparison to Messi, we all suffer.

We are brought up short because Messi is a man who has always known his own voice. Messi has long since known that, at the level of self-expression, there is never any need for violence. Messi did not need to break any "bones." After all, he'd been on the receiving end of enough bad tackles to develop a distaste for those whose intention it has long been to "break his bones."

Lionel Messi has always, with his immense control of the ball and himself, with his capacity for scrutinizing the world intensely, known something very important. That moment in which he surveys the scene of what is surely his last appearance on football's biggest stage, suggests to me now, as I write it, write about it, that Leo Messi has been master of his own voice.

The problem, as it were, has always been us. The problem has always been us in one of two ways: either we have been so clamorous in asserting our own voices that we have drowned out his, or (and this is the line of thinking I favor) we simply have no facility for listening in the registers in which Messi operates.

Much as we have never fully been able to command a language to describe how it is he plays, how it is he has changed our expectations of the game, how it is he sees—his vision, his, imagination, his stamina, and his creativity—possibilities available within the game.

We have, as it were, been not only insufficiently alert to the visual, architectural, and geometric beauties of his play, we have also, maybe especially in that final moment, been deaf to the many modulations of his voice.

The loss, then, is ours. On many levels, in several registers.

Or, perhaps, our loss is the consequence of a more painful reality. We could not, we cannot now, hear Messi, because for all the public nature of his play, he has never truly granted us access.

All this while, he has kept us, those who watch him, have watched him, for these many years, steadfastly at a remove, kept us at arm's length.

No wonder, then, that when he seemed most out of character to us, he was being nothing more than absolutely felicitous to himself.

But then again, hasn't that always been true of him?

# NOTES

PREFACE

1 Rüdiger Safranski, *Martin Heidegger: Between Good and Evil*, trans. Ewald Osers (Cambridge, MA: Harvard University Press, 2002).
2 Safranski, *Martin Heidegger*, 429.
3 In July, 2018, James left the Cleveland Cavaliers to sign for the Los Angeles Lakers.
4 In *"Bauen Wohnen Denken"* ("Building Dwelling Thinking"), one of his most famous essays, Heidegger establishes "dwelling" as not only distinct from but elevates it above (mere) "building." For Heidegger, "dwelling" might very well be the closest approximation we get to Being, even if "dwelling" can only be achieved through and because of our "building." Fittingly, for the paradoxical purposes of my thinking here, Heidegger declares: "Bridges and hangars, stadiums and power stations are buildings but not dwellings" (Heidegger, "Building Dwelling Thinking," Martin Heidegger, *Basic Writings*, edited by David Farrell Krell, New York: HarperPerennial, 2008, 347). How great are Lionel Messi's (philosophical) accomplishments.
5 Love, that is, on the order Friedrich Nietzche's Zarathustra, especially that moment when Zarathustra refuses any possibility of loving human beings. Zarathustra declares that the "human being is for me too incomplete an affair. Love of human beings would be the death of me" (Friedrich Wilhelm Nietzsche, *Thus Spake Zarathustra*, translated by Graham Parkes, Oxford: Oxford University Press, 2005, 10). It is precisely Suárez's "imperfections" that make Tabárez's love for his player such a salient response in the face of Suárez's transgressions. In fact, we could say that is a love on the order of the New Testament.
6 Safranski, *Martin Heidegger*, 425.

INTRODUCTION

1   I am, of course, invoking the title of Nancy's work *Being Singular Plural*, trans. Robert D. Richardson and Anne E. O'Byrne (Stanford, CA: Stanford University Press, 2000).
2   The title of this essay might be translated as "The Order of the Monarchs." The term "Baselius" (βασιλεύς) is best understood as referring to the Byzantine monarchs, locating the honorific firmly within the Greek experience. In English "Baselius" is most easily rendered as "king" or "emperor." Nancy's use of *Nomos* evokes, intentionally or not, Carl Schmitt's *Nomos of the Earth*, a work in which Schmitt seeks to provide a framework of "order" that organizes the world, a notion of "order" that is especially interested in how the project of dominion over the seas (oceans) is engaged. For his part, Nancy is interested in how to achieve "infinite justice" (Nancy, *Being Singular Plural*, 188).
3   Nancy, *Being Singular Plural*, 185.
4   Nancy, *Being Singular Plural*, 185.
5   *Elective Affinities* is the English title of Goethe's 1809 novel *Die Wahlverwandtschaften*, which was translated into English in 1854. It is sometimes also translated as *Kindred by Choice* and deals with the difference between those who have affinity for each other, and mix like "water and wine," and those who do not, and separate into "water and oil." Goethe takes the term *Wahlverwandtschaft* from 18th century chemist, where "elective affinities" marks the preference that chemical species demonstrate for certain other species or substances. "Elective affinities" is also a term that Max Weber borrows for sociology from Goethe. In this scientific vein, Goethe's main male protagonist, Eduard (his female counterpart is Charlotte, his wife), explains: "'Just as each thing has an adherence to itself, so it must also have a relationship to other things. . . . Sometimes they will meet as friends and old acquaintances who hasten together and unite without changing one another in any way, as wine mixes with water. On the other hand, there are others who will remain obdurate strangers to one another and refuse to unite in any way even through mechanical mixing and grinding, as oil and water shaken together will a moment later separate again'" (Johann Wolfgang von Goethe, *Elective Affinities*, translated by R.J. Hollingdale, London: Penguin Books, 1971, 52). It should be noted, as accurately as Eduard describes the scientific principles of "elective affinities," it is knowledge put to idle use. That is, the *Novelle* (a "fictional narrative longer than a short story . . . but shorter than a novel") *Elective Affinities* is Goethe's critique of the "state of idleness" of the landed aristocracy (Hollingdale, *Elective Affinities*, 11, 15). The transient, largely useless labor of Eduard, Charlotte and their intimates (the Captain and Ottilie chief among them), whether it is their attempts to reshape the landscape or in their pursuit of love and passion, is ceaselessly mocked by

Goethe. The use of the concept of "elective affinities" in regards to Messi is, then, used in its scientific and not "Platonic" sense.

6 Ta-Nehisi Coates, *Between the World and Me* (New York: Spiegel & Grau, 2015), 28.

7 (Self-)"will" is understood here in the sense that Heidegger deploys Nietzsche's concept in *Was Heißt Denken?* Heidegger writes, "all philosophy strives to find the highest expression for primal being as the will" (Heidegger, *Was Heißt Denken?*, 109). For Heidegger, in this moment, Nietzsche's "will to power"—read in relation to *Zarathustra*—is the "bridge" that can get us closer to Being. However, it is also important—arguably, more important—to keep in mind the distinction Nietzsche insists on between "two kinds of philosopher." On the one hand we have the archivists or the assiduous collectors—"those who want to ascertain a complex fact of evaluations (logical or moral)"—and the "*legislators* of such evaluations" (Friedrich Nietzsche, *The Will to Power*, trans. Walter Kaufmann and R.J. Hollindale, New York: Random House, 1967, 509). Nietzsche warns against, taking clear aim at Plato "and the "founders of religion," what he names the "will to blindness" (Nietzsche, 510).

8 The Real Madrid striker and Portugal captain Cristiano Ronaldo is preferred by some fans. I pay these fans of "Scuba Ron" (in other words, "See grass, will dive") no mind.

9 In fact, his full name is Lionel Andrés Messi Cuccittini.

10 Pablo Aimar, Messi's favorite player as a boy, represented River Plate from 1996 to 2000. Messi has said that Aimar is the player who had the most influence on him as a footballer. Aimar played in La Liga from 2000 to 2008, first for Valencia, and then Zaragoza, so that Aimar's and Messi's careers in Spain would have overlapped. Messi debuted for Barcelona in 2005. Their international careers also coincided—Aimar played for Argentina from 1999 to 2009, and Messi made his senior bow with Argentina in 2005.

11 The FC Barcelona management was reluctant to sign Messi because in 2000 it was still unusual for European clubs to recruit players as young as Messi. He was only thirteen and registered with Newell's Old Boys.

12 Two of Messi's contemporaries at La Masia were native Catalans, Gerard Piqué and Cesc Fàbregas. Piqué and Fàbregas left Barça for England's Premier League, Manchester United and Arsenal, respectively. Messi remained. First Piqué and then Fàbregas returned to Barça, but Fàbregas, unable to command a regular place in what was (and continues to be) a very talented but now aging side, has since returned to England for a second time, and he now plies his trade with Chelsea.

13 The transformation of La Masia from club headquarters into training academy was the brainchild of former Ajax Amsterdam, Holland, and Barça great Johan Cruyff, who both played for and managed Barça. Himself a graduate of the famed Ajax Youth Academy, whose graduates include Piet Keizer; Ruud Krol; Marco van Bas-

ten; Frank Rijkaard; the de Boer brothers, Frank and Ronald; Wesley Sneijder; and Maarten Stekelenburg (a massively abbreviated list, it should be cautioned), Cruyff set about proposing the establishment of a similar structure in his adopted Catalunya. Once renowned throughout the world for its production of good footballers, the Ajax Youth Academy has since been surpassed by the alumni of La Masia.

14 Nine of the players on Spain's 2010 Copa Mundial–winning squad passed through La Masia. In addition to Piqué, Pedro, and Fàbregas, there were Xavi Hernández, Andrés Iniesta, Carles Puyol, Sergio Busquets, Pepe Reina (Liverpool, Inter Milan, Bayern Munich), and Victor Valdés. Seven of these players were, at the time of the 2010 Copa Mundial, at Barça (Reina and Fàbregas, then playing for Arsenal in the English Premier League, were not), a record for a single club in a World Cup final, and the first six of those listed above started, another record for a final.

15 See Ian Hawkey, "Friends Reunited: Cesc Fàbregas and the Class of 1987," *Times*, March 28, 2010.

16 In 2010, for the first and thus far only time in the award's history, all three of the finalists, Messi, Iniesta, and Xavi, were from the same club.

17 The third chapter of *In Motion, At Rest: The Event of the Athletic Body* (Minneapolis: University of Minnesota Press, 2013) posits the former French captain, Zinedine Zidane (current Real Madrid coach), as an état *voyou*. Like Suárez, although it must be said that Zidane was much more successful as a player, leading France to victory in the 1998 World Cup, Zidane was a player with a known capacity for falling foul of the law. He was sent off for club (Juventus, during his time in Italy) and country, much more famously, of course, for head butting, an event that became known as the *coup de boule*, in the final of the 2006 World Cup. Against, as historical irony would have it, Italy.

18 The *vuvuzela*, as most football fans know, is a long plastic horn (generally about 65 centimeters long), unrelentingly monotone, that is blown regularly at football matches in South Africa. Traditionally, the *vuvuzela* was made of kudu horn (the "kudu," or "koodoo" as the indigenous Khoisan people named them, belongs to the antelope genus; it is part deer and part zebra) and used to summon villagers to community gatherings.

19 Suárez was also banned from any football-related activities for four months, a ban so uncompromising that it included a complete prohibition on entering football stadia for those four months.

20 "José Mujica en el recibimiento a la Celeste, Los de la FIFA son una manga de viejos hijos de puta," June 30, 2014. www.marca.com/2014/06/30/fctbol/mundial/uruguay /1404129785.html.

21 "El Maestro Seeks to Restore the Tradition of a Forgotten Footballing Identity," *Guardian*, October 2009. https://www.theguardian.com/football/blog/2009/oct/14 /uruguay-forgotten-football-identity-world-cup.

22  Eduardo Galeano, *Football in Sun and Shadow*, trans. Mark Fried (London: Fourth Estate, 2003).
23  Fonseca began his career in Uruguay with Nacional before moving on to Cagliari, AS Roma, Napoli, and finally Juventus in Italy. He currently works as a football agent. Forlán was a youth player with Peñarol in Uruguay before making his name as a striker for Independiente in Argentina, after which he moved to Manchester United in England and then on to Villarreal and Atlético Madrid in Spain; from there he went to play for Inter Milan, after which his career petered out with stints in Mexico, Japan, and back to his boyhood club before ending up with Mumbai City in the Indian Premier League. The highlight of his career was winning the Golden Ball award at the 2010 World Cup in South Africa—the FIFA award for the best player of the tournament.
24  The Victorian Web. http://www.victorianweb.org/authors/mooreg/bio.html. Last accessed November 2013.
25  Andrzej Diniejko, "George Moore: A Biographical Sketch."
26  Under apartheid, the South African population was divided into four racial categories. In hierarchical order these were: whites, Asians (more pejoratively known as "Indians" but generally referring to subjects of South Asian origin, many of whom came to South Africa in the late nineteenth and early twentieth century as indentured laborers), coloreds (South Africans of "mixed" racial ancestry), and "blacks" (those who traced their roots, with greater "physiognomic ease," shall we say, to the indigenous population).
27  Deleuze, as we know, is a critic of Hegel, and his *Nietzsche and Philosophy* may contain his sharpest line of disagreement.
28  The Victorian Web. http://www.victorianweb.org/authors/mooreg/bio.html. Last accessed November 2013.
29  Elspeth Probyn, *Blush: Faces of Shame* (Minneapolis: University of Minnesota Press, 2005), ix.
30  In an articulation that gives one cause for pause, especially in light of the acknowledgment (admission? confession?) just offered, Probyn tries to account for why it might be difficult to write about that which is at the root of our shame. "My argument," Probyn writes, ".s that a form of shame always attends the writer" (Probyn, *Blush*, xvii). While this may be valid in some instances, one wonders what distinguishes "shame" as such from, say, reluctance? Or what if overcoming "shame" so conceived serves not to strengthen but to detract from the critique being offered? What if the writer's shame is not in the least disabling but is precisely what sustains the argument, keeps the critique in and as the focus? What if shame makes of the writer an author more responsible to the project?
31  Nancy, *Being*, 11.
32  It is possible here to think of the "un-spoken" on the order, if not on the same

order of magnitude, of Jacques Derrida's notion of "under erasure." That is, for everything we say, we, per force, leave several things unsaid—or, in truth, which is where the provocation to thinking resides, it is precisely in their condition of being unsayable that they demand to be said. Derrida's notion of "under erasure" derives from Heidegger's *sous rature* (which is usually rendered as "under erasure") in which a word is crossed out in a text but remains visible so that it must be accounted for, confronted, thought. *Sous rature* is developed by Derrida into a critique of "presence" ("presence" as an impossibility) and, most specifically, as an insistent argument against univocity—no word can claim to have a single meaning; univocity, then, as an illusion or a desire that stands against thinking. See, in this regard, Nicole Anderson's *Derrida: Ethics under Erasure*, New York: Bloomsbury, 2012.

33  Afrikaans is a language that derives from colonial Dutch and was for a long time considered a bastardized version of the European tongue. It was sometimes referred to, in an obvious pejorative, as *kombuis Nederlands*, "kitchen Dutch," a moniker that at once domesticized and politicized Afrikaans, and is historically recognized as the language of the apartheid regime. The Cape Flats version of the language I grew up with in Hanover Park, as my second language, was marked by a different sense of inferiority. Its "impurity" was attributed to, as I have already argued, class and race, so that it was meant to mark its speakers of a lesser, grammatically compromised version of formal—or pure—Afrikaans (*pure Afrikaans*, in which "pure" is pronounced very differently, as something like "PeeRer").

34  Nancy, *Being*, 25.
35  Nancy, *Being*, 27.
36  Jean-Luc Nancy, *Hegel: The Restlessness of the Negative*, trans. Jason Smith and Steven Miller (Minneapolis: University of Minnesota Press, 2002), 15.
37  Nancy, *Hegel*, 15.
38  Nancy, *Being*, 186.
39  Nancy, *Hegel*, 22.
40  Nancy, *Hegel*, 19.
41  Nancy, *Hegel*, 28.
42  Nancy takes a moment, even though he does so parenthetically, to explain the syntax of being-with-the-other. ("By the way, the logic of 'with' often requires heavy-handed syntax in order to say 'being-with-one-another.' . . . But perhaps it is not an accident that language does not easily lend itself to showing 'with' as such, for it is itself the address and not what must be addressed"); Nancy, *Being*, xvi.
43  For Rastafarians, "I-and-I" designates the plural form of "communing-with"; that is, being-with. This form of the plural is a hallmark of reggae music, made popular as a concept most notably by Bob Marley and the Wailers. It is often used to articulate the relationship of human beings ("mortals," Heidegger would say)—the Rastafarians—to "Jah" ("God").

44  See my discussion of the singular plurality of the concept of "I-and-I" in Grant Farred, *What's My Name? Black Vernacular Intellectuals*, Minneapolis: University of Minnesota Press, 2003

45  It is here that Nancy differs from Heidegger, for whom the "bridge"—a "bridge" to—is less a critical possibility than an absolute philosophical necessity. The "bridge" is, Heidegger's lexicon, second only to the "leap" as that force that might get us to Being and thinking.

46  And, as we know from Heidegger, the richness of a thinker's thought resides in her or his unthought. For Heidegger there is a quantitative and qualitive commensurability: the more unthought that a thinker's thinking possesses, the greater the thinker. In this regard, see Heidegger's explication of Nietzsche via his critique of metaphysics in Lecture X, Part I, of *Was Heißt Denken?*

47  In short, the project is to "possess language" in such a way as to give language to the constitutive, sustaining violence of/in relation. This is, of course, an impossible undertaking, to "possess language." In *Sein und Zeit*, Martin Heidegger is clear that we are "possessed by language." I am thinking here particularly of the "Idle Talk" section in *Being and Time*, in which Heidegger stresses the need to take care with language (Heidegger, *Being and Time*, trans. Joan Stambaugh, Albany, NY: State University of New York Press), 157–159.

48  Nancy, *Being*, 3; emphasis in original.

49  G. W. F. Hegel, *Phenomenology of Spirit*, trans. A. V. Miller (New York: Oxford University Press, 1977), 2.

## CHAPTER ONE · A CONDEMNED MAN

1  Charles Dickens, *A Christmas Carol* (New York: Fall River Press, 2013), 86.

2  Around the time of the 2014 World Cup, the Brazil sports paper *Lance!* named Messi the "sixth greatest footballer ever." Ahead of Messi were Pelé, Garrincha, Romário, Ronaldo (Brazil), and Maradona. There are few judgments in football that carry as much weight as this one, not because of *Lance!* but because this is a singular honor for a Brazilian outlet to bestow on Messi, not only because of the deep antipathy that marks the history of Argentine-Brazilian relations but also because Messi is the only player on the list never to have won a World Cup

3  Jean-Luc Nancy, *Hegel: The Restlessness of the Negative*, trans. Jason Smith and Steven Miller (Minneapolis: University of Minnesota Press, 2002), 70.

4  Nancy, *Hegel*, 70.

5  Nancy, *Hegel*, 70, 71.

6  See Grant Farred, *In Motion, At Rest: The Event of the Athletic Body* (Minneapolis: University of Minnesota Press, 2013).

7  Nancy, *Hegel*, 71.

8   Jean-Luc Nancy, *Being Singular Plural*, trans. Robert D. Richardson and Anne E. O'Byrne (Stanford, CA: Stanford University Press, 2000), 7.
9   Nancy, *Being*, 5.
10  Nancy, *Being*, 5.
11  Nancy, *Being*, 5.
12  Friedrich Nietzsche, *Thus Spoke Zarathustra: A Book for Everyone and Nobody*, trans. Graham Parkes (Oxford: Oxford University Press, 2008), 80. In this denunciation, Nietzsche is clear: he finds that "even the greatest" among those whom he encounters are "all-too-human" (80).
13  In recent years a number of players have been lured to the Chinese Super League with the promise of huge paydays. Some of these players, such as Mascherano, Lavezzi, Ricardo Carvalho (Portugal), Nicolas Anelka (France), or Didier Drogba (Côte d'Ivoire), are approaching the end of their careers. Some, of course, can no longer compete in the European or Latin American leagues. But this is not true of all of those who choose to ply their trade in the Chinese league, a league that is far inferior to its European and Latin American counterparts. Players such as Carlos Tevez (Argentina), Oscar (Brazil), Jackson Martínez (Colombia), and Axel Witsel (Belgium) are hardly over the hill superstars in search of one last payday. Although, it must be said, the remuneration that the likes of a Tevez or an Oscar received in China is not to be sniffed at.
14  Nancy, *Hegel*, 79; emphasis in original.
15  Nancy, *Hegel*, 2.
16  In recent times, the French have excelled in this kind of "chaos." During the 2010 World Cup in South Africa, then-national captain Patrice Evra led a walkout during training before their third match against the hosts. The mutiny that Evra spurred was in response to the disciplinary measures enacted against striker Nicolas Anelka, which ensued after France's second match against Mexico. According to the players, much of the animosity between the players and management emerged from tensions that were racial in origin. Issues of race, ethnicity, and nationality were on display again during the 2016 Euros, hosted by the French. This time, however, it came from outside the camp, spearheaded by disgraced former national team player Eric Cantona, who charged that the exclusion of certain players by the manager, Laurent Blanc ("White") was based on their "names" (that is, their ethnic origins). According to Cantona, certain players, such as Karim Benzema, were left out because they were not "recognizably French," to phrase it delicately.
17  Nancy, *Hegel*, 9.
18  "Not Everybody in Argentina is Rooting for Messi," Cork Gaines, June 26, 2014. https://www.businessinsider.com.au/argentina-lionel-messi-2014-6.
19  Nancy, *Hegel*, 9.
20  Hernán Claus, quoted in "Lionel Messi Has Few Fans in Argentina," *Guardian*, March 27, 2010.

21 Nat Hentoff, liner notes *Sketches of Spain*, Miles Davis, Columbia Records, 1959; emphasis in original.
22 Claus, "Lionel Messi Has Few Fans in Argentina."
23 Judith Butler, *Precarious Life: The Powers of Mourning and Violence* (New York: Verso, 2006), 22.
24 Rendering Butler's work as a critique of the internal evokes the way in which Carl Schmitt, seeking to rehabilitate his reputation as a philosophical jurist, posits himself as a thinker of "civil war." Like "his 'brothers' Jean Bodin and Thomas Hobbes—both thinkers of the state and both 'entirely formed by civil wars'"—Schmitt saw himself as writing about "politics and law during civil wars"; "Introduction" by Andreas Kalyvas and Federico Finchelstein, in Carl Schmitt, *Ex Captivitate Salus*, trans. Matthew Hannah (Medford, MA: Polity Press, 2017, 11). It is what is "internal," as it were, that is the most likely and therefore the most (potentially) terrifying form of (self-)destruction. In Derrida's work, this political concern is given the name "autoimmunity," and while it too advocates a kind of caution against/within the self, "autoimmunity" is explicated as a much less malignant political force.
25 The language that Claus uses suggests a kind of assault on the self—especially through his use of "battery"—but it also manages to evoke a kind of domestic violence; as though, to offer this speculatively and hesitantly, Messi were a kind of abused child or even a "battered" spouse.
26 Butler, *Precarious Life*, 49.
27 Butler, *Precarious Life*, 25.
28 Gilles Deleuze and Félix Guattari, *A Thousand Plateaus: Capitalism and Schizophrenia*, trans. and foreword by Brian Massumi (Minneapolis: University of Minnesota Press, 2003), 6.
29 "Why Messi Is Such a Great Footballer!" @Royal Myscre Walks.
30 Quoted in "Lionel Messi Has Few Fans."
31 "La Bombanera" is now officially known as Estadio Alberto J. Armando; it was previously called Estadio Camilo Cichero.
32 "El Gran Capitán" is the moniker by which the Argentine independence hero José de San Martín is known. Passarella is afforded this titular mark because he captained Argentina to its first Copa Mundial triumph in 1978, under, as I have written elsewhere, dubious circumstances. See Grant Farred, *Long-Distance Love: A Passion for Football* (Philadelphia, PA: Temple University Press), 2007.
33 Charles Bukowski, "A Smile to Remember," http://bukowski.net/poems/a_smile_to_remember.php.
34 There are, thus, between Yeats and Owen, two distinct arguments against war, colonization and antimilitarism, arguments that are mutually interrogative. Would it be in order for the "Irish Airman" to fight in the Irish cause? Can patriotism ameliorate the imminent death that the "Irish Airman foresees" or does it simply condemn him for his participation in the war?

35 Butler, *Precarious Life*, 49.
36 Nietzsche, 51.
37 Together with, of course, "eternal recurrence of the same."
38 *Webster's Unabridged Dictionary*, Second Edition, New York: Random House, 2001, 425.
39 Nancy, *Hegel*, 78.
40 Jacques Lacan, *The Ethics of Psychoanalysis: 1959–1960: The Seminar of Jacques Lacan Book*, book 7, ed. Jacques-Alain Miller, trans. with notes by Dennis Porter (New York: Norton, 1997), 172.
41 Lacan, *Ethics of Psychoanalysis*, 172.
42 Lacan, *Ethics of Psychoanalysis*, 194.
43 This is what passes for "loyalty" (which is proximate to patriotism, in our case) and it is precisely "loyalty" of this order that Zarathustra condemns: "'To practise loyalty and for the sake of loyalty to risk honour and blood even for evil and dangerous causes'" (Nietzsche, 51).
44 *Webster's*, 425.
45 The syntactic rendering of Catalan in his soul would be Catalá d'animá, but that would have no resonance within this context. I am indebted to Alberto Moreiras for the Catalá phrasing I use in the chapter.
46 Lacan, *Ethics of Psychoanalysis*, 184.
47 *Webster's*, 425.
48 *Webster's*, 425.
49 Jonathan Culler, *Theory of the Lyric* (Cambridge, MA: Harvard University Press, 2015), 300.
50 In arguing for *Aufhebung*, this chapter, while privileging Lacan's conception of it, will be subtended by Nancy's contention that it must be understood as the "conjoined suppression of two possible significations, the sublation or upheaval of one by the other"; Nancy, *Hegel*, 51. Critical also is what extends from *Aufhebung* for Nancy: "upheaval . . . the most serious penetration of thought," for which Nancy offers the possibility of "upsurge," the forceful emergence of something—thought, political action, an act—that can re- or disarticulate things as they are (51).
51 Butler, *Precarious Life*, 49.
52 On the pathological relationship between Maradona and Argentina, see Lacan, *Ethics of Psychoanalysis*, 192, 183. On the "lovable rogue," see Farred, *In Motion, At Rest*.
53 Lacan, *Ethics of Psychoanalysis*, 203.
54 Nancy, *Hegel*, 51, 52; emphasis in original.
55 Lacan, *Ethics of Psychoanalysis*, 200.
56 Lacan, *Ethics of Psychoanalysis*, 199.
57 Lacan, *Ethics of Psychoanalysis*, 202.

58 Lacan, *Ethics of Psychoanalysis*, 203.
59 Nancy, *Hegel*, 68.
60 Nancy, *Hegel*, 49.
61 Lacan, *Ethics of Psychoanalysis*, 200.
62 Nancy, *Hegel*, 36.
63 Nancy, *Hegel*, 59.
64 Lacan, *Ethics of Psychoanalysis*, 172.
65 Lacan, *Ethics of Psychoanalysis*, 173.
66 Nancy, *Hegel*, 62.
67 See Farred, *Long-Distance Love*.
68 *Cules* translates roughly as "half-asses," the name given to the club's fans when it played at its previous home, Camp des Les Corts, and the fans who sat on the wall—mainly men, one imagines—showed "half" of their posterior to the world while watching the game.
69 Carole Slade, *St. Theresa of Avila: Author of a Heroic Life* (Berkeley, CA: University of California Press, 1995) 135.
70 Lacan, *Ethics of Psychoanalysis*, 202.
71 Nancy, *Hegel*, 22.
72 Nancy, *Hegel*, 22.
73 Nancy, *Hegel*, 24.
74 Agamben's rendering is, of course, "zones of indistinction," a concept that is at the core of critique of biopolitics and the difference that Agamben claims for the "distinction" between "bare life" and "political life." See Agamben's *Homer Sacer: Sovereign Power and Bare Life*, trans. Daniel Heller-Roazen (Stanford, CA: Stanford University Press, 1998). To extrapolate analogically (and pejoratively, I hasten to add), one might say that for Messi, Argentina is the site of "bare life" (the accidental but not place of origin), and Barcelona, wrapped into the entire Catalan project (the desire for independence, the scars and the bitterness that emanates from defeat in the *guerra civil*, the anti-Castillian politics, the insufficiency of its *autonomista* status, and so on), is where his "political life" (the "fuller expression of self") is articulated.
75 I am intrigued, in this regard, by J. L. Austin's critique of the "statement"; of the ways in which the "statement," as the bearer of truth or fact, is not at all a reliable marker of either. Austin's critique incorporates, it can even be said to begin with, the notion of "nonsense" and the ways in which the "misstatement" (also designated as an "utterance") can be issued in "*bad faith*," could be "misleading, probably deceitful and doubtless wrong," but can still not be deemed a "lie or a misstatement"; J. L. Austin, *How to Do Things with Words* (Cambridge, MA: Harvard University Press, 1975), 11. How can we make a "statement" about Messi? More precisely, in this attempt to craft a "language" for Messi how does one avoid the pitfalls

of "nonsense" ("deceitfulness, lies," and so on) and remain, as it were, felicitous—in order to avoid the trap of the "truth"—to Messi and the ways in which he makes us think about, enjoy, watch, and agonize over football?

76  In contemporary football it is known as an "assist," a statistical way to keep track of who provides the pass that allows the goal scorer to convert the opportunity. This is a recent statistical innovation. In the past, it was not recorded—midfielders, let us say, or wingers, were simply doing their job when they created the opportunity for, say, the central striker.

77  It is also possible, of course, to render Austin's "distinction"—the "act" which creates the potential for the "unintended"—as agency. Broadly conceived, our capacity to act in the world is always counterbalanced, contingent, upon the world's—the context in which we find ourselves, the time, the people, the various circumstances that construct a moment—ability to "act," in ways intended or not, on us; the interrupt the "act," to "malform" it, even to destroy or utterly consume our "act." The "act" guarantees nothing, certainly not the "effect" it envisages. Every "act" must, in this way, be understood as subject to that which it does not know.

78  I am borrowing here from genealogy of *Dasein* offered by Michael Inwood's *A Heidegger Dictionary* (Oxford: Blackwell Publishing, 1999, 42).

79  For Heidegger, as is his wont, there remains an inveterate tension that surrounds *Dasein*. He addresses this in relation to the question that preoccupies *An Introduction to Metaphysics* his critique of metaphysics: "Why are there beings at all and not nothing?" In contemplating this question, Heidegger writes, "Our Dasein, too, as it questions, comes into suspense, and nevertheless maintains itself, by itself, in this suspense"; Martin Heidegger, *An Introduction to Metaphysics*, trans. Gregory Fried and Richard Polt (New Haven, CT: Yale Nota Bene, Yale University Press, 2000), 31. Following Heidegger's fidelity to the question, then, means that any designation of Messi as *Dasein* is always articulated in the shadow, the possibility, of the very "suspense" that enables this designation in the first place.

80  In my essay "Cum Deus Calculat Fit Mundus: When God Plays, a World Comes to Be," http://cargocollective.com/OppositionalConversations_Ii/Cum-Deus-Calculat-Fit-Mundus-When-God-plays-a-world-comes-to-be; also translated into Croatian by Stipe Grgas (under the same title), in *Quorum* 3/4 (2011): 251–64, I use Martin Heidegger's *Was Heißt Denken?* to produce a language for the very particular way in which FC Barcelona played during Guardiola's time at the club. (Guardiola, of course, was a Barça player before he became the coach.)

81  Thinking beyond metaphysics, from "being" as such to "Being," is the project Heidegger undertakes in *An Introduction to Metaphysics*; an argument that is also taken up in *Kant and the Problem of Metaphysics*, a work in which Heidegger makes the case that Kant's *Critique of Pure Reason* is the foundation of metaphysics. Kant scholars describe Heidegger's work as a "violent" attack on Kant.

82  "Route 1" football is the term used to describe the robust kind of game played by English side Wimbledon FC during the late 1980s and early 1990s. It was, to be euphemistic, a take-no-prisoners approach to the game. Unsightly, to say the least, and effective for only so long, thank goodness.

83  Messi is now the Barça captain. In his time with the club, the only club he has represented, he has played under the leadership of Carles Puyol, Xavi Hernández, and Andrés Iniesta. Such is the way that the Catalan club plays, such is the culture at Barça, that leadership is spread among the senior players, among whom Messi most certainly ranks. Iniesta, Messi, and Gerard Piqué would, in the 2016–17 team, together with, say, Javier Mascherano (Messi's Argentine teammate), constitute that leadership core. Messi's talents are augmented, complemented, intensified through his relationship with this wonderfully talented Barça team—with the several iterations of talented Barça teams on which he has played. For all Hernández's, Iniesta's, Suárez's and Neymar's gifts, for me Messi stands above them, which is in no way a disparagement of their talents. Messi is simply that good. He ranks with the greatest players in the history of football—Alfredo Di Stéfano, Pelé, Johan Cruyff, and Diego Maradona.

84  This is of course by no means an exhaustive list. But, by its very nature, players such as Messi have very few peers. I must add, however, that even by these standards there are players, in the various sports codes, whom I could have included. To lengthen the list just a little with some personal favorites: Magic Johnson (basketball), Franz Beckenbauer (football), Lawrence Taylor (gridiron), Learie Constantine and Richie Benaud (cricket), Zinzan Brooke, Billy Beaumont, and Morné du Plessis (rugby).

85  There remains, however, a signal difference between Cruyff, who named his son Jordi in honor of the patron saint of Catalunya, and Messi. Unlike Cruyff, who joined Barcelona only after he was deposed as Ajax (Netherlands) captain in the buildup to the 1973 season, Messi, as we know, has never represented another club as a professional.

86  In one of his more self-deprecating moments, and there are many of those, Nortje dubs himself "too nominal an exile." Arthur Nortje, "Autopsy," in *Dead Roots: Poems* (London: Heinemann, 1973), 52.

87  Adam Bate, http:www.skysports.com/football/news/15241/9381511/world-cup-was-lionel-mess-really-a-disappointment-in-brazil-or-have-we-just-become-numb-to-his-genius.

88  Adam Bate, "Was Lionel Messi really a disappointment in Brazil or have we just become numb to his genius?," "Sky Sport," https://www.skysports.com/football/news/15241/9381511/world-cup-final-was-lionel-messi-really-a-disappointment-in-brazil-or-have-we-just-become-numb-to-his-genius.

89  Lacan, *Ethics of Psychoanalysis*, 176.

90  Nancy, *Hegel*, 59.
91  Nancy, *Hegel*, 4.
92  Lacan, *Ethics of Psychoanalysis*, 202.
93  Lacan, *Ethics of Psychoanalysis*, 202.
94  Nancy, *Hegel*, 6.

INTERLUDE · "*NOG LANSUR!*"

1  Ta-Nehisi Coates, *Between the World and Me* (New York: Spiegel & Grau, 2015), 124.
2  Coates, *Between the World and Me*, 52.
3  Jean-Luc Nancy, *Hegel: The Restlessness of the Negative*, trans. Jason Smith and Steven Miller (Minneapolis: University of Minnesota Press, 2002), 35.
4  I am reminded here of Arthur Ashe's reflections on growing up in pre-Civil Rights Richmond, Virginia. After Althea Gibson, Ashe was the first African American tennis player to win a Grand Slam title. In fact, Ashe won three of the four Grand Slam events (Wimbledon, the US Open, and the Australian Open, with only the French Open eluding him). By no means an outspoken champion against US racism in his playing days (1960s–1970s), Ashe rose to the occasion in the 1980s as a stalwart in the antiapartheid movement. His boyhood experiences in Richmond found clear resonances with the apartheid educational and political system: "'I went through a segregated school system and a segregated society'"; Arthur Ashe and Arnold Rampersad, *Days of Grace: A Memoir* (New York: Alfred A. Knopf, 1993), 112.
5  Jean-Luc Nancy, *Being Singular Plural*, trans. Robert D. Richardson and Anne E. O'Byrne (Stanford, CA: Stanford University Press, 2000), 9.
6  Nancy, *Hegel*, 19.
7  On *Rastlosigkeit/Ruhelosigkeit*, I would like to thank Dirk Uffelmann for suggesting that I think "restlessness" in terms of the German translations he offered me. Nancy, in delineating his notion of "creation," offers a critique of Heidegger's conception of "curiosity." According to Nancy, for Heidegger "curiosity is the frantic activity of passing from being to being in an insatiable sort of way, without ever being able to stop and think"; Nancy, *Being*, 19. Ironically, Nancy himself fails to advocate for a moment's rest, a moment to stop and think. Moreover, it is worth recognizing that taking the time to think, to think thinking, is precisely what Heidegger does in *Was Heißt Denken?* This is important to acknowledge because for Heidegger there is no greater or sustaining curiosity than "thinking" and "Being," than thinking Being in relation to thinking.
8  In establishing, even if only temporarily, "restlessness" in relation to "being at rest," it is possible, if only mischievously, to suggest that there might be precisely such

a possibility located in Nancy's understanding of "separation" and its "alterity": "Separation is henceforth the posited present of the thing: its alterity"; Nancy, *Hegel*, 22. (Thinking) at rest is the "alterity" of "separation."

9  Nancy, *Hegel*, 18.
10 Nancy, *Being*, 14.
11 Nancy, *Being*, 9; emphasis in original. Nancy is deliberate in distinguishing his concept of the "everyday" from Heidegger's *existentielle*, which Nancy critiques as "undifferentiated, statistical and anonymous"; Nancy, *Being*, 9.
12 Nancy, *Being*, 25.
13 Nancy, *Being*, 9; emphasis in original.
14 Nancy, *Hegel*, 24.
15 Under SACOS (see note 18 for a history of SACOS), all the clubs within its structures played their games either at their own, racially segregated (that is, racially enclosed) venues or against clubs that shared their racial designation. In effect this meant that the disenfranchised competed only among themselves. Clubs such as Lansur played other clubs in Hanover Park; clubs in other townships, such as Heideveld, and middle-class colored communities, such as those in Wynberg, did the same. We never, until the end of apartheid, played against predominantly white clubs. I must admit that the first time Lansur traveled to play in Green Point against a white club, we were all a little shell-shocked—at the quality of their facilities (they took it for granted, it seemed). The fields were green, as opposed to the scrub brown of Die Veld, the grass neatly trimmed, and their changing rooms were spacious, well maintained, and clean.
16 Bruce Springsteen, *Born to Run* (New York: Simon & Schuster, 2016), 262.
17 For his part, Coates has the following to say about his mother teaching the value of reading, of reading and writing for the interrogative: "She also taught me to write, by which I mean not simply organizing a set of sentences into a series of paragraphs, but organizing them as a means of investigation"; Coates, *Between the World and Me*, 29.
18 SACOS was founded in 1973 on the principle of nonracialism. The organization worked to highlight the structural inequities that derived directly from apartheid. SACOS provided an important mode of political education, in no small part because its structural effects reached down to, or began, in the school system itself. So, all disenfranchised children, but especially those in the Western and Eastern Cape, the border region (around the city of East London), and in the hinterland (cities such as Kimberley), were raised on the SACOS demand for the franchise and equality in all aspects of society. That is to say that SACOS was especially strong in South Africa's colored communities. It had also had something of a toehold in the "Indian" (South Asian) community, in what was then the province of Natal, but it had little traction in the black community as such (the Eastern Cape was the exception, but not much of an exception, I hasten to add). SACOS also had

an international arm, SANROC (the South African Non-Racial Olympic Committee), whose brief it was to isolate the apartheid regime, to prevent apartheid teams from competing internationally, not only in the Olympics or the World Cup but in general. SANROC, supported as it was by antiapartheid activists in Britain, New Zealand, and elsewhere, was a major success in making apartheid sports teams international pariahs. SACOS is the sports structure under which I played my entire career; I played football and cricket under its umbrella, critical as I sometimes was of its middle-class leadership. See Douglas Booth, "The South African Council on Sport and the Political Antinomies of the Sports Boycott," *Journal of Southern African Studies* 23, no. 1 (March 1997): 51–66.

19 Young Pirates of Hanover Park were named after a black professional team, Orlando Pirates, from the massive township of Soweto in Johannesburg, and they mimicked the black-and-white strip of their professional idols. The Pirates' colors were, I must admit, the coolest in our league.

20 W. H. Auden, "The Dark Years," *Collected Poems* (New York: Vintage International, 1991), 283.

21 Dylan Thomas, "I See the Boys of Summer in their Ruin," https://www.poemhunter.com/poem/i-see-the-boys-of-summer/. Last accessed November 2018.

22 Fine Young Cannibals, "She Drives Me Crazy," https://www.youtube.com/watch?v=osw54Pdh_m8.

23 Jacques Derrida, *Learning to Live Finally: The Last Interview*, an interview with Jean Birnbaum), trans. Michael Naas and Pascale-Anne Brault (Hoboken, NJ: Melville Publishing House, 2007), 17.

24 Derrida, *Learning*, 23.

25 Later scientific video replay has shown that Hurst's shot did not, in fact, cross the line so the goal should not have counted. Today there is technology (the ball is equipped with a sensor to indicate whether or not it completely crosses the line) to make such a determination. No matter, Hurst entered the history books and there Sir Geoffrey Charles Hurst remains.

26 See, in this regard, Jimmy Burns's *Barça: A People's Passion* (London: Bloomsbury, 1999) for an incisive discussion about the relationship between the Catalan desire for sovereignty and the role that FC Barcelona plays in this (political) movement. I have also addressed this issue in the chapter *Som Més que un Club, però Menys que una Nació*: More Than a Club, but Less Than a Nation (*Long Distance Love: A Passion for Football*, Philadelphia: Temple University Press, 2008).

27 Springsteen, *Born to Run*, 264.

28 Coates, *Between the World and Me*, 108.

29 Nancy, *Being*, 7.

30 Nancy, *Hegel*, 35.

31 Billy Joel, "Everybody Has a Dream," https://www.azlyrics.com/lyrics/billyjoel/everybodyhasadream.html. Last accessed November 2018.

32  Nancy, *Hegel*, 35.
33  As quoted in Nancy, *Hegel*, 42.
34  Nancy, *Hegel*, 57.
35  Jacques Lacan, *The Ethics of Psychoanalysis: 1959–1960: The Seminar of Jacques Lacan*, book 7, ed. Jacques-Alain Miller, trans. Dennis Porter (New York: W. W. Norton, 1992), 200.
36  Lacan, *Ethics of Psychoanalysis*, 200.
37  Lacan, *Ethics of Psychoanalysis*, 201.

CHAPTER TWO · THE SHAME OF LOVING THE CONDEMNED

1  When I began to write this project Guardiola was in his first season as Manchester City coach, so the jury is still out on what he might, or might not, accomplish in the Premier League. Manchester City started out his first season with ten straight wins in all competitions at the beginning of the 2016–17 season, faded in January and February, eventually losing the Premier League to Chelsea. In the 2017–2018 season, however, Guardiola's Manchester City vanquished all before them, winning the Premier League, in style, I hasten to add. At the moment that I am completing this project (late-October, 2018), Guardiola's Manchester City and my beloved Liverpool top the Premier Leagues, separated only by goal difference. Manchester City have 10 more goals than us. Watching a Guardiola-coached team, especially in Spain and England (Germany's level of competition never seemed to challenge Pep), is never anything short of an absolute delight.
2  Eduardo Galeano, *Football in Sun and Shadow*, trans. Mark Fried, London: Fourth Estate, 2003, 1.
3  Tabárez has had two stints with the Uruguayan under-twenties, once in 1983, and then again in 1987. During his first time in charge, he was appointed directly from Bella Vista (1980–83). During his initial term, his Uruguayan team won the Pan American games in Caracas, beating Guatemala.
4  Like many coaches, Tabárez has had a peripatetic career, moving among his native Uruguay (Danubio and Peñarol [one of the two most famous clubs in the country, the other being Nacional]), neighboring Argentina (Boca Juniors [the most popular team in Argentina, whom he managed twice] and Vélez Sársfield), and Colombia (Deportivo Cali); in Europe he has managed in Italy (Cagliari [twice] and Inter Milan [a spell that lasted only a few short months, in many ways the nadir of his career]) and Spain (Oviedo).
5  Bob Marley, "Redemption Song," https://www.lyrics.com/lyric/7166186/Manfred+Mann/Redemption+Song+%28No+Kwazulu%29.
6  Jean-Luc Nancy, *Being Singular Plural*, trans. Robert D. Richardson and Anne E. O'Byrne (Stanford, CA: Stanford University Press, 2000), 25. "First philosophy," of

course, is the (posthumous) name given to Aristotle's work that followed *Physics*. As such, *Physics* is of limited scientific use, but its value resides in its interrogative philosophical propensities. "First philosophy" is today most recognizable as "metaphysics," a term that Aristotle does not use but would speak to his study, a line of philosophical inquiry taken by a host of modern thinkers, from René Descartes (see his 1641 text *Meditations on First Philosophy*) to Emmanuel Levinas and Heidegger.

7   Nancy, *Being*, 25.
8   Jean-Luc Nancy, *Hegel: The Restlessness of the Negative*, trans. Jason Smith and Steven Miller (Minneapolis: University of Minnesota Press, 2002), 47, emphasis in original.
9   Nancy, *Hegel*, 52.
10  In this regard, we might think about Martin Luther King Jr.'s "Letter from a Birmingham Jail," https://www.africa.upenn.edu/Articles_Gen/Letter_Birmingham.html, in which King explains his commitment to "justice"—the "disease of segregation"—as what motivates his sacrifice.
11  Derrida, as we know, argues stringently against such a prospect. We cannot, in his terms, take on the suffering of the other.
12  In John's Gospel, the promise and prophecy of the New Testament is clear: "The next day he saw Jesus coming toward him and declared, 'Here is the Lamb of God who takes away the sins of the world!'" (John 1:29).
13  Jacques Derrida, *The Gift of Death*, trans. David Wills (Chicago: University of Chicago Press, 1996), 114, (original emphasis).
14  Friedrich Nietzsche, *On the Genealogy of Morals*, trans. Walter Kaufmann (New York: Vintage Books, 1969), 92.
15  Nietzsche, *On the Genealogy of Morals*.
16  In Derrida's work on the Abrahamic tradition, especially *The Gift of Death*, as we have seen, Derrida argues that it is Abraham's refusal to be responsible to his wife, his family, his community, his faith, and, of course, his son, that makes him irresponsible, that is, absolutely, radically felicitous to God.
17  Nancy, *Being*, 13.
18  Nancy, *Hegel*, 45.
19  In his "Trembling" chapter, Nancy argues for a relation between "trembling" and "negativity" insofar as the former initiates a restlessness that disturbs everything, throws everything into relief. "Negativity," he writes, "makes all determinateness tremble, all being-all-to-itself: it injects it with a shudder and an unsettling agitation." Nancy, *Hegel*, 45.
20  Nancy, *Hegel*, 45.
21  See Marcel Mauss, trans. W.D. Halls, *The Gift: Forms and Reason for Exchange in Archaic Societies* (New York: W.W. Norton, 1990). Here we can trace Derrida's thinking in *The Gift of Death* to Mauss's work.

22 Carl Schmitt, *Ex Captivitate Salus*, trans. Matthew Hannah (Medford, MA Polity Press, 2017), 56. The notions of "instantaneous copresence" and "immediate simultaneity" emerge out of Schmitt's argument for "recuperating," for the purposes of "delivering" himself from postwar "captivity," Jean Bodin and Thomas Hobbes as fellow travelers; Schmitt *Ex Captivitate Salus*, 56. That is, as thinkers assaulted on all sides by the different partisans in the "civil wars" of their time. It is a politically troubling claim, to say the least, given Schmitt's support for National Socialism, but all the more provocative for that as Schmitt tries to redeem himself as a scholar of legal jurisprudence.

23 Nancy, *Hegel*, 43.

24 Nancy, *Hegel*, 60. In *Being Singular Plural*, Nancy (intentionally or not, it is difficult to know) raises the discussion about the "gift," in the form of the "given," to the level of Being. He does so by positing what is given as follows: "*Being itself is given to as meaning*"; Nancy, *Being*, 2. Understood as such, we could say that every gift is the gift of meaning; of seeking to make meaning in the world; or the gift is the meaning that is inscribed in this commitment, the gift that is not-only a gift, as such, to the other.

25 Judith Butler, *Precarious Life: The Powers of Mourning and Violence* (New York: Verso, 2006).

26 Nancy, *Hegel*, 59.

27 Jean-Luc Nancy, *The Inoperative Community*, trans. Peter Connor, Lisa Garbus, Michael Holland, and Simona Sawhney (Minneapolis: University of Minnesota Press, 2015), 104. In *The Inoperative Community*, Nancy critiques Heidegger for his inability to write about love. "It is not at all by chance that Heidegger is silent about love," he asserts; even Levinas, whom Nancy holds up as *the* philosopher of love, praised here for "clearing the path toward . . . a metaphysics of love," is not spared because he "remains *equivocal*" about love; Nancy, *Inoperative Community*, 104, 105. However, it might be possible that love takes a distinct articulation in Heidegger's work. For Heidegger, I would argue, love as such manifests itself as fidelity to thinking. It is worth recalling that for Heidegger, "only philosophy thinks," and his entire oeuvre is, in one way or another, dedicated to the relation between Being and thinking. As such, while love might not be spoken by Heidegger, a good argument can be made for Heidegger's corpus as a labor of love in the name of thinking/Being, of thinking Being. All Heidegger's writing, as such, inclines in the direction of love; the speaking of love takes, then, many forms. But, Nancy cautions in his recognition of the limits of writing love, "it might well be appropriate that a discourse on love—supposing that it still has something to say—be at the same time a communication of love, a letter, a missive, since love sends itself as much as enunciates itself. But the words of love, as is well known, miserably repeat their one declaration, which is always the same, always already suspected of lacking love because it declares it"; Nancy, *Inoperative Community*, 82. If it is indeed the

case that love is, a priori, always, the word that constitutes its own lack, so that to declare "I love you" is to know, before itself, the inadequacy, the repetition, maybe even the ventriloquization, of love, its constitutive insufficiency. "Love," as such, is always in search of the word "love," that word that can instill the truth of love, that can retrieve love into truth.

28  Nancy, *Inoperative Community*, 82.
29  "I know," Derrida writes, "that I will never deliver the other from his death, from the death that affects his whole being"; Jacques Derrida, *The Gift of Death*, 43. Indeed, it is impossible to "deliver the other from his death." However, what if we propose death not as the "delivery from death" as such but the "staying" of (the) death intended for the other. That is, death, as the self's political decision, to die not so much in the place of but to die in the moment of the "other's" death. If death is conceived as such then sacrifice as we know it imbues the political decision with the force, not the power, mind, the possibility, of postponing the other's death to another moment, the moment that is not now. Death as sacrifice, in such a rendering, "regains" its Heideggerian imperative—all being is indeed toward death—but sacrifice becomes the act of temporal intervention; as such, of course, it can return us to Derrida if we posit sacrifice, so conceived, as *différance*.
30  Nancy, *Inoperative Community*, 84.
31  The Bee Gees, "How Deep is Your Love?," https://youtu.be/XpqqjU7u5Yc.
32  Of course, the late 1970s to early 1980s are marked, in the Dylan canon, by three albums exploring his newfound interest in and conversion to evangelical Christianity. In 1979 Dylan released the first of his Christian trilogy LPs, *Slow Train Coming*. He followed this with two further LPs in the next two years, *Saved* (1980) and *Shot of Love* (1981). The trilogy was panned by critics, no one more so than John Lennon, who lambasted *Slow Train Coming*. However, for our purposes, it is worth remembering the opening track on that much-maligned LP. Its title is "Gotta Serve Somebody."
33  The Bee Gees, "How Deep is Your Love?"
34  Jacques Lacan, *The Ethics of Psychoanalysis: 1959–1960: The Seminar of Jacques Lacan Book*, book 7, ed. Jacques-Alain Miller, trans. with notes by Dennis Porter (New York: Norton, 1997), 203.
35  Lacan, *Ethics of Psychoanalysis*, 193.
36  Nancy, *Hegel*, 51.
37  Lacan, *Ethics of Psychoanalysis*, 173.
38  See, for example, *The Random House Webster's Unabridged Dictionary* (New York: Random House, second edition, 2001), which lists, among other definitions, the ethical as "pertaining to or dealing with morals or the principles of morality; pertaining to right or wrong in conduct."
39  Galeano, 1.

40 Jacques Derrrida, *On Touching—Jean-Luc Nancy*, trans. Christine Irizarry (Stanford, CA: Stanford University Press, 2005), 93. In the chapter titled "Tenderness," from which the quote about Levinas is drawn, Derrida offers a gentle, he would say, of course, "tender," reflection on Nancy's work on touching. Just a small sample: "—And in an aside you tell yourself: what a funny, admiring, and grateful salutation you're addressing to him, to Jean-Luc Nancy. What a peculiar way to pretend you're touching him while acting *as if* from now on you wanted to put his lexicon about touch out of service, or even banish it to the *Index librorum prohibitorum*"; Derrida, *On Touching*, 107; emphasis in original.

41 Nancy, *Hegel*, 57.

42 See Suárez: "Yo no mordí a nadie," June 24, 2015. https://www.youtube.com/watch?v=jhwkFwOh5uI.

43 Fútbol internacional Suárez habló de su mordisco en el Mundial y le apuntó a la FIFA http://www.clarin.com/futbol-internacional/Suárez-mordisco-chiellini-trataran-delincuente_0_Sko7iYE7x.html. Last accessed November 2018.

44 Fútbol internacional Suárez habló. Last accessed November 2018.

45 Fútbol internacional Suárez habló. Last accessed November 2018.

46 Uruguay Football Team. The Telegraph, http:/www.telegraph.co.uk/sport/football/teams/Uruguay/1087526/World-Cup-2014-How. This page is no longer active.

47 On this date, Tabárez spoke against FIFA and the media. He talked about a "media artillery" and affirmed that during the first conference press journalists who condemned Suárez's behavior only "spoke English." ("I do not know what their nationality was, but all of them spoke English"). In essence, he says, FIFA needed a scapegoat for the event. "Óscar Tábarez jumps to the defence of Luis Suárez," https://www.theguardian.com/football/2014/jun/28/world-cup-2014-oscar-tabarez-luis-suarez.

48 Tabárez en conferencia: "Más que nunca para el partido de mañana, vamos que vamos." See https://www.youtube.com/watch?v=CsxGqsE7VP0 Tabárez en conferencia: "Más que nunca para el partido de mañana, vamos que vamos."

49 Derrida, *On Touching*, 129.

50 In this regard, Michael Hardt and Sandro Mezzadra's understanding of the 1917 Bolshevik Revolution is instructive. Hardt and Mezzadra write that the "transformative powers of the event carry beyond the impossible to the unthinkable, opening new and vast horizons for the political imagination, allowing us to desire what we previously could not even imagine. That is where the highest power of the event lies"; Michael Hardt and Sandro Mezzadra, "October! To Commemorate the Future," *South Atlantic Quarterly*, 116, no. 4, 2017: 650.

51 Hardt and Mezzadra, "October!," 650.

52 In the twelve-nation World Cup, the United States finished third, beating out Yugoslavia. That remains the United States' best showing at the Copa Mundial to date.

53  Galeano relates a wonderful tale about sacrifice during that first World Cup that the Uruguayans hosted. Every time the Uruguayans played their neighbors and included Adhemar Canavessi in the team, they lost. Without him, they won. So, before the 1928 Olympic final in Amsterdam, Canavessi got off the team bus taking the team to the match, and Uruguay won. Such is the nature of "sacrifice"; Eduardo Galeano, *Football in Sun and Shadow*, trans. Mark Fried (London: Fourth Estate, 2003), 51.
54  Galeano, *Football*, 54.
55  Galeano, *Football*, 86.
56  Galeano, *Football*, 86. Tabárez is speaking, in this context, about Suárez as exemplifying El Proceso, the national football structure that facilitated Suárez's development from the youth level through to the senior side. What is also clear, however, is that Tabárez thinks about this process as a philosophy, as a series of thinkings about football, its organization, and, most important, how it can make possible the "maturation" of a player; that is, a player such as Suárez is valued, treasured, surely, because he is recognized in terms of, as Nancy would say, the "singular plural" of his "origins." In this way, we might say, El Proceso is nothing other than a synonym for nurturing the singular individual talent—the talent that is, in this case, Suárez, but could, with allowance for difference, as easily be another player.
57  Galeano, *Football*, 86.
58  Galeano, *Football*, 86.
59  *The Guardian*, "Luis Suárez: Uruguayans are Hurting But We Can't Go on Defending Him at Any Price." https://www.theguardian.com/football/2014/jun/28/luis-suarez-uruguayans-hurting. Accessed November 15, 2018.
60  *The Guardian*, "Luis Suárez: Uruguayans are Hurting." Accessed November 15, 2018.
61  Entorno Inteligente, "El 'Maestro' Tabárez Rechazó Contestar Sobre Denuncias Contra Miguel Zuluaga." http://www.entornointeligente.com/articulo/3745768/El-maestro-Tabárez-rechazo-contestar-sobre-denuncias-contra-Miguel-Zuluaga. All the quotes in this "section" are from this source. It is not noted as such because such a "technicality" would interfere with the "flow" of the section. Last accessed November 15, 2018.
62  "El 'Maestro' Tabárez defendió con furia a Luis Suárez," http://elcomercio.pe/deporte-total/brasil-2014/mundial-brasil-2014-copa-mundo-2014-uruguay-italia-mundial-maestro-Tabárez-defendio-furia-luis-Suárez-noticia-1738345. See also, http://www.leftvoice.org/. Following this, Tabárez then went on to say, "No he visto la jugada y no acepto consejos de nadie. No sé de dónde sacaron eso de que a Suárez lo sacarán del Mundial. Hay gente escondida que está lista para pegarle a Suárez. Es cierto que ha cometido errores, pero él de a pocos ha ido intentando cambiar su actitud. Él es el blanco perfecto de cierta prensa,' dijo muy molesto" ("I have not seen the play

and I do not accept advice from anyone. I do not know where they got that from Suárez will get him out of the World Cup. There are hidden people who are ready to beat Suárez. It is true that he has made mistakes, but he has been trying to change his attitude. He is the perfect target of certain press," he said, very annoyed.)

63 "El 'Maestro' Tabárez defendió con furia a Luis Suárez."

64 On government apology, see then-Australian prime minister Kevin Rudd's apology for the violence done to the indigenous people, which included a moving speech to the "stolen generation" of Aboriginal children—and by extension to their families, communities, to their entire people—in his February 2008 address to the Australian parliament. http://parlinfo.aph.gov.au/parlInfo/search/display/display.w3p;query=Id%3A%22chamber%2Fhansardr%2F2008-02-13%2F0003%22; Elspeth Probyn, *Blush: The Faces of Shame* (Minneapolis: University of Minnesota Press, 2005), x.

65 See Alyosha Goldstein and Alex Lubin, eds., "Settler Colonialism," *South Atlantic Quarterly* 107, no. 4 (2008); a collection of essays that deals with the various iterations of settler colonialism that marks life in Palestine, several locations in Africa (among them South Africa and Eritrea), the United States, and Argentina.

66 Probyn, *Blush*, 8.

67 Nancy, *Being Singular Plural*, 99.

68 *Entrée-nous* is Nancy's spelling of the term. Nancy, *Hegel*, 78.

69 Consonant with this thinking, or finding philosophical echoes in this claim, is Probyn's assertion that shame "emerges as a kind of primal reaction to the very possibility of love—either of oneself or of another"; Probyn, *Blush*, 3. If there is no longer the imperative to tack to the logic of the self-other dialectic, then love as a "primal possibility," the love that shows its face, repeatedly, in public, as love, is much more likely to manifest itself. And if one extends these "primal" possibilities, then it might just be that there need be no distinction between the love of and for the self and love of and for the other. Love too becomes open to as such. Nancy, *Hegel*, 48.

70 Nancy, *Hegel*, 62.

71 Nancy, *Hegel*, 69.

72 Nancy, *Hegel*, 76; emphasis in original.

73 Probyn, *Blush*, x.

74 Probyn, *Blush*, x.

75 Probyn, *Blush*, xiii.

76 I have wondered, in the course of writing this chapter (especially in its earliest articulation), what Galeano, doyen of football writers the world over, and the keenest observer of football his native land has ever produced, made of the entire episode? Was he glad to be in retirement for this? Surely he admires Suárez as a player; his impish brilliance is just the thing that Galeano so celebrates in *Football in Sun and Shadow*. But the racism? The repeated biting? Galeano, who is so proud of Uruguay's history of producing and exalting its black players, who so abhors the ugly

physicality that so often ruins the game, Suárez's behavior, this must surely trouble him. Writing on Suárez and Tabárez on the day that the most beautiful footballer the game has ever known, Alfredo di Stéfano (born in neighboring Argentina), has passed on, Galeano, I have no doubt, would interrupt his mourning to call for more beauty, for less racism, and, if at all possible, for outlawing of all violence. Galeano (1940–2015; he was born and died in Montevideo) passed on about a year after the event of Suárez's third bite.

77 Probyn, *Blush*, xvi.
78 Probyn, *Blush*, xvi.
79 An explication of Suárez's "motivations" as such will not be sought, beyond the acknowledgment offered in the introduction. This is not because his "motivations," insofar as it is possible to delineate them (an impossible project, of course, which is what makes of the event such a constitutive philosophical difficulty, and why every philosopher seeks to offer an account of it), are unimportant; it is, rather, that the focus of this book is to understand what the effects of Suárez's actions are in relation to the concept of *entre-nous*.
80 Probyn, *Blush*, xviii.
81 There was a clutch of movies, most prominent among them *Boyz n the Hood* and *Menace II Society*, in the early 1990s, that directly addressed this issue. Or, as its critics would insist, these depictions of life in the "ghetto" (the "projects" or its socioeconomic equivalent) fed the stereotype of the young African American boy/teenager abandoned by his father, left to fend for himself in the "ghetto," usually with very little success. The overdetermination of death by poverty, violence, and paternal abandonment, so to speak.
82 See Hortense Spiller's essay "Mama's Baby, Papa's Maybe: An American Grammar Book," *Diacritics* 17, no. 2 (summer 1987): 64–81, which takes the author of the report, the late New York senator Daniel Patrick Moynihan, to task for his critique of the African American family. Spillers's essay has spawned a number of works in a mode similar to hers.
83 Miroslav Holub, "Ode to Joy," trans. Ewald Osers, George Theiner, Ian and Jarmila Milner, *The Fly* (Newcastle-upon-Tyne: Bloodaxe Books, 1987), 45.
84 Watching Suárez commit his transgression, there is about him—and, again, this is not to pathologize but to find a means of expressing the helplessness of the fans who admires him—a tragic quality. (Again, this line of argument is developed more fully in the chapter.) I was reminded of this sense of helplessness, the protagonist-who-can't-but-act-self-destructively, watching *Manchester by the Sea*. Lee Chandler (Casey Affleck), the tragic focus of the movie, is utterly helpless before the fact of the event—the death of his three children in a fire that he caused by throwing an extra log on the fire to keep his kids warm; he cannot turn up the heat because his wife, Randy (Michele Williams), has trouble breathing when the furnace is running; so, it is a tragedy that he accepts responsibility for that leaves

him a shell of a human being. He is unable to form any meaningful bonds with anyone. The closest he comes is when he is compelled, after his brother's death, to become his nephew Patrick's (Lucas Hedges) guardian. It is a task that he executes only for a matter of months. When Patrick asks his uncle why, all "Lee" can offer is, "I can't beat this, I can't beat this." The Suárez bite, for all kinds of reasons (helplessness, the sense of bowing one's head before the world, in shame, no doubt, are first among these reasons), came back to me in watching Affleck's Lee utter these painful words, the words of a man struggling to defeat himself, the man unable to face down his demons.

85  Reuters, "FIFA defends Suarez Biting Ban That Many Call Excessive." http://www.reuters.com/article/us-soccer-world-Suárez-idUSKBN0F213B20140627.

86  1 Corinthians 15:10.

87  In understanding Tabárez's insistence to recognize the other through the essential force of being-with, it is worth, if only for a moment, acknowledging the ways in which this raises the question of the "consciousness of the other" á la Jean-Paul Sartre. In "The Existence of Others," Sartre presents the difficulty (for the "idealist," ostensibly) of the problematic of the Other. For the "idealist," the alternative is either to "get rid of the concept of the Other completely" or to "affirm the real existence of the Other" (Jean-Paul Sartre, *Being and Nothingness: A Phenomenological Essay on Ontology* trans. Hazel E. Barnes (New York: Citadel Press, 2001), 205.

88  Ephesians 2:8.

# BIBLIOGRAPHY

Agamben, Giorgio. *Homer Sacer: Sovereign Power and Bare Life*. Translated by Daniel Heller-Roazen. Stanford, CA: Stanford University Press, 1998.
Ashe, Arthur, and Arnold Rampersad. *Days of Grace: A Memoir*. New York: Alfred A. Knopf, 1993.
Auden, W. H. "The Dark Years." *Collected Poems*. New York: Vintage International, 1991.
Austin, J. L. *How to Do Things with Words*. Cambridge, MA: Harvard University Press, 1975.
Burns, Jimmy. *Barça: A People's Passion*. London: Bloomsbury, 1999.
Butler, Judith. *Precarious Life: The Powers of Mourning and Violence*. New York: Verso, 2006.
Coates, Ta-Nehisi. *Between the World and Me*. New York: Spiegel & Grau, 2015.
Culler, Jonathan. *Theory of the Lyric*. Cambridge, MA: Harvard University Press, 2015.
Deleuze, Gilles, and Félix Guattari. *A Thousand Plateaus: Capitalism and Schizophrenia*. Translation and foreword by Brian Massumi. Minneapolis: University of Minnesota Press, 2003.
Derrida, Jacques. *The Gift of Death*. Translated by David Wills. Chicago, IL: University of Chicago Press, 1996.
Derrida, Jacques. *Learning to Live Finally: The Last Interview*. An interview with Jean Birnbaum. Translated by Michael Naas and Pascale-Anne Brault. Hoboken, NJ: Melville Publishing House, 2007.
Derrida, Jacques. *On Touching—Jean-Luc Nancy*. Translated by Christine Irizarry. Stanford, CA: Stanford University Press, 2005.
Dickens, Charles. *A Christmas Carol*. New York: Fall River Press, 2013.

Farred, Grant. *In Motion, at Rest: The Event of the Athletic Body*. Minneapolis: University of Minnesota Press, 2013.

Farred, Grant. *Long-Distance Love: A Passion for Football*. Philadelphia, PA: Temple University Press, 2008.

Galeano, Eduardo. *Football in Sun and Shadow*. Translated by Mark Fried. London: Fourth Estate, 2003.

Hardt, Michael. *Gilles Deleuze: An Apprenticeship in Philosophy*. Minneapolis: University of Minnesota Press, 1993.

Hegel, G. W. F. *Phenomenology of Spirit*. Translated by A. V. Miller. New York: Oxford University Press, 1977.

Heidegger, Martin. *Being and Time*. Translated by Joan Stambaugh. Albany, NY: State University of New York Press, 1996.

Heidegger, Martin. *An Introduction to Metaphysics*. Translated by Gregory Fried and Richard Polt. New Haven: Yale Nota Bene, Yale University Press, 2000.

Heidegger, Martin. *Was Heißt Denken?*. Translated by Fred W. Wieck and J. Glenn Gray. New York: Harper & Row, 1968.

Lacan, Jacques. *The Ethics of Psychoanalysis, 1959–1960: The Seminar of Jacques Lacan*. Book 7. Edited by Jacques-Alain Miller. Translated with notes by Dennis Porter. New York: Norton, 1997.

Nancy, Jean-Luc. *Being Singular Plural*. Translated by Robert D. Richardson and Anne E. O'Byrne. Stanford, CA: Stanford University Press, 2000.

Nancy, Jean-Luc. *Hegel: The Restlessness of the Negative*. Translated by Jason Smith and Steven Miller. Minneapolis: University of Minnesota Press, 2002.

Nancy, Jean-Luc. *The Inoperative Community*. Translated by Peter Connor, Lisa Garbus, Michael Holland, and Simona Sawhney. Minneapolis: University of Minnesota Press, 2015.

Nietzsche, Friedrich. *Thus Spoke Zarathustra: A Book for Everyone and Nobody*. Translated by Graham Parkes. Oxford: Oxford University Press, 2008.

Nortje, Arthur. *Dead Roots: Poems*. London: Heinemann, 1973.

Probyn, Elspeth. *Blush: Faces of Shame*. Minneapolis: University of Minnesota Press, 2005.

Safranski, Rüdiger. *Martin Heidegger: Between Good and Evil*. Translated by Ewald Osers. Cambridge, MA: Harvard University Press, 2002.

Sartre, Jean-Paul. *Being and Nothingness: A Phenomenological Essay on Ontology*. Translated by Hazel E. Barnes. New York: Citadel Press, 2001.

Schmitt, Carl. *Ex Captivitate Salus*. Translated by Matthew Hannah. Medford, MA: Polity Press, 2017.

Schmitt, Carl. *Nomos of the Earth*. Candor, NY: Telos Press Publishing, 2006.

Slade, Carole. *St. Theresa of Avila: Author of a Heroic Life*. Berkeley, CA: University of California Press, 1995.

Springsteen, Bruce. *Born to Run*. New York: Simon & Schuster, 2016.

# INDEX

Aboriginals, 197, 201, 204; Ayers Rock, 198; children, 197; communities, 198; culture, 197; land, 198; Rudd, Kevin (Apology), 201, 247; Uluru, 198
Adidas, 89
Africa, 114, 132, 186, 191, 247
African National Congress (ANC), 97, 98, 118, 128; Pan African Congress (PAC), 97
Afrikaans (*pure*), 18, 19, 26, 101, 110, 114, 115, 116, 122, 133, 147, 155–157, 230; Indonesia, 116; Kaaps, 19, 26, 27; *kombuis Nederlands*, 230; Raj, 116; township Afrikaans, 18, 115, 116
Agamben, Giorgio, 73, 235, 251; "zones of distinction," 73, 235
Agüero, Sergio "Kün," 36, 37, 85
Aimar, Pablo, 227; Valencia, 227; Zaragoza, 227
Ajax Amsterdam, 8, 9, 80, 213, 228, 237; Ajax Youth Academy, 228; de Boer, Frank and Ronald, 228; Keizer, Piet, 228; Krol, Rudi, 228; Stekelenburg, 228
Algeria, 89
Alonso, Xabi, 89

Anaximander, 76
Anderson, Nicole, 230; *Derrida: Ethics Under Erasure*, 230
Apartheid, xxiv, 5, 12–16, 18, 19, 82, 97, 98, 101, 109, 116, 118–123, 127, 151, 152, 159, 229; antiapartheid, 118, 123; coloured, 15, 16, 101, 117–119, 127, 151, 152, 229; National Party (NP), 98; postapartheid, 5, 14, 19, 118, 121, 139, 152
Appels, 124; Clive, 124; John, 124; Ivan, 124; Willie, 124
Amsterdam, 246
Andes, 71; Pampas, 71; Patagonia, 71
Arendse, Shaheed "Puppets," 155–159, 161
Arendse, Shahied "Pung," 127, 130, 134–138, 141–144, 149, 150, 154, 155; Nathaniel, 137
Argentina, xx, xxi–xxii, xxiv, 3, 6, 11, 12, 29–33, 35, 36, 38, 39, 41, 42, 44, 45, 47, 49, 52–54, 56, 58, 60–62, 64, 65, 68, 69, 71, 73, 80–84, 86, 90–93, 163, 165, 185, 192, 208, 219–221, 227, 229, 232–234, 241, 247; Argentine, xiii, xv, xxi, xxii, 7, 30–35, 37, 33, 40–43, 45, 48, 52, 53, 59, 61, 63, 68, 69, 74, 80, 81, 85, 86, 90, 92, 151, 219, 233;

Argentina (continued)
Argentine national team, xx, 43; *guerra sucia*, 90, 91; La Plata, 40, 68; "Los Celestes" (Los Albicelestes), xx–xxii, 64, 71, 73, 84; revolutionary, 10; Videla, 91
Aristotle, 200, 242; "First Philosophy," 242
Arsenal, 227
Ashe, Arthur, 238, 251; *Days of Grace: A Memoir* (Rampersad, Arnold), 238, 251; Richmond, Virginia, 238
Asia, 186
Atlantic Ocean, 101, 102, 106, 117
Atlético de Madrid, 187, 229
Aubemeyang, Pierre-Emerick, 85
Auden, W. H., 125, 240, 251; *Collected Poems*, 240
Austin, J. L., 74, 77, 235, 236; *How to Do Things with Words*, 74, 236
Australians (white), 197, Rudd, Kevin (prime minister), 204
*Autonomista*, xxiii, 12, 29, 45, 48, 80, 208, 235; anti-, 41

Bakkal, Otman, 186
Ballon d'Or, 7, 10, 36
Barcelona, Football Club (Barça), ix, x, xiv, xvii–xix, xxi, xxiii, 3, 6, 8, 30–32, 37, 41, 44, 45, 49, 51, 55, 59, 60, 62, 64, 65, 67, 69, 70, 76, 78–82, 92, 93, 95, 149, 164, 181, 207, 209, 212, 227, 228, 236, 237; *blaugrana*, xiv, 30, 62, 69, 93; Camp Nou, x, xvi, xvii, xix, xx; *cules*, xix, 235; Gardel, Carlos, 69, 70; Greenwell, Jack, 69; Kamper, Joan (Hans Kamper), 69; La Masia, 6, 227, 228; Les Corts, 70; Parsons, John and William, 69; Rexach, Charly, 6; Samitier, Josep "Pep," 69; *Som més que un club*, 68, 149
Barnes, John, 60, 61
Bayern, München, xii, xvi, 75, 164, 228
Beaumont, Billy, 237

Beardsley, 213
Beckenbauer, Franz, ix–xiv, xxiii, 76, 80, 237
Bee Gees (Brothers Gibb), 177, 244; "How Deep is Your Love," 244; *Saturday Night Fever*, 177
Begović, Asmir, 205; Bosnian goalkeeper, 205
Benaud, Richie, 237
Berlin, West, x, 85
Best, George, 51
Black River (Rondebosch East), 102
Boca Juniors, 6, 31, 39, 41, 54, 59, 241; Estadio Alberto J. Armando, 233; Estadio Camilo Cichero, 233; La Boca Stadium ("La Bombanera"), 31, 39–42, 51, 52, 233
Borges, Jose Luis, 31, 91
Botha, P. W., 98
Bourdieu, Pierre, 206; habitus, 206, 207
*Boyz n the Hood*, 248
Brazil, xix, 11, 53, 82, 87, 88, 185, 196, 207, 212, 217; Estádio das Dunas, 212; *joga bonito*, 11, 33, 182; *Lance!*, 231; Maracanã, 54, 185; Rio, 54, 182; Natal, 212
Britain, 240; British colonial rule, 57
Brooke, Zinzan, 237
Buenos Aires, xxi, 6, 31, 39, 40, 82; "Barrio Norte," 31, 40; Palermo, 31; Recoleta, 31, 39, 40; Retiro, 31
Bukowski Charles, 55, 56, 233; "A Smile to Remember," 55, 233
Burns, Jimmy, *Barça: A People's Passion*, 240, 251
Busquets, Sergio, 7, 228
Butler, Judith, 43, 44, 57, 64, 106, 108, 125, 172, 180, 233, 234, 243, 251; *Precarious Life: The Powers of Mourning and Violence*, 43, 233, 234, 243, 251

Cáceres, Martín, 187
Cagliari, 229, 241

Camus, Albert, x
Cape Flats, xxxiv, 18, 19, 26, 39, 100, 121, 124, 128, 129, 132, 135, 150, 152, 230; Heideveld, 239; Mitchells Plain, 118, 119, 155; Rocklands, 122, 155
Cape Peninsula, 117, 139
Cape Town, xxiv, 14, 97, 98, 100–102, 107, 119, 120, 122, 132, 137, 142, 143, 150; Athlone Stadium, 142; "Cape of Good Hope," 114; "Cape of Storms," 114; Claremont, 143; D. F. Malan Airport (Cape Town International), 97, 99; Grand Parade, 99, 100; Green Point, 239; Groote Schuur Hospital, 142; Mowbray, 143; Western Cape, 14; Wynberg, 143, 230; Table Mountain, 14, 99, 117
Caracas, 241; Pan American Games, 241
Caribbean, 216
Castro, Fidel, 166
Catalunya, xx, xxi, xxiii, 6, 12, 30, 33, 34, 45, 46, 59, 61, 62, 69, 71, 80, 82, 109, 151, 181, 208, 212, 237; Senyera, xxii
Cavani, Edinson, xvi, xvii, xix
Celan, Paul, xxiv; *Litchzwang*, xxiv
Champions League, ix, xvi, xvii, 7, 36, 85
Charlton, Bobby, xii
Chelsea, 241
Chicago's South Side, 158
Chiellini, Giorgio, 9–11, 180–185, 195, 204, 205, 210, 212
Chile, 53, 54, 192; Estadio Nacional, 54; Santiago de Chile, 54
Chinese Super League, 232; Anelka, Nicholas, 232; Carvalho, Ricardo (Portugal), 232; Drogba, Didier (Côte d'Ivoire), 232; Martínez, Jackson, 232; Oscar, 232; Witsel, Axel (Belguim), 232
Christian (Christianity), 66, 87, 159, 171; Abraham (Abrahamic tradition), 169, 170, 215, 242; Apostle Paul (Paul/Pauline), 214, 217, 218; Corinthians, 214, 249; Crucifixion, 166; Ephesians, 214, 249; ethical Judas, 200; Gospel of John, 170, 242; Isaac, 215, 169; Jesus-the-Christ, 166, 169; Judas, 200; Judeo-Christian, 156; New Testament, 242; Resurrection, 166, 215; Romans, 214; Roman Catholic, 50, 52, 66; Saint Peter, 212; Trinity, 215
Cillesen, Jesper, 79
Cleveland Cavaliers, xviii
Claus, Hernán, 40, 41, 43, 44, 46, 233
Coates, Ta-Nehisi, 4, 5, 97, 98, 151, 158, 227, 238–240, 251; *Between the World and Me*, 4, 227, 238–240, 251; Samori, 151; West Baltimore, 4, 158
Cobain, Kurt, 82
Cold War, 69; 192; *desaparacidos*, 192; Operación Cóndor, 192, 193; Southern Cone, 192
Colombia, 93, 180, 182, 195, 197, 215, 232, 241
Columbia University, 103, 111, 115; Philosophy Hall, 103
Constantine, Learie, 237
Copa America, 29, 30
Cornell University, 103
Costa Rica, 196
Croatia, 76, 220
Cruyff, Johann, 8, 46, 80, 82, 89, 228, 237
Culler, Jonathan, 63, 251; *Theory of the Lyric*, 251
Cupido, Errol "Aalee," 108, 122, 130, 131, 135, 139, 141–143, 150, 155–159
Cupido, Michael ("Mike"), 126, 127, 130, 131, 133, 138–140, 142, 145, 150, 155

Dalglish, "King" Kenny, 213
D'Amato, Cus, 182
Daniels, Clive "Kai," 140, 141, 161
Davis, Miles, 43, 233; *Sketches of Spain*, 43, 233; Hentoff, Nat, 43, 233
de Klerk, F. W., 98, 99

Deleuze, Gilles, 13, 15, 47, 50, 61, 68, 72, 229, 233, 251; *A Thousand Plateaus: Capitalism and Schizophrenia*, 233, 251; Deleuzian possibility, 15; Guattari, Félix, 47, 50, 233, 251; *Nietzsche and Philosophy*, 229

de Mann, Paul, 50; *Allegories of Reading*, 50

Demichelis, Martín, 86

Democracy, xiii

Derrida, Jacques, x, 3, 60, 109, 128, 169, 170, 173, 176, 179, 180, 183, 184, 230, 233, 240, 242–245; *différance*, 244, 251; "infinite hospitality," 109; *Learning To Live Finally: The Final Interview*, 240, 251; *On Touching: Jean-Luc Nancy*, 179, 180, 245, 251; *The Gift of Death*, 176, 242–244, 251

Descartes, René, 242; *Meditations on First Philosophy*, 242

*Diacritics*, 248

Diaspora, xxii

Dickens, Charles, 22, 29, 30, 43, 46, 48, 49, 231, 251; *A Christmas Carol*, 29, 231, 251; "Humbug," 94; *Oliver Twist*, 22; Scrooge, 49, 94; Tiny Tim (Cratchit), 29, 43, 46, 48, 49

di María, Angel, 36, 38, 44, 84–86

Dirks, Henry, 118, 119, 138–140, 156 ; Julian, "Brother," 131–134, 138, 143, 155

Di Stéfano, Alfredo, xxi, 46, 70, 93, 237; Madrid, 93

Don Quixote, 212

Dortmund, 85; BVB, 78, 164; Signal Iduna Park, 85; Westfalenstadion, 85

Duke University, 103; Art Museum (Friedl Building), 103

Duncan, Aarie (Arawaan), 118, 127, 133, 134, 139, 141, 143, 150, 154; Abraham, 142; Hamat, 118, 119, 122, 126, 127, 131–134, 137–140, 142, 143, 154–156; Shaheeda, 119, 122, 132, 150, 151, 153, 155, 161; Wakes (Abdulwazi), 118, 127, 133–135, 139, 141, 142, 144, 150, 154; Wazi, 142

du Plessis, Morné, 237

Dylan, Bob, 175, 177, 244; Christian trilogy, 244; *Saved*, 244; *Shot of Love*, 244; *Slow Train Coming*, 244; *Street Legal*, 177; "Where Are You Tonight?," 175

Ecuador, 31, 38; Quito, 31, 38

England, xii, xvi, 51, 60, 146, 181, 207, 227–229, 241; English Premier League, 8, 85, 164, 204, 207, 227–229, 241

*entre*, 23

*entre-eux*, 12, 13, 17, 39, 53, 81, 167, 169; *il y a de l'animosité entre eux*, 39

*entre-deux*, 33

*entre-moi-et-moi*, 33, 42

*entre-moi-et moi-même*, 13–15, 22, 46, 55, 64, 69, 71, 105–107, 122, 153, 158, 172

*entre-nous*, xxi, xxii, 3, 4, 6, 8, 10, 12–27, 32–35, 42, 46, 53, 57, 59–61, 64, 69, 98, 102, 106, 107, 112–114, 121, 125, 128, 146–148, 150–153, 157, 158, 160, 162, 167, 169, 177–179, 199, 200, 206, 208, 209, 212, 215, 217, 218

Eritrea, 247

Europe, 8, 36, 37, 185, 207, 208, 241; European low countries, 114

Eusébio, 46, 80

Evra, Patrice, 9, 232

Fábio Aurélio, 205

Fàbregas, Cesc, 7, 227, 228; Chelsea, 228

Farred, Andrea, 42, 51, 99

Farred, Ezra, 119, 122, 137, 150, 151, 155, 156

Farred, Grant, 119, 231–236, 252; G. F., 142; *Long Distance Love: A Passion for Football*, 233, 235, 240, 252; *In Motion, At Rest: The Event of the Athletic Body*, 228, 231, 234, 252; *Quorum*, 236; *What's*

*My Name? Black Vernacular Intellectuals*, 231
FIFA, 7, 67, 71, 180–182, 186, 190–192, 195, 210, 229, 249
Fine Young Cannibals, 126, 240: Gift, Roland, 126; "She drives me crazy," 240
Football, European, ix, 232
Fonseca, Daniel, 11, 229
Forlán, Diego, 11, 229
Fortuin, Gerhard "Gert," 126, 151
Foucault, Michel, 115
France, 219, 221, 232; Benzema, Karim, 232; Blanc, Laurent, 232; Cantona, Eric, 232
Franco, 70
Freiburg, theater, x
Friaça, 185
Freire, Paolo, 165, 188; *Pedagogy of the Oppressed*, 165

Gago, Fernando, 86
Galeano, Eduardo, 10, 11, 165, 179, 185, 190, 191, 218, 229, 241, 245–247, 252; Canavessi, Adhemar, 246; *Football in Sun and Shadow*, 11, 165, 229, 241, 246, 247, 252
Garay, Ezequiel, 86
*Garra*, 187
Garrincha, 54, 231
German, West, x, xii–xiv, xvi, 81, 146; Germany, 9, 33, 53, 75, 80, 83, 86, 87, 89–92, 164; *Bundesliga*, 164; Munich, 81, 85; Tikowski, Hans, 146
Gerrard, Steven, 76, 79, 212, 213
Ghiggia, 185
Gietzman, Anthony, 126, 131, 138, 143, 145
Goethe, Johan Wolfgang von, 3, 4, 38, 226; *Elective Affinities* (*Kindred by Choice*), "elective affinities," 3, 39, 226, 227; *Wahlverstandschaft*, 12, 38, 49, 226
Godín, Diego, 187

Götze, Mario, 80, 84–86, 89, 92; Dortmund Technische Universität, 84
Gramsci, Antonio, 115; *Prison Notebooks*, 115
Greenwood, Ron, 182
Gregory, Lady, 12
Guardiola, Josep "Pep," 78, 164, 236, 241; *tiki-taka*, 78, 164
Guevara, Ernesto "Che," 10, 166, 188, 190, 216, 218; Tania, 10
Gullit, Ruud, 89
Gyan, Asamoah, 9

Hanover Park, xxiv, 13, 14, 17, 18, 100–102, 104, 108, 112 115–123, 127, 129, 132–139, 141–145, 147–150, 153, 156–158, 239, 240; Amerdien, Saleem, 154, 155; Athwood Road, 137, 133, 154, 155; Celtic Spurs, 133, 141; Die Veld, 117, 123, 127, 129, 150, 152, 239; Etosha Court, 137, 153; Football Association, 129, 146; High School (Crystal), 102; Lansdowne Industrial, 143; Leeds United, 142, 144, 145; Melchester Rovers, 138; Mountview High School, 102, 132; Premier United, 141, 142, 150; Summit Primary, 105, 121, 154; "The Americans," 127; "The Backstreets" (*die backstreets*), 127, 135; "The Cisco Yakkies," 127
Hardt, Michael, 13, 15, 184, 245; 1917 Bolshevik Revolution, 245; *Gilles Deleuze. An Apprenticeship in Philosophy*, 252
Hegel, G. W. F., 14, 28, 39, 157, 252; *die Sache selbst*, 28, 30, 31, 33; *Phenomenology of Spirit*, 231, 252
Heidegger, Martin, ix–xvi, xix, xxi, xxiii, xxiv, 20, 23, 31, 33, 39, 40, 52, 74, 77, 78, 103, 115, 166, 173, 176, 225, 227, 231; 235–238, 242–244, 252; *An Introduction to Metaphysics*, 236, 252; "Bauen Wohnen Denken," 225; *Being and Time*, 252;

Heidegger, Martin (*continued*)
  *Ereignis*, 77; *Kant and the Problem of Metaphysics*, 236; Meβkirch, ix, xii; *Mitsein*, ix–xii, xiv–xvi, xviii, xix–xxii, xxiv, 20, 35, 38 107–109; rectoral address, xi; *Sein und Zeit*, 110, 231; *Sous rature*, 40, 45, 50, 55, 113, 153, 168, 199, 230; *Was Heißt Denken?*, 23, 231, 238, 252
Hendrix, Jimmy, 82
Hesse, Herman, xiii, xxiii, 97, 100; "Cosmic Spirit," 100; "Stages," 97
Higuaín, Gonzalo, 35–38, 41, 44, 59, 83, 84, 90; Brest, France, 36
Hitler, xii
Hodges, Craig, 182
Holub, Miroslav, 207, 248; "Ode to Joy," 207, 248
Hugo, Victor, 48; *Le Dernier jour d'un condamné*, 48
Hungarians, 69, 70; Kocsis, Sándor, 69, 70; Kubala, László, 69, 70
Hurst, Sir Geoffrey Charles, xii, 146, 240

Independiente, 229
Indian ocean, 117
Indian Premier League, 229
Iniesta, Andrés, 79, 89, 164, 228, 237
Inter Milan, 84, 164, 228, 229, 241
Inwood, Michael, 236; *A Heidegger Dictionary*, 236
Ireland, 57
Irving, Kyrie, xviii
Italy, 33, 78, 180, 190, 196, 204, 228, 229, 241; *calcio*, 78; Rome, 88
Ivanović, Branislav, 186

Jackson, Phil ("Zen meister"), 182
James, C. L. R., 103
James, LeBron, xviii, 79, 225; Los Angeles Lakers, 225

Japan, 229
Jean, Wyclef, 209
Joel, Billy, 153, 241; "Everybody has a dream," 153, 241
Johnson, Magic, 237
Joplin, Janis, 82
Jordan (country), 196
Jordan, Michael, 79, 182
Joyce, James, 220; Dublin, 220
Juffer, Jane, 119, 122, 150, 155, 156
Juventus (Turin), 36, 84, 187, 228, 229

Kant, Immanuel, 194, 237; *Critique of Pure Reason*, 237
Keats, 62; Keatsian, 58, 61, 74
Keegan, Kevin, 213
Kempes, Mario, 54, 87
Kierkegaard, Søren, 170, 171, 176; *Fear and Trembling*, 170
King, Martin Luther Jr., 242; "Letter from a Birmingham Jail," 242
Klopp, Jürgen, 78, 164
Krol, Rudi, 89
Kurzawa, Layvin, xvi
Kuyt, Dirk, 204, 205

Lacan, Jacques, xxiii, 56, 59, 61, 63–69, 71, 74, 82, 88, 90, 91, 93, 94, 97, 150, 159, 234, 235, 244, 252; *Aufhebung*, 63, 64, 66, 69, 72, 82, 177, 178, 234, 238, 241; ethical, 72; Freud, 159; Marquis de Sade, 67, 93, 94, 159; numen ("numinous"), 59, 64, 68, 73; *The Ethics of Psychoanalysis*, 56, 63, 234, 235, 238, 241, 244, 252; "The *Jouissance* of Transgression," 97
Lamm, Philipp, 89
Lansur United Amateur Football Club (AFC), xxiv, 13, 16–18, 23, 100, 102–105, 108, 110–112, 114–119, 121–123, 129, 130,

133, 136–142, 144, 148–152, 154, 156–159, 161, 174, 239
Latin America, 7, 10, 36, 38, 82, 165, 183, 184, 186, 207, 216
Lavezzi, Ezequiel, 36, 85, 232
Lear, 212
Levinas, Emmanuel, 109, 179, 197, 242
Liverpool FC, xvi, 8, 9, 60, 78, 85, 92, 147, 164, 181–183, 186–188, 204, 205, 207, 210–213, 228; "ALLEZ ALLEZ ALLEZ," 147; Anfield, 212; Gerry and the Pacemakers, 182; Merseyside, 188; Scouser(s), 182, 188, 213; "You'll Never Walk Alone," 147, 182
Livingstone High School, 98, 103
Löw, Jachem "Jochi," 89
Lugano, Diego, 10, 184, 185, 187, 190, 191, 195, 202
Luiz, David, 88
Lumumba, Patrice, 166

McEnroe, John, 50
Macbeth, 51
*Manchester by the Sea*, 248
Manchester City, 36, 37, 85, 164, 241
Manchester United, 227, 229
Mandela, Nelson, 99, 100
Maradona, Diego Armando, 36, 41, 42, 46, 51, 52, 55, 59–62, 65, 67, 68, 72, 80, 81, 90, 93, 212, 222, 231, 234, 237; "La mano de Dios" ("Mano de Dios"), 51–55, 60, 90
Marcus, "Boeta," 161
Marley, Bob, 46, 166, 231, 241; Jah, 231; Rastafarian, 46, 231; "Redemption Song," 241
Marx, Karl, 103, 112, 208; lumpenproletariat, 208
Martinon, Jean-Paul, 1, 3, 24
Mascherano, Javier ("Masch"), 36, 37, 59, 79, 86, 92, 207, 237; Hebei Fortune (China), 36–38, 232

Mauro, Claudio, 35
Mauss, Marcel, 242; *The Gift: Forms and Reasons for Exchange in Archaic Societies*, 242
*Menace II Society*, 248
Mertesacker, Per, 89
Messi, Lionel, ix–x, xiv–xxiv, 3, 5–8, 12–17, 20, 23, 27, 29–95, 109, 151, 152, 164, 208, 209, 218–222, 225, 227, 228, 231, 233, 236, 237; Arnold, Benedict, 45; Jorge, 71; Newell's Old Boys, 6, 40, 41, 57, 209, 227; Rosário, 6, 34, 35, 40, 41, 45, 68, 81, 109, 208; Rosario Central (FC), 40, 41, 57, 209
Mexico, 88, 163, 165, 186, 229, 232; Mexico City, 61; Estadio Azteca, 61
Mezzadra, 184, 245
Michels, Rinus, 80, 81
Middle East, 186
Moćrić, Luka, 76
Molotov cocktail, 99
Mona Lisa, 55
Moore, George Augustus, 12, 14, 15, 22, 229; *Confessions of a Young Man*, 12; County Mayo, 12; Irish Literary Revival, 12; Sir Thomas, 12
Moreiras, Alberto, 234
Mourinho, José, 78; 164; Chelsea, 164; Porto, 164
Moynihan Report, 207
Müller, Thomas, 75, 87, 89, 93

Nacional, 229, 241
Nadal, Rafael, 50
Nancy, Jean-Luc, xxii, xxiv, 1, 2, 14–16, 18, 19, 21–35, 37, 57, 58, 59, 64, 67–69, 72, 91, 92, 100, 101, 106, 107, 109–111, 152, 156, 157, 166–176, 179, 183, 184, 199, 201, 203, 208, 226, 230–235, 238–247, 252; *Being Singular Plural*, 23, 27, 33, 149, 166, 199, 226, 230–232, 238, 240, 242, 252;

Nancy, Jean-Luc (*continued*)
"Cosmos Baselius," 2, 4, 21, 226; *entrée nous*, 199, 247; *Hegel: The Restlessness of the Negative*, 14, 27, 29, 91, 100, 110, 230–235, 238, 240–245, 247, 252; singular plural, 8, 13, 16, 17, 27, 48, 128, 175, 208; *The Inoperative Community*, 170, 243, 244, 252
Napoli, 36, 51, 59, 229
National Basketball Association, xviii
National "Football" League (NFL), 54
National Socialists, xii
Netherlands, x, 8, 9, 73, 80, 87, 101, 186, 207, 237
Neuer, Manuel, 83, 90
New Jersey, 100, 101, 106, 113, 114, 121, 151; Freehold, 121, 151
New York (City), 100, 104, 114, 139, 140, 150; Morningside Heights, 100, 104
New Zealand, 240
Neymar, xvii, xviii, xxiv, 75, 87, 88, 207, 237
Nietzsche, Friedrich, 5, 23, 34, 35, 63, 94, 115, 169, 170, 172, 173, 214, 225, 227, 232, 234, 242, 252; eternal return of the same, 34, 94; "genius of Christianity," 171, 214; *On the Genealogy of Morals*, 242; *Thus Spoke Zarathustra: A Book for Everyone and Nobody*, 23, 35, 57, 63, 92, 225, 232, 234, 252; will, 20; *Will to Power*, 227
Nigeria, 85; Ibadan, 191; Lagos, 191; Port Harcourt, 191
Nike, xiv
*Nog Lansur!*, 97, 147, 153, 158, 161, 162; "C'mon Lansur," 147; "More Lansur," 147; "We are Lansur," 147
Nortje, Arthur, 80–82, 237, 252; *Dead Roots: Poems*, 237, 252; "Song for a Passport," 80

O'Neal, Shaquille, 182
Obama, Barack, 139
Olympics, 246
Othello, 212; Desdemona, 212; Moor, 212
Owen, Wilfred, 53, 55, 57, 68, 88, 234; "Dulce et decorum est pro patria mori," 57; Horace, 57; "Smile, Smile, Smile," 55

Palacio, Rodrigo, 83, 84
Palestine, 247
Pamuk, Orhan, 219, 220, 222; Istanbul, 220, 222; *Other Colors: Essays and a Story*, 219
Paris, xviii, 82
Paris Saint-Germain (PSG), ix, xvi–xx, xxii, 36, 85
Passarella, Daniel, 54, 91, 233; de San Martín, José, 233; "El Gran Capitan," 233
Pedro, 7, 228
Pelé, xii, 46, 54, 80, 231
Peñarol, 187, 229, 241
Perry, "Bags," 124, 141
Peru, 39
Petersen, Mark, 140
Picasso, Málaga, 70; Catalan, 70
Piqué, Gerard, xvii, 7, 227, 228, 237
Poe, Edgar Allen, 188, 190, 209, 210; "The Imp of the Perverse," 188, 190, 209
Portia Primary, 102
Princeton United, 101, 102, 104, 105, 111; "Groot Man," 101, 113, 114; Mercer County league, 100, 113
Princeton University, 100, 102, 103, 111, 112; McCosh Hall, 103
Probyn, Elspeth, 17, 190, 197, 198, 202–204, 206, 229, 247, 248, 252; *Blush: Faces of Shame*, 190, 229, 247, 248, 252
Puskás, Ferenc, 46, 70
Puyol, Carles, 228

*Rastlosigkeit*, 14, 28, 37, 39, 58, 66, 95, 104
Real Madrid, xvi, 36, 164, 227, 228
Reina, Pepe, 228
Richards, Viv, 79

Rijkaard, Frank, 89, 228
Ríos, Arévalo ("El Cacha"), 187
River Plate, 6, 36, 41, 185
Robben, Arjan, 87, 88, 92, 93, 185
Roberto, Sergio, xvii, xix
Rodgers, Brendan, 205
Robson, Bobby, 164, 182
Rodríguez, Maxi, 79
Rodríguez, Marco Antonio, 180; "Dracula," 180
Roma, AS, 229
Romário, 231
Romero, Sergio, 54, 84, 86, 92
Ronaldo (Brazil), 231
Ronaldo, Cristiano, 7, 50, 75, 227; Portugal, 75
Roux, Luis, 191, 194
Rudolph, "Cavalla" ("Cavakes"), 124–127, 156
*Ruhelosigheit*, 14, 37, 104
Russia, xxi, 31, 38, 219, 220, 222

Sabella, Alejandro, 75, 85
SACOS (South African Council on Sport), 117, 239; SANROC (South African Non-Racial Olympic Committee); 240; Booth, Douglas, 240
Safranski, Rüdiger, x, xiv, 225, 252; *Martin Heidegger: Between Good and Evil*, 252
Santana, Carlos, 209; "Maria, Maria," 209
Sartre, Jean-Paul, x, 249, 252; *Being and Nothingness*, 249, 252
Schmitt, Carl, xii, 44, 172, 226, 233, 243, 252; Bodin, Jean, 233, 243; *Ex Captivitate Salus*, 233, 243, 252; Hobbes, Thomas, 233, 243; National Socialism, 243; *Nomos of the Earth*, 226, 252
Schweinsteiger, Bastian, 87, 89; Chicago Fire, 89; Manchester United, 89
*Sein*, 20, 26, 35, 38, 68, 70, 78, 109; *Dasein*, 20, 78, 79, 90, 91, 103, 236; *Zeit*, 79

Shakespeare, 128, 160, 173, 215; *Hamlet* (Hamlet), 51, 128, 160, 212; Marcellus, 128
Shankly, Bill, 188, 189
Shelford, Wayne, 79
Shiri, Jeremiah "Nontjies," 108, 141
Silva, Francisco, 54
Silva, Thiago, xix
Sisyphean, 72
Slade, Carole, 71, 235, 252; Saint Theresa of Avila, 71; *St. Theresa of Avila: Author of a Heroic Life*, 235, 252
Sneider, Wesley, 86, 228
Sócrates, 54
Souness, Graeme, 213
South Africa, 9, 15, 51, 81, 82, 89, 97–101, 109, 110, 114, 116, 118, 121, 123, 126, 128, 142, 150, 151, 228, 229, 232, 247; "Casspirs," 128, 129; Eastern Cape (East London), 239 Kimberley, 239; *machine á habiter*, 99; Natal, 239; "ungovernable," 128
*South Atlantic Quarterly*, 245, 247; Goldstein, Alyosha, 247; Lubin, Alex, 247; "Settler Colonialism," 247
Soweto (Johannesburg), 98, 240; June 1976, 98
Spain, xvi, 9, 30, 70, 89, 228, 229, 241; Castillia, 30, 36, 70; La Liga, 227
Spillers, Hortense, "Mama's Baby, Papa's Maybe: An American Grammar Book," 248; Moynihan, Daniel Patrick, 248
Springsteen, Bruce, 121, 151, 152, 239, 240, 252; *Born to Run*, 121, 239, 240, 252
Stoke City, 204, 205
Suárez, Luis, xvi, xviii, xxii–xxiv, 3, 5, 7–17, 20, 23, 49, 65, 71, 75, 79, 87, 93, 151, 152, 173, 174, 177, 178, 180–191, 194–220, 225, 228, 237, 245–249; Benjamin (son), 217; Delfina (daughter), 217; "El Pistolero," 183; *etat voyou*, 9; Groningen, 8;

Suárez, Luis (*continued*)
  *Guardian*, 246; "Lou," 205, 206, 209, 211; Nacional, 8; Salto, 7, 182, 187, 189, 207, 208, 213
Swartz, Steven "Scarra," 154, 161

Tabárez, Óscar Washington, xxii-xxiv, 5, 8–17, 22, 23, 151, 152, 163, 164, 172, 173, 177–207, 210–218, 225, 241, 245–249; Bella Vista, 165; Danubio, 241; Deportivo Cali, 241; "El Maestro," 10, 189, 194, 215, 217, 218, 229, 246, 247; "El Proceso," 11, 16, 184, 193, 196; *el ténico*, 163, 178, 183; Fénix, 165; Montevideo Wanderers, 165; Puebla, 165; Sportivo Italiano, 165; Sud América, 165; UNESCO, 165; Vélez Sársfield, 241
Taylor, Lawrence, 237
Tevez, Carlos, 83, 84
Theunis, Charlie, 154, 161
Third World, 216
Thomas, Dylan, 125, 126, 240; "I see the boys of summer in their ruin," 125, 240
Tottenham Hotspur, 85
Trappist monastery, 134
Trotsky, Leon, 103
Tyson, Mike, 182

United States, 14, 53, 54, 105, 118, 121, 139, 146, 149, 151, 191, 207, 245, 247; African American athletes, 207; Delaware; Haitian immigrants, 192; inner-city, 120, Lloyd, Carli, 146; Major League Soccer, 89; Metlife Stadium, 54; neo-Nazi, 192; New Jersey, 54; New York, 54
University of Cape Town (UCT), 132, 143
University of the Western Cape (UWC), 102, 111
*Unruhig*, 14
Uruguay, xvi, 8, 11, 12, 151, 163, 165, 180, 183–185, 189, 194, 196, 202, 204, 205, 208, 211–213, 219, 220, 241, 246, 247; Areco,

Jorge Pacheco (Tupamaro National Liberation Movement), 192; Bordaberry, Juan Mariá, 192; "Civil Dictatorship," 199; Demicheli, Alberto, 192; Football Association, 10; Gestido, Óscar Diego (Left; Communist movement), 192; Guaraní, 11; "JOG" (Junta Officiales Generales), 192; "Libertad o muerte," 195; "Los Charrúas," 11; Montevideo, 7–10, 182, 185, 189, 196, 217, 248; president, Mujica, José, 10, 191, 192, 195, 228; República Oriental del Uruguay, 10; Sanguinetti, Julio María (Ley de Amnistía), 192; "Switzerland," 10; Valdez, Wilmar, 10

Valdés, Victor, 228
van Basten, Marco, 89, 228
van Heerden, Lyndon "Lynnie," 134, 135, 141, 143, 144
van Riebeeck, Jan, 101
Van Wyk, Stan "Sailor," 133, 140, 141, 143–147
Varela, Obdulio, 185
Villarreal, 71, 229
Vlaar, Ron, 86
*vuvuzela*, 9, 228; Khoisan, 228; "koodoo/kudu," 228

*Webster's Unabridged Dictionary*, 58, 62, 190, 234, 244
Wembley, xii, 146, 147; London, 146
West Bromwich Albion, 187
Western Province's Virginia Super League, 142; Thornhill United, 142
Wilkinson, Andy, 205
Williams, Raymond, 103
Wordsworth, William, 72, 74; "Tintern Abbey," 72
World Cup, ix, x, xii, xxi, xxii, 9, 17, 18, 29–31, 36, 39, 49, 51, 60, 73, 79–83, 87–90, 93, 142, 146, 152, 182, 185, 190, 217–222, 228, 229, 231, 232, 240, 245, 246;

Bahramov, Tofiq (Azerbaijan), 146; Coup du monde, 17; Copa Mundial, 6, 8, 10–12, 16, 17, 31, 38, 53, 60, 66, 73, 81–83, 90, 91, 187, 196, 233, 245; Dienst, Gottfried (Switzerland), 146; Weltmeisterschaft, 17
World War I, 55, 57; Great War, 57

Xavi, (Hernández), 79, 89, 164, 228, 237

Yeats, William Butler, 12, 29, 54, 56, 57, 61, 63, 234; "Irish Airman," 54, 55, 57, 61, 63

Yorick, 74, 209
Young Pirates, 125, 147, 156, 240; Lewis, Chris "Gunny," 125, 147

Zabaleta, Pablo, 86
Zidane, Zinedine, 76, 80, 228; *coup de boule*, 228; état *voyous*, 228
*Zu sein wie*, x–xv
Zuluaga, Miguel, 192–194, 198–201, 203, 218; el Juzgado Penal de 17 Turno, 193

www.ingramcontent.com/pod-product-compliance
Lightning Source LLC
Chambersburg PA
CBHW070755230426
43665CB00017B/2364